*Projections
and Interface
Conditions*

Projections
and Interface
Conditions

Essays on Modularity

Edited by
ANNA-MARIA DI SCIULLO

New York   Oxford
Oxford University Press
1997

Oxford University Press

Oxford   New York
Athens   Auckland   Bangkok   Bogota   Bombay   Buenos Aires
Calcutta   Cape Town   Dar es Salaam   Delhi   Florence   Hong Kong
Istanbul   Karachi   Kuala Lumpur   Madras   Madrid   Melbourne
Mexico City   Nairobi   Paris   Singapore   Taipei   Tokyo   Toronto
and associated companies in
Berlin   Ibadan

Library of Congress Cataloging-in-Publication Data
Projections and interface conditions : essays on modularity / edited
by Anna-Maria Di Sciullo.
    p.   cm.
Includes bibliographical references and index.
ISBN 0-19-510414-5
1. Psycholinguistics.   2. Grammar, Comparative and general—
Syntax.   3. Modularity (Psychology).   4. Generative grammar.   I. Di
Sciullo, Anne-Marie, 1951–
P37.P744   1996
415—dc20   96-32092

Preface

The modular approach to grammar developed in Generative Grammar has been shown to have important consequences for the study of language. Within such an approach, the properties of specific rules (PASSIVE, NOMINALIZATION, and so on) are derived from the interaction of general principles, and in this way a greater explanatory adequacy is obtained. Another important aspect of the modular approach is that it focuses research on the properties of the modules, the interface levels, and the overall architecture of the grammar, making these notions more precise. Although specific hypotheses have emerged with respect to the form of a fully modular grammar, many questions remain unanswered.

In Chomsky (1981), the modularity of the grammar resides in the coexistence of autonomous components (phonological, syntactic, morphological, semantic) as well as in the interaction of given sets of principles (Theta theory, Case theory, Binding theory, and so on) at given levels of representation (D-structure, S-structure, Logical Form, and so on). The properties of linguistic expressions follow from the interaction of the principles at given levels of representation, and it is possible to dispense with the notion of "linguistic construction," as well as with the notion of "construction-specific rules." With the Minimalist framework (Chomsky 1993, 1994), the organization of the grammar is simplified, both with respect to the levels of representation and with respect to the modules. The levels of representation are reduced to the two external interface levels with the performance systems — the Conceptual-Intentional system and the Acoustic-Perceptual system: Logical Form and Phonetic Form. The internal interface levels, D-structure and S-structure, are dispensed with together with the problems they posed. In this framework, a derivation is driven by the conceptual necessity to satisfy the interface conditions, some of which can be subsumed under general economy conditions on representations, such as the principle of Full Interpretation. Economy conditions on derivations, such as the principles of Last Resort and Greed, ensure optimal derivations.

The Minimalist program provides a general framework for the formulation of a fully modular theory of grammar. In this framework, the grammar includes a small set of interacting modules, components, and interface levels. Beyond the general assumptions, there is an ongoing debate on the nature and the interaction of each of the building blocks of the grammar. Of particular interest are the following questions, which are addressed in this collection. What are the components of the grammar? What are the autonomous modules? What modules can be derived from the properties of the configuration? How does variation follow from the theory of grammar? The following paragraphs point out the salient features of the chapters in this collection, which offer original ways to handle these questions.

The question of identifying the components of the grammar has been addressed in radically different terms in the last decade; intermediate positions ranging from the strict lexicalist hypothesis (Di Sciullo and Williams 1987) to the strict syntactic hypothesis (Lieber 1992) have also been sustained. In the Minimalist framework, the debate resolves itself: morphology is an independent component of the grammar, while there is only one computational component for the generation of linguistic expressions, either X^0 or XP expressions. The first two chapers of this collection address this topic.

In "On Word-structure and Conditions," Anna-Maria Di Sciullo develops a theory of word-formation in which X^0 expressions are restricted to head-adjunction structure at the interface with the Conceptual-Intentional system, and X-bar structure is virtually projected in the derivation, given a configurational theory of argument structure. The proposed theory preserves a configurational treatment of the argument structure restrictions in word-structure, while it accounts for word-internal opacity effects. The argument structure restrictions are checked in the virtual X-bar projection, while the opacity effects follow from the head-adjunction properties of word-structure at the interface. The discussion focuses on the properties of denominal and deadjectival verbs in French, as well as on the properties of deverbal compounds in English. It is shown that the restrictions on these expressions follow from their configurational properties and not from Theta conditions. The author discusses the application of the principle of Full Interpretation to XP structure and to word-structure and provides evidence to the effect that this principle is relativized to the properties of the interface to which it applies. When it applies to X^0 expressions, Full Interpretation identifies X^0 heads and X^0 adjuncts as legitimate interface objects; when it applies to Logical Form, it identifies legitimate XP chains. The proposal reinforces the modularity of the grammar, in that X-bar structure and head-adjunction structure participate in distinct ways in the derivation of linguistic expressions.

In "On Some Syntactic Properties of Word-Structure and Modular Grammars," Paul Law investigates the issue of projection of argument structure in nominalization and argues that although there is good reason to assume an X-bar theoretic approach to deverbal nominals, as discussed in Selkirk (1982), principles of Theta theory as generally assumed for syntax can be shown to be inoperative in derivational morphology. Drawing data from -*er* and -*ion* nominalizations and those concerning control in nominals, the author shows how apparent incompatibility of X-bar theory and Theta theory in derivational morphology can be resolved in an independent theory of projection of argument structure according to which Theta-positions are syntactically projected if the head having the Theta-structure projects maximally to an XP.

In "Prefixed-verbs and Adjunct Identification," Anna-Maria Di Sciullo considers the properties of prefixed verbs in French under the hypothesis that prefixed verbs give rise to head-adjunction structures at the interface between word-structure and the Conceptual-Intentional system. It is shown that the restrictions on the occurrences of prefixes of the same configurational sort follow from the interaction of a general condition pertaining to the interpretation of adjunct structures, the Adjunct Identification Condition, which can be reduced to general economy considerations in the Minimalist framework. This principle applies to word-structure according to the properties of these structures, as is generally the case for the other interface conditions. Given that prefixed verbs are adjunct-head structures, it follows that the interpretation of the adverbial and prepositional prefixes will be attributive and not descriptive. The author also considers the variation between French and Italian with respect to verb-formation. The observed variation is expected if, as suggested in Chomsky (1993), linguistic variation in word-order can be reduced to morphological variation. This chapter provides guidelines to an approach of variation in derivational morphology.

The question of the projection of conceptual categories in syntactic positions has also given rise to a lively debate in the literature. Several hypotheses have been developed within generative grammar, ranging from more conceptual approaches (Jackendoff 1990) to more syntactic approaches (Hale and Keyser 1993). Elizabeth Klipple's chapter, "Prepositions and Variation," bears on this question, as it addresses how language variation may arise with respect to the projection of aspectual categories. The author pursues the hypothesis that cross-linguistic variation does not arise from changes in parameter settings, but principally from differences in the morphological properties of the languages. A close comparison is made of the behavior of prepositions in English and French. It is proposed that there is a universal set of conceptual functions available to natural language, which are arrayed in a certain configuration in Lexical Conceptual Structure (LCS). There exists a mapping between this level and the level of syntactic structure; cross-linguistic variation is possible in this mapping. It is argued that a difference in the representation of the "direction/aspect" function found in English prepositions but not in French prepositions accounts for several differences between the two languages. The modular nature of the theory adopted by the author and the parallel but not isomorphic nature of the levels are essential to the account. In addition, it is shown that the notion of category must be relativized to each level of the grammar.

The question of the autonomy of the modules of the grammar is discussed in Mireille Tremblay's chapter, "On the Modularity of Case Theory." Within a fully modular theory of grammar, Theta theory and Case theory are seen as independent modules interacting at specific levels of representation. A modular approach thus excludes any principle or well-formedness condition making reference to more than one module. However, formal interaction between the above-mentioned theories has been proposed in the Visibility hypothesis, the inherent Case hypothesis, and Burzio's generalization. The discussion is based on the behavior of *have* and *be* in a number of different constructions. The author argues against the Visibility hypothesis by showing that the Case Filter and the Theta Criterion apply to two distinct classes: [+N] elements (predicates or arguments) and arguments (NPs, PPs, and CPs), respectively. The relevant data drawn from copular constructions also provide evidence against the notion of inherent Case. It is also shown that the verb *have* constitutes a counterexample to Burzio's generalization and that Burzio's discussion on auxiliary selection in passive and ergative constructions was misled. A better understanding of the different Case properties of *have* and *be* provides an account that derives the empirical generalization, rather than assigning it a formal status.

The interaction of the modules in the explanation of the properties of linguistic expressions is a central aspect of the modularity of the grammar and has given rise to fruitful research. The following chapters bear on this issue.

In "Argument Projection, Thematic Configurationality, and Case Theory," by Jeffrey S. Gruber and Chris Collins, a cross-modular approach to the representation and projection of Theta-roles is shown to account for asymmetries in the correspondence between subjects and objects and the Theta-roles they can express. The approach involves the elimination of the concept of Theta-role "assignment": that is, the correspondence between arguments in a syntactic structure and thematic roles in a structure apart from syntax (Stowell 1980, Williams 1984, Jackendoff 1990). Concomitantly, primitive thematic relations are derived configurationally, in accordance with principles of X-bar theory, and the derivation of overt forms through the operation of principles of syntax. The proposed account then involves the interaction of X-bar theory, Movement theory, and Case theory. Chomsky's (1993) Minimalist Program, in which derivations are constrained by principles of economy and conditions on the syntactic interfaces, provides a framework to their approach. A limitation in Hale and Keyser's (1993) model — allowing the projection of only two arguments — is overcome by the representation of the elemental event structure by a form of asymmetric conjunction. The possibility of movement for structural Case-assignment into Agreement Phrase from basic structural positions constrains the projection of arguments as subject and object. The account also characterizes the variation between the serializing and the non-serializing languages; all languages are serializing in underlying form, while differences between languages reduce to the stage at which "conflation" of the serial form takes place.

In Jeff Gruber's "Modularity in a Configurational Theta Theory," the interaction of three theoretic modules of syntax with a configurational Theta theory is shown to be necessary to account for the asymmetries of Case and Theta-role assignments. These include the modules of X-bar theory and Case theory, as well as a module of Event Linkage. Event Linkage is independently required for the licensing of elemental event representations in complex configurations. Thematic relations are inherent in the basic positions of arguments in configurations composed according to X-bar theory in a Minimalist framework. Argument projection is movement to positions in which arguments are licensed according to conditions on morphological features. Semantic Case is generalized to structural Case as movement into Agreement Phrases for the checking of Case-features. Event Linkage, related to Event Binding (see, among others, Higginbotham 1985), involves the Colinking of thematic roles between elemental event representations. Movement within the structure for Colinking interacts with movement for the discharge of Case-features, resulting in source/goal asymmetries. The presence of inner aspectual phrases associated with elemental event representations may alter basic configurations. This affects the possibility of Movement for Colinkage and structural Case, resulting in asymmetries of subject and object projection with respect to the Theta-roles they express. For instance, the differences in the "punctuality" or the "durativity" within the event structure correlate with the possibility of projecting a Theta-role as subject or complement/object.

In "On Passive as Partitive Quantification," Johan Rooryck considers the modular account of passive of Chomsky (1981), in which passive is reduced to the interaction of various principles involving Case theory, Movement theory, and Theta theory, and provides evidence to the effect that it is empirically inadequate. The overgeneration of Chomsky's theory can be overcome not in thematic terms but from an even more modular approach where the passive morphology and the role of the copula play a central role. It is proposed that the constraints on passive are determined by partitive properties of the verb *be/être* that is used as a passive auxiliary. The author proposes an analysis of quantificational *be* versus predicational *be* along the lines of Kayne (1992) and Hoekstra (1993). A quantificational analysis of passive is developed in which no reference is made to thematic roles to explain the "exceptions" to passive. According to this analysis, passive is the only way an internal NP argument can be syntactically construed in such a way as to express a constitutive property of that NP.

Finally, Pierre Pica and William Snyder's "On the Syntax and Semantics of Local Anaphors in French and English" argues for an account of local anaphors that distinguishes the separate contributions of syntax, morphology, semantics, and the conceptual-interpretive component of human cognition. The authors analyze the English anaphor *himself* as composed of the pronominal element *him* in combination with the morpheme *-self*. In sharp contrast to standard Binding theory, but in keeping with an extensive philosophical literature, they take *-self* to denote a function that takes as its arguments (a contextually salient aspect of) an individual and returns as its semantic value a distinct aspect of the same individual. Thus, in *John washed himself*, *John* as agent is understood psychologically, whereas *himself* as patient is understood physically. Evidence is provided to the effect that the range of partitions (such as mental/physical) that license a local anaphor is tightly constrained by properties of extralinguistic cognition. Moreover, the authors demonstrate that the relevant partition must be introduced by the lexical semantics of the predicate. The similar but distinct properties of French local anaphors are explained in terms of differences in morphology and lexical semantics.

We thank the Social Sciences and Humanities Research Council of Canada for funding the Modularity project, from which most of the contributions in this volume originate, and the Fonds pour la Formation de Chercheurs et l'Aide à la Recherche for funding the Interface project, which is related to the Modularity project, as well as the Fonds Institutionnel de Recherche of the Université du Québec à Montréal for the financial support provided. Many thanks to the members of these projects and to the external participants for their contributions to this volume. Special thanks to Noam Chomsky, Ken Hale, Jay Keyser, Jim Higginbotham, and Tom Roeper for their helpful comments at different stages of the development of the ideas presented here.

Montreal   A.-M. D.
June 1996

Contents

*Projections
and Interface
Conditions*

ONE

On Word-structure
and Conditions

ANNA-MARIA DI SCIULLO

1. THE DERIVATION OF WORDS

The derivation of words gives rise to a lively debate in generative grammar. The debate is actual and important, not only because the differences and the relations between words and phrases are not yet well understood but also because it has consequences for the internal architecture of the grammar. The central questions in this debate are whether the derivation of words is performed by the laws of the syntax or by the laws of another component, that is, the morphology, the phonology, or the lexicon; whether the derivation of words includes phrasal categories or is restricted to lexical categories; and whether word-structures are subject to the conditions that apply on syntactic structures, or to completely different or partly different conditions.

A variety of hypotheses have been considered that offer partial solutions to these questions. Let us mention two current views here, which reflect, at least in part, the early lexicalist versus transformationalist debate (cf. Chomsky 1970, Lees 1970). One view is that word-structure is generated by the laws of the morphological component of the grammar (cf. Williams 1981, Selkirk 1982, Di Sciullo and Williams 1987, Law 1990, and Borer 1990, among others); another view is that word-structure is derived by the laws of the syntax and is subject to syntactic conditions (cf. Baker 1988, Lieber 1992, Hale and Keyser 1992, and Ackema 1995, among others). In favor of the syntactic approach is the fact that no further stipulations are needed to account for the syntactic properties of words, provided the syntax is extended to cover both words and phrases. In favor of a more lexical approach is the fact that no movement is required in the derivation of words, and thus there are fewer steps in the derivation.

Assuming that there is only one computational space, as in Chomsky (1993, 1994), we would like to consider here an approach to word-structure that brings together the lexicalist and the transformationalist hypotheses within a fully modular theory of grammar.

In this perspective, we will take word-structure to be the set of the X^0 expressions derived by the morphological component of the grammar, as is the case in Di Sciullo and Williams (1987), as well as in Chomsky (cf. 1993, 1994), and consider the configurational and interpretative properties of X^0s within what we will call the Modular hypothesis (cf. Di Sciullo 1990a). According to this hypothesis, words and phrases are both different and similar grammatical objects. They differ configurationally as well as with respect to interpretation, and they are subject to the interface conditions according to their configurational properties, assuming that the interface conditions are strictly configurational conditions (cf. Chomsky 1994). However, words and phrases are similar objects, we claim, because the derivation of words includes asymmetrical X-bar projections, and it is the presence of these projections in the derivation of words that allows for the relatedness of word-internal constituents to phrasal structure. If we allow asymmetrical X-bar projections to be part of the derivation of X^0s without being part of what we will call their canonical target configuration, it is possible to account both for the atomicity of words as well as for their relatedness to phrases.

The Modular hypothesis allows us to maintain a configurational representation of argument structure under the word-level and to derive the opacity of words from their canonical target configuration, as defined in section 2.1. We show that our hypothesis is empirically motivated in considering the properties of X^0 expressions in different languages. As was the case for the early lexicalist and transformationalist hypotheses, our hypothesis has consequences for the architecture of the grammar and leads to the formulation of a fully modular theory of grammar, in which modularity ranges over the configurations, as well as over the components and the conditions of the grammar.

The organization of this chapter is the following. In section 2, we define the canonical target configuration for X^0 expressions. In section 3, we show that the principle of Full Interpretation applies to X^0s according to the properties of their canonical target configuration. In section 4, we consider conditions that make reference to Theta-roles and show that they do not apply to X^0s. In the last section, we point out some consequences of our proposal for the architecture of the grammar.

2. WORD-STRUCTURE

2.1. Head-adjunction Structure

Let us take the grammar to generate types of linguistic expressions, that is, structural descriptions, such as X^0 and XP expressions, defined in terms of "canonical target configurations" (CTC). A CTC for a type of linguistic expression is a configuration that must be obtained at the interface for that expression to be interpretable by the performance systems, even if other configurations are obtained in the derivation. We assume, as in Chomsky (1993, 1994), that the Conceptual-Intentional (C-I) system and the Acoustic-Perceptual (A-P) system are the only performance systems that interpret linguistic expressions at the interfaces by conceptual necessity. In the Minimalist framework, Logical Form (LF) is the interface between linguistic expressions and the C-I system, whereas Phonetic Form (PF) is the interface between linguistic expressions and the A-P system. Assuming that the grammar defines CTCs for types of linguistic expressions, we will take Morphological Form (MF) to be the interface between X^0 expressions and the performance systems (cf. Di Sciullo 1993a). We will focus here on the configurational and semantic properties of X^0s at the MF interface with the C-I system.

We posit that the CTC for X^0 expressions is a head-adjunction structure at the MF interface. A head-adjunction structure takes the form in (1), in which Y, the adjunct, is contained in the two-segment category X, the head of the structure.[1]

(1) $[_X Y \ X]$

Adjunction does not project a new category, as is the case in a head-complement or a specifier-head structure, but forms a configuration in which a two-segment category X includes a category Y (cf. May 1985, Chomsky 1994). This configurational difference between adjunction structure, on the one hand, and asymmetrical X-bar structure, on the other, is, in our view, the structural basis upon which fundamental differences between words and phrases can be derived. The following paragraphs bring motivations to this effect.

In favor of the hypothesis that X^0 expressions are canonical head-adjunction structures is the fact that the adjunct in these expressions does not generally project onto an XP structure, as is the case for a complement or a specifier. In fact, neither the adjunct nor the head in an X^0 expression generally projects an XP. Both the head and the adjunct generally project an X^0 category, which combine to form another X^0 category. Thus, the structure in (1) qualifies as a CTC for X^0 expressions, but not the structures in (2).

(2)   a. $[_X X \ YP]$
     b. $[_X YP \ X]$

We argued elsewhere (Di Sciullo 1994b) that X^0 expressions including overt XP structures, such as the deverbal compounds of Romance languages, as illustrated in (3), must be reduced to a head-adjunction structure, such as in (1), at the interface between word-structure and the C-I system. Syntactic and semantic properties of these expressions justify their being head-adjunction structures at MF.

(3)   a. $[_N [_{VP} \text{V-DP}]]$,   trompe-l'oeil, crève-la-faim
     b. $[_N [_{PP} \text{P-PP}]]$,   prêt-à-porter, hors-la-loi
     c. $[_N [_{AP} \text{A-PP}]]$,   dur-à-cuire, bon-à-tirer
     d. $[_N [_{NP} \text{N-PP}]]$,   homme-de-paille, table-de-chevet

One property of these expressions is that their parts are not interpreted compositionally, as is the case for the constituents of XP structures. Another property is that their internal syntactic structure is not accessible to overt syntactic operations. These two properties are typical of X^0 expressions. They can be observed in compounds, as well as in derived forms that may not freely be affected by overt syntactic operations, such as MERGE and MOVE, as defined in Chomsky (1994). This is illustrated in the examples in (4), in which in (4a, b) MERGE applied word-internally, and in (4c, d), in which MOVE applied into or out of a word.

(4) a.   *the [write-novel-er] that you know
    b.   *you know the [John's-writer]
    c.   *the [who-writer] did you meet
    d.   *who did you meet the [write t]

The opacity of X^0s can be seen as following from the properties of their CTC, since we have independent evidence to take adjunction structures to be opaque domains for overt syntactic operations (cf. Huang 1982, Lebeaux 1988). Assuming that the properties of adjunction structures are constant and that they hold for XP and X^0 derivations, it follows that in a head-adjunction structure there are no accessible specifier and complement positions that can be the target for overt syntactic operations or the origin of such operations.

Further support for our hypothesis comes from the fact that word-structure is not subject to regular phrase-structure interpretation (see, among others, Chierchia and McConnel-Ginet 1990). In fact, descriptive (predicate-argument) meaning cannot be obtained in X^0 expressions; only attributive (predicate) meaning can be obtained in X^0s, as proposed in Di Sciullo (1993a) and illustrated here in (5).

(5) a.   to saddle a horse with a blanket
    b.   #to saddle a horse with a shoe
    c.   #to saddle a horse with a saddle
    d.   to shelve the books on a windowsill
    e.   #to shelve the books on a nail
    f.   #to shelve the books on a shelf

The complement of a denominal verb must have part of the attributes of the noun included in the verb, as in (5a) and (5d); otherwise the expressions are interpreted as gibberish. They may not have the same attributes, as illustrated in (5c) and (5f), where both have indefinite reference. The noun included in the denominal verb does not describe an entity, as is the case for the complement of the verb; rather, it denotes certain attributes of an entity. Thus, the noun *saddle* in the derived verb *to saddle* no longer refers to a saddle, but rather denotes certain basic attributes of that entity, such that *a blanket* may satisfy them. This suggests that in an X^0, an adjunct contributes only part of its semantic features to the whole X^0 expression.

In our model, the semantic opacity of words also follow from their CTC, which is a head-adjunction structure at the MF interface. The fact that the categories that are a part of X^0s do not have a descriptive (predicate-argument) content is a consequence of the fact that they are not interpreted as if they were in an asymmetrical X-bar structure at MF.

The difference in the interpretation of X^0s and XPs follows from the configurational properties of their CTCs and not from the categorial properties of the elements they include. Thus, the opacity of X^0s does not follow from the absence in X^0s of functional categories, such as the determiner (D), which otherwise determine the referential properties of nominal expressions in XP structures (cf. Higginbotham 1985, Abney 1987). In fact, compounds from different languages include a determiner. This is the case for complex reflexive pronouns in English and French, such as *himself* and the like, assuming that pronouns are determiners (cf. Abney 1987); and in deverbal compounds in French and Hebrew (cf. Borer 1990, Di Sciullo 1990a, 1994a, b), as well as complex conjunctions including complementizers and wh-words such as *whatever, however,* and *whenever*. The functional categories in X^0s are not analyzed as if they were in XPs. The syntactic and semantic properties of wh-words, determiners, and other functional categories are opaque when they are a part of X^0s because, we claim, the CTC for these expressions is a head-adjunction structure. The functional categories in X^0 expressions are not analyzed as if they were a part of an asymmetrical X-bar structure, but as being a part of a head-adjunction structure.

2.2. Asymmetrical X-bar Structure

While opacity effects are observed in X^0 expressions, parts of X^0s may be related to parts of XPs, as discussed in Lieber (1992), Ackema (1995), and Di Sciullo (1995), giving rise to the X^0/XP relatedness effect. The relatedness effect can be observed in (5a, c) above, in which the noun in the denominal verb and the complement of that verb are related. The relatedness between parts of X^0s and part of XPs is possible, we claim, because of the projection of an asymmetrical X-bar projection in the derivation of X^0 expressions. One way to express the relatedness is to take the head-adjunction structure to be included in an asymmetrical X-bar structure, as in (6).

(6)

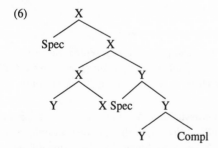

In this structure, X is the head and its adjunct Y is linked to a position in the complement domain (cf. Chomsky 1993) of X.

Motivation for the presence in X^0s of an asymmetrical X-bar structure comes from the fact that word-formation affects argument structure (Williams 1981, Di Sciullo and Williams 1987) and that argument structure takes the form of an asymmetrical X-bar projection.[2]

In fact, X^0 expressions including category-changing suffixes differ as to whether they project argumental or non-argumental specifier or complement positions, as evidenced in Di Sciullo (1995). For example, verbal affixes may project an argumental specifier position, as is the case for the verbal suffix *-ize*, contrary to nominal suffixes such as *-er*. Category-changing suffixes also differ with respect to their selectional properties, that is, whether they select projections including or not including certain argumental positions. For example, the adjectival suffix *-able* requires a verbal complement with argumental specifier and complement positions, since it does not productively combine with unergatives and unaccusatives, for example, *likeable*, **leaveable*, **snoreable*. On the other hand, the nominal suffix *-er* requires a VP complement with an argumental specifier position as it combines productively with unergatives but not with ergatives, for example, *worker*, **leaver*. These differences can be expressed in terms of a configuration in which a derivational affix both projects and takes in its complement domain an asymmetrical X-bar structure. Such projections are motivated, given a configurational theory of argument structure. However, the asymmetrical X-bar structure is not accessible to XP derivation and is not interpreted at the MF interface, where the CTC for X^0 expressions takes the form of a head-adjunction structure.

In our model, the central difference between an X^0 and an XP is a configurational difference at the interface. An X^0 is a head-adjunction structure at MF, even though an asymmetrical X-bar structure is projected in its derivation. On the other hand, an XP is an asymmetrical X-bar structure at LF, even though a head-adjunction structure is projected in its derivation.

The existence of a configurational difference between word-structure and phrase-structure is related to the fact that the derivation of words is driven by the conceptual necessity to form complex predicates on the basis of more elementary ones; this can be achieved via adjunct-head structure in our model, whereas the derivation of phrases is driven by the conceptual necessity to derive predicate-argument structures and that this can be achieved via asymmetrical X-bar projections.

2.3. Verb-formation

The properties of French denominal and deadjectival verbs, which we discuss in this section, bring support to our Modular hypothesis, according to which the CTC for X^0s is a head-adjunction structure while an asymmetrical X-bar structure can be projected in their derivation.[3]

We claim that the properties of denominal and deadjectival verbs in French, such as *accrocher*, "to hook" and *embellir*, "to embellish," can be accounted for if verb formation targets head-adjunction structures while it also allows asymmetrical X-bar structures in the derivation, as depicted in (7). These projections differ with respect to linear order of the constituents, as well as with respect to the dominance relations. While the linear order of the constituents is obtained in the projections in (7a, b), this is not the case for the projections in (7c, d), which provide the argument structure properties of the expressions. These projections are both motivated, as we will see here.

(7) a.

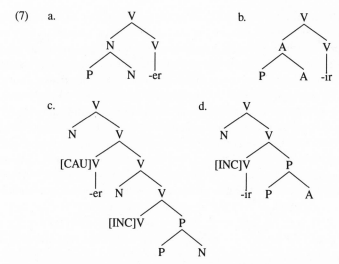

The projections in (7a, b) express the generalization that the verbal suffix *-er* composes with a lexical noun rather than with an adjective, for example, *timbrer*, "to stamp," *poster*, "to post," and *remiser*, "to store," while the verbal suffix *-ir* composes with an adjective rather than with a noun, for example, *faiblir*, "to weaken," *grandir*, "to grow," and *rougir*, "to redden."[4] The projections in (7c, d) also express the generalization that prefixed *-er* verbs are causatives [CAU], while prefixed *-ir* verbs are inchoatives [INC]. Furthermore, the projections in (7a, b) express the generalization that a prefix (P) is required in French denominal and deadjectival verbs, for example, *accrocher* versus **crocher*, *embellir* versus **bellir*, whereas the projections in (7c, d) express the generalization that the prepositional prefix is the relational category heading a change of location or a change of state phrase in the argument structure of the verbal projection. Motivation for the more complex structure in (7c, d) comes from the fact that the two verbal suffixes differ with respect to their argument structure, including conceptual and aspectual structure. In these projections, *-er* heads a projection with two subevents, an action event and a resulting inchoative event, whereas *-ir* heads an inchoative event. The difference in argument structure between *-er* and *-ir* verbs is supported by the difference in transitivity between these verbs. It is generally the case that denominal *-er* verbs are transitives, while deadjectival *-ir* verbs are generally intransitives, for example, *beurrer*, "to butter," and *rougir*, "to redden." This generalization is confirmed by the fact that when there is an *-er* as well as an *-ir* form for the same base, as is the case for *atterrer*, "to overwhelm," and *atterrir*, "to land," the *-er* verb is transitive/causative, whereas the *-ir* verb is intransitive/inchoative. Likewise, deadjectival verbs with *-er* are generally transitive/causative, as is the case for *majorer*, "to raise," whereas denominal verbs with *-ir* are intransitive/inchoative or have an intransitive/inchoative variant, as is the case for *fleurir*, "to bloom." Thus, the difference in transitivity and in the causative/inchoative semantics between *-er* and *-ir* denominal and deadjectival verbs constitutes evidence for the structural difference between *-er* and *-ir*-derived verbs, which is depicted in (7c, d).

Our hypothesis allows for the following predictions. First, it is possible to predict the categorial nature of the category that combines with the verbal suffix in the head-adjunction structures in (7a, b) if that category is related to a complement position in the argument structure projections of the suffixes in (7c, d). Assuming that places are mapped onto nouns and states are mapped onto adjectives, given the Canonical Structural Realization (cf. Grimshaw 1981, Pesetsky 1982, Rochette 1990), it follows that the category that combines with the verbal suffix *-er* is a noun, while the category that combines with the verbal suffix *-ir* is an adjective.

Furthermore, given that the complement domain of the verbal suffix *-ir* does not include a specifier position, as in (7d), we also predict that *-ir* may combine with intransitive adjectives, but not with transitive ones. In fact, deadjectival verbs are computable on the basis of ergative adjectives, but they may not combine with indirect transitive adjectives, for example, *certifier*, "to certify," versus **fièrifier*, "to proudify." This is to be expected in view of the fact that derivational affixes select on the basis of the ergative/transitive/unergative distinction, as discussed in Di Sciullo (1993a).

Thus, the properties of French denominal and deadjectival verbs bring support to the claim that, given a configurational theory of argument structure, a category-changing suffix has two domains, a head-adjunction domain and an asymmetrical X-bar domain.

The head-adjunction structure for the derived verbs would be a structure in which the noun or the adjective is adjacent to the verbal head, as in (7a, b) above. However, if these structures are related to the ones in (7c, d), they include abstract categories: the abstract verb V[INC], in the case of *-er* verbs, and the directional prefix P[D], as in the following head-adjunction structures.

(8)   a.   b.

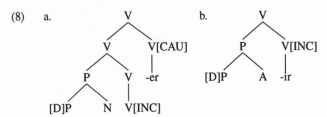

The abstract categories are interpreted by the C-I system at the MF interface; these categories are not interpreted by the A-P system, given that they lack phonetic features.[5]

The presence of abstract categories in these expressions allows for the following predictions. First, we predict that the verbal categories are spelled out in that order at PF: the inchoative affix *-ir* must precede the causative affix *-er*, but the former may not precede the latter. This is exactly what we find — *terreuriser*, "to terrorize," and *formaliser*, "to formalize," are possible, but not **terreuresir* and **formalesir*. Second, we predict that the abstract prepositional categories may not be spelled out at PF, as in *coller*, "to glue," and *rougir*, "to redden."

Futhermore, given that a category-changing suffix has a head-adjunction domain expressing word/predicate formation, we predict that such a suffix may not combine with a stem that is categorially and/or semantically of the same type.

We have shown elsewhere (Di Sciullo 1993a) that a category-changing suffix changes every dimension of argument structure, not only the categorial dimension (e.g., Noun → Verb → Adjective) but also the conceptual (e.g., Entity → Event → Attribute) and the aspectual dimension (e.g., Individual-level → Stage-level/Stage-level → Individual-level). To illustrate this point, let us consider the distinction between stage- and individual-level predicates (Carlson 1977, Kratzer 1984, Diesing 1992) in verb-formation. We observe that the suffix *-ir* typically composes with individual-level adjectives, yielding verbs that are generally interpreted as stage-level predicates. For example, the adjectival predicate *grand*, "big," in expressions such as *il est grand*, "he is tall," denotes a constant property of an individual that does not change through time. This is no longer the case with the deadjectival verb *grandir*, "to grow tall," in expressions such as *il grandit*, "he grows tall," denoting a transitory property, that is, a property in which changes are seen as progressing through time. The fact that a verbal affix selects on the basis of the aspectual properties of a predicate is the general case for derivational suffixes.[6]

2.4. Summary

According to our Modular hypothesis, the CTC for X^0 expressions is a head-adjunction structure at the MF interface with the C-I system, while an asymmetrical X-bar structure may be projected in their derivation. The head-adjunction structure is motivated under a configurational representation of word/predicate formation, while the asymmetrical X-bar structure is motivated under a configurational representation of argument structure.

Our hypothesis provides a way to express in configurational terms the fact that word-formation affects argument structure as well as gives rise to opacity effects. It allows for a unified account of the restrictions observed in French verb-formation with respect to the linear order of constituents, as well as with respect to the argument structure restrictions imposed by the verbal suffixes on the projections with which they combine. In the case of prefixed denominal and deadjectival verbs, neither the specifier-head-complement structure nor the head-adjunction structure alone is sufficient to account for the full range of restrictions in configurational terms, for instance, the fact that *-ir* does not combine with transitive adjectives but does combine with intransitive ones, and the fact that *-ir* does not form a verb on the basis of a verbal or a nominal predicate, but on the basis of an adjectival predicate.

3. EXTERNAL INTERFACE CONDITIONS

We now turn to the conditions applying to word-structure. We discuss the effects of both external and internal interface conditions in order to show that purely configurational conditions apply to X^0 expressions at MF.

Assuming, as in the Minimalist framework, that the only conditions of the grammar are external conditions, we pursue the hypothesis that the conditions are relativized to the configurational properties of the interfaces to which they apply (cf. Di Sciullo 1990a, b). In the following paragraphs we discuss the application of the Principle of Full Interpretation at MF.

3.1. Full Interpretation

The Principle of Full Interpretation proposed in Chomsky (1986–1993) applies at LF and PF and requires that every element in a linguistic expression be a legitimate object. In order to be interpreted at LF, a linguistic expression must only be constituted of elements that have a uniform language-independent interpretation at that interface.

(9)   *Full Interpretation (FI)*
      At Logical Form, each legitimate object is a chain: either a head, an argument, a
      modifier, or an operator-variable construction. (Chomsky 1993)

We propose that FI applies to X^0 expressions, as well as to XP expressions. We show, however, that the properties of legitimate objects in X^0 and XP expressions are not coextensive. This leads us to conclude that FI is relativized to apply to head-adjunction structures at MF.

3.2. Head

We assume that both XP and X^0 expressions include a head, given their X-bar format. However, the head of an X^0 and the head of an XP have partially different formal properties.

In XP structure, a head projects a higher level category; in X^0 structure, a morphological head is a two-segment category and thus does not project a different type of category. This constitutes a first formal difference between a X^0 head-adjunction structure, on the one hand, and an XP structure, on the other.

Second, languages such as French and English exhibit linear-order asymmetries with respect to the position of the head in XP and in X^0 expressions. The asymmetries are expected if the notion of head is relativized to CTCs.

Third, assuming that heads are predicates and that predicates can either be XP or X^0, an X^0 predicate differs from an XP predicate with respect to the following properties. On the one hand, an XP predicate is an open function requiring an external argument for saturation within its XP domain (cf. Williams 1980, Rothstein 1983); on the other hand, an X^0 predicate is not subject to such a requirement in its X^0 domain. If predication is defined, as in Williams (1980), in terms of a symmetrical c-command relation between two maximal categories, this relation does not hold in head-adjunction structures, as depicted below.

(10)   a.   b.

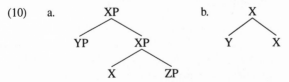

If YP in (10a) is the external argument or the logical subject of XP, this is not the case for Y with respect to X in (10b). Furthermore, a predicative head in an X^0 expression is not interpreted as if it was part of a specifier-head structure; otherwise it would be impossible to account for the fact that X^0 expressions generally exclude the overt projection of the external argument (cf. Halle 1990). This is the case in French denominal verbs, in which the overt non-head is never interpreted as the external argument or the logical subject, even though the nominal category precedes the verbal head, as is generally the case for external arguments in XP structure. Thus, a predicative head in an X^0 expression differs formally from a predicative head in an XP expression. This suggests that a predicate is an open function only if it is part of an asymmetrical X-bar structure at the interface. In a X^0 head-adjunction structure, a predicative head is not an open function requiring an external argument or logical subject for saturation within its X^0 domain. The configurational difference between X^0 and XP predicates correlates with the difference between the attributive versus descriptive interpretation of categories (cf. Di Sciullo 1993c).

Thus, the notions of head of an X^0 and head of XP are not coextensive. They differ with respect to their projection, interpretation, and, in some languages, with respect to their distribution.

3.3. Operator-Variable

If the CTC for an X^0 expression is a head-adjunction structure, there is no visible operator-variable chain in that expression at the interface with the C-I system. Consequently, a suffixal head may not be interpreted as an operator at MF even though there is a close semantic relation between a derived nominal, such as the one in (11a), and a relative clause, such as the one in (11b), including an operator-variable at LF.

(11) a. a writer
     b. someone who writes (by profession)

As expected, the semantic parallelism between (11a) and (11b) does not correspond to a parallelism in structure. Evidence to this effect comes from the fact that a parasitic gap may not be licensed in the XP projection of a derived nominal, whereas this is possible in a relative clause.

(12) a. *a writer without publishing
     b. someone who writes without publishing
     c. The book he wrote without publishing

This fact also brings support to our hypothesis that the CTC for an X^0 expression is a head-adjunction structure at the interface, even though an asymmetrical X-bar structure may be projected in the derivation. In the case at hand, the nominal suffix *-er* must be linked to the specifier (external argument) of the VP in its complement domain and saturate this position, since this argument may not be saturated outside the deverbal noun, as in **the writer by John*, in which *John* is the one who writes. Furthermore, the existence of a semantic relation between expressions such as (11a) and (11b) suggests that the structure of *-er* nominals may include both an XP predication relation and an XP operator-variable relation at some point in the derivation. However, these relations licensed in the asymmetrical X-bar projection of the suffixal head are not visible at MF.

Here again, as was the case for heads and predicates, operator-like elements do not have the same properties in XP and in X^0 expressions. If the nominal suffixes *-er* and *-ee* are quasi operators, the variable they bind in their asymmetrical X-bar domain is no longer accessible in their X^0 head-adjunction domain. Operator-variable chains may be licensed via an asymmetrical X-bar structure. Operator-variable chains are not licensed in a adjunct-head structure.

3.4. Modifier

Assuming Kayne's (1995) theory, the non-head in an X^0 expression may be interpreted as a modifier, since it precedes the head. However, if this were the case, the interpretation of the non-head and the interpretation of the head would be conjoined, assuming as in Higginbotham (1985) that modification results in the conjunction of two attributes predicated of a single individual. However, this is not necessarily the case in X^0 expressions, since the non-head may be linked to an argument position, as in denominal verbs, or to a head position, as in prefixed verbs.

Prefixes provide aspectual modification to the projection they are adjoined to. Some prefixes modify an entire event by iterating it or inverting it, as in (13a); other prefixes modify some internal parameter of the event, such as the direction or the orientation of an event, as in (13b).

(13) a. restructurer/déstructurer quelque chose
          "restructure/unstructure something"
      b. apporter/emporter quelque chose
          "bring to/bring away something"

The analysis of prefixes as adjuncts provides the configurational basis for their interpretation. However, the licensing of prefixes in word-structure differs from their licensing in XP structures. Support for this claim comes from the fact that in some cases it is not always possible to modify an event word-internally, whereas it is possible to do so with XPs.

(14) a. désirer quelque chose à nouveau
          "to desire something again"
      b. *redésirer quelque chose
          "to redesire something"
      c. courir à travers la forêt
          "to run through the forest"
      d. *transcourir la forêt
          "to transrun the forest"

In our model, (14b) is excluded because the aspectual attributes of the stative verb *désirer*, "to desire," may not be identified by the iterative prefix *re-*, which may only identify accomplishments (cf. Di Sciullo, in this volume). On the other hand, adverbial XPs such as *à nouveau* are not restricted in such a way. They are possible in these structures and provide the actual iteration of the event. Likewise, in (14d), the aspectual attributes of the activity verb *courir*, "to run," are not specified for a path, contrary to verbs such as *porter*, "to carry," which may combine with a prefix, for example, *transporter*, "to transport." On the other hand, prepositional XPs expressing paths, such as *à travers,* are not restricted in such a way. They are possible in structures such as (14c), and they identify the trajectory of the event. A directional prefix, such as the prefix *a-* in the French verb *apporter*, "to bring to," identifies the spatial orientation of the event; it does not describe the actual spatial endpoint of the event, which can be done by a PP complement, as in *apporter les livres à l'école*, "to bring the books to school." This, again, is typical of the difference in interpretation between categories in an X^0 head-adjunction structure, as opposed to categories in an asymmetrical X-bar structure.

We will thus take the non-head in X^0 expressions to be interpreted as an adjunct without being necessarily interpreted as a modifier, since some adjuncts are linked to argument positions, as is the case for the non-head in denominal verbs, while other adjuncts are linked to a predicative head, as is the case for the prefix in prefixed denominal verbs. Complex X^0 expressions may include more than one adjunct, as depicted in (15) with Z and Y, each adjunct identifies a feature of the head it is adjoined to.

(15)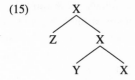

3.5. Argument

The adjunct in an X^0 head-adjunction structure is not an argument of the head. The properties of the adjunct differ from the properties of arguments in XP structure.

According to Chomsky (1993), an argument is a narrowly L-related XP category. It is a chain originating in an argument position within the VP and headed by the specifier of an agreement phrase. A head-adjunction structure does not include such a chain. The non-head in an X^0 expression is an adjunct and thus cannot be an XP argument of the head at MF, even if it is related to an argument position in its asymmetrical X-bar projection. Consequently, the non-head exhibits some of the properties of arguments, even though it is not an argument of the head at MF.

It has been proposed, however, that selectional restrictions, both categorial and semantic, hold between a suffixal head and the non-head in an X^0 expression (cf. Borer 1990, Lieber 1992, Roeper 1987, Booij 1992). If correct, the non-head would be an argument of the suffixal head and not an adjunct, since heads select arguments and not adjuncts. We argued in Di Sciullo (1995) that the selection is configurational in nature and that the adjunct in an X^0 head-adjunction structure is not an argument of the head on the basis of the properties of deverbal nouns and adjectives. The properties of denominal verbs and deverbal compounds also bring evidence to this effect, as we will see next.

In French denominal verbs, the verbal suffix *-er* may combine with a nominal expression it c-commands in its X-bar projection, one of the two lower N positions in (16). In change-of-place verbs, the nominal expression can be related to the Theme role, as in *timbrer*, "to stamp," or to the Location role, as in *remiser*, "to store."

(16)

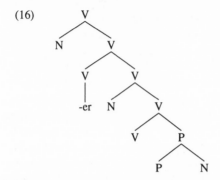

However, the noun that composes with the verbal causative suffix *-er* is not the external argument of the verbal suffix, that is, the higher verb in (16). It is either an argument of the inchoative predicate, that is, the lower verb in (16), as in *timbrer*, or an argument of the directional head, the prepositional head in (16), as in *remiser*. If the selectional restrictions holding between the suffixal head and the projection with which it combines are not local relations, they may be stated configurationally in terms of linking to X-bar positions in its complement domain, as proposed in Di Sciullo (1995). The adjunct in the X^0 head-adjunction projection of denominal verbs is not an argument of the verbal head. It is related to a directional predicate IN in the asymmetrical X-bar projection of that suffixal head.[7] The adjunct is not an argument of the causative or the inchoative predicate, spelled out as *-er* and *-ir*, respectively. Thus, there is no direct "argument of" relation between the adjunct and the verbal suffixal head at MF, while the adjunct is linked to an argument position in the derivation.

Thus, the selectional properties of derivational suffixes provide evidence for our proposal. In denominal verbs, the non-head is not an argument of the head; it is an adjunct and thus exhibits opacity with respect to overt movement. This is also what we observe in English deverbal compounds, in which the non-head is related to an argument position in the asymmetrical X-bar projection of the head, but is no longer an argument in its X^0 head-adjunction structure. As expected, the non-head manifests opacity with respect to overt movement and anaphora.

Giorgi and Longobardi (1991) argue that arguments are excluded from compounds for the following reasons. First, the internal noun does not induce the same truth-value as a referential DP in object position. Hence, (17b) is a contradiction, but (17a) is not. Second, the noun included in the compound cannot bind any A-position, although a regular internal argument can, as evidenced in (17c, d, e). Third, the noun can be doubled, as in (17f), and if it is the case that the genitive phrase discharges the internal argument (cf. Higginbotham 1985), the noun included in the compound cannot be licensed by Theta-marking.

(17) a. John is a Nixon-hater, but he does not hate Nixon.
     b. John is a hater of Nixon, but he does not hate Nixon.
     c. The informers of a person about himself.
     d. A person's informers about himself.
     e. *Person-informers about himself.
     f. The bar-tender of Bill's bar.

This is compatible with our view that a nominal expression in an X^0 expression is not directly Theta-related to the head, even though it may be indirectly related to an argument position projected via an asymmetrical X-bar structure in the derivation.

If we assume that thematic XP arguments are not part of deverbal compounds at MF, it is possible to account more directly for the restrictions they are subject to. It is possible to account for the fact that phrases are generally excluded word-internally, since thematic arguments are XPs. It is also possible to account for the fact that overt case features are generally excluded in deverbal compounds in languages such as Modern Greek, in which XP arguments have overt case features. This is what we find, as illustrated in (18), in which the non-head *kapn-*, "tobacco," has no overt case features (cf. Di Sciullo and Ralli 1994).

(18) kapnokaliergia   kapn-   kaliery-   -i-   -a
     "tobacco cultivation" "tobacco" "cultivate" "-ion" nominative

Thus XP arguments are not legitimate objects at MF, in which X^0 expressions are head-adjunction structure, and in which the adjunct may but needs not be related to an argument position in the asymmetrical X-bar projection of the head.

3.6. Summary

If FI applies at MF, X^0 expressions must be constituted of legitimate objects. These objects are reduced to heads and adjuncts in our model. The head projects its features as being part of a segment, and the non-head is an adjunct identifying some features of the head.

The parts of an X^0 expression may be related to asymmetrical X-bar positions in the derivation; however, they are not interpreted as if they were in these positions at MF. This is a desirable result, given that an asymmetrical X-bar projection includes XP arguments, XP predicates and XP modifiers with descriptive meaning, and that these categories are not part of X^0 expressions at MF.

In the next section, we show that internal interface conditions proposed to apply in the derivation of XP expressions fail to apply in the derivation of X^0 expressions. This provides additional support to our hypothesis, according to which the conditions applying at MF are strictly configurational conditions on X^0 expressions, that is, conditions on head-adjunction structures given X^0's CTC.

4. INTERNAL INTERFACE CONDITIONS

The Projection principle, the Aspectual Interface hypothesis, and the Uniformity of Theta Assignment hypothesis proposed in the Government and Binding framework (cf. Chomsky 1981–1986) are internal interface conditions. They apply to D-structure, the interface between the lexicon and the syntax. They are basically conditions on the linking of Theta-roles to syntactic positions. If these conditions fail in part as conditions on XP structures (Chomsky 1993, 1994; Browdy 1993), they also fail as conditions on X^0s, as we show here by considering the properties of English deverbal compounds.

Assuming that Theta-roles can be projected only via an asymmetrical X-bar structure, as is the case in configurational theories of thematic structure, the fact that Theta-based conditions such as those mentioned above do not apply to X^0 expressions also points to the conclusion that X^0 expressions are not asymmetrical X-bar projections at the point where the conditions apply. According to our hypothesis, the only conditions they are subject to are conditions on the licensing of heads and adjuncts.

4.1. The Projection Principle and the Theta Criterion

The Projection principle (PrPr) governs the mapping of categories from the lexicon to the syntax. In particular, it ensures the presence of D-structure positions for the projection of the Theta-roles of a predicative head.

(19) *Projection Principle*
      The thematic properties of lexical items must be present at all levels of syntactic representation. (Chomsky 1981)

Several problems have been noted in the literature with respect to the PrPr,[8] as well as with the related principle, the Theta Criterion (ThC) of Chomsky (1981), imposing a biuniqueness relation between arguments and Theta-roles and requiring that every role be saturated in the syntax.[9]

(20) *Theta Criterion*
      Each argument bears one and only one Theta-role, and each Theta-role is associated to one and only one argument. (Chomsky 1981)

The fact that in eventive deverbal compounds, such as those in (21), there is at least one role — the external role — that must be projected in XP structures suggests that X^0 expressions are not subject to conditions such as the PrPr and the Theta Criterion.

(21) a. John hates exam-giving.
      b. Exam-giving to students is dull.
      c. He likes letter-writing.
      d. Letter-writing to a friend is fun.

In the Minimalist program (cf. Chomsky 1993, 1994) there is no condition that bears on the mapping of the complete set of Theta-roles of a predicative head onto syntactic positions. However, this does not undermine the requirement that the thematic structure be represented configurationally in the derivation. The absence of principles such as the PrPr and the ThC, on the one hand, and the requirement that the thematic structure be represented configurationally, on the other, are not incompatible if we assume the CTC hypothesis. Thus, even though more complex structures may be projected in the derivation of an X^0 expression, only a subpart of the projection is interpreted at MF, the head-adjunction structure.[10] That only a part of the projection is visible or interpreted at a given interface is crucial in the derivation of words, in which argument structure positions are affected in the derivation. Thus, with agentive compounds such as that in (22), the non-head saturates the Theme role and the nominal suffix saturates the Agent role of the verb included in the compound. These roles may not be saturated outside of the compound, as illustrated in (22b, c). Assuming a configurational representation of thematic structure, the Theta-roles must be projected in terms of an asymmetrical X-bar structure in the derivation of these compounds.

(22)   a.   John is a book-buyer.
       b.   *He is a book-buyer of novels.
       c.   *This is a book-buyer by John.

However, these positions are not interpreted as argument positions at MF, since the noun included in the compound is not the direct projection of a Theta-role; rather, it is indirectly related to the thematic structure of the verb, as is the case for adjuncts originating in argument positions. This can be seen in (22a), in which the nominal category included in the compound *book* does not denote an entity that actually undergoes a change of place, as it is the case for a Theme in XP structure, as in *John buys a book*. The nominal category *book* identifies the attributes or type of entity satisfying the predicate *buy* it composes with. If this is the case, and if Theta-roles may only have a descriptive meaning via an asymmetrical X-bar projection, deverbal compounds are not subject to the PrPr or the ThC at MF.

4.2. The UTAH and the Thematic Hierarchy

Another internal interface condition ensuring the mapping of Theta-roles from the lexicon to the syntax is the Uniformity Theta Assignment hypothesis (UTAH).

(23)   *Uniformity of Theta Assignment Hypothesis*
       Identical thematic relationships between items are represented by identical struc-
       tural relationships between those items at the level of D-structure. (Baker 1988)

The UTAH is a descendant of Perlmutter and Postal's (1984) Universal Alignment Hypothesis (UAH), according to which the initial relation borne by each argument in a given clause is predicted from the meaning of the clause. The UTAH specifies that there is a direct mapping between thematic roles and syntactic structure and that each thematic role must be linked to a single position in D-structure. Therefore, any deviation from that position must be accomplished by movement. The UTAH restricts the position of arguments at D-structure and forces a syntactic movement in constructions in which a change occurred in grammatical functions (noun-incorporation, passivization, causativization, and so on).

Along with PrPr and the ThC, the UTAH is problematic.[11] It faces further problems when we consider its application to deverbal compounds, as we will see directly.

It has been observed that deverbal compounds are subject to restrictions with respect to the projection of Theta-roles. In particular, the Agent and the Goal may not be projected within deverbal compounds, while the non-head is generally related to the Theme role.

(24)   a. *student-giving of exams
       b. *professor-giving of exams to students
       c. exam-giving to students by professors

Attempts have been made to account for the thematic restrictions on deverbal compounds in terms of the thematic hierarchy. However, these attempts do not provide convincing explanations.

According to Grimshaw (1990), the exclusion of the Agent, as well as the Goal, from deverbal compounds follows from the thematic hierarchy in (25a) in conjunction with the assumption that Theta-role assignment is cyclic, the lowest Theta-role in the hierarchy being assigned first. This proposal is problematic on theoretical grounds, in view of the fact that several thematic hierarchies have been proposed in the literature (Jackendoff 1972, Larson 1988, Grimshaw 1990), some of which make opposite predictions with respect to the admissibility of Goal and Themes in compounds.

(25)   a. (Agent (Experiencer (Goal/Source/Location) (Theme))) (Grimshaw 1990)
       b. Agent > Theme > Goal > Obliques (Manner, Location, Time ...) (Larson 1988)

The fact that it is generally the Theme that is projected and not the Goal or the Agent is correctly predicted by Grimshaw's hierarchy but not by Larson's hierarchy. However, a purely configurational approach leads to a more straightforward account of these restrictions.

Notice that a nominal expression that bears a given role in an XP structure, say, the Goal, the Experiencer, or the Location role, may no longer be related to that role when part of a deverbal compound. Thus, in the examples in (26), compound formation is possible if a Goal, an Experiencer, or a Location interpretation for the nominal non-head is not forced by an XP complement.

(26)   a. To give a present to a child is fun.
       b. *child-giving of presents is fun.
       c. Child-giving by parents is not so frequent.
       d. Man fears sharks.
       e. *Man-fearing of sharks is frequent.
       f. Man-fearing by sharks is rare.
       g. To load hay into a truck is not fun.
       h. *Truck-loading of hay is not fun.
       i. Hay-loading of trucks is not fun.

This indicates that the thematic restrictions on deverbal compounds are configurational conditions and not conditions that make reference to specific Theta-roles or to linear organizations of Theta-roles.

4.3. The Aspectual Interface Hypothesis

According to the Aspectual Interface hypothesis (AIH), the direct object of a verb can be defined in aspectual terms as the argument that delimits the event. The prominence of the direct internal argument in the delimitation of an event is used as a general mapping principle relating thematic and syntactic structures.

(27) *Aspectual Interface Hypothesis*
      The mapping between thematic structure and syntactic argument structure is governed by aspectual properties. A universal aspectual structure associated with internal (direct, external, and oblique) arguments in syntactic structure constrains the kinds of event participants that can occupy these positions. Only the aspectual part of thematic structure is visible to syntax. (Tenny 1989)

The AIH fails in part for XP structures, as noted in Filip (1990) and elsewhere.[12] It also fails for word-structure. Considering English deverbal compounds, we observe that the noun included in the compound, even if it is related to the internal argument position of the verbal head, does not delimit the event denoted by that verb. This can be seen in the examples in (28), using durative and punctual adverbials, in which the noun included in a deverbal compound is non-delimiting in (28a), whereas the object of the verb may be, if it includes a definite determiner, as in (28c).

(28) a. John proofread for an hour/*in an hour.
      b. John read proofs for an hour/ *in an hour.
      c. John read the proof *for an hour/in an hour.

If we assume that the noun included in the deverbal compound is an adjunct at MF, the fact that it does not delimit the event denoted by the verbal projection of which it is part follows from the properties of the configuration of which it is part.

4.4. Summary

We identified some problems with a set of internal interface conditions based on Theta-roles. These conditions are already problematic when considering their application to XP structures. We provided evidence to the effect that these conditions do not apply to X^0 structures. If thematic structure projects via asymmetrical X-bar structure, the fact that Theta-based conditions do not apply to word-structure points to the conclusion that X^0 expressions are not interpreted in terms of asymmetrical X-bar structures at MF.

5. CONSEQUENCES FOR THE ARCHITECTURE OF THE GRAMMAR

Our work supports a model of grammar in which conditions apply only at the interfaces between the grammar and the performance systems. The expressions generated by the grammar are not isomorphic at the interfaces, even though they may share projections in their derivation.

We argued that X^0s and XPs have distinct properties: they both differ configurationally and with respect to the interpretation of their parts. With respect to configuration, X^0 expressions are adjunct-head structures at the MF interface with the C-I system; they are not asymmetrical X-bar projections. With respect to interpretation, the parts of X^0 expressions have an attributive interpretation and not a descriptive one, as is the case for XP expressions.

Our work also supports a model of grammar in which the conditions apply to the external interfaces according to the properties of these interfaces. We proposed that FI applies at the interface between X^0 expressions and the C-I system, legitimizing heads and adjuncts. On the other hand, syntactic conditions that make reference to Theta-roles do not apply to word-structure, given that Theta-roles may only be projected via an asymmetrical X-bar structure and that the latter is not part of word-structure at the MF interface.

If MF is part of the right branch of the grammar, as discussed in Halle and Marantz (1993a), our work suggests that it is also part of the left branch of the grammar.

NOTES

Earlier versions of this chapter were presented at the GLOW Colloquium at the University of Lisbon in 1990, and at the Linguistic Symposium on Romance Languages at UCLA in 1993. We thank the participants to these conferences for their questions and comments. We also thank Noam Chomsky, Ken Hale, Jeff Gruber, Pierre Pica, and Tom Roeper for discussions. This study was supported by the Social Sciences and Humanities Research Council of Canada grant #411-92-0012 (La modularité de la grammaire: arguments, projections et variations), by the Fonds pour la formation de Chercheurs et l'Aide à la Recherche grant #94ER401 (Interfaces: invariants et relativisation), and by the Fonds Institutionnel de Recherche of the Université du Québec à Montréal.

1. Adjunction is either to a minimal or a maximal category in the derivation of X^0 expressions, as evidenced in Di Sciullo and Klipple (1994), according to which certain prefixes must adjoin to V^0 while others must adjoin to VP in French verb-formation.

2. See Sportiche (1988), Speas (1990), Hale and Keyser (1992), Di Sciullo (1993b), Gruber (in this volume), and Gruber and Collins (in this volume) for motivations in favor of the projection of argument structure in terms of an asymmetrical X-bar structure.

3. For other analyses of denominal and deadjectival verbs, see Hale and Keyser (1992) for an analysis of English denominal verbs, Borer (1990) for an analysis of English deadjectival verbs, Labelle (1992) and Lieber (1992) for an analysis of French denominal verbs, and Di Sciullo (1990) for an analysis of Italian deadjectival verbs.

4. There is, however, a small set of counterexamples to this generalization, including -*e*-(*r*) verbs with adjectives, such as *hausser*, "to raise," and *baisser*, "to lower"; as well as a small class of -*i*-(*r*) verbs with nouns, such as *finir*, "to finish," and *fleurir*, "to flower." However, the denominals and deadjectivals that escape our generalization come from Latin and earlier stages of French. In fact, they are no longer productive in modern French, in which new -*e*-(*r*) verbs are not currently formed from adjectives and new -*i*-(*r*) verbs are no longer formed from nouns. a. *hausser*: from *halcer*, XIIe s. Latin vul. *altiare*, from *altus*, "high"; b. *fleurir*: from *florir*, XIIe s. Latin vul. *florire*, from *flos*, "flower." See Houle (1993) for an extensive description of these facts.

5. Note that categorial selection for derivational affixes, assumed in Lieber (1992) and elsewhere, becomes an epiphenomenon in our view. See Di Sciullo (1995) for a way to derive subcategorization features for derivational affixes.

6. Likewise, the adjectival suffix *-able*, "-able," may only combine with verbs with a stage-level interpretation yielding adjectives with an individual-level interpretation. Thus, when a verb has the two interpretations available, one individual and the other stage, as for *peser*, "to weigh," *-able* may only be suffixed to the stage-level variant, that is, with the interpretation of the verb, which may vary through time — for example, *ceci/*un kilo est pesable*, "this/*one kilo is weighable." This is expected in our model, in which selectional restrictions are configurational restrictions covering all the dimensions of the argument structure of a predicate, including the aspectual dimension, projected in terms of asymmetrical X-bar structure.

7. The directional predicate IN is not the only predicate to be projected in these structures. Other directional predicates may be present, such as AT, TO, or ON, depending on the argument structure properties of the verbal projection.

8. Chomsky (1993) points out that complex adjectival constructions such as those in (i) are problematic for the PrPr as well as for the level of D-structure at which the PrPr applies. In these structures, the overt subject, here, *John*, is in a non-Theta position and therefore cannot appear in that position at D-structure, even though it must appear in that position given the structure in (ii).

   i. John is easy to please.

   ii. John is easy [CP O [IP PRO to please *t*]]

If it does appear in that position, the structure violates the PrPr requirement that the elements participating to interpretation at Logical Form be present at D-structure. If it were to be inserted at a later stage in the derivation, as suggested in Chomsky (1981), D-structure would still not be isomorphic to LF, and the PrPr would still be violated.

Chomsky (1993) suggests that we eliminate the PrPr and view the projection of items from the lexicon to the syntax in purely configurational terms, as the projection of a lexical item from the lexicon onto one of the positions licensed in asymmetrical X-bar head-complement and specifier-head structure.

9. On the basis of the properties of indefinite object constructions, Rizzi (1986) proposed to revise the PrPr as in (i). According to (i), Theta-roles may be saturated in the lexicon. This is also assumed in Hale and Keyser (1986) and Guerssel (1986), for instance, as well as in Di Sciullo (1990), in which an earliness principle is proposed, here in (ii), which has the consequence that not all roles selected by a predicative head are projected onto categorial structure.

   i. Categorial structure reflects lexically unsaturated thematic structure.
      (Rizzi 1986)
   ii. If an argument can be saturated at a level L, then it must be saturated at L.
      (Di Sciullo 1990)

10. The idea that certain projections are not visible or interpreted at LF is suggested in Chomsky (1994), in which intermediate level categories are not visible; only maximal categories are.

11. Borer (1990) argues that the UTAH makes wrong predictions with respect to the projection of the argument selected by verbal passives as opposed to adjectival passives. The thematic nature of the selected argument is the same — it is a Theme — however, it is an internal argument in the first case and an external argument in the second.

    i. The vase was broken (by John).
    ii. The vase is broken.
    iii. *The vase is broken by John.

Assuming that Borer (1990) as well as Levin and Rappaport (1986) are right in their analysis of passive structures, UTAH fails at D-structure.

12. Filip (1990) notes that the singular/plural distinction of the external argument has an effect on the properties of the sentence. Another problem with the AIH is that the aspectual properties of the predicate have an effect on the possibility for the object to be delimiting, as in (i). A further problem with the AIH is that the direct object may be delimiting, depending on the mass/count features of the object, as in (ii), as well as on the singular/plural features of the object, as in (iii).

    i. a. A/the bird flew in./He drank a bottle of beer.
        b. Birds flew in./He drank many bottles of beer.
    ii. a. to paint a wall/to eat a cake
        b. to wash a shirt/to push a cart
    iii. a. John loaded the hay onto the wagon.
        b. John loaded hay onto the wagon.
        c. John loaded the wagon with hay.
        d. John loaded wagons with hay.

These facts suggest that the residue of the AIP should be viewed as a condition on LF and not a condition on D-structure.

REFERENCES

Abney, Steven. 1987. "The English noun phrase in its sentential aspect." Doctoral diss., MIT, Cambridge, Mass.

Ackema, Peter. 1995. *Syntax below zero*. Utrecht: OTS Publications.

Aronoff, Mark. 1976. *Word formation in generative grammar*. Cambridge, Mass.: MIT Press.

Baker, Mark. 1988. *Incorporation: A theory of grammatical function changing*. Chicago: University of Chicago Press.

Borer, Hagit. 1990. "Derived nominals and the causative-inchoative alternation: Two case studies in parallel morphology." Ms. University of California at Irvine.

Booij, Geert. 1992. "Morphology, semantics, and argument structure." In *Thematic structure: Its role in grammar*, ed. Iggy Roca, 47–63. Dordrecht: Foris.

Browdy, Michael. 1993. "Theta-theory and arguments." *Linguistic Inquiry* 24:1–23.

Carlson, Greg. 1977. "Reference to kinds." Doctoral diss., University of Massachusetts, Amherst, Mass.

Chierchia, Gennaro, and Sally McConnell-Ginet. 1990. *Meaning and grammar*. Cambridge, Mass.: MIT Press.

Chomsky, Noam. 1970. "Remarks on nominalizations." In *Readings in English transformational grammar*, ed. Roderick A. Jacobs and Peter S. Rosenbaum, 184–221. Waltham, Mass.: Ginn.

———. 1981. *Lectures on government and binding*. Dordrecht: Foris.

———. 1986a. *Knowledge of language: Its nature, origin, and use*. New York: Praeger.

———. 1986b. *Barriers*. Linguistic Inquiry Monograph 13. Cambridge, Mass.: MIT Press.

——. 1988. "Some notes on economy of derivation and representation." In *Principles and parameters in comparative grammar*, ed. Robert Freidin, 417–454. Cambridge, Mass.: MIT Press.

——. 1993. "A minimalist program for linguistic theory." In *The view from Building 20: Essays in linguistics in honor of Sylvain Bromberger*, ed. Kenneth Hale and Samuel Jay Keyser, 1–52. Cambridge, Mass.: MIT Press.

——. 1994. "Bare phrase structure." In *MIT Occasional Papers in Linguistics* 5. Department of Linguistics and Philosophy, MIT, Cambridge, Mass.

Cinque, Guglielmo. 1990. "Agreement and head-to-head movement in the Romance noun phrase." Paper presented at the XXth Linguistic Symposium on Romance Languages, University of Ottawa.

——. 1991. "A null theory of phrasal stress." *Linguistic Inquiry* 24:239–297.

Diesing, Molly. 1992. *Indefinites*. Cambridge, Mass.: MIT Press.

Di Sciullo, Anna-Maria. 1990a. "Modularity and the mapping from the lexicon to the syntax." *Probus* 2:257–290.

——. 1990b. "Multi-level saturation." *Lexicon Project Working Papers* 33. Center for Cognitive Science, MIT, Cambridge, Mass.

——. 1991. "On the structure of deverbal compounds." *University of Venice Working Papers in Linguistics* 3:1–25. Centro linguistico interfacoltà, Università degli studi di Venezia.

——. 1992. "Deverbal compounds and the external argument." In *Thematic structure: Its role in grammar*, ed. Iggy Roca, 65–78. Dordrecht: Foris.

——. 1993a. "The Complement domain of a head at morphological form." *Probus* 5:95–125.

——. 1993b. "Selection and derivational affixes." Paper read at the 1992 International Morphology Meeting in Krems. To appear in *Progress in Morphology*, ed. Martin Prinzhorn, Berlin: Walter de Gruyter, forthcoming.

——. 1993c. "Prefixes and suffixes." Paper presented at the XXIVth Linguistic Symposium on Romance Languages held at USC and UCLA. To appear in *Romance Linguistics in Los Angeles: Selected papers from the XXIVth linguistic symposium on Romance languages at USC and UCLA*, ed. Claudia Parodi, Carlos Quicoli, Mario Saltarelli, and Maria Luisa Zubizarreta, Georgetown University Press, forthcoming.

——. 1994a. "Word-internal pronouns and reflexives." Paper presented at the Conference on Anaphoric Relations at the University of Antwerp. To appear in *Proceedings of the conference on anaphoric relations*, University of Antwerp, Belgium, forthcoming.

——. 1994b. "Modularity." Paper read at the XXth International Linguistic Conference at Moscow Lomonosov State University. To appear in *Proceedings of the XXth international conference in linguistics*, Moscow Lomonosov State University, forthcoming.

——. 1995. "X-bar Selection." In *Phrase structure and the lexicon*, ed. Johan Rooryck and Laurie Zaring, 77–107. Dordrecht: Kluwer.

Di Sciullo, Anna-Maria, and Edwin Williams. 1987. *On the definition of words*. Cambridge, Mass.: MIT Press.

Di Sciullo, Anna-Maria, and Elizabeth Klipple. 1994. "Modifying affixes." In *Proceedings of the Western Conference on Linguistics XXIII*. University of Washington, Seattle.

Di Sciullo, Anna-Maria, and Angela Ralli. 1994. "Theta-role saturation in Greek deverbal compounds." To appear in the *Proceedings of the first international workshop on Modern Greek syntax*, Dordrecht: Kluwer, forthcoming.

Dowty, David. 1979. "On the semantic content of the notion of thematic role." In *Property theory, type theory, and natural language semantics*, vol. II: *Semantic issues*, ed. Gennaro Chierchia, Barbara Partee, and R. Turner. Dordrecht: Kluwer.

Filip, Hanna. 1990. "Thematic role and aspect." Ms. University of California at Berkeley.

Giorgi, Alessandra, and Giuseppe Longobardi. 1991. *The syntax of noun phrases.* Cambridge: Cambridge University Press.

Grimshaw, Jane. 1981. "Form, function, and the language acquisition device." In *The logical problem of language acquisition*, ed. Charles Lee Baker and James McCarthy. Cambridge, Mass.: MIT Press.

———. 1990. *Argument structure.* Cambridge, Mass.: MIT Press.

———. 1991. "Extended projection." Ms. Brandeis University, Waltham, Mass.

Gruber, Jeffrey. 1965. "Studies in lexical relations." Doctoral diss., MIT, Cambridge, Mass.

Guerssell, Mohamed. 1986. "On Berber verbs of change: A study of transitivity alternations." *Lexicon Project Working Papers* 9. Center for Cognitive Science, MIT, Cambridge, Mass.

Hale, Kenneth. 1990. "The syntax of lexical word formation." Ms. MIT, Cambridge, Mass.

———. 1991. "On argument structure and the lexical expression of syntactic relations." Ms. MIT, Cambridge, Mass.

Hale, Kenneth, and Samuel Jay Keyser. 1992. "The syntactic character of thematic structure." In *Thematic structure: Its role in grammar*, ed. Iggy Roca, 107–141. Dordrecht: Foris.

Halle, Morris, and Alec Marantz. 1993. "Distributed morphology and the pieces of inflexion." In *The view from Building 20: Essays in linguistics in honor of Sylvain Bromberger*, ed. Kenneth Hale and Samuel Jay Keyser, 111–176. Cambridge, Mass.: MIT Press.

Higginbotham, James. 1985. "On semantics." *Linguistic Inquiry* 16:547–595.

Houle, Jocelyne. 1993. "Analyses lexicales des ergatifs." In *La modularité de la grammaire: arguments, projections et variation*, ed. Anna-Maria Di Sciullo, 235–246. CRSH report.

Huang, James. 1982. "Logical relations in Chinese and the theory of grammar." Doctoral diss., MIT, Cambridge, Mass.

Jackendoff, Ray. 1972. *Semantic interpretation in generative grammar.* Cambridge, Mass.: MIT Press.

———. 1990. *Semantic structures.* Cambridge, Mass.: MIT Press.

Kayne, Richard. 1995. *The antisymmetry of syntax.* Cambridge, Mass.: MIT Press.

Keyser, Samuel Jay, and Tom Roeper. 1992. "Re-: the abstract clitic hypothesis." *Linguistic Inquiry* 23:89–127.

Koopman, Hilda. 1984. *The syntax of verbs: From verb movement rules in Kru languages to universal grammar.* Dordrecht: Foris.

Kratzer, Angelika. 1989. "Stage-level and individual-level predicates." Ms. University of Massachusetts, Amherst, Mass.

Krifka, M. 1986. "Massenterme, individualterme, aktionsarten." Doctoral diss., University of Munich, Federal Republic of Germany.

———. 1989. *Nominalreferenz und zeitkonstitution: Zur semantik von massentermen, individualterme, aspektklassen.* München: Wilhelm Fink Verlag.

Labelle, Marie. 1992. "La structure argumentale des verbes locatifs à base nominale." In *Linguisticae Investigationes* 14:267–315.

Larson, Richard. 1988. "On the double object construction." *Linguistic Inquiry* 19:335–391.

Law, Paul. 1990. "Heads, arguments, and adjuncts in derivational morphology." In *MIT Working Papers in Linguistics* 12, *Papers from the second student conference in linguistics*, ed. Thomas Green and Sigel Uziel. Cambridge, Mass.

Lebeaux, David. 1988. "Language acquisition and the form of grammar." Doctoral diss., University of Massachusetts, Amherst, Mass.

Levin, Beth, and Malka Rappaport. 1986. "The formation of adjectival passives." *Linguistic Inquiry* 17: 623–662.

Lees, Robert B. 1960. *The grammar of English nominalizations*. The Hague: Mouton.

Lieber, Rochelle. 1983. "Argument-linking and compounds in English." *Linguistic Inquiry* 14:251–285.

———. 1992. *Deconstructing morphology: Word-formation in syntactic theory*. Chicago: University of Chicago Press.

May, Robert. 1985. *Logical form: Its structure and derivation*. Cambridge, Mass.: MIT Press.

Perlmutter, David, and Paul Postal. 1984. "The 1-advancement exclusiveness law." In *Studies in relational grammar*, ed. David Perlmutter, 3–29. Chicago: University of Chicago Press.

Pesetsky, David. 1982. "Paths and categories." Doctoral diss., MIT, Cambridge, Mass.

Rappaport, Malka, and Beth Levin. 1986. "What to do with Theta-roles?" *Lexicon Project Working Papers* 11. Center for Cognitive Science, MIT, Cambridge, Mass.

Rizzi, Luigi. 1986. "Null objects in Italian and the theory of pro." *Linguistic Inquiry* 17: 501–557.

———. 1990. "Residual verb-second and the wh-criterion." Ms. University of Geneva.

Rochette, Anne. 1990. "Semantic and syntactic aspects of Romance sentential complementation." Doctoral diss., MIT, Cambridge, Mass.

Roeper, Thomas. 1987. "Implicit arguments and the head-complement relation." *Linguistic Inquiry* 18:267–311.

———. 1988. "Compounds, syntax, and head movement." *Yearbook of Morphology*. Dordrecht: Foris.

Roeper, Thomas, and Dorothy Siegel. 1978. "Transformations and the lexicon." *Linguistic Inquiry* 9:199–260.

Rothstein, Susan. 1983. "The syntactic form of predication." Doctoral diss., MIT, Cambridge, Mass.

Scalise, Sergio. 1990. "La formazione delle parole." Ms. Università degli Studi di Venezia.

Selkirk, Elizabeth O. 1982. *The syntax of words*. Cambridge, Mass.: MIT Press.

Speas, Margareth. 1990. *Phrase structure in natural language*. Natural Language and Linguistic Theory. Dordrecht: Kluwer.

Sportiche, Dominique. 1987. "Structural invariance and symmetry in syntax." Doctoral diss., MIT, Cambridge, Mass.

———. 1990. "Movement, agreement, and case." Ms. University of California at Los Angeles.

Sproat, Richard. 1985. "On deriving the lexicon." Doctoral diss., MIT, Cambridge, Mass.

Tenny, Carol. 1989. "The aspectual interface hypothesis." *Lexicon Project Working Paper* 24. Center for Cognitive Science, MIT, Cambridge, Mass.

Williams, Edwin. 1980. "Predication." *Linguistic Inquiry* 11:203–238.

———. 1981. "On the notions 'lexically related' and 'head of a word.' " *Linguistic Inquiry* 12:245–274.

———. 1989. "The anaphoric nature of Theta-roles." *Linguistic Inquiry* 20:425–457.

TWO

On Some Syntactic Properties
of Word-structure and
Modular Grammars

PAUL LAW

In a theory of modular grammar as a system of several independent components (for example, syntax, phonology, semantics, and so on), each of which is governed by its own principles (and parameters) as originally conceived by Chomsky (1981), an issue of central concern is the delimitation of these grammatical components and the connection between them. To this end, I examine in this chapter some properties of nominalization, in the hope that the conclusions drawn from this study would shed some light on the issue of where the dividing line between syntax and morphology is.

Recent work on nominalization makes extensive use of syntactic principles of X-bar theory (Selkirk 1982), Theta-role assignment (Burzio 1981, Roeper 1987), and control (Roeper 1985) in nominalization. If this syntactic approach to word-structures with derivational morphology[1] is correct, then the syntactic component of the grammar covers a larger ground than is ordinarily thought of, including not only phrasal but also word-level syntax. I would like to argue that while word-structures with derivational morphology have the categorial properties of phrase-level syntax (section 1), there are good reasons to suppose that principles of Theta and Control theories as observed in phrasal syntax do not hold of word-structures (section 2). In fact, if argument structure of a predicative head is projected only if all other properties of the head are projected, then Theta-roles cannot possibly be assigned in word-structures. Thematic interpretation in derived nominals is therefore not obtained by means of Theta-marking, but is a consequence of the principle of Full Interpretation (FI; Chomsky 1986a) requiring every constituent part of an expression to be interpreted as related to some other constituent (section 3). The conclusion that word-structures with derivational morphology are generated by the same component of the grammar that generates phrase-structures is entirely expected in Chomsky's (1993, 1994) Minimalist conception of grammar, according to which there is but one computational system that generates syntactic structures (section 4). Space limitation and the complex nature of the issues involved prevent me from getting at a definitive answer to the question of where the division is between syntax and morphology. I nevertheless hope that the present chapter has some positive light to shed on the study of syntax/morphology interface in showing why certain properties hold of word-structures but not of phrase-structures, and vice versa.

1. CATEGORIAL PROPERTIES OF NOMINALIZATION

In the generative tradition, the idea that words have internal structures with formal categorial features dates back at least to Chomsky and Halle (1968), Halle (1973), and subsequent works by Aronoff (1976), Roeper and Siegel (1978), and Lieber (1980) (see also Marchand 1969 for an extensive description of English morphology), but the first systematic study of derivational and compounding morphology that explicitly links word- and phrase-level syntax in terms of the same subtheory of grammar was Selkirk's (1982:6ff) proposal, according to which word- and phrase-structures are both generated by the schemata of X-bar theory.[2] The same idea can be implemented in Chomsky's (1993) Minimalist framework as well. That is, word-structures with derivational morphology are generated by the computational component of the grammar, drawing elements from the lexicon, in the same way that phrase-structures are generated.

It is not difficult to see why word-level and phrase-level syntax should be subsumed under one subtheory of grammar. Consider the pair *confuse-confusion*. It is clear that the first has a verbal and the second a nominal distribution. What is particularly significant here is that the relationship between such verb-noun pairs is quite systematic. Thus, when the suffix *-ion* is attached to a (latinate) verb, the result is a noun. Moreover, it does not attach to other categories (for example, *promote-promotion*; *remote-*remotion*; *with-*withion*; *concert-*concertion*). The categorial relationship between the verb-base and the nominalizing suffix can thus be taken as subcategorization (Lieber 1980), or selection (Grimshaw 1979, Pesetsky 1982, Fabb 1988), the same notion that is prevalent in phrasal syntax (cf. Chomsky 1965).

There are various ways to account for the categorial property of morphologically derived words by affixation. Either the categorial feature of the affix percolates in some specific way, as suggested by Lieber (1980), or an affix is inserted in a position in a morphological structure independently generated by X-bar theory, provided that the affix has the categorial feature specified for that position (cf. Selkirk 1982:60ff for specific technical details, and also Williams 1981):

(1)   a.

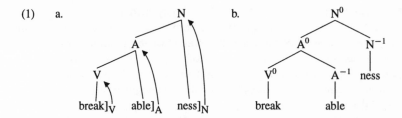

The representations in (1) come close to the notion of categorial projection in syntax (Chomsky 1981) if we take the categories Adjective and Noun in these cases as projecting their categorial features. In the Minimalist framework, the structures in (1) would be generated by the computational system of the grammar, drawing the elements *break*, *-able*, and *-ness* from the lexicon. The structures thus generated must respect lexical properties. For instance, *-able* has the property that it must occur with a verb, and *-ness* with an adjective.

From the perspective of complementation, the morphological structure in (2a) of the nominal *promotion* resembles that of the phrasal structure in (2b) of the verb phrase *saw John*:

(2)   a.

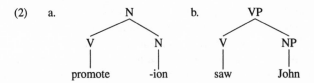

As *promotion* has nominal distribution and *promote* is a verb, it must be that the nominal category of *promotion* comes from the suffix *-ion* (cf. Williams 1981). In other words, the categorial feature of the nominal suffix *-ion* projects when it combines with a verb under the operation MERGE (Chomsky 1994),[3] the same way that the categorial feature of a transitive verb such as *saw* projects when it combines with a noun phrase. In terms of complementation, the nominal suffix *-ion* takes the verb *promote* as its complement in (2a) just as the verb *saw* takes *John* as its complement in (2b). The suffix *-ion* thus resembles a transitive verb in that it must take a complement. Thus, except for the difference in the position of the complement (see note 5), the morphological structure in (2a) has the same complementation relation as that in the phrasal structure in (2b).

Apart from categorial projection, word-structures also resemble phrase-structures in another respect. Law (1990) argues that the distribution of the diminutive suffix *-ito/-ita* in Spanish[4] is evidence for the argument/adjunct distinction in word-structures, a distinction that figures most prominently in syntax since Huang's (1982) work. As Jaeggli (1980) points out, the diminutive suffix *-ito/-ita* can attach to adjectives, nouns, or adverbs, but the resulting category is the same as that of the base to which the suffix attaches:

(3)   a.   Adjectives: poco, "little"   poquita, "little, diminutive"
       b.   Nouns: chica, "girl"   chiquita, "little girl"
       c.   Adverbs: ahora, "now"   ahorita, "now, diminutive"

The categorial property of the suffix *-ito/-ita* is thus similar to the prefix *counter-* in English, which may attach to verbs, nouns, or adjectives. The category of the resulting structure is the same as that of the base to which the prefix attaches (Lieber 1980; compare also the Russian diminutive suffixes *-ushka/-ushek*, discussed in Marantz 1984):

(4) a. Verbs: sign   counter-sign
     b. Nouns: example   counter-example
     c. Adjectives: intuitive counter-intuitive

If the suffix *-ito/-ita* and the prefix *counter-* are adjuncts to the base to which they attach, then the fact that the category of the resulting structure must be the same as the base follows directly from the syntactic principle of adjunction (Chomsky 1986b), according to which the category resulting from adjoining a category X to a category Y is Y (since the category of the adjuncts are irrelevant to that of the resulting structure, it is ignored in [5] and [6]):[5]

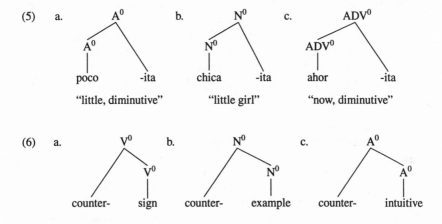

(5) a. A^0 b. N^0 c. ADV^0
         A^0 N^0 ADV^0
         poco   -ita   chica   -ita   ahor   -ita
         "little, diminutive"   "little girl"   "now, diminutive"

(6) a. V^0 b. N^0 c. A^0
                   V^0 N^0 A^0
         counter- sign   counter- example   counter- intuitive

If the component of grammar that sanctions word-structures involving derivational morphology of the type we just discussed is entirely distinct from that of phrase-structures, then it would be a remarkable coincidence that they have the same categorial properties. By contrast, if they are in fact generated by the same component of grammar, namely, the computational system, and are therefore subject to the same constraints, then it would be just as expected that they project their categorial features the same way.

2. ON THETA THEORY AND CONTROL IN NOMINALIZATION

In this section, I consider two modules of grammar that are apparently of some relevance to word-structures with derivational morphology: Theta theory and Control theory. I argue, however, that properties of these two theories do not hold of word-structures.

2.1. Locality Constraint on Theta-role Assignment

The suffix *-er* attaches to verbs to form nouns. According to the X-bar theoretic approach to nominalization discussed in section 1, the representation for a noun such as *employer* would be something like that in (7):

(7)

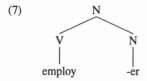

employ   -er

Now, it is clear that *employer* refers to the property of employing someone, in more formal terms, the property of being the Agent of *employ*. Given that the verb *employ* independently has an Agent role, one might naturally ask how the Agent role of the verb is related to the Agentive interpretation of the noun *employer*.

In the structure in (7), the morpheme *-er* is a sister to the verb. Given that the principle of Theta-role assignment in syntax is subject to the sisterhood condition (Chomsky 1986b), it thus appears that *-er* in (7) might be assigned the Agent role of *employ*, since it does meet the sisterhood condition on Theta-role assignment. That the syntactic principle of Theta-role assignment might be relevant in word-structures can apparently explain the impossibility of the examples in (8a), on the same grounds as those for the examples in (8b), with raising verbs such as *appear* and *seem*. The latter are standardly taken to be instances of Theta Criterion violation, since the matrix subject *John* is not assigned a Theta-role:

(8)   a. *seemer, *appearer
      b. *John seems/appears that Bill is intelligent.

Therefore, if the nominalizing suffix *-er* must also receive a Theta-role, then the impossibility of the examples in (8a) follows from the fact that raising verbs have no Theta-role to assign to *-er* (Burzio 1981). The same explanation can also be extended to the account of the ungrammaticality of (9a), on a par with that of (9b):

(9)   a. *The employer of Bill by John.
      b. *Mary employed Bill by John.

Here, the Agent role of *employ* has been assigned to *-er* in (9a) and to *Mary* in (9b); it therefore cannot be also assigned to the argument *John* in the *by*-phrase.

2.2. Control in Derived Nominals

Control theory apparently has some bearing on word-structures with derivational morphology as well. Manzini (1983) points out the grammatical contrast in (10), in which the Agent of the passivized verb *sink* in (10a) can control the PRO in the infinitival, but the intransitive use of the same verb without an Agent cannot:

(10) a. The ship was sunk [PRO to collect the insurance]
      b. *The ship sank [PRO to collect the insurance]

Roeper (1987) thus suggests that the grammatical contrast in (10) be accounted for by assuming that PRO is controlled by an implicit Agent in (10a), but not in (10b).

The same explanation can thus be given to account for the grammatical contrast in (11), if Theta theory is assumed to be relevant to word-structures:

(11) a. John$_i$ employed Bill [PRO$_i$ to prove a point]
      b. *The employer$_i$ of Bill [PRO$_i$ to prove a point]

The argument *John* bearing the Agent role c-commands and thus can control PRO in (11a). By contrast, *-er* in (11b) is assigned the Agent role but does not c-command PRO; it therefore cannot control PRO (Roeper 1987:296). The impossibility of the example in (11b) can thus be attributed to the lack of a c-commanding controller, as required by the structural constraint on control relationship (cf. Larson 1991).

2.3. Theta Theory and Complementation

Despite the apparent relevance of Theta theory to word-structures with derivational morphology, several issues arise. First, in syntax, a Theta-role is assigned to a position, regardless of the intrinsic lexical property of the category occupying that position. Thus, whether *dogs* or *cats* appears as the complement of the verb *hit* in (12), they are both interpreted as the Theme of *hit*:

(12) a. Bill hit dogs.
      b. Bill hit cats.

Second, an argument in a position may be assigned a different Theta-role according to the lexical property of the Theta-role assigner. In (13), the argument *John* is apparently in the same structural relation with respect to the verb, and the Theta-role that it receives is different in the two cases, a Theme in (13a) but an Experiencer in (13b) (Gruber 1965):

(13) a. Bill saw John.
      b. Bill surprised John.

These two Theta theoretic properties observed in syntax do not hold in word-structures with derivational morphology. Consider the structure in (14) with the morpheme *-ee*:

(14)
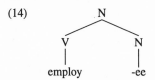

The morpheme *-ee* apparently is in the same structural position with respect to the verb-base in (14), just as the morpheme *-er* in the structure in (7). But the two resulting forms have quite different interpretations. While *employer* is the property of being someone who employs people, *employee* is the property of being someone who is employed. Given that they have the same verb-base, their semantic difference must come from the nominalizing suffix: *-er* versus *-ee*.

Thus, if Theta-role assignment is pertinent in word-structures with derivational morphology, then we must say that morphemes with different intrinsic lexical properties may receive different Theta-roles. This is in contrast to syntax where the intrinsic lexical property of the argument is not pertinent to Theta-role assignment (cf. [12]).

Third, Theta-role assignment of the sort in (7) is not what we observe in phrasal syntax. The Agent role is typically assigned to a Specifier position (or, equivalently, it is checked in that position; cf. Chomsky 1993), not to a complement position. As the morpheme *-er* appears to be in the same structural position as that of *-ee*, we would have to assume that the Agent role is assigned to *-er* in the complement position. Although we might say that Theta-role assignment in phrasal syntax (for example, Baker's [1988] Uniform Theta Assignment Hypothesis) differs from that in word-structures, a new question arises. Why should the locality condition on Theta-role assignment in syntax and morphology be this way, but not otherwise?

Fourth, the direction of Theta-role assignment in word-structures with derivational morphology would be exactly opposite to that in syntax, from the complementation point of view. In the structures in (7) and (14), the nominalizers *-er* and *-ee* are X-bar theoretic heads and the verb-bases are their X-bar theoretic complements. Theta-role assignment in word-structures with derivational morphology, as discussed earlier, would be from the argument to the selecting head. This is exactly the reverse of Theta-role assignment in syntax, where it is from the selecting head to the arguments. Apart from the issue of the direction of Theta-role assignment, the most serious problem with assignment of Theta-roles from arguments to heads is that it undermines much of the idea of selection, according to which the selector imposes restrictions on the category that it selects.

Last, there is good semantic reason for not assuming that the affixes are assigned a Theta-role. Although one might have the impression that the morpheme *-er* is similar to phrasal arguments in that, depending on the co-occurring verb, it has different Theta-roles (for instance, *employer* versus *copier* and the examples in [13]), the fact is that it is the derived nominal as a whole (for example, *employer* or *employee*), not the nominalizing affix itself (for example, *-er* or *-ee*), that is understood to denote a property that is related to a Theta-role of the verb-base. For instance, it is the derived nominal *employer*, not the suffix *-er*, that is understood to be related to the Agent role of the verb-base *employ*; it denotes the property of being a person bearing the Agent role of the verb *employ*. However one is to account for the way in which the resulting derived nominal is thematically related to the verb-base (see section 4), it is certainly not the kind of Theta-role assignment we see in syntax.

2.4. On Determining Nominal Reference

Let us now return to the examples in (8a) and (9a), repeated here in (15), to see how one might go about accounting for their ungrammaticality:

(15)   a. *seemer, *appearer
      b. *The employer of Bill by John.

Suppose that the morphemes *-er* and *-ee* have some lexical information such as that in (16) (Di Sciullo and Williams 1987:41), a lexical stipulation that we could independently assume, given the semantic difference between the two nouns *employer* and *employee*:[6]

(16)   *-er*:   (R), R controls external argument of the predicate.
         -ee: (R), R controls internal argument of the predicate.

The ungrammaticality of the example in (15a) would then be due to the fact that raising verbs such as *seem* and *appear* do not have an external argument to be controlled, and the impossibility of the example in (15b) woud also follow from the fact that the external argument of the verb *employ* is already controlled by *-er*, so the argument in the *by*-phrase cannot be assigned the Agent role of the verb, just as in (9b) (see also sections 3 and 4.3.4). With lexical specifications like those in (16), Theta-role assignment of the sort in syntax would no longer be necessary in word-structures.

The lexical specification of the morpheme *-er* as stated in (16a) apparently does not explain the ungrammaticality of the example in (17), repeated from (11b):

(17)   *The employer$_i$ of Bill [PRO$_i$ to prove a point]

We might attribute the impossibility of the example to the lack of a c-commanding argument bearing the Agent role and the subsequent absence of a controller for PRO. In (17), the Agent role is already assigned to the morpheme *-er*, which does not c-command PRO. Nevertheless, there is good reason to suppose that the ungrammaticality of (17) has nothing to do with the structural condition on control. As shown in (18), *Bill* is not an Agent but a Theme of the verb *employ*, yet it can control PRO, which shows that PRO needs not be controlled by an Agent:

(18)   John$_i$ employed Bill$_j$ [PRO$_{i/j}$ to prove a point]

Instead of appealing to Theta-marking in word-structures, one might argue that the impossibility of the example in (17) is due to the fact that the PRO is part of a constituent that determines the reference of the whole noun phrase. To see this, let us consider the structure of the example in (17), which is either as in (19a), where the infinitival is an N′-adjunct, or as in (19b) (if noun phrases are headed by a determiner; cf. Barwise and Cooper 1981, Abney 1987), where the infinitival is an NP-adjunct:

(19)   a.   The [$_{N'}$ [$_{N'}$ employer of Bill] [PRO to prove a point]]
        b.   [$_{DP}$ The [$_{NP}$ [$_{NP}$ employer of Bill] [PRO to prove a point]]]

Clearly, the reference of the whole noun phrase *the employer of Bill* to prove the point cannot be determined without the semantic value of the infinitival. Therefore, the reason for which the PRO in the infinitival cannot have the same reference as that of the whole noun phrase is that the PRO is part of a constituent that determines the reference of the whole noun phrase. A similar explanation can be given to account for the ungrammaticality of (9a); the *by*-phrase is part of a constituent that determines the reference of the whole noun phrase (see section 4.3.4).

There is some independent reason to think that this is correct. Consider the examples in (20):

(20)   a.   [The employer of Bill]$_i$ is here [PRO$_i$ to prove a point]
       b.   [The man]$_i$ is here [PRO$_i$ to prove a point]

Clearly, PRO can be controlled by the subject in (20a), since the infinitival containing PRO is not part of the subject. This is just like the example in (20b), in which PRO is controlled by *the man*. In the two examples, the controller of PRO is not an Agent argument of any predicate, showing again that an argument need not be an Agent in order to be a controller, at least in these cases. In fact, one might even argue that PRO in (10b) is actually controlled by the unaccusative subject *the ship*. Since ships cannot be naturally interpreted as Agents of collection, the example has a pragmatically odd interpretation.[7]

Let us now return to the examples in (15) to see how we can account for their ungrammaticality without appealing to assignment of Theta-roles. The morpheme -*er* need not attach to a verb that has an Agent role in its argument structure (for instance, *hearer, lover, receiver, thinker*, and so on). It is not entirely clear what Theta-roles verbs such as *hear, love*, and *think* have; it is therefore rather difficult to characterize the class of verbs to which the morpheme -*er* attaches. However, it is certainly not true that the morpheme -*er* may attach to just any verb that has an external Theta-role, as the examples in (21) show (these forms remain impossible with the alternative orthography -*or*):

(21)   *amazer, *baser, *calmer, *delighter, *easer, *freeer, *glarer, *hoper, *initialler, *knower, *liver, *meeter, *needer, *obliger, *placer, *querier, *resembler, *smogger, *tieer, *vacater, *worrier, *yielder

In a few rare cases, the morpheme -*er* can also attach to a variety of categories that clearly have no argument-structures, with the resulting expressions denoting different properties (the X in [22] has some connection, sometimes very loose, with the expression to which the morpheme -*er* attaches):

(22)   a.   A person who practices X or makes X:
            lawyer, geographer, footballer, potter
       b.   A person who resides in X:
            rancher, New Yorker, northerner, westerner
       c.   A person or thing that has some X property:
            airliner (a large passenger aircraft),
            appetizer (something to eat before the main dish),
            fifth-grader (someone who is in fifth grade),
            teenager (someone who is teenaged),
            goner (someone who will soon die),
            forty-niner (someone who went to California in 1849),
            three-wheeler (something that has three wheels),
            fiver (a five-pound bill)

If the morpheme -*er* must receive a Theta-role, then it is not obvious from where it could receive one in (22). In fact, cases like these are not specific to the morpheme -*er*. Suffixes such as -*ese*, -*i*, -*ian*, -*ist*, and -*ite* exhibit the same property in attaching to a base that apparently has no argument structure:

(23)   a.   Assamese, Japanese, Nepalese, Senegalese, Sudanese
       b.   Bangladeshi, Israeli, Kuwaiti, Omani, Paskistani, Yemeni

    c.   Grammarian, Iranian, librarian, magician, parlementarian, theoretician
    d.   Communist, guitarist, journalist, Marxist, socialist, theorist
    e.   Clintonite, Mennonite, Moscovite, Reaganite, Trotskyite

What seems to be true is that to the extent that one can tell that the X of the combination $X + er$ is a verb, then the verb has an external argument. But this need not have anything to do with Theta-role assignment, which cannot at any rate predict when a $X + er$ combination is good, and when it is bad.

If we take the semantics of the $V + er$ combination as denoting a property of being a person or an instrument that Vs (cf. note 6), then the reason the examples in (15a) are impossible is because they denote non-sensible properties, namely, the property of being a person or an instrument that seems or appears. A similar explanation can be given for the impossible example in (15b). Clearly, the semantic function of the morpheme *-er* is to send a property to a property. For instance, in the expression *runner, -er* takes the property of running to the property of being someone who runs. Thus, on the one hand, if the argument in the *by*-phrase in (15b) is the Agent of the verb *employ*, then there would be no property for the morpheme *-er* to nominalize. On the other hand, if the *by*-phrase is not part of the property of employing Bill that the morpheme *-er* nominalizes, then a problem of a different sort arises. There seems to be no natural way to relate the *by*-phrase with the rest of the expression (for instance, *The employer of Bill by the window*, with the locative *by*). The resulting expression would then be uninterpretable, and would consequently violate FI. Admittedly, this sketchy explanation does not cover cases in (21) through (23), but it seems clear that the impossible examples in (15) need not have anything to do with Theta-role assignment.

I therefore see no reason to assume that principles of Theta-role assignment and those of Control theory are operative in word-structures. Their apparent relevance either is misconstrued, as in the first case, or can be explained independently in terms of reference determination for nominals, as in the second case.

3. ON PROJECTION OF ARGUMENT STRUCTURE IN DERIVED NOMINALS

The parallelism between sentences and derived nominals, first studied by Lees (1960), is well illustrated by the oft-cited doublet of Chomsky's (1970):

(24)   a.   The enemy's destruction of the city.
       b.   The enemy destroyed the city.

The question we will be discussing in this section is whether we should consider the subject and object of the nominalized verb in (24a) as arguments of the head noun on a par with the corresponding verb in (24b).

From the point of view of selectional restriction, derived nominals apparently impose selectional restrictions on the occurring *of*-phrase:

(25)   a.   #The employer of life.
       b.   #John employed life.

(26)   a.   #The trainer of the bananas.
       b.   #John trained the bananas.

However, when we look at the interpretation of derived nominals and the semantic relationship between the *of*-phrase and the verb-base, it turns out that the *of*-phrase is in fact a semantic argument of the verb, not of the derived noun. The examples in (27) clearly have the interpretations in (28), where the objects of the verbs correspond to the objects in the *of*-phrases of the derived nominals:

> (27)   a.   The employer (of the students) (was stingy).
>   b.   The trainer (of the athletes) (was lazy).

> (28)   a.   The person who employs the students.
>   b.   The person who trains the athletes.

In other words, the object in the *of*-phrase in a derived nominal is semantically an argument of the verb-base, not of the derived noun.

If we are to insist on Theta-marking of the argument in the *of*-phrase or the *of*-phrase itself, then we would inevitably complicate Theta theory. In the structures in (29) for the examples in (27), neither the argument in the *of*-phrase nor the *of*-phrase itself is in a Theta-position; it is in neither a complement nor a specifier position of the verb:

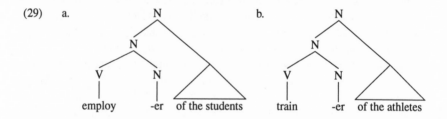

Expressions of the type in (30) are possible, where the *of*-phrase clearly bears no thematic relation to the verb-base:

> (30)   a.   The employer of the year.
>   b.   The trainer of the nineties.

The *of*-phrases in (30) are apparently in the same syntactic position as those in (29). If the *of*-phrase or the argument within the *of*-phrase is assigned a Theta-role, then one would have to explain why the ones in (30) may apparently occupy the same position, even though they are not Theta-marked.

The matter is much worse in cases like that in (31a) (some morpho-phonological rule presumably turns the sequence *read* + *able* + *ity* into the surface form *readability*), where the *of*-phrase and the argument in the *of*-phrase are nowhere near being a sister to the verb-base, even though the *of*-phrase or the argument in the *of*-phrase is a semantic argument of the verb, as its interpretation in (31b) indicates:[8]

(31)   a.

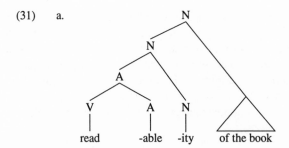

   b.   The degree to which one can read the book.

So, in order for the same principle constraining the locality of Theta-role assignment in phrasal syntax to be applicable in word-structures, we would need either to make some additional assumption about the projection of argument structure, or to derive them from some representation in which the *of*-phrase is in either a complement or a specifier position. We will consider these two cases in turn.

3.1. Inheritance of Argument Structure

Randall (1984) suggests that nominalizing affixes may inherit the argument structure of the verb-base (see also Williams 1981, Lieber 1983, Booij 1986, Levin and Rappaport 1988). The selectional restriction of the verb-base would then become a property of the nominalizers, and of the derived nominals as a whole. There are various ways to implement this view (see Roeper 1987 for an extension of it to other affixes). For instance, one might adopt the structures in (32) as representations for the examples in (27), in which the suffix *-er* inherits the argument-structure of the verb-base:

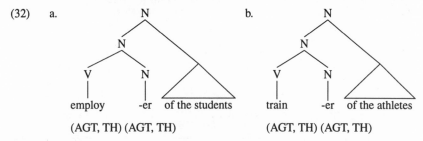

The *of*-phrase is still not in a complement or specifier position with respect to the nominalizing affix *-er* in these structures; therefore, we need to assume that the derived nominal as a whole, for example, *employer* or *trainer*, has the argument structure of the head. From these additional assumptions, it would follow that the *of*-phrase must obey the selectional restriction of the verb-base. This is because the *of*-phrase is now in the complement position of the derived noun $V + er$, which has the argument structure of the verb-base, and is Theta-marked by it (cf. also $V + ee$).

As argument structure is semantic in nature, we must look at the semantics of derived nominals to see whether the notion of argument structure inheritance is warranted. It turns out that there is no reason to suppose that head nouns such as *employer* and *trainer* in (27) take the *of*-phrase as their argument. In contrast to relational nouns such as *friend, brother, sister, top,* and so on (for example, *friend of Bill, top of the table*), it makes no sense to say that a noun like *person* in (28) takes *the students* or *the athletes* as argument. By parity of reasoning, there is no reason to claim that nouns such as *employer* or *trainer* take the *of*-phrase (or the noun phrase in the *of*-phrase) as argument either, given that the interpretations of the examples in (27) are as in (28).[9]

3.2. Nominalization as Head-movement

Another possibility of accounting for the selectional restriction in derived nominals is to derive the examples in (27) from some representation in which the *of*-phrase is in complement position of the verb so that it can be Theta-marked by it. The verb subsequently undergoes head-to-head movement to the nominalizing affix, deriving the correct surface form, as shown in (33):

(33)   a.   b.

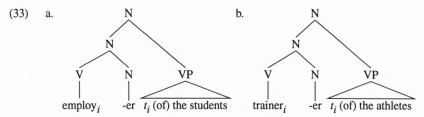

However, there are several problems with this view. First, VPs may take adverbial modifiers. Therefore, if there were a VP inside a nominalized verb, then we should expect a VP-adverb to be possible, contrary to fact:

(34)   a. *   b. *

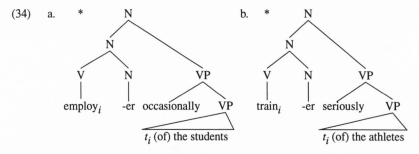

The problem can be solved if one makes the assumption that attachment of adverbs is done exclusively in the syntax, barring structures of the sort in (34), as they are in morphology. This solution, of course, raises further questions as to why, in contrast with VPs, which may be generated in both syntax and morphology, adverbs are only generated in syntax but not in morphology, and why the constraint does not hold the other way around.[10]

Second, if a VP is indeed present inside derived nominals, then there is no reason the preposition (or Case-marker) *of* is necessary. The argument in the VP should be able to receive Case from the verb, just like it does in syntax.

Third, the *of*-phrase is optional in (27) (see section 4.3.3), contrary to the obligatory presence of the argument of the corresponding verbs:

(35) a. John employed *(the students).
     b. John trained *(the athletes).

It is thus not clear how one can explain the optionality of the *of*-phrase in derived nominals (see section 3.3.2) if deverbal nouns are derived from some representation with a VP inside them. The same problem also arises if derived nominals have the argument structure of the verb-base (see section 3.1).

3.3. On Projecting Argument Structure

In this section, we first see how the problems with the notion of argument structure inheritance and with the head-to-head movement derivation for deverbal nominals can be resolved in a principled way, especially the issue of the optionality of the *of*-phrase that is problematic in both approaches. We then proceed to see how the suggested solution can be extended to other types of derived nominals that have a bearing on the process/result interpretation distinction.

3.3.1. *Syntactic Projection of Lexical Properties*

We have seen some conceptual and empirical reasons for thinking that derived nominals do not have the argument structure of the verb-base (sections 2.1, 2.3, 3.1, and 3.2). As a consequence of this, the *of*-phrase in these cases can only be an adjunct, as it cannot be related to an argument structure (see section 3.3.3 on the adjunct status of the *by*-phrase). The fact that the *of*-phrase is optional would follow immediately. One might wonder, however, why it should be that the argument structure of the verb-base is not projected in derived nominals.

It is not too difficult to see how this question can be answered, if one considers argument structure to be an inherent property of lexical items, and supposes that projecting of argument structure onto syntax is effected only if all other lexical properties are projected. Now, the fact that the verb-base does not take syntactic arguments in derived nominals would be just as expected, since it does not project its lexical properties; in particular, it does not project its categorial feature maximally to an XP. Consequently, the verb-base does not project its argument positions. The *of*-phrase in derived nominals therefore cannot occupy a Theta-position, as there is none. It therefore follows immediately that the *of*-phrase is an adjunct.

Deverbal nominals are thus exactly like concrete nouns with respect to the optionality of the *of*-phrase. The problem of adverbs inside derived nominals would no longer arise, since there is simply no VP inside these structures. Moreover, the obligatoriness of the preposition or the Case-marker *of* is also expected, as the argument in the *of*-phrase is never a sister to the verb.

3.3.2. *On the* Of-*phrase in Derived Nominals*

The claim that the *of*-phrase in derived nominals is generally optional, a consequence of the non-projection of the argument structure of the verb-base, is apparently in direct conflict with Grimshaw's (1990) claim according to which the *of*-phrase is obligatory in process-denoting derived nominals. I argue, however, that the claim does not hold in general, and that cases in which the *of*-phrase is seemingly necessary can be attributed to independent factors.

Grimshaw (1990:49) points out that although the noun *examination* has both the process and result interpretations, the noun *exam* only has the result interpretation. As the examples in (36) show, the process interpretation appears to require an *of*-phrase, while the result interpretation does not:

(36)   a.   The examination/exam was on the table.
     b.   The exam (*of the patients) was on the table.
     c.   The examination/*exam of the patients took a long time.

The process interpretation can be brought out by a co-occurring process-denoting predicate such as *take a long time*, or by adding a prenominal adjective such as *constant, frequent, deliberate*, or *intentional*, as in (37a), or by adding an (Agentive) *by*-phrase, as in (37b):

(37)   a.   The intentional examination *(of the papers) took a long time.
     b.   *The intentional examination was on the table.
     c.   The examination *(of the papers) by the instructor.

In these cases, the *of*-phrase seems necessary.

In Grimshaw's analysis, result nominals lack argument structures (A-structures), but process nominals have the A-structure of the verb-base except that the external argument, the most prominent argument in her theory, is suppressed. This is illustrated in (38) for the verb *repress* and the related deverbal noun *repression* in its process interpretation (*Ev* is an event argument, and the $\emptyset$ next to the argument *x* means that the argument has been suppressed; Grimshaw 1990:137):

(38)   a.   *repress* $(x\,(y))$
     b.   *repression* $(Ev\,(x\text{-}\emptyset\,(y)))$

On the one hand, the reason the *of*-phrase is obligatory in (39) is because the a-structure of *repression* has an argument, represented in (38b) as the variable *y*, that must be satisfied just as it must be in the case of the corresponding verb (see Zubizarreta and van Haaften [1988] for an alternative account of the obligatoriness of the *of*-phrase):

(39)   a.   They (constantly) repressed *(human rights).
     b.   The CIA's constant repression *(of human rights).
     c.   The constant repression *(of human rights) (by the CIA).

On the other hand, the *x* argument in (38b) may license, although does not require, a *by*-phrase, since the *x* argument has been suppressed.

There are both conceptual and empirical problems with this account. Conceptually, although we might take the representation in (38b) as specifying how the variables are projected onto syntax, just as the representation in (38a) does, the semantic relationship between the variables and the predicate in (38b) is rather different from that in (38a). Whereas in (38a) we can certainly take the category that fills the position that the variable *x* projects onto syntax as a person who represses someone, and that of the variable *y* as a person who is repressed, no such construal seems possible for the representation in (38b). That is, it makes no sense to say that the category that fills the position that the variable *x* projects onto syntax as a person who "repressions" someone, and that of the variable *y* as a person who is "repressioned" by someone. After all, *repression* denotes an event (see section 3.1 for a similar problem in *-er-* and *-ee*-nominalization).

In fact, the process interpretation of the derived nominal *repression* can be taken to be something like that in (40), in which the argument *human rights* is clearly an argument of the verb *repress*, semantically:

(40)   The process of repressing human rights.

Thus, if the noun phrase *human rights* in the *of*-phrase or the *of*-phrase itself in (39) is an argument of anything at all, it ought to be the semantic argument of the verb-base *repress*. The intention of the representation in (38b) seems to be to ensure that the *y* variable be projected onto syntax, and consequently filled by an *of*-phrase, even though the variable is, from the semantic point of view, an argument of the verb-base. But this is exactly the view of argument structure inheritance, which is itself problematic (see section 3.1). It thus seems that in *-ion*-nominalization too there is no reason to suppose that the argument in the *of*-phrase or the *of*-phrase itself is an argument of the deverbal noun *repression*. (In section 3.3.3, we will discuss the issue of how the noun phrase in the *of*-phrase is ordinarily taken to be the object of the verb-base to which the morpheme *-er* attaches.)

Empirically, there are cases in which a process nominal need not have an *of*-phrase. Alongside Williams's (1985:301) examples in (41), those in (42) are quite acceptable:

(41)   a.   John underwent an operation.
       b.   John submitted himself to her scrutiny.

(42)   a.   Human rights in third world countries are subject to constant repression.
       b.   The poor are susceptible to constant exploitation by the rich.
       c.   A very strong will for survival helped the villagers sustain such heavy bombardment.
       d.   Political dissidents in the ex-USSR were under constant surveillance by the KGB.
       e.   The sea water was sent to the plant for desalination.
       f.   The analysis needs further refinement.
       g.   The UN officials appeared to be in constant negotiation.
       h.   Constant exposure to the sun is harmful to the skin.

The deverbal nouns in (42), as they are modified by adverbials such as *constant*, *heavy*, and *further*, appear to have the process interpretation. However, these examples are possible without an *of*-phrase. The *of*-phrase is thus not strictly obligatory in process nominals either. This is just what we should expect if deverbal nouns do not have the *of*-phrase as an argument, and the *of*-phrase is in fact an adjunct.

Nevertheless, we still have the question of why an *of*-phrase is seemingly necessary in process nominals in (39). It appears that, in a case such as (39c), the presence of a prenominal adjective such as *constant, intentional,* and so on adds some specific information about the act involved in the process, but nothing about its participants. It might well be that some pragmatic factor is at work to the effect that information about the participants of the process should be specified before other details. Although it is not clear why this should be so, the grammaticality of the examples in (41) and (42) suggests that something along this line is probably correct.

In these examples, the semantic argument of the verb-base in the derived nominal (that is, the *of*-phrase) is not in a position Theta-marked by it; in fact, they are nowhere close to each other. Nevertheless, information about the argument can be recovered from other parts of the sentence. For instance, in (41a) we understand the subject *John* as being operated, and the subject *the poor* in (42b) as being exploited. In these examples, however, they are clearly not syntactic arguments of the base-verbs. Since the information about the participants can be recovered, other details of the process as specified by prenominal adjectives such as *constant, heavy,* and so on can therefore be added.

Quite apart from the nominalization contexts, more or less the same sort of pragmatic factor appears to be at work in sentences as well. Without a discourse context, the sentence in (43a) appears to be infelicitous where the adverb provides some particular information about the act involved in the process of staring, but one of the participants of the process is syntactically missing:

(43)   a.   John constantly stared.
       b.   John constantly stared at the ceiling.

Adding some information about what it is that John stared at as in (43b) would render the example much better.

While a full account for the optionality of the *of*-phrase remains to be worked out, it seems clear what approach one should take. It must be that the *of*-phrase is optional in general and that some other (possibly pragmatic) factors in contexts like (39) require that an *of*-phrase be present. If the *of*-phrase were obligatory as a lexical property of process nominals (see the lexical representation in [38b]), then it would be very unclear how one could explain why the examples in (41) through (42) are possible. As the *of*-phrase is evidently missing, one would have to make some additional assumption to the effect that the *of*-phrase may be absent in these cases.

3.3.3. *On Thematic Interpretation in Derived Nominals*

An issue that immediately arises in the analysis of the *of*-phrase in derived nominals as an adjunct is that one must explain why the same selectional restriction apparently holds of both word- and phrase-structures, as shown in (25) and (26), repeated here as (44) and (45):

(44)   a.   #The employer of life.
       b.   #John employed life.

(45)   a.   #The trainer of the bananas.
       b.   #John trained the bananas.

As we saw in section 2, the structural condition for Theta-role assignment does not obtain in word-structures. The impossibility of the examples in (44a) and (45a) must then be due to something else, not to Theta theoretic reasons.

When we look at FI (Chomsky 1986a), we can see why these examples are impossible. One interpretation of FI is that every constituent part of an expression must be interpreted as related to some other constituent as argument or modifier. Thus, on the one hand, if the argument in the *of*-phrase in (44a) and (45a) is taken to be the object of the predicative base of the derived nominal, then it would give rise to a pragmatically anomalous interpretation, just like their sentential counterparts in (44b) and (45b). On the other hand, there seems to be no natural way to construe the *of*-phrase in these examples as modifying the derived nominal either (for example, *an employer for life, the employer of the year, the trainer with the bananas*). The net result is that no pragmatically sensible interpretations can be obtained, violating FI.

This approach to thematic interpretation in derived nominals can also account in a simple fashion for why *the book*, in (46a), repeated from (31a), is taken to be the object of the predicate *read* even though it does not appear in a syntactic configuration in which Theta-role assignment is possible:

(46)   a.

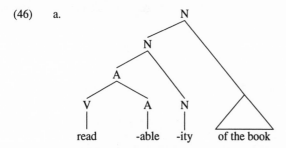

   b.   The degree to which one can read the book.

As books are pragmatically natural objects of predicates such as *read*, rather than (adjunct) modifiers, the thematical interpretation of *the book* as the object of the predicative verb-base *read* is obtained.

Moreover, as thematic relations do not formally hold between the constituent parts of a derived nominal, we can also explain why examples of root compounding such as those in (47a) are possible when the first members of the compounds are not thematically related to the second members, in contrast to those in (47b), in which the first members of the compounds are naturally taken to be objects of the second (some of these examples are from Selkirk 1982; see also Lieber 1980):

(47)   a.   Bathroom, garage sales, toilet seat, coffee shop, apron string
       b.   Hair brush, paper clip, bookshelves, car wash, crime watch

That is, whereas *hair* is clearly understood to be the object of *brush* in *hairbrush* (cf. *to brush hair*), *garage* is not understood to be the object of *sales* in *garage sales* (cf. *to sell the garage*). In fact, as *garage* can naturally be understood to be a Location, it seems to function as an adjunct modifier. The reason the examples in (47) are allowed regardless of whether the two members of the compounds are thematically related is that FI only requires that constituent parts be related, leaving open the precise relationship between them. The relationship in (47a) is one of modification; that in (47b) is thematic in the sense that the relationship involves an argument of a predicate.

A question that immediately arises in this non-syntactic account of thematic interpretation in derived nominals is why we must take *Bill* in (48) as the object of *employ* rather than as the subject, even though *Bill* can be the subject of the verb *employ* in phrasal syntax:

(48)   The employment of Bill

The answer to this question is quite straightforward if we consider the semantic function of the suffix *-ment*. Clearly, it is a property-nominalizer, turning a property into another property (cf. Di Sciullo and Williams's [1987:33ff] role R for the resulting property). In order for the expression in (48) to have the interpretation in which *Bill* is the Agent of *employ*, the suffix *-ment* would have to nominalize a property that is denoted by the expression *Bill employs* or *Bill employed*. But these latter expressions are not possible surface forms, and as a result have no interpretation corresponding to them. Thus, the failure of supplying a property for the suffix *-ment* to nominalize is the reason we cannot take *Bill* as the subject of *employ* in (48).

4. CONCLUSION

As word-structures with derivational morphology have the categorial properties of phrasal syntax, there is thus reason to assume that they are generated by the same grammatical component that generates phrase-structures, in spite of the fact that the syntactic principles of Theta-role assignment and Control do not hold for the word-structures. Insofar as the principles of Theta theory have a more precise form, in that argument structure is projected only if the head projects all its lexical properties, we have an explanation for why Theta theoretic principles do not apply to X^0s, even though they are built by the same computational system that generates XPs.

From the perspective of Chomsky's (1993) Minimalist program for linguistic theory, in which there is but one computational system that generates syntactic structures, the conclusion that word-structures with derivational morphology are in fact no more special than those in syntax is especially welcome. In fact, if we abstract away from bar-levels (Chomsky 1994), then it would become clear that word-structures with derivational morphology are built in the same way as phrase-structures. Elements like *-er*, *employ*, and *John* are on the same footing with respect to the categorial property, and their distribution is constrained by syntactic principles governing their mode of combination.

If word-structures with derivational morphology are in fact generated by the same grammatical component that generates phrase-structures, we might naturally ask why word-structures notably do not have the same property of syntactic movement (Chomsky 1977, Travis 1984). For instance, in contrast with phrasal syntax where maximal projections may undergo movement, neither a derivational affix like -*ness* or -*er* nor the predicative base to which the affix attaches may move away, stranding the other.[11] The answer to this question is quite straightforward in a model of grammar in which movement must be justified by feature-checking (see Chomsky 1993). The reason the predicative base does not move away from the affix is that there is no motivation for such movement. By economy considerations, it cannot move. A similar explanation can be given for the affix as well. To illustrate, consider the examples in (49):

(49) a. John and Mary employ writers of children's books.
      b. *John and Mary [$_V$ [$_V$ employ] ers$_i$] write-t_i of children's books.

As its subcategorization requirement is already satisfied by *write* and there is no need for feature-checking, the affix -*ers* cannot move. Thus, movement of either the predicative base or the affix is automatically ruled out on independent grounds.

Despite the justification for word-structures with derivational morphology being generated by the same grammatical component that generates phrase-structures, the properties considered in the present study are not in and of themselves sufficient to argue against an independent grammatical component just for word-structures. Such a component can be motivated, if some properties can be shown to have no natural syntactic analysis. Complex verbal morphologies in languages such as Georgian, in which the distribution of Person-Number agreement affixes depends on Tense and the lexical properties of the verb stem (Anderson 1984), or those in the Semitic family, in which the verb forms are obtained from projecting tri-consonantal roots and vocalic melodies of Aspect-Voice onto morphological templates (McCarthy 1981), come to mind as being good cases for a separate component of grammar, as there appears to be no obvious syntactic treatment for them. A detailed analysis of these cases is evidently beyond the scope of my concerns here.

NOTES

I am indebted to Anna-Maria Di Sciullo and Ingo Plag for extensive discussion, comments, and suggestions on earlier versions of this chapter, parts of which were presented in the Fourth Canadian Workshop on Lexical Syntactic Relations in the University of Toronto in February 1993, at the Heinrich-Heine-Universität Düsseldorf and the Philipps-Universität Marburg. I would also like to thank the audiences of these occasions for penetrating comments. All inadequacies are my responsibility.

1. As I will be concerned with the specific structures and the particular issues that are pertinent to them, I will not attempt to approach the problem of defining what derivational morphology is (cf. Williams 1981).

2. The X-bar theoretic view of derivational morphology was originally conceived by Elizabeth Selkirk in the mid-1970s.

3. The structure in (2a) without the bar-level representation may give the impression that the V is an adjunct to the N. However, as bar-levels can be defined relationally, for example, a one-bar level projection is the level at which the head combines with a complement, and a two-bar level is the result of combining a one-bar projection and an argument of the head, and so on (cf. Chomsky 1994), no confusion should arise as to the bar-level of a given node. One can decide what bar-level it is in examining its daughter

nodes. Structures of the sort in (2a) would henceforth be used without representing the bar-levels. I differ from Chomsky (1994) in retaining the categorial labels in the syntactic representations for reason of familiarity.

4. The same argument holds for the Italian diminutive suffix *-inolina* (Scalise 1988).

5. There are three relevant issues that I cannot deal with here. First, it is not clear of what category these adjuncts are. Since they do not have independent syntactic distribution, it is quite difficult to settle this issue independently. Second, why do these adjuncts not project maximally to XPs, so that phrasal distribution is possible? Third, why should these adjuncts attach to the left? Notice that it is simply a restatement of facts if one says that they are suffixes, and therefore must attach to something to their left.

6. Diane Massam (personal communication) points out the example *standee* as a problematic case for the semantics of the suffixes *-er* and *-ee*, a full account of which is clearly beyond the scope of this chapter (cf. Levin and Rappaport 1988). Lexical specifications of the sort in (16) are stipulative, but the point is that selectional restrictions in derivational morphology can be imposed without resorting to Theta-role assignment (cf. Di Sciullo 1993 for a principled theory of selection in derivational morphology).

The notion of Control in (16) is unlikely to be the same as that in syntax, where both the controller and the controlled argument are syntactically projected as XPs. What is intended in (16) is probably something like that in (i), where we specify the syntactic category with which these morphemes combine:

    i. a. *-er*:
        Syntax: N, [V ____]
        Semantics: Being a person of which the thematic role of the external
                   argument of V is predicated.

      b. *-ee*:
        Syntax: N, [V ____]
        Semantics: Being a person of which the thematic role of the internal
                   argument of V is predicated.

In addition, if there is a structural condition on the control relationship (cf. Larson 1991), then the fact that *-er* does not c-command anything other than the verb-base might explain the impossibility of (9a) and (11b) (Roeper 1987).

7. It remains to be explained why the example in (7a) is possible with an interpretation in which the implicit Agent of the verb *sink* controls the PRO. The correct description of control seems to be that PRO is controlled by a syntactic controller, if it satisfies the selectional restriction of the predicate in the infinitival clause; otherwise, it would be controlled by the Agent, syntactically implicit or explicit, of the matrix clause (Roeper 1987). It is not clear why this should hold.

8. The expression in (31a) is perhaps better paraphrased as "the degree to which the book can be understood." In any event, *the book* is clearly understood to be the object of the verb-base *read*.

9. Hoekstra and van der Putten (1988) reach the same conclusion, but on different grounds.

10. Compounds such as *well-intentioned*, *often-repeated*, and *once-popular* show that adverbs may be part of an X^0. Note that the issue here is not whether adverbs may or may not appear inside X^0s; rather, the point is that the structures in (34) with an adverb should be possible if there is indeed a VP inside them.

11. Cf. Lapointe's (1981:230) Lexical Integrity Hypothesis, according to which no syntactic rule can refer to an element of morphological structure, and Selkirk's (1982:70)

Word Structure Autonomy Condition, which bars deletion and movement transformation that involve categories of both W-structure and S-structure.

REFERENCES

Abney, Steven. 1987. *The English noun phrase in its sentential aspect.* Doctoral diss., MIT, Cambridge, Mass.

Anderson, Stephen R. 1984. "On representations in morphology: Case marking, agreement, and inversion in Georgian." *Natural Language and Linguistic Theory* 2:157–218.

Aronoff, Mark. 1976. *Word formation in generative grammar.* Cambridge, Mass.: MIT Press.

Baker, Mark. 1988. *Incorporation: A theory of grammatical function changing.* Chicago: University of Chicago Press.

Barwise, Jon, and Robin Cooper. 1981. "Generalized quantifiers and natural language." *Linguistics and Philosophy* 4:159–219.

Booij, Geert. 1986. "The relation between inheritance and argument linking: Deverbal nouns in Dutch." In *Modularity and morphology*, ed. Martin Everaert, Arnold Evers, Riny Huybregts, and Mieke Trommelen, 57–73. Dordrecht: Foris.

Burzio, Luigi. 1981. *Intransitive verbs and Italian auxiliaries.* Doctoral diss., MIT, Cambridge, Mass.

Chomsky, Noam. 1965. *Aspects of the theory of syntax.* Cambridge, Mass.: MIT Press.

———. 1970. "Remarks on nominalization." In *Readings in English transformational grammar*, ed. Roderick A. Jacobs and Peter S. Rosenbaum, 184–221. Waltham, Mass.: Ginn.

———. 1981. *Lectures on government and binding.* Dordrecht: Foris.

———. 1986a. *Knowledge of language: Its nature, origin, and use.* New York: Praeger.

———. 1986b. *Barriers.* Cambridge, Mass.: MIT Press.

———. 1993. "A minimalist program for linguistic theory." In *The view from Building 20: Essays in linguistics in honor of Sylvain Bromberger*, ed. Kenneth Hale and Samuel Jay Keyser, 1–52. Cambridge, Mass.: MIT Press.

———. 1994. "Bare phrase structure." In *MIT Occasional Papers in Linguistics* 5, Department of Linguistics and Philosophy, MIT, Cambridge, Mass.

Chomsky, Noam, and Morris Halle. 1968. *The sound pattern of English.* New York: Harper & Row.

Di Sciullo, Anna-Maria. 1993. "The complement domain of a head at morphological form." *Probus* 5:95–125.

Di Sciullo, Anna-Maria, and Edwin Williams. 1987. *On the definition of words.* Cambridge, Mass.: MIT Press.

Fabb, Nigel. 1988. "English suffixation is constrained only by selectional restriction." *Natural Language and Linguistic Theory* 6:527–539.

Grimshaw, Jane. 1979. "Complement selection and the lexicon." *Linguistic Inquiry* 10:279–326.

———. 1990. *Argument structure.* Cambridge, Mass.: MIT Press.

Gruber, Jeffrey S. 1965. "Studies in lexical relations." Doctoral diss., MIT, Cambridge, Mass. In *Lexical structures in syntax and semantics*, Part I, Amsterdam: North Holland, 1976; and *MIT Working Papers in Linguistics*, Department of Linguistics and Philosophy, MIT, Cambridge, Mass.

Halle, Morris. 1973. "Prolegomena to a theory of word formation." *Linguistic Inquiry* 4:3–16.

Hoekstra, Teun, and Jean Putten. 1988. "Inheritance phenomena." In *Modularity and morphology*, ed. Martin Everaert, Arnold Evers, Riny Huybregts, and Mieke Trommelen, 163–186. Dordrecht: Foris.

Huang, James C.-T. 1982. *Logical relations in Chinese and the theory of grammar*. Doctoral diss., MIT, Cambridge, Mass.

Jaeggli, Osvaldo. 1980. "Spanish diminutives." In *Contemporary studies in Romance languages*, ed. Frank H. Nuessel, Bloomington, Ind.: IULC.

Lapointe, Steven. 1981. "A lexical analysis of the English auxiliary verb system." In *Lexical grammar*, ed. Teun Hoekstra, Harry van der Hulst, and Michael Moortgat, 215–254. Dordrecht: Foris.

Larson, Richard. 1991. "Promise and the theory of control." *Linguistic Inquiry* 22:103–139.

Law, Paul. 1990. "Heads, arguments, and adjuncts in derivational morphology." In *MIT Working Papers in Linguistics* 12, *Papers from the second student conference in linguistics*, ed. Thomas Green and Sigal Uziel. Cambridge, Mass.

Lees, Robert B. 1960. *The grammar of English nominalizations*. The Hague: Mouton.

Levin, Beth, and Malka Rappaport. 1988. "Non-event -*er* nominals: A probe into argument structure." *Linguistics* 26:1067–1083.

Lieber, Rochelle. 1980. *On the organization of the lexicon*. Doctoral diss., MIT, Cambridge, Mass.

———. 1983. "Argument-linking and compounds in English." *Linguistic Inquiry* 14:251–285.

Manzini, Rita. 1983. "On control and control theory." *Linguistic Inquiry* 14:421–446.

Marantz, Alec. 1984. *On the nature of grammatical relations*. Cambridge, Mass.: MIT Press.

Marchand, Hans. 1969. *The categories and types of present-day English word-formation: A synchronic and diachronic approach*. München: C.H. Beck.

McCarthy, John. 1981. "A prosodic theory of nonconcatenative morphology." *Linguistic Inquiry* 12:373–418.

Pesetsky, David. 1982. "Paths and categories." Doctoral diss., MIT, Cambridge, Mass.

Randall, Janet. 1984. "Thematic structure and inheritance." *Quaderni di Semantica* 4:91–109.

Roeper, Thomas. 1985. "Copying implicit arguments." In *The proceedings of the 4th West Coast Conference on Formal Linguistics*, ed. J. Goldberg, S. MacKaye and M.T. Westcoat, 273–283. Stanford, Calif.: SLA.

———. 1987. "Implicit arguments, and the head-complement relation." *Linguistic Inquiry* 18:267–310.

Roeper, Thomas, and Dorothy Siegel. 1978. "A lexical transformation for verbal compounds." *Linguistic Inquiry* 9:199–260.

Scalise, Sergio. 1988. "The notion of head in morphology." In *Yearbook of morphology* 1, ed. Geert Booij and Jaap van Marle, 229–245. Dordrecht: Foris.

Selkirk, Elizabeth O. 1982. *The syntax of words*. Cambridge, Mass.: MIT Press.

Sproat, Richard. 1985. "On deriving the lexicon." Doctoral diss., MIT, Cambridge, Mass.

Travis, Lisa. 1984. "Parameters and effects of word order variation." Doctoral diss., MIT, Cambridge, Mass.

Williams, Edwin. 1981. "On the notions 'lexically related' and 'head of a word.' " *Linguistic Inquiry* 12:245–274.

————. 1985. "PRO and subject of NP." *Natural Language and Linguistic Theory* 3:297–315.

Zubizarreta, Maria-Luisa, and Ton van Haaften. 1988. "English *-ing* and Dutch *-en* nominal constructions: A case of simultaneous nominal and verbal projections." In *Modularity and morphology*, ed. Martin Everaert, Arnold Evers, Riny Huybregts, and Mieke Trommelen, 361–393. Dordrecht: Foris.

THREE

Prefixed-verbs and Adjunct Identification

ANNA-MARIA DI SCIULLO

1. THE PUZZLE

Prefixes pose an interesting puzzle. In some cases, they seem to determine the category as well as the argument structure of the projections they are a part of, and in other cases they do not seem to have this effect. The question then arises of whether prefixes are heads or not, and if not, what kind of categories they are. Also puzzling is how to determine the licensing conditions they are subject to. Even though they are bound morphemes, they share properties with prepositions and adverbs, and the question arises of whether prefixes, prepositions, and adverbs are subject to the same conditions. Another piece of the puzzle to explain is why there is variation in prefixation among languages that do not exhibit major differences with respect to the distribution of prepositions and adverbs. A modular theory of grammar, along the lines of Chomsky (1993, 1994) and Di Sciullo (1990, 1993), provides a principled approach to this set of questions.

We will consider these questions in the light of our configurational theory of morphology (cf. Di Sciullo 1995a, 1995b, and in this volume), the main features of which are the following. In our theory, words and phrases are grammatical objects, given that they are both subject to the principles of the grammar. They are, however, different grammatical objects, given that they are derived by the laws of different components and that they are subject to the conditions of the grammar according to their configurational properties. The canonical configuration for a word is a non-ambiguous head-adjunction structure, whereas the canonical configuration for a phrase is an asymmetrical X-bar structure, that is, a specifier-head-complement structure. Asymmetrical X-bar structure may be a part of word-structure, but only head-adjunction structure is visible, that is, interpreted, at the interface between X^0 expressions and the Conceptual-Intentional (C-I) system. We termed this interface Morphological Form (MF) to distinguish it from Logical Form (LF). The MF/LF distinction is motivated on formal as well as conceptual grounds, as discussed in Di Sciullo (1993). The head-adjunction/asymmetrical X-bar structure distinction correlates with the difference in the type of interpretation, attributive/descriptive, of the expressions generated by the grammar.

We will focus here on the properties of prefixes in French verbs and claim that the restrictions on the occurrences of prefixes follow from a condition on the interpretation of adjuncts. This condition, as well as the condition on the identification of heads in X^0 expressions, such as the Relativized Head (RH) (cf. Di Sciullo and Williams 1987), can be subsumed under a general economy condition in a framework such as that of Chomsky (1993, 1994). Furthermore, the variation between languages with respect to prefixation is expected in our model, in which linguistic variation is reduced to morphological variation (cf. Chomsky 1993, 1994; Di Sciullo and Ralli 1994).

The organization of this chapter is as follows. In section 2, we discuss the properties of prefixed verbs in French and motivate the existence of two sorts of prefixes on configurational grounds. In section 3, we formulate a condition on the licensing of adjuncts and show how it accounts for the restrictions on the occurrences of prefixes of the same configurational sort. In section 4, we provide evidence that the variation between French and Italian in verb formation is possible given the underspecification of aspectual features. Finally, we consider some differences in the interpretation of prefixes and the interpretation of prepositional and adverbial phrases, which point to the correctness of a modular approach to the grammar.

2. PREFIXES AS ADJUNCTS

In our theory, the parts of X^0 expressions are non-ambiguously heads or adjuncts. Assuming that heads are the rightmost categories in X^0 expressions (cf. Di Sciullo and Williams 1987, Kayne 1994), prefixes must be adjuncts since they precede the other constituents in the expressions they are a part of.

The analysis of prefixes as adjuncts in verbal structures excludes the possibility of analyzing them as verbal heads providing the causative/inchoative semantics to the structure they are a part of. The adjunct analysis is motivated on empirical grounds, as we will show in considering the properties of prefixes in French verbs.[1]

The adjunct analysis has several advantages over the head analysis. One advantage is that it allows for a unified treatment of prefixed verbs. Another advantage of this analysis is that it leads to the formulation of a licensing condition for non-heads in X^0 expressions, which also applies to other prefixed categories.

2.1. Internal and External Prefixes

If prefixes are adjuncts, there are reasons to distinguish two sorts of prefixes. This distinction cuts across the categorial distinctions between prefixes, separating adverbial prefixes such as *re-* and *dé-* from prepositional ones such as *a-* and *-en*.

The prefixes *a-* and *en-* have prepositional properties, as they may, for instance, also be projected as prepositions; the prefixes *re-* and *dé-* have adverbial properties, as they are related to iterative and inverse adverbs. These prefixes differ with respect to their position and interpretation, as we will see. However, these differences cannot be reduced to categorial differences, since some prefixes have in some cases adverbial properties and in other cases prepositional properties; this is so for *dé-*, as in *déconstruire*, "to deconstruct," and *dériver*, "to derive from," a point to which we will return later.

We propose that prefixes are distinguished on configurational grounds. They are adjoined either outside or inside the verbal projection, as depicted in (1), in which the specifier (Spec) and the complement (Compl) positions are not visible or interpreted at MF.

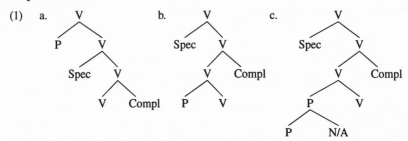

(1)   a.   b.   c.

In (1a), a prefix P is adjoined outside the verbal projection, while in (1b, c) it is adjoined inside the verbal projection. The prefix is directly adjoined to the verbal projection in (1a, b), while it heads an adjunct structure to the verbal projection in (1c).[2]

The structure in (1a) corresponds to verbal projections including the external prefixes *re-* and *dé-*, as in *recomposer*, "to recompose," and *décomposer*, "to decompose." The structure in (1b) corresponds to verbal projections including internal prefixes such as *a-* and *en-* in verbs such as *apporter*, "to bring to," and *emporter*, "to bring in." The structure in (1c) corresponds to denominal and deadjectival verbs including internal prefixes, as in *accrocher*, "to hook," and *embellir*, "to embellish."

The difference between external and internal prefixes allows us to make a substantive set of predictions with respect to the properties of prefixed verbs, as we will see next.

2.2. Predictions

The configurational difference between prefixes accounts for the linear order properties of prefixes. It correctly predicts that an external prefix must precede an internal one, the reverse sequence of prefixes being excluded.

(2)   réapporter, réemporter, *areporter, *enreporter
       "to bring again," "to bring from again"

Since external prefixes are adjoined outside the maximal projection of a verb and that internal prefixes are adjoined inside that projection, external prefixes precede internal ones. Thus, the configurational difference accounts for the linear order of adverbial and prepositional prefixes.

Second, the configurational differences between prefixes account for the fact that prefixed denominal and deadjectival verbs differ from prefixed verbs in that they may not generally take an external prefix without an intervening internal prefix.

(3)   réembarquer, *rebarquer, *emrébarquer
      "to embark again"

According to our analysis, in prefixed denominal and deadjectival verbs, the prepositional prefix is the head of an adjunct structure to the verbal head, as depicted in (1c). The obligatory presence of the internal prefix follows then from the fact that it is a head, even though the structure it heads is an adjunct to the verbal suffix. On the other hand, in prefixed verbs, that is, in structures such as (1a, b), the prefix is a bare adjunct, and consequently its presence is not forced. Thus, the configurational differences in (1) account for the cases in which a prefix must be projected in the verbal structure.

Third, the configurational differences account for the fact that external prefixes may be iterated and may co-occur, as is the case for adjuncts. This is not so for internal prefixes, which are more closely related to the argument structure of the projection they adjoin to, as in (4).

(4)   rerefaire, redéfaire, *aa/enemporter, *aem/enapporter
      "to redo again," "to undo again"

If prefixes are aspectual categories (cf. Di Sciullo 1993, Di Sciullo and Klipple 1993), internal prefixes may not be iterated because there is only one position for aspectual categories within the verbal projection (cf. Keyser and Roeper 1992). On the other hand, external prefixes may iterate, but, as we will see, only under certain conditions.

Fourth, assuming that the VP constitutes the argument structure domain of a verb (cf. Chomsky 1993, 1994), the configurational differences also account for the fact that external prefixes may not affect the argument structure of the verbal projection, whereas internal prefixes may do so, since they are a part of the argument structure domain of the verb. Thus, the external iterative prefix does not affect the argument structure of the verbal projection it is adjoined to. On the other hand, the adjunction of an internal prefix to a verbal projection may have this effect.

(5)   a.   Il a (re)fermé le donjon.
           "He locked the dungeon (again)."
      b.   Il a enfermé le dragon dans le donjon.
           "He locked the dragon in the dungeon."

Thus our configurational analysis allows us to predict that argument structure alternation occurs only in certain cases of verbal prefixation and not in other cases. Only internal prefixation may give rise to argument structure alternations.

Fifth, assuming that the VP is the *aktionsart* domain of the verb, that is, the internal structure of the event denoted by the verbal projection, we predict that the configurational difference between internal and external prefixes correlates with aspectual differences. This is what we find considering the aspectual properties of verbs in French. Prefixes provide internal or external aspectual specifications to a verbal projection. External prefixes provide external specifications to their projection by iterating an event or inversing it. Internal prefixes provide internal aspectual specification to the event; they specify internal parameters of the event such as the direction and the orientation of the event. Thus, external prefixes may not affect the *aktionsart*, whereas internal prefixes may do so, given that they are a part of the internal structure of the event. While *courir*, "to run," denotes an activity, *accourir*, "to hasten up," denotes an accomplishment. As expected, *courir* allows durative adverbs such as "for five minutes," but not frame-temporal adverbials such as "in five minutes." The reverse is true for *accourir*.[3]

(6) a. Pierre a couru pendant cinq minutes/?en cinq minutes.
   "Pierre ran for five minutes/?in five minutes."
   b. Pierre est accouru ?pendant cinq minutes/en cinq minutes.
   "Pierre hastened up ?for five minutes/in five minutes."

On the other hand, external prefixes do not affect the internal properties of the event denoted by the projection they adjoin to. This is evidenced in (6), in which both *peindre*, "to paint," and *repeindre*, "to repaint," are accomplishments. Both verbs allow frame-temporal expressions, but not durative adverbs and they may occur in the complement of verbs such as *to finish*, as it is typical of accomplishments.

(7) a. ?Il l'a (re)peint pendant une heure.
   "He (re)painted it for an hour."
   b. Il l'a (re)peint en une heure.
   "He (re)painted it in an hour."
   c. Il a fini de le (re)peindre.
   "He finished (re)painting it."

These aspectual differences are expected given the structural differences depicted in (1a, b). External prefixes are outside the internal aspectual structure of a verb and thus do not have an effect on its internal structure, whereas internal prefixes are a part of the internal aspectual structure of a verb and thus have a direct effect on that structure. As for the structure in (1c), in which the prefix is the head of an adjunct structure to the verb, the prefix contributes directly to the argument structure as well as to the internal event structure of the projection it is a part of.

Moreover, if an internal prefix provides a direction to the event denoted by the verbal projection it is adjoined to, we expect that such prefixation is excluded for telic verbs. This is exactly what we find. Internal prefixes may not be adjoined to verbs that have an inherent natural endpoint, such as *naître*, "to be born," and *exploser*, "to explode." On the other hand, an external prefix may do so given that it does not have access to the internal aspectual structure of the verb.

(8) a. renaître, réexploser, regagner
   "to be born again," "to explode again," "to win again"
   b. *anaître, *aexploser, *agagner
   "to be born at," "to explode at," "to win at"

Thus our configurational analysis of prefixes makes the correct predictions with respect to the aspectual contribution of a prefix in the verbal projection they are a part of.

2.3. Summary

To sum up, prefixes are aspectual adjuncts, internal or external to the verbal projection. This hypothesis allows for a unified treatment for prefixes in French verbs, including adverbial and prepositional prefixes. It makes the relevant structural and semantic differences between prefixes, in terms of internal and external prefixes. Internal prefixes may affect the argument structure and the internal event structure of the projection to which they adjoin, external prefixes affect the whole verbal projection, but not the internal aspectual structure of the verbal projection.

3. ADJUNCT IDENTIFICATION PRINCIPLE

The configurational distinction between external/internal prefixes allows for a substantial set of predictions. However, it does not account for the fact that only given prefixes may occur in given verbal projections. This fact holds for external as well as internal prefixes, as can be observed in the following examples.

(9) a. apposer, atterrir, embellir
         "to place," "to land," "embellish'
      b. *emposer, *enterrir, *abellir
         "to place in," "to land in," "to atbellish"

(10) a. refaire, défaire
          "to do again," "to undo"
      b. *resavoir , *désavoir
          "to know again," "to unknow"
      c. rerefaire, redéfaire
          "to do again and again," "to undo again"
      d. *dédéfaire, *dérefaire
          "to undo again," "to undo again"

These facts do not follow from the configurational difference between prefixes that we discussed above, since the restrictions on the occurrences of prefixes hold for prefixes of the same configurational sort. We propose that these restrictions follow from a local condition on the licensing of adjuncts, the Adjunct Identification principle (AIP), that we formulate as follows.

(11) *Adjunct Identification*
      An adjunct Y to a category X is licensed if it identifies an underspecified feature of X.

      Y identifies X iff
      Y is immediately contained in X, and
      X is underspecified.

The AIP is part of a general economy condition on interfaces, the principle of Full Interpretation (FI), assumed in Chomsky (1986–1994). FI requires that every element be a legitimate object and thus have a language-independent interpretation at the interface. At LF, FI requires that each legitimate object be a head, an argument, a modifier, or an operator-variable construction. We will take FI to apply also at MF and to require that each legitimate object be a head or an adjunct at the interface. Thus, the AIP holds for head-adjunction structures, that is, for configurations in which an adjunct Y is contained in a two-segment category X, as in (12).

(12)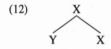

The AIP is not a condition on the licensing of categories in asymmetrical X-bar positions. It is a condition on the licensing of adjuncts. Complement, specifiers, and adjuncts differ with respect to their licensing conditions. In a head-complement structure, the features of the complement must satisfy the selectional features of the head. In the specifier-head structure, the features of the specifier and the head must be checked. However, in an adjunction structure, some under-specified feature of the head must be identified by the adjunct.[4] We claim that the AIP applies at MF for the interpretation of adjuncts, including aspectual adjuncts.

The traditional literature on aspect (cf. Vendler 1967, Dowty 1979) distinguishes different aspectual classes of verbs on the basis of different syntactic and semantic properties.[5] We propose here that the grammar analyzes aspectual classes in terms of features, as it does for other grammatical properties, including inflection. We posit that the aspectual classes of verbs are defined by the two binary aspectual features: Terminal, [T], indicating if the event has a terminus or not, and Subinterval, [S], indicating if the event has subintervals or not. The following specifications obtain. States are $[-T, -S]$, achievements are $[+T, -S]$, activities are $[-T, +S]$, and accomplishments are $[+T, +S]$. We will propose other aspectual features below to account for event iteration and inversion. We will also take categories other than verbs to be specified for aspectual features. This is the case for prepositions, whether they head an XP projection or take the form of a prefix. If aspect is analyzed in terms of features, we expect certain lexical items to be underspecified for aspectual features, as is the case for phonological features. We will take the basic assumptions of underspecification theories proposed for phonological features (cf. Archangeli 1988, Archangeli and Pulleyblank 1995) to cover aspectual features as well. That is, we will assume that unmarked aspectual feature values are filled in the derivation.

We claim that in prefixed verbs, the restrictions on the occurrences of external prefixes, as well as the occurrence of internal prefixes, follow from the AIP, given the presence of underspecified aspectual features in the derivation. Thus, in order for a prefixed verb to be interpreted by the C-I system, a prefix must have the relevant aspectual features to identify the verbal projection to which it is adjoined; otherwise the structure is interpreted as gibberish. In sections 3.1 and 3.2, we discuss the effects of the AIP on prefixed verbs; denominal and deadjectival verbs are discussed in section 3.2.2.

3.1. External Prefixes

According to our analysis, *re-*, and in some cases, *dé-* are instances of prefixes adjoined outside of the maximal projection of the verb, as in (13), where the dummy △ represents the argument structure of the verbal projection. In (13a), the structure includes only one external prefix, and in (13b), the structure includes two external prefixes.

(13)   a.   b.

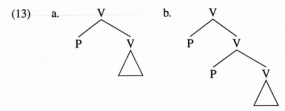

The examples in (14) show that the iterative prefix generally combines with accomplishments, that is, with [+T, +S] verbs in our system, as in (14d), but generally not with other aspectual classes of verbs, such as states, as in (14a); achievements, as in (14b); and activities, as in (14c).

(14)   a. *Il resait l'italien.
          "He reknows Italian."
       b. *Il est réarrivé.
          "He rearrived."
       c. *Il a reconduit une auto.
          "He redrived a car."
       d. Il a reconstruit la structure.
          "He rebuilt the structure."

This fact brings evidence to the effect that there are aspectual restrictions on the combination of the iterative prefix with a verbal projection. This is also the case for English, according to Wechsler (1989), in which the iterative prefix also generally combines with accomplishments. Furthermore, it is also the case that the inverse prefix generally combines with verbal projections denoting accomplishments, as the examples in (15) illustrate. Thus, the iterative and the inverse prefixes compose with [+T, +S] verbs in our system.

(15)   a. *Il désait l'italien.
          "He unknows Italian."
       b. *Il est déarrivé.
          "He unarrived.'
       c. *Il a déconduit une auto.
          "He undrove a car.'
       d. Il a déconstruit la structure.
          "He deconstructed the structure."

The aspectual restrictions involved in the combination of the iterative or the inverse prefix within a verbal projection range over the aspectual properties of the whole event denoted by that projection.[6] These prefixes do not affect the internal aspectual structure of the verbal projection they are a part of, as evidenced above.

They do not identify the [T] feature of a verb. They do, however, identify an underspecified aspectual feature outside of the *aktionsart* domain of that verb.

(16)   a.   (re)composer quelque chose en cinq min./*pendant cinq min.
             "to (re)compose something in five min./*for five min."
       b.   (dé)composer quelque chose en cinq min./*pendant cinq min.
             "to (de)compose something in five min./*for five min."

These facts suggest that external prefixes range over the aspectual properties of the whole verbal projection. If this is the case, the verbal projection of [+T, +S] verbs includes an underspecified aspectual feature, say, the feature [I], to be identified in the derivation. We will take *re-* and *dé-* to be specified positively for [I], and to differ with respect to other aspectual features.[7] These prefixes identify underspecified aspectual features of the verbal projection, as exemplified in the partial representation in (17) including the iterative prefix. The latter identifies the [I] feature of the [+T, +S] verb as being [+I].

(17)

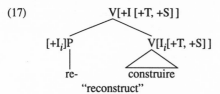

"reconstruct"

The aspectual features of external prefixes do not affect the internal aspectual features of a verbal projection, defined in terms of the [T] and [S] features in our system. The iterative feature [+I] identifies an underspecified aspectual feature of the verbal complex, and the complex aspectual features project, since the verb is both the categorial head and the head with respect to aspectual features.

We noted above that external prefixes exhibit adjunct-like properties to the extent that they may in some cases be iterated and may co-occur. However, the iteration of *re-* is possible, as in (18a), while the iteration of *dé-* is not, as in (18b). Furthermore, *re-* precedes *dé-*, as in (19).

(18)   a.   Elle a rerecomposé la structure.
             "She recomposed the structure again."
       b.   *Il a dédécomposé la structure.
             "He decomposed the structure in reverse."

(19)   a.   Elle a redécomposé la structure
             "She decomposed the structure again."
       b.   *Il a dérecomposé la structure.
             "He recomposed the structure in reverse."

These facts do not follow from the external/internal difference between prefixes, given that the iterative as well as the inverse prefix are both external prefixes. The restrictions on the iteration and the occurrence of the inverse prefix follow from the locality of the AIP. The adjunct identification is obtained under strict inclusion, as specified in (11) above. Thus the inverse prefix must be a sister to the verbal projection. Consequently, the inverse prefix may not be iterated, may not precede the iterative prefix, as illustrated above, as well as may not precede an internal prefix, as in (20a). The fact that it may not co-occur with an internal prefix suggests that it may in some cases be projected within the verbal projection. This is, in fact, the case in the examples in (20b) and (20c), in which the prefix *dé-* has a directional but not an inverse value.

(20)   a. *déapporter, *déamener, *déapposer
           "to uncarry," "to unbring," "to unplace"
      b. déporter, délivrer, déposer
           "to deport," "to deliver," "to deposit"
      c. dériver, débarquer, débourser
           "to derive," "to disembark," "to disburse"

On the other hand, the iterative prefix *re-* differs from the inverse prefix *dé-* in this respect, as illustrated in (21a). This is due to the fact that the iterative prefix may only be adjoined outside of the verbal projection and thus is not in a position at which an internal prefix can be projected. As expected, the iterative prefix may not occur in denominal verbs, as in (21b), since it cannot be projected within a verbal structure.

(21)   a. réapporter, réamener, réapposer
           "to carry again," "to bring again," "to place again"
      b. *reriver, *rebarquer, *rebourser
           "to rederive from," "to rebark," "to relay down"

Thus the AIP, in conjunction with the configurational differences between prefixes, accounts for the restrictions on the iteration and the co-occurrence of external prefixes in French verbs.

3.2. Internal Prefixes

Although an external prefix may not affect the internal aspectual features of an event, internal prefixes may do so. We will see that the restrictions observed on the occurrences of internal prefixes also follow from the AIP.

3.2.1. *Prefixed Verbs*

Recall that internal prefixes may not be iterated, they may not co-occur, and they typically follow external prefixes. Internal prefixes do not affect a whole event structure but are a subpart of that structure. As seen above, internal prefixes may, in some cases, change the *aktionsart* as well as the argument structure of the projection they are adjoined to. These facts follow from their being projected within the verbal structure.

(22)

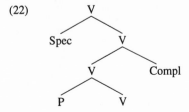

As is the case for external prefixes, the adjunction of an internal prefix to a verbal projection does not necessarily give rise to an interpretable structure. There are aspectual restrictions on the combination of internal prefixes, such as *a-* and *en-*, with a verbal projection. These prefixes may generally combine with verbs denoting activities, that is, with [−T, +S] verbs, in our system. In fact, they provide an endpoint to unbounded events, including subintervals; they do not generally combine with states, that is, with [−T, −S] verbs, with achievements, that is, [+T, −S] verbs, or with accomplishments, that is, [+T, +S] verbs.

(23) a. *Il a-/en-sait l'italien.
          "He to-/in-knows Italian."
      b. *Il est a-/en-arrivé.
          "He to-/in-arrived."
      c. Il est accouru./ Il a encouru des risques.
          "He hastened up."/"He took risks."
      d. *Il a a-/en-construit la structure.
          "He to-/in-built the structure."

Internal prefixes affect the internal aspectual structure of the verbal projection they are a part of.[8] While durative adverbials but not punctual adverbials may modify an activity, only punctual adverbials may do so when the verbal projection includes an internal prefix.

(24) a. porter quelque chose *en cinq min./pendant cinq min.
          "to carry something in five min./for five min."
      b. apporter quelque chose en cinq min./*pendant cinq min.
          "to bring something in five min./for five min."
      c. emporter quelque chose en cinq min./*pendant cinq min.
          "to bring something in five min./for five min."

Internal prefixes have the aspectual effect of specifying the [T] feature of a verbal projection, provided that the verb is underspecified for that feature. This is the case for verbs such as *porter*, "to carry," and *mener*, "to lead," but not for verbs for which the [T] feature is specified, such as *sauter*, "to jump," and *plonger*, "to dive," which are [−T, +S] verbs, for example, *assauter*, "to tojump," *ensauter*, "to injump," *applonger*, "to todive," and *emplonger*, "to indive."

The aspectual features of internal prefixes affect the internal aspectual features of a verbal projection they are adjoined to. The [+T] feature of these prefixes identifies the underspecified [T] feature of the verb and the features of the verbal head project, as depicted in (25).

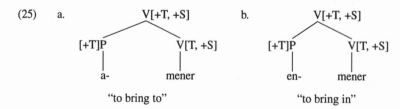

(25) a.   V[+T, +S]   b.   V[+T, +S]

      [+T]P   V[T, +S]   [+T]P   V[T, +S]
       | | | |
       a-   mener   en-   mener

           "to bring to"   "to bring in"

These structures include only legitimate objects at the MF interface, that is heads and adjuncts. They satisfy FI, including the AIP and the RH.

3.2.2. *Prefixed Denominal and Deadjectival Verbs*

In prefixed denominal and deadjectival verbs, it is the adjunct structure that identifies the aspectual features of the verbal projection of which it is a part. An internal prefix provides the spatial orientation of the event in a space, as in (26a), or on a scale, as in (26b).

(26)   a.   Il l'a accroché/enterré.
            "He hooked/buried it."
        b.   Elle est embellie/appauvrie.
            "She is embellished/empoverished."

We assume that in denominal and deadjectival verbs, the internal prefix is the head of a structure including a noun or an adjective, and that this structure is an adjunct to the verbal head, which is an overt suffix in French.

(27)   a.   b.

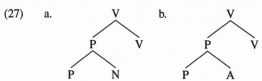

The [+T] feature of an internal prefix projects to the P complex adjunct structure, and the latter identifies the [T] feature of the verbal head and the aspectual features of the verbal head, including [+T], project. Prefixed denominal verbs generally denote accomplishments, [+T, +S] verbs, whereas prefixed deadjectival verbs generally denote achievements, [+T, −S] verbs. This is a point to which we will return later.

(28)   a.   b.

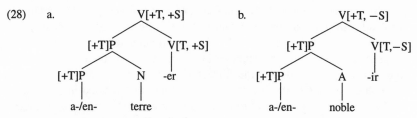

The aspectual features are visible in adjunct-head structure at MF, in which FI applies, ensuring that every category is interpreted either as an adjunct or as a head. If a category is an adjunct, it is subject to the AIP; if it is a head, it is subject to the RH.

However, the presence of an internal prefix does not necessarily give rise to an interpretable structure, as illustrated here:

(29)   a.   emboîter/*aboîter, accrocher/*encrocher
            "to box," "to hook"
        b.   embellir/*abellir, appauvrir/*empauvrir
            "to embellish," "to become poor"

These facts follow if we assume that the internal prefix structure must provide a proper aspectual identification to the event denoted by the verbal projection of which it is a part, as is the case for the related PP structures, for example, *mettre en/*à boîte*, "to put in/at box," *devenir en/*à beauté*, "to become in/*at beauty." This suggests that the interpretation of a prefix is a function of the interpretation of the verbal projection of which it is a part. For example, in *apporter*, "to bring to," and *emporter*, "to bring in," the prefixes denote a direction. This is not the case in *emboîter*, "to box," and *accrocher*, "to hook," in which the prefixes denote a physical relation of enclosure or contact; in *enamourer*, "to enamour," and *acclimater*, "to acclimatize," the prefixes denote a change in a state, whereas in *enrichir*, "to make rich," and *appauvrir*, "to impoverish," the prefixes denote a high or a low value on a scale.

Di Sciullo and Klipple (1993) observed that the interpretation of prefixes, as well as of prepositions, varies according to the conceptual pseudospace (cf. Gruber 1965; Jackendoff 1972, 1983; Hale 1984) of the verbal projection they are a part of. Assuming that the conceptual pseudospaces include directional (D), physical (P), abstract state (A), and scalar (S) pseudospaces, prefixes may be underspecified for certain pseudospaces, or may be specified, as is the case for French *a-* and *en-*.

(30)   en-:   a.   away from   (D)
                b.   enclose in   (P)
                c.   into a state   (A)
                d.   in high point   (S)

(31)   a-:   a.   toward   (D)
                b.   contact with   (P)
                c.   in a state   (A)
                d.   in low point   (S)

Now, the restrictions on the occurrence of given internal prefixes in denominal and deadjectival verbs can be accounted for as follows. With change of position (P) verbs such as *emboîter*, the prefix *en-* may combine with a noun such as *boîte*, the prefix *en-* providing the "enclose in" relation, as specified in (30b), and the adjunct structure may identity the [T] features of the verbal suffix; with *accrocher*, the prefix *a-* provides the 'contact with' relation, as specified in (31b); it may combine with a noun such as *crochet*, and the adjunct structure may identify the [T] feature of the verbal projection. On the other hand, *aboîter* and *encrocher* are interpreted as gibberish, since the prefix structures may not identify the [T] feature of the change-of-place projection they are a part of. Likewise, with change of state (S) verbs, the prefix *a-* provides the "in low point" relation, as in (31d), and may combine with an adjective such as *pauvre*. This is also the case for the prefix *en-*, which provides the "in high point" relation; it may combine with adjectives such as *riche*, and the adjunct structure may identify the [T] feature of the verbal projection. Thus, *appauvrir* and *embellir* are interpretable, but not *empauvrir* and *abellir*, in which the prefix structures cannot identify the [T] feature of the change of state projection of which they are a part. Thus, the restrictions on the occurrences of prefixed structures in denominal and deadjectival verbs follow from the AIP. In these expressions, it is the complex adjunct structure that identifies the [T] feature of the verbal head.

Our analysis also accounts for the fact that denominal verbs are generally headed by *-er* and not by *-ir*, whereas deadjectival verbs are generally headed by *-ir* and not by *-er*, as in (32).

(32) a. accrocher/*ir, emboîter/*ir
           "to hook," "to box"
      b. appauvrir/*er, embellir/*er
           "to impoverish," "to embellish"

Assuming, as in Di Sciullo (1993), that the verbal suffix *-er* may head a change of location verb and the verbal suffix *-ir* may head a change of state verb, it is possible to account for the fact that a change of location verb headed with *-ir* and a change of state verb headed with *-er* are generally interpreted as gibberish.

With *-er* denominal verbs, such as *emboîter*, "to box," a physical (P) position (PT) adjoined structure (P/PT) may identify the [T] feature of the event denoted by the verb it is adjoined to, which is a change of position (CPT) verb. With *-ir* deadjectival verbs such as *appauvrir*, "to empoverish," a scalar (S) state (ST) adjunct structure (S/ST) may identify the [T] feature of the event denoted by a change of state (CST) verb. Conversely, a P/PT adjunct structure may not identify the [T] feature of a CST verb. Likewise, a S/ST adjoined structure may not identify the [T] feature of a CPT verb.

(33) a.   b.

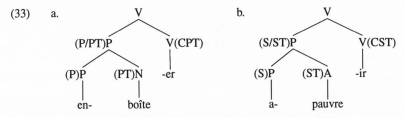

Thus the properties of prefixes in conjunction with the principle pertaining to the interpretation of adjuncts, the AIP, accounts for the interpretability of prefixed verbal constructions and prefixed denominal and deadjectival verbs.

3.3. Summary

The contribution of prefixes to verbal projections is aspectual in nature. Prefixes may iterate or inverse an event, as in *refaire*, "to do again," and *défaire*, "to undo," or they may affect a part of the internal structure of an event, indicating the direction of the event in a space, as in *apporter*, "to carry to," and *emporter*, "to carry away," *atterrir*, "to land," and *enterrer*, "to bury," or on a scale, as in *appauvrir*, "to impoverish," and *embellir*, "to embellish." External prefixes have scope over the whole event denoted by a verbal projection, while internal prefixes affect a subpart of the event. The restrictions observed on the occurrence of prefixes of the same configurational sort follow from the AIP. A prefix structure can be licensed only if it identifies an underspecified aspectual feature of the event denoted by the projection to which it adjoins. If this is not the case, the expression it is a part of is interpreted as gibberish.

4. SOME DIFFERENCES BETWEEN FRENCH AND ITALIAN

There is variation among languages with respect to prefixation. We will briefly consider Italian verbal prefixed structures and contrast them with French. These differences may follow from independent properties of the languages, as we will see.

Italian prefixes include *ri-*, *dis-*, *di-*, *in-*, *a-*, and *s-*, as illustrated in (34). These examples include cases of external prefixation, as in (34a), cases of internal prefixation to verbs, as in (34b), and cases of internal prefixation in denominal and deadjectival verbs, as in (34c, d, e).

(34) a. rifare, ricominciare, distendere, scomporre
          "to remake," "to begin again," "to distend," "to decompose"
      b. immettere, inscrivere, imporre
          "to put in," "to write in," "to impose"
      c. affossare, incollare, infuriare, scarcerare
          "to ditch," "to glue," "to enrage," "to release"
      d. approfondire, arricchire, abbellire
          "to deepen," "to enrich," "to make beautiful"
      e. imbruttire, inasprire, indurire, impoverire
          "to make ugly," "to embitter," "to harden," "to impoverish"

Even though there is variation between French and Italian in the shape of the prefix (for example, in Italian, *s-* is similar to French *dé-*), it is possible to observe similar restrictions with respect to prefixation. For instance, external prefixes may be iterated; they may co-occur and precede internal prefixes. Only the former may change the argument structure of the verbal projection.

(35) a. ririfare, *disdisfare
          "to remake again"
      b. ridisfare, *disrifare
          "to undo again"
      c. riimportare, riscatenare
          "to import again," "to unchain again"
      d. Gianni ha rubbato i documenti di Paulo.
          "Gianni stole the papers of Paulo."
      e. Gianni ha dirubbato Paulo dei suoi documenti.
          "Gianni stole Paul from his papers."
          "Gianni stole Paulo's papers."

However, Italian differs from French with respect to the licensing of prefixes in certain verbal structures. Typically, denominal and deadjectival verbs carry a prefix in Italian, as illustrated in (36a, c). This is generally the case with deadjectivals; however, there are some denominals without a prefix in both languages, as is the case for *salare*, *saler*, "to salt," and *secare*, *scier*, "to saw."[9]

(36) a. imburrare, inchiodare, incollare
          beurrer, clouer, coller
          "to butter," "to nail," "to glue"

    b.   inscatolare, imbottigliare, agganciare
         emboîter, embouteiller, accrocher
         "to box," "to bottle," "to hook"
    c.   arrossire, annerire, imbianchire, invecchiare, ingrassare
         rougir, noircir, blanchir, vieillir, grossir
         "to blush," "to blacken," "to whiten," "to age," "to fatten"
    d.   impoverire, amorbidire, allargare, digrossare
         appauvrir, amollir, largir, dégrossir
         "to impoverish," "to soften," "to enlarge," "to refine"

These facts show that in Italian, contrary to French, aspectual identification is generally projected as an independent morpheme. This difference between Italian and French is corroborated by the fact that particles are licensed in Italian, but not in French, particles also being aspectual categories.

(37) a. Gianni ha portato su/giu il piano.
      b. Gianni a monté/descendu le piano.
         "Gianni brought up/down the piano."
      c. Paulo ha portato via il quadro.
      d. Paulo a emporté le tableau.
         "Paulo brought the painting away."
      e. Maria ha buttato via i documenti.
         "Paulo brought the painting away."
      f. Marie a jeté les documents.
         "Mary threw away the documents."

The fact that denominal and deadjectival verbs generally carry a prefix in Italian, whereas this is not necessarily the case in French, could be due to a difference in the projection of aspect onto categories.[10] However, the fact that the variation in prefixation is localized in deadjectival verbs suggests that it is a function of feature underspecification. While in French the prefixes *en-* and *a-* are specified for the scalar field, *en-* pointing toward a high point and *a-* pointing toward a low point, in Italian, the equivalent prefixes, *in-* and *a-*, are not specified with respect to a high or low point in a scale. Evidence to this effect comes from the fact that in French *en-* generally combines with scalar adjectives with high value, while *a-* combines with low-value ones, as pointed out above and further evidenced in (38); however, in Italian, *in-* and *a-* occur with high- as well as low-valued adjectives, as illustrated in (39). This suggests that the prefixes *a-* and *in-* in Italian are not specified for the scalar dimension.

(38) a. enrichir, appauvrir
         "to become rich," "to impoverish"
      b. endurcir, amollir
         "to harden," "to soften"
      c. élargir, amincir
         'to enlarge," "to thin"

(39) a. impiccolire, ingrandire
         "to make small," "to make bigger"
      b. invecchiare, ringiovanire
         "to age," "to rejuvenate"

c. appaciare, aguerrire
    "to make peace," "to harden to war"

Thus, variation in derivational morphology with respect to verbal prefixation can be viewed as a consequence of the underspecification of aspectual features.

5. X^0 AND XP ASPECTUAL INTERPRETATION

There are reasons to believe that X^0 and XP structures differ with respect to the interpretation of aspect. We claim that aspectual features are interpreted under a head-adjunction relation in X^0 expressions, while aspectual features are interpreted under a specifier-head relation in XP structures.

Locative PPs may modify verbs denoting activities, such as the verb *conduire*, "to drive," but not states, such as the verb *savoir*, "to know." The PP in the example in (40a) provides a spatial endpoint to the event denoted by the verb, and a terminative reading results, as evidenced in (40b, c). However, the PP in (41) is not legitimate, since stative verbs may not be bounded, and thus a terminative reading cannot be obtained.

(40) a. Il a conduit Paul à Paris.
          "He drove Paul to Paris."
      b. Il a conduit Paul pendant un jour/*en un jour.
          "He drove Paul (around) for a day/*in a day."
      c. Il a conduit Paul à Paris *pendant un jour/en un jour.
          "He drove Paul to Paris *for a day/in a day."

(41) a. *Il sait le français à Paris.
          "He knows French in Paris."
      b. *Il lui ressemble à Paris.
          "He looks like him in Paris."

These facts follow from the AIP, according to which an aspectual adjunct must identify some aspectual features of the event denoted by the category it is adjoined to; otherwise the structure is interpreted as gibberish. However, the properties of the determiner in the PP determines the aspectual properties of the verbal projection. This can be seen considering the examples in (42). In (42a), the PP includes an indefinite determiner, and a terminative reading is not available for the verbal projection. On the other hand, in (42b) the PP includes a definite determiner and a terminative reading is obtained.

(42) a. Il l'a conduit à des cités interdites pendant un an/*en un an.
          "He drove him to forbidden cities for a year/*in a year."
      b. Il l'a conduit à la cité interdite *pendant un an/en un an.
          "He drove him to the forbidden city *for a year/in a year."

These facts indicate that the terminative reading is interpreted via the specifier-head relation and thus the head-complement relation in XP structure. This is not the case for X^0 expressions, in which the terminative reading is interpreted in adjunct-head relation, as we have seen above.

Moreover, we observe that there is a relation between the presence of a prefix on a verb and the presence of a PP complement, as in (43b), in which the prefix and the head of the PP have the same form. This is a consequence of the fact that internal prefixation affects the internal aspectual structure as well as the argument structure of a verbal projection.

(43) a. Il a collé la photo dans l'album.
       "He glued the picture into the album."
    b. Il a décollé la photo de/*dans l'album.
       "He unglued the picture from/*into the album."

In (43b), the interpretation of the prefix and the interpretation of the head of the PP complement are very close. They denote the orientation of the event away from a spatial source. However, the interpretation of the prefix is not identical to the interpretation of the whole PP. The prefix provides only part of the meaning that is conveyed by the PP. The actual spatial source of the event is given by the PP and not by the prefix, which only provides the spatial orientation of the event denoted by the verb to which it is adjoined. This follows from our assumption that the interpretation of a prefix is an attributive rather than a descriptive one. Thus, we expect that prefixes may specify the orientation of the event denoted by the verbs to which they are adjoined, but not the actual spatial endpoint or beginning-point of the event they modify, which is provided by XP complements. The difference between an attributive and a descriptive interpretation is, we claim, a basic difference distinguishing word-internal from phrasal interpretation.

The attributive interpretation of the parts of an X^0 expression can also be observed in denominal verbs. The interpretation of the noun included in the expression is attributive and not descriptive. Consequently, it may not refer to an entity in a domain of interpretation. The only interpretation for this expression is attributive, that is, the expression is interpreted as a set of features. For example, in the prefixed denominal verbs in (44), it is only the features defining the internal semantics of a noun that are interpreted. If this were not the case, it would be impossible to account for the fact that PP complements of the same form are not acceptable.

(44) a. Il a accroché le tableau au mur/*au crochet.
       "He hooked the painting to the wall/*to the hook."
    b. Il a encodé la grammaire en LISP/*en code.
       "He encoded the grammar in LISP/in code."

These facts bring support to the hypothesis that the interpretation by the C-I system of categories in X^0 expressions and XP expressions is different. The differences, we claim, follow from the configurational difference between the two sorts of expressions.

6. SUMMARY

We proposed a way to account for restrictions on the occurrence and the co-occurrence of prefixes in French verbs. The hypothesis that prefixes are internal or external adjuncts to a verbal projection accounts in part for the restrictions. We proposed that they followed from the AIP, a licensing condition subsumed under FI, in conjunction with the aspectual underspecification of categories.

The incidence of the AIP in derivational morphology clarifies the role of a prefix in the structure it is a part of and correlates its structural and semantic properties. Prefixes do not generally affect the argument structure of their projection, but they do affect the aspectual features of their projection. A prefix in a verbal projection may be interpreted if it identifies an underspecified aspectual feature of the verbal projection it is adjoined to. The variation between French and Italian with respect to the presence or absence of a prefix in verbal structures is expected in a model of grammar that reduces variation to morphological variation and is possible given feature underspecification.

The fact that the properties of prefixes are partially distinct from the properties of prepositional phrases in XPs suggests that the notion of relativized modularity of Di Sciullo (1990) is on the right track. Given the configurational differences between X^0 and XP expressions, aspectual features are visible in different structural relations. Moreover, in head-adjunction structures, the aspectual specification conveyed by the prefix can only be attributive, while the aspectual specification conveyed by the aspectual PP will have a descriptive content. This, again, is expected, given the configurational differences between X^0s and XPs at the interface with the C-I system.

NOTES

An earlier version of this paper was presented at the Going Romance conference in Utrecht in December 1993. We thank the participants to this conference for their questions. We also thank Noam Chomsky, Ken Hale, and Pino Longobardi for helpful comments. This study was supported by the Social Sciences and Humanities Research Council of Canada grant #411-92-0012 (La modularité de la grammaire: arguments, projections et variations), by the Fonds pour la formation de Chercheurs et l'Aide à la Recherche grant #94ER401 (Interfaces: invariants et relativisation), and by the Fonds Institutionnel de Recherche of the Université du Québec à Montréal.

1. See Di Sciullo and Klipple (1993), Labelle (1992), Lieber (1992), and Di Sciullo (1990) for the analysis of prefixed verbs in Romance languages. As for the analysis of prefixed verbs in Germanic languages, see Borer (1990), Keyser and Roeper (1992), Walinska de Hackbeil (1985), Stiebels and Wunderlich (1992), Neeleman and Schipper (1992), Lieber and Baayen (1993).

2. The structures in (1) contain no minimal or maximal categories, as we take these notions not to be primitives of the grammar (cf. Speas 1990, Chomsky 1994) but derived from the configuration.

3. The argument structure change observed in the example (5b) above can be seen as a consequence of the fact that the directional prefix adds a direction to the event denoted by the verb it adjoins to, here a movement verb, and a PP referring to a spatial endpoint is licensed, which in turn licenses an internal argument — the entity undergoing the change of place — by predication.

4. The AIP is distinct from Theta-identification proposed in Higginbotham (1985) as one way to discharge Theta-roles in XP structures, including AP or PP modifiers. The AIP does not apply to Theta-roles. Furthermore, it applies under the word-level.

5. Different proposals are available in the literature for the representation of event structure. In Pustejovsky (1988), the properties of the traditional aspectual classes (cf. Vendler 1967, Comrie 1976, Dowty 1979) are represented in terms of X-bar projections differing in internal complexity and embedding. It is also possible to represent the geometry of events in terms of the mathematical notion of vector, as in Di Sciullo and Klipple (1993), as defining the parameters of the event. We will take the parameters of an event to include the temporal (cf. Tenny 1978, Pustejovsky 1988), the spatial (cf. Hale 1984, Kipka 1990, Klipple 1991) and the scalar properties (cf. Di Sciullo and Klipple 1993) defining the shape of that event. We are departing from the traditional view of aspect here, which is generally limited to the determination of the state of completion of an event or a situation, in taking the geometry of the event to be defined in terms of a set of temporal, spatial, and scalar features characterizing its beginning point, its internal structure, and its endpoint, if it has one.

6. See Wechsler (1989) and Keyser and Roeper (1992) for analyses of the iterative prefix in English.

7. We will take the iterative prefix to be specified positively for the feature [I] as well as for the feature [N] for Negative; thus, *re-* is [+I, +N]. We will take the inverse prefix to be specified as follows: [+I, +N]. The features [I] and [N] are associated with other prefixes, including *anti-*, which is [−I, +N] and *pro-*, which is [−I, −N]. We will not provide justifications for the aspectual features here. See Di Sciullo (1995b) for discussion.

8. For different analyses of directional prefixes, see Walinska de Hackbeil (1985) and Borer (1990) for English; Labelle (1990) for French; Kipka (1990) for Polish; Olsen (1992) for German; and Stiebels and Wunderlich (1992) and Neeleman and Schipper (1992) for Dutch.

9. In French, an internal prefix must be present in some cases and not in other cases, as illustrated in the examples in (i) and (ii).

i . a. emboîter/*boîter, accrocher/*crocher
   "to box," "to hook"
   b. beurrer, saler, seller
   "to butter," "to salt," "to saddle"

ii. a. enrichir/*richir, appauvrir/*pauvrir
   "to become rich," "to become poor"
   b. *enrougir/rougir, *adoubler/doubler
   "to redden," "to become pale"

A prefix is required in denominal verbs including a location, as in (ia). No prefix is required in denominal verbs including an entity undergoing a change of position, as in (ib). A prefix specified for the scalar pseudospace is required in deadjectival verbs, as in (iia), including scalar adjectives, such as *riche* and *pauvre*. This is not the case in (iib), in which the adjectives are not scalar.

10. The difference between French and English with respect to the projection of aspectual categories is discussed in Klipple (in this volume). In French, aspectual categories may be conflated into the verb, whereas they may be projected independently as particles in English.

REFERENCES

Archangeli, Diana. 1988. *Underspecification in Yawelmani phonology and morphology*. New York: Garland.

Archangeli, Diana, and Doug Pulleyblank. 1994. *Grounded phonology*. Cambridge, Mass.: MIT Press.

Baayen, H., and Rochelle Lieber. 1993. "Verbal prefixes in Dutch: A study in lexical conceptual structure." In *Yearbook of Morphology*, ed. Geert Booij and Jerome van Marle, 1993.

Broman Olsen, Mari. 1992. "Aspectual marking and English 'verb-forming' prefixes." In *Proceedings of Console* 1, ed. Peter Ackema and M. Schoorlemmer, Dordrecht: Kluwer.

Chomsky, Noam. 1993. "A minimalist program for linguistic theory." In *The view from Building 20: Essays in linguistics in honor of Sylvain Bromberger*, ed. Kenneth Hale and Samuel Jay Keyser, 1–52. Cambridge, Mass.: MIT Press.

———. 1994. "Bare phrase structure." In *MIT Occasional Papers in Linguistics* 5, Department of Linguistics and Philosophy, MIT, Cambridge, Mass.

Comrie, Bernard. 1976. *Aspect*. Cambridge, Mass.: Cambridge University Press.

Di Sciullo, Anna-Maria. 1990. "Modularity and the mapping from the lexicon to the syntax." *Probus* 2:257–290.

———. 1991. "Interfaces in a modular grammar." *GLOW* paper, University of Lisbon.

———. 1993. "Prefixes and suffixes." Paper presented at the XXIVth Linguistic Symposium on Romance Languages held at USC and UCLA. To appear in *Romance Linguistics in Los Angeles: Selected papers from the XXIVth linguistic symposium on Romance languages at USC and UCLA*, ed. Claudia Parodi, Carlos Quicoli, Mario Saltarelli, and Maria Luisa Zubizarreta, Georgetown University Press, forthcoming.

———. 1995a. "X-bar Selection." In *Phrase structure and the lexicon*, ed. Johan Rooryck and Laurie Zaring, 77–107. Dordrecht: Kluwer.

———. 1995b. "Atomicity and relatedness in configurational morphology." In *Configurations and X-bar structure*, ed. Anna-Maria Di Sciullo. Somerville, Mass.: Cornell Cascadilla Press.

Di Sciullo, Anna-Maria, and Edwin Williams. 1987. *On the definition of word*. Cambridge, Mass.: MIT Press.

Di Sciullo, Anna-Maria, and Elizabeth Klipple. 1994. "Modifying affixes." In *Proceedings of the Western Conference on Linguistics XXIII*. University of Washington, Seattle.

Di Sciullo, Anna-Maria, and Angela Ralli. 1994. "Theta-role saturation in Greek deverbal compounds." To appear in the *Proceedings of the first international workshop on Modern Greek syntax*, Dordrecht: Kluwer, forthcoming.

Dowty, David. 1979. *Word meaning and Montague grammar*. Dordrecht: Reidel.

Gruber, Jeffrey S. 1965. "Studies in lexical relations." Doctoral diss., MIT, Cambridge, Mass. In *Lexical structures in syntax and semantics*, Part I, Amsterdam: North Holland, 1976; and *MIT Working Papers in Linguistics*, Department of Linguistics and Philosophy, MIT, Cambridge, Mass.

Hale, Kenneth. 1984. "Notes on world view and semantic categories: Some Warlpiri examples." Ms. MIT, Cambridge, Mass.

Hale, Kenneth, and Samuel Jay Keyser. 1992. "The syntactic character of thematic structure." In *Thematic structure: Its role in grammar*, ed. Iggy Roca, 107–141. Dordrecht: Foris.

Heinrichs, E. 1985. "A compositional semantics for aktionsarten and NP reference in English." Doctoral diss., Ohio State University, Columbus.

Higginbotham, James. 1985. "On semantics." *Linguistic Inquiry* 16:547–595.

———. 1989. "The elucidation of meaning." *Lexicon Project Working Papers* 19. Center for Cognitive Science, MIT, Cambridge, Mass.

Jackendoff, Ray. 1972. *Semantic interpretation in generative grammar*. Cambridge, Mass.: MIT Press.

———. 1983. *Semantics and cognition*. Cambridge, Mass.: MIT Press.

————. 1990. *Semantic structures*. Cambridge, Mass.: MIT Press.

Kayne, Richard. 1994. *The antisymmetry of syntax*. Cambridge, Mass.: MIT Press.

Kearns, Kate. 1988. "Light verbs in English." Ms. MIT, Cambridge, Mass.

Keyser, Samuel Jay, and Tom Roeper. 1992. "Re-: the abstract clitic hypothesis." *Linguistic Inquiry* 23:89–127.

Kipka, Paul. 1990. "Slavic aspect and its implications." Doctoral diss., MIT, Cambridge, Mass.

Kuroda, S.-Y. 1985. "Whether you agree or not: Rough ideas about the comparative grammar of English and Japanese." Ms. UCSD.

Labelle, Marie. 1992. "La structure argumentale des verbes locatifs à base nominale." In *Linguisticae Investigationes* 14:267–315.

Lieber, Rochelle. 1992. *Deconstructing morphology: Word-formation in syntactic theory*. Chicago: Chicago University Press.

Lieber, Rochelle, and Harald Baayen. 1993. "Verbal prefixes in Dutch: A study in lexical conceptual structure." In *Yearbook of Morphology 1993*, ed. Geert Booij and Jaap van Marle, Dordrecht: Kluwer, 51–79.

Neeleman, Ad, and Joleen Schipper. 1992. "Verbal prefixation in Dutch: Thematic evidence for conversion." In *Yearbook of Morphology 1992*, ed. Geert Booij and Jerome van Marle, Dordrecht: Kluwer, 57–92.

Pustejovsky, James. 1988. "The geometry of events." In *Studies in generative approaches to aspect*, ed. Carol Tenny, *Lexicon Project Working Papers* 24, Center for Cognitive Science, MIT, Cambridge, Mass., 19–39.

Stiebels, Barbara, and D. Wunderlich. 1992. "A lexical account of complex verbs." In *Theorie des Lexikons* 30. Düsseldorf: Heinrich Heine Universität.

Tenny, Carol. 1987. "Grammaticalizing aspect and affectedness." Doctoral diss., MIT, Cambridge, Mass.

————. 1989. "The aspectual interface hypothesis." *Lexicon Project Working Papers* 24. Center for Cognitive Science, MIT, Cambridge, Mass., 1–18

Travis, Lisa. 1992. "Inner aspect and the structure of VP." *Cahiers de linguistique de l'UQAM* 1/1:130–147.

Vendler, Zeno. 1967. *Linguistics in philosophy*. Ithaca, N.Y.: Cornell University Press.

Walinska de Hackbeil, Hanna. 1985. "En-prefixation and the syntactic domain of zero derivation." In *Proceedings of the 11th annual meeting of the Berkeley Linguistics Society*.

Wechsler, S. 1989. "Accomplishments and the prefix *re-*." In *Proceedings of the 19th annual meeting, NELS*, GLSA, University of Massachusetts, Amherst.

Williams, E. 1981. "Argument structure and morphology." *The Linguistic Review* 1:81–114.

FOUR

Prepositions and Variation

ELIZABETH KLIPPLE

The question of how language variation may arise is central to the theory of grammar. Recent proposals by Chomsky (1993) and Di Sciullo (1993) suggest that cross-linguistic differences do not arise from changes in parameter settings, but that variation arises principally from differences in the morphological properties of the languages. This paper supports these proposals.

We examine the category preposition cross-linguistically. A close comparison is made of the behavior of prepositions in English and French. It is shown that prepositions serve several different functions, which may be divided up differently on a language-particular basis. We argue that a difference in the representation of the "direction/aspect" (D/A) function found in English prepositions but not in French prepositions accounts for several differences between the two languages.

This research is set within a modular theory of grammar, following Di Sciullo (1993). In this framework, there are three levels of grammar: syntax (LF), Morphological Form (MF), and Lexical Conceptual Structure (LCS). These levels of structure are delineated on essentially morphological grounds: their domain is either the decomposition of phrases into words, the decomposition of words into morphemes, or the decomposition of morphemes or lexemes into primitive categories. All of these levels have an X-bar structure, and are subject to the application of the same principles or modules of the grammar.[1]

However, the principles are relativized to each level. Each level of the grammar is opaque to the other levels; for instance, the syntax cannot "see inside" the morphological structure, and so processes occurring at the syntactic level cannot involve parts of the morphological structure.

We claim that there are grammatical categories at both LCS and syntax, and that the categorial structures are parallel, although not isomorphic. Thus, LCS, as understood in this paper, is not just "lexical"; functional as well as lexical categories are assumed to have an LCS representation, and the entire sentence has a representation at conceptual structure as well. This view is in keeping with that of Hale and Keyser (1991) in their view of their "Lexical Relational Structure"; Abney (1987) also holds that functional categories have lexical representations.

We propose that LCS is composed of conceptual categories that are universal, and that map onto syntactic (and morphological) categories in every language. However, we argue that the mapping between conceptual categories and syntactic categories is not one-to-one, but that a syntactic category may correspond to several conceptual categories. Moreover, this correspondence differs from language to language. Thus, the division of the grammar into levels based on lexical and morphological patterns is central to the study of variation.

In particular, we argue that the category preposition corresponds to three conceptual categories in English. In French, one of these conceptual categories, direction/aspect (D/A), is not encoded as part of the syntactic category preposition, but instead is mapped to the category verb. We claim that this difference accounts for a wide range of differences between the two languages. This in turn bears on the articulation of functional and lexical categories as collections of grammatical features. The "conceptual categories" are taken to be distinctive features at LCS.

It is important to note that we are dealing not with variation in the linear order of elements, but in the properties and identification of categories. This variation, of course, influences the syntactic behavior of the elements concerned, specifically with regard to constructions such as preposition-stranding and the pseudopassive. It also allows (or disallows) certain constructions involving the category preposition, including verb-particle constructions and resultative complex predicates. However, a significant emphasis of this study will concern what Talmy (1985) calls "Lexicalization Patterns," that is, regularities in the possible lexical semantic content of lexical items, in this case, prepositions and certain classes of verbs. That this is an important issue for syntax is implied by our hypothesis, following Hale and Keyser (1991), that there is a level of lexical structure that has syntactic properties.

In addition, we assume that the notion of "event," in the sense of Davidson (1967) and Higginbotham (1985), has a central role in the semantic relations in a clause. We adopt the hypothesis of Klipple (1991) that the internal aspectual structure of the event corresponds to the syntactic constituent VP, and that elements are licensed as complements within the VP if they participate semantically in this internal aspectual structure. We will argue that the direction/aspect node is, universally, licensed as part of the VP, because it is inherently aspectual; cross-linguistic differences lie in what syntactic categories it may be mapped onto.

The chapter is organized as follows. In section 2, we consider motivation for our claim that there are three different functions that prepositions perform, at least in English. In section 3, we examine variation between French and English in verb + preposition constructions. In section 4, we propose certain minimal differences in the mapping between LCS and syntax that can account for this variation. Section 5 deals with the structure of the three prepositional conceptual categories proposed. We extend our analysis to preposition-stranding and pseudopassive constructions in section 6, and to resultative constructions in section 7. In section 8, we discuss the possibility that the conceptual categories proposed might reduce to syntactic features, and outline how this might be captured. Finally, in section 9, we summarize our view on the semantics of prepositions, in which underspecification is central.

1. THE CATEGORY PREPOSITION

In comparing a category across languages, the first questions to ask are: What is the category? What does it do? The question "What is a preposition?" is not simple to answer. According to Hale and Keyser (1990), a preposition essentially expresses an "interrelation" between, typically, a place and a thing; Curme (1931) also states that prepositions express a relation. Many linguists take the basic function of a preposition to be to express a *spatial* relation, although prepositions are found in many non-spatial contexts (in fact, we claim that the spatial meaning is not basic).

It should be noted at the outset that we take this category to include postpositions, so that the more appropriate name for this syntactic category is "adposition." There is no a priori reason to distinguish the two (although we will see that the identification of the category cross-linguistically is more complicated than this view suggests). However, for most of the chapter, we will be dealing only with languages that have adpositions that are ordered before their complements; the term "preposition" will be retained except where it would cause confusion.

There is disagreement over what sort of a category a preposition is. Prepositions are clearly "closed class" items, rather than "open class"; that is, there is a limited, relatively fixed number of them. It is striking that almost any grammar of any language will give a list of prepositions. In the case of languages such as English and French, about thirty prepositions are usually listed; the lengths of the lists vary as to how many complex prepositional elements (e.g., *in spite of*) are admitted.[2]

Despite their limited number, prepositions are often listed among the lexical rather than the functional categories in the current literature. However, they are recognized to have hybrid properties, in some ways resembling lexical categories and in some ways operating like functional categories. We discuss this question further in section 8.

We will argue that prepositions in both English and French are combinations of primitive conceptual categories, or a basic set of distinctive features, available to all languages. We propose that the class of prepositions is not totally homogeneous, because not all include all of the primitive categories possible in a preposition. Finally, we argue that differences between English and French result from a different combination of primitive categories underlying the syntactic category preposition.

2. THREE "CONCEPTUAL CATEGORIES" ASSOCIATED WITH PREPOSITIONS

Prepositions serve at least three different functions in a language such as English. These three functions will be referred to as "spatial functor" (henceforth SF), "(locative) relation" (REL) and "direction/aspect" (D/A), respectively.

We claim that these constitute three "conceptual categories" that can be associated with prepositions and preposition-like particles. These conceptual categories are linguistically relevant, but they do not necessarily map directly to syntactic categories. In fact, the mapping is usually not one-to-one, and it is not universal; we will argue that it is in fact one of the principal areas of language variation.

Spatial functors are functors that take a thing, and yield a place that is determined in relation to that thing; for instance, in *on the table*, at least part of what the preposition *on* does is to refer to a space above (and probably touching) the table. Actually, temporal functors are part of this category as well; they include notions such as reference to a prior time, as in *before 5 o'clock*, or to the interval of the complement, as in *during class*. For simplicity of reference, we will use the label SF for all members of this category. Since SFs make direct reference to an area, point, or interval, I assume that SF is a category with nominal properties.

Relations, such as *at* in *at school*, are two-place predicates, taking a place as internal argument and yielding a one-place predicate, the property of being at that place. The relations represented by English *to, from, by,* and *with* are probably also in this category. Temporal and abstract relations, such as those found in *at noon* or *with Mary*, are also expressed by this category.

Direction is the trajectory of an event of motion or orientation, often indicated by particles, such as *up* in *the balloon went up*. Directions also sometimes are interpreted as a place that is "in the direction" specified; for instance, in *put the book down, down* seems to indicate the final resting place as well as the direction. I take this category to have non-spatial uses, or aspectual uses, as well; for instance, the function of *up* in *eat up the cake* is completive, and that of *away* in *work away at a problem* is to emphasize duration. Hence the name direction/aspect; I discuss the relation between the two below in section 8.

I will argue that at an abstract level these categories are separate, and arranged in the following hierarchy.

(1)

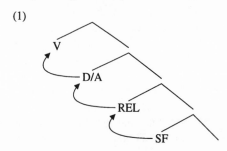

They may be joined together in syntax through an operation called "conflation" at Lexical Conceptual Structure (LCS). Following Hale and Keyser (1990), who adapted the idea of Talmy (1985), we take conflation to be incorporation, or head-to-head movement, at LCS. We will assume the representation of conceptual categories at LCS to be a linguistic universal. As a result of which conceptual categories they allow to conflate, languages vary in their inventory of syntactic categories.

In section 8, I will suggest that these conceptual categories are more properly seen in terms of distinctive grammatical features that operate at the interface between a non-linguistic conceptual component and the linguistic component of grammar, much in the same way that phonological features operate between a non-linguistic component of sound perception and the linguistic phonological component.

2.1. Spatial Functors versus Relations

First we consider evidence that the functions of spatial functor and relation should be distinguished at some level of grammar.

The SF and REL components of prepositions, although they are almost never separate in a language like English, have been analyzed by Jackendoff as two separate conceptual categories. He represents the semantics of the PP *on the table* as in (2):

(2) $[_{path}$ AT $[_{place}$ ON $[_{thing}$ the table]]]

Jackendoff calls the two categories "Path-functions" and "Place-functions." Place-functions are identical to SF; Path-functions, according to Jackendoff, take a place and yield a "Path." Note that I depart from this use of "Path," and treat these functions instead as locative predicates.[3]

In French, Ruwet (1982) argues that prepositions such as *sur*, "on"; *sous*, "under"; *dans*, "in," and the like should be analyzed as *à*, "at," + a nominal expression of place, for example:

(3)   sur: à + dessus

This corresponds precisely to the REL-SF division. In this regard, French prepositions are similar to English ones, although as we have hypothesized above, they are different with respect to the category D/A.

Furthermore, Ruwet has a number of arguments to show that *à* does not have exactly the same syntactic properties as the other prepositions he considers, including *sur*, *dans*, *sous*, and others. This is easily explained if *à* is posited to represent only the category REL, while the other prepositions are a conflation of REL and SF.

There are languages in which SF and REL are expressed by separate morphemes. For instance, Mandarin Chinese expresses SF with particles ("post-positions") that occur at the end of the VP, and conveys REL by means of verb-like "prepositions," or "coverbs" (cf. Li and Thompson 1981, Ernst 1987, Klipple 1991):

(4)   zai zhuozi shang
      AT table ONK
      "on the table"

The "postpositions," or SF, include *shang*, "on"; *li*, "in"; *xia*, "under"; *hou*, "behind"' and *wai*, "outside." These elements cannot serve to head a PP that functions as a VP complement or modifier (although they can be found as NP modifiers). By itself, a phrase such as *zhuozi shang* means something closer to "top of the table," indicating that SF is a nominal category in Chinese as well.

To form a full PP in Chinese, a "preposition" must be used. This class includes prepositional elements that double as full verbs, exemplified in (5):

(5)   zai   "at/be at"
        dao   "to/arrive"
        gei   "to (transfer)/give"

There are also prepositional elements such as *cong*, "from," and *wang*, "toward," that cannot serve as independent verbs, at least not for most speakers.[4]

It is interesting from the point of view of language typology that Chinese seems to have two kinds of adpositions, those that precede and those that follow their complement; the answer to the question of whether it has prepositions or postpositions is that it has both. However, as we are arguing, the proper way to understand these facts is to see that the functions of these elements are not the same, and that in fact they constitute different categories.[5]

A cursory glance at an unrelated and typologically different language, West Greenlandic Eskimo, suggests that similar divisions can be found between two classes of adposition-like elements. In this language,[6] REL and D/A seem to be encoded in extensive case system, which includes the oblique cases of locative, allative (motion to, purpose), ablative (source), prosecutive (motion through, via) and instrumental. Postpositions, themselves considered nominals and usually occurring in possessed form and following a case-marked NP, are necessary to represent the variety of meanings (in, out, under, on, over, and so on) denoted by SF. This is illustrated in (6):

(6)   a.   illup qaani
           house-rel top-poss.
           on top of the house
    b.   umiap ataani
           boat-rel under
           under the boat

According to Fortescue (1984), these postpositions "indicate more specific locational functions than simple case inflections" (p. 209). This separation of tasks between oblique case, marking the concepts of being at and going to, from, and via (exactly those subsumed by REL), and postpositions indicating various SF, suggests that this language draws the same categorial distinction between SF and REL found in Chinese.[7]

English prepositions may sometimes occur with only their SF meanings, stripped of the REL component. Consider (7):

(7)   a.   Under the table is my cat's favorite spot.
    b.   At the zoo is a nice place to be.

These sentences equate the PP in the subject with an NP referring to a place. From the meaning, it is clear that the P in question is not expressing a relation, but only SF.[8] The fact that the PP is equated with a nominal expression supports the hypothesis that SF is a nominal category.

French prepositions also seem to be able to function in this way:

(8)   Sous la table est l'endroit favori de mon chat.
      under the table is the place favorite of my cat
      "Under the table is my cat's favorite place."

A similar case occurs when one preposition expresses SF, and another expresses REL:

(9)   This oil sample came from under the streets of Paris.

2.2. Relations versus Direction/Aspect

The category of direction/aspect is motivated as a separate conceptual category first by the simple fact that there exist notions such as "up," "down," "in," "out," "left," "right," and so on that do not fit the semantic characteristics of either spatial functors (SF) or relations (REL). One may speak of a direction independently, without relating its position directly to anything else, as REL does, and without reference to the spatial characteristics of an object, as SF does.

Furthermore, the corresponding lexical items do not pattern with the prepositions we have seen; they often stand alone, as directional particles.[9]

(10)   a.   The balloon floated up.
       b.   I walked away.

They also appear either directly after the verb before the direct object, the two options being related by what is called "Particle Movement."[10]

(11)   a.   The cat ate up its dinner.
       b.   The cat ate its dinner up.

Full PPs cannot occur before the direct object, presumably because they would block case assignment to this element. Thus, particles seem to have the property of not blocking case assignment, for some reason. This is easier to explain if they can in fact be instances of only the features underlying D/A.[11]

We call this category direction/aspect, rather than just Direction, because the same particles can be used to indicate some characteristic of the internal aspectual structure of the event, or *aktionsart*.[12] The aspectual notions indicated include telicity, duration, iteration, and intensity, among others.

(12)   a.   Billy ate up his dinner.
       b.   Jane threw out her old shoes.
       c.   Tom worked away at the problem.
       d.   Vicky read over her paper.
       e.   Bill gave in to the pressure.

Particles can sometimes behave like relational prepositions, as in:

(13)   The cat climbed up the tree.

However, the interpretation of the relation to the NP is not the same. NP seems to define, to specify the trajectory of the direction, unlike SF. This is an example of D/A combined with REL, without SF. Not all particles can function as REL; for instance, *out* and *away* must occur with another preposition if they are to relate to an NP.

(14) a. We ran out *(of) the house.
      b. We ran away *(from) the lion.

However, there are also morphemes that can function as D/A alone, as REL and SF conflated, or even perhaps as a conflation of all three. *In* and *on* are the chief examples of this.

(15) a. Come in!
      b. Get on!
      c. Put the book on the table/in the box.

Once again, Mandarin Chinese provides evidence to identify D/A as a separate category: this notion is encoded in a third type of preposition-like morpheme. These are separate directional verbal elements that sometimes stand alone, but often combine with other verbs with a similar function as English particles. They include *jin*, "in, enter"; *chu*, "out, go out"; *qi*, "up"; and *xia*, "down."[13]

(16) Zhan qi lai!
      stand up come
      Stand up!

(17) Qing jin lai.
      please enter(in) come
      Please come in.

It is interesting to note that Chinese seems to distinguish the SF properties of *in* from its D/A properties, by having two different morphemes to express these.

2.3. Combinations of the Prepositional Conceptual Categories

The three conceptual categories may be expressed by separate lexical items, or two or more may be conflated in a single lexical item. The preposition *at*, in (18), is a simple locative predicate, REL; *to* and *from* are more complex examples of REL. Prepositions such as *on* and *onto* normally express SF and REL predications, as in (19). D/A can be expressed alone in a particle, as in (20), or conflated with REL, as in (21).

(18) REL:
      a. John is at the store.
      b. Jane is with Bill.
      c. Bill went to school.
      d. The residents ran from the burning building.

(19) SF + REL:
      a. Benny walked onto the ship.
      b. Lightning jumped into the box.

(20) D/A:
    a. The balloon went up.
    b. The lion ran away.
    c. Lily climbed down.

(21) D/A + REL:
    a. Benny walked down the street.
    b. Lily climbed up the tree.

It is possible to find all three conceptual categories indicated separately, as in (22), or all three conflated into one preposition, as in (23). The latter example is ambiguous; the PP can indicate the location of the event of walking, and in this case has roughly the semantics interpretation in (23b); or it may indicate the goal of the action, in which case it has the interpretation in (23c).

(22) The mouse ran out from under the clock.

(23) a. Benny walked on the ship.
    b. Benny walked around and this happened on the ship.
    c. Benny went onto the ship by walking onto it.

It is important to note that a verb may have several PP complements, occurring in series:

(24) Joey walked from his school down the street to his grandma's house.

Some researchers, notably Jackendoff (1983), treat these as part of a single, semantic constituent called Path. Syntactically, they are usually considered to be separate constituents.

Multiple particles, or a combination of several particles and PPs, are also possible:

(25) Go on over along the river to Grandma's house!

3. VERB-PREPOSITION INTERACTION IN ENGLISH AND FRENCH

We will now consider variation between English and French, which lies mainly in the interaction between verbs and prepositions, and in the existence of prepositional particles. We consider how the expression of conceptual categories, that is, their mapping from conceptual structure to syntactic structure, may vary from language to language. We claim that the variation found between English and French with respect to the properties of prepositions lies in a difference of the mapping of the conceptual category D/A to syntax. This claim supports the view that cross-linguistic variation in general reduces to variation in the properties of morphemes, for we propose that the differences are located in the properties of prepositions themselves.

3.1. Motion Verbs and Directional Particles

There are regular differences between French and English in the way that they express the notions of direction, directed motion, goal, and telicity. These differences lie primarily in which categories indicate the concepts of direction and several aspectual notions. English uses a variety of directional particles, such as *up*, or *out*, to express direction with a motion verb, and also to express aspect. French does not have this kind of directional particle, but usually expresses the notions of direction and aspect in the meaning of the verb itself.

Whereas English often uses a verb plus a directional particle to express a directed action, French may use just a verb to express the same situation, as shown in (26) and (27):

(26) a. *Edwidge threw her old shoes.[14]
      b. Edwidge threw her old shoes out.

(27) Edwidge a jeté ses vieux souliers.
      Edwidge has thrown her old shoes
      "Edwidge threw out her old shoes."

Normally, the verbs *put* and *mettre* both require a locative PP, but if the location is absolutely clear from the context, the PP may be left out. For instance, in a context in which there is a pot of boiling water on the stove, the sentences in (28b) and (29) may be used:

(28) a. *Put the noodles!
      b. Put the noodles in!

(29) Mets les pâtes!
      put the noodles
      "Put the noodles in!"

What is interesting is that although English may leave the location elliptical, it must still use a directional particle, as shown by the ungrammaticality of (28a); French can use just the verb alone.

A different use of *put* and *mettre* that is inherently reflexive, exemplified in (30) and (31), displays the same pattern. A PP is not required in either case, for the verb is understood to mean "put on oneself"; that is, there is an inherent Goal that is coreferential with the subject. Yet, the English version must still use a directional particle.

(30) a. *John put his coat.
      b. John put on his coat.

(31) Jean a mis son manteau.
      Jean has put his coat
      "Jean put his coat on."

This difference is also found with verbs indicating transfer, but not necessarily physical movement.

(32) a. *Paul gave his old coat.
      b. Paul gave away his old coat.

(33) Paul a donné son vieux manteau.
      Paul has given his old coat
      "Paul gave away his old coat."

Explicit direction is often encoded in the verb in French, but in a particle in English, as illustrated in (34) and (35). This pattern is similar to that above; French has separate lexical verbs to express what in English is most naturally expressed by *go* or *come* plus a directional particle:

(34) a. John came in.
      b. Jean est entré.
          Jean is entered
          "Jean entered."

(35) a. Edwidge went up the stairs.
      b. Edwidge a monté l'escalier.
          Edwidge has gone-up the stairs
          "Edwidge went up the stairs."

The French verbs in this class include *entrer*, "enter"; *sortir*, "exit"; *monter*, "go up"; *descendre*, "descend"; and *passer* "pass." There are many other English V + particle constructions which correspond to single verbs in French, for example:

(36) get up   se lever
      sit down   s'asseoir
      walk around   se promener
      turn over   renverser
      get out   s'en aller/se sortir
      go down   descendre
      give away/up   donner
      stand up   se lever/se tenir debout
      take out   retirer
      take off (clothing)   se déshabiller
      take off   décoller (airplane)/partir
      run away   s'échapper/s'évader

Note that the presence of the reflexive clitic *se* is generally related to the transitivity of the verb; most of the verbs given are basically transitive, and the addition of the clitic satisfies the internal argument, resulting in a reflexive construction. According to Di Sciullo (in this volume), *se* can have an aspectual function as well; however, this possibility is not a crucial factor in this discussion. The arguments here carry over to English transitive verbs and their non-reflexive French counterparts.

There are many other verb + particle constructions in English that do not express directed motion, but have an aspectual significance. The existence of these in English, and the absence of them in French, follows straightforwardly from the statements above, if we assume that the particles here are the same as those in the above constructions, in spite of the different interpretation. These constructions are often said to be idiomatic, and may partially be so; however, the particle concerned generally has a rather consistent interpretation. *Up*, *out*, and *down* usually have a telic interpretation, stressing the completion of an activity; *away*, *over*, and *through* indicate intensity or thoroughness throughout the duration of the event. In addition, *over* can indicate repetition of the event.

(37)   a.   finish up
     b.   work away
     c.   calm down
     d.   eat up
     e.   chill out (relax)
     f.   think through
     g.   read over
     h.   do over

The recent coining of (37e) indicates that the verb + particle construction is still very productive in English.

We take these examples to be the same as the spatial verb + particle constructions. The difference between the spatial and aspectual interpretation, we claim, lies chiefly in the verb with which the particle occurs. That is, the particles are semantically underspecified, and it is the other constituents with which they occur that determine how their meaning is completed. Aspect and spatial direction, furthermore, are two sides of the same coin. We discuss this further in section 9.

There is no real correlate in French for the aspectual senses of the particles *up* and *out*; to achieve the same effect, some other means must be found.[15]

(38)   a.   The boy ate up the cake.
     b.   Le garçon a mangé tout le gâteau.
        the boy has eaten all the cake
        "The boy ate all of the cake."
     c.   Le garçon a mangé le gâteau au complet.
        the boy has eaten the cake to completion
        "The boy ate the cake completely."

(39)   a.   Marie worked out today.
     b.   Marie s'est entraînée aujourd'hui.
        Marie refl is trained today
        "Marie worked out today."

Many correlates of these constructions are, again, single verbs in French.

(40) | | |
|---|---|
| calm down | se calmer |
| shut up | se taire |
| pass up | se passer |
| look up | chercher/verifier |
| break up | s'amorceler/ se séparer |
| pick out | sélectionner |
| stand out | se démarquer (du reste du groupe) |
| put up with | tolérer |
| work out | s'entraîner |

We will treat these as exactly parallel to the situation with motion verbs and directional particles; the only difference is that here the particles are interpreted in the temporal/aspectual domain rather than in the spatial domain. Once again, note that the French *se* indicates that a reflexive has been formed from a transitive and is not directly related to the issue of the presence of a particle.

3.2. Directional Verbs

A problem is raised by verbs that seem to incorporate prepositional notions into their meaning in English. English and French both have verbs like *enter*, in which the direction of the motion seems to be included in the motion verb, suggesting that D/A is conflated with the verb in both languages. However, as we see in (41) and (42), the French versions take a PP, whereas the English versions normally take an NP:[16]

(41) a. He entered (*into) the room.
      b. He exited (from) the room.

(42) a. Il est entré *(dans) la salle.
          he is entered (in) the room
          "He entered the room."
      b. Il est sorti *(de) la salle.
          he is exited (from) the room
          "He exited the room."

At first glance, these verbs seem to go against the pattern; for while the French verbs as usual include D/A, the English verbs also include it, which is not the norm. However, the English verbs seem to carry more information than the corresponding French verbs, and to incorporate the entire prepositional meaning. These verbs normally take only an NP; supplying a PP is at least redundant, and sometimes ungrammatical.

In the next section, we propose a way that the facts we have seen in section 3 can be accounted for with simple assumptions about the mapping between the conceptual category D/A and categories at the syntactic level.

4. CONSTRAINTS ON THE MAPPING OF D/A TO SYNTAX

The simple fact that French uses separate verbs for the notions of direction and aspect suggests that the content of the D/A node is encoded in the verb in this language. That is, the D/A node that is present universally at LCS is subjected to a language-particular restriction on its mapping to syntax, stated in (43):

(43) In French, the conceptual D/A node must be conflated with the verb at syntactic structure. D/A cannot be expressed outside of V in syntax.

It follows from this that D/A cannot be conflated with the preposition or stand alone in a separate morpheme in French. Thus, in French, the category of prepositional particle can not exist.[17]

The prevalence of prepositional particles suggests that the converse mapping holds in English:

(44) In English, the conceptual D/A node does not have to be conflated with the verb at syntactic structure. D/A can be expressed outside of verb in syntax.

This principle implies that D/A in English can be expressed by other conceptual categories in the syntactic category P, or it can be expressed alone in a prepositional particle.

Before we can discuss the full structure of a PP, we also need a statement about the expression of SF in both languages:

(45) In English and French, SF must conflate with REL in syntax.

This does not hold for all languages, of course; in Chinese, for instance, SF constitutes its own category and does not conflate with any other. However, English and French do not seem to differ at all on this point.

The phenomena we saw in section 3 follow straightforwardly from these mapping principles.

First, the lack of directional particles in French syntax is explained directly: these particles express D/A, but they are not part of the verb in syntax.[18] Thus, they cannot exist in French. They are predicted in English, since D/A is fully separable from the verb in syntax.

Second, the preponderance of directional verbs in French, and of V + particle constructions in English, also follows directly from the mapping constraints. That is, the contrast between the English and French constructions in (34), (35), and (36) is accounted for.

Third, we can account for differences in the requirements of verbs which involve movement or transfer to an endpoint like *put/mettre*, *throw/jeter*, and *give/donner*, in (26) through (31). For this, we must assume that such a situation, one which involves a process terminating in an endpoint, requires the expression of the endpoint (or rather, the boundedness of the event) in conceptual structure. Moreover, the property of boundedness is one of the aspectual properties expressed by the conceptual category D/A. Thus, in the case that such a property is intended by the speaker, D/A must be expressed in the structure.

Many motion verbs, such as *throw*, are essentially process verbs, although in English they can be used as accomplishment verbs if they occur with a PP or a particle. In this use, they require the PP or particle, as we saw in (26) and (36) above. Many non-motion verbs, as in the English examples in (37), (38), (39), and (40), have a similar behavior: they are essentially simple process verbs, but can have other aspectual properties, including telicity, added to them by a PP or particle. However, if the meaning intended includes one of these other aspectual properties, then the PP or particle is required; that is, D/A must be expressed in the structure.

Unlike most verbs, *put* and *give* actually always require a third argument, usually assumed to be a PP.[19] However, what is actually required is more specifically D/A; the PP may be elliptical or omitted altogether. This is shown by (28) and (32) (repeated here), in which the PP need not be supplied for *put* or *give*, but the D/A component must still be supplied:

(28) a. *Put the noodles!
      b. Put the noodles in!

(32) a. *Paul gave his old coat.
      b. Paul gave away his old coat.

In English, the expression of D/A here requires a particle or a PP.[20]

In French, according to the statement in (43), the interpretation must be part of the verb. This implies that many verbs in French must include in their definition the interpretation of D/A, that is, their LCS must include a specification of D/A. This is true of directional verbs and the others we have seen above. It is interesting to note that *jeter*, unlike *throw*, seems to imply a goal; if the process meaning of "throw" is wanted, *lancer* must be used.

It also is possible, at least for some classes of verbs, for a verb optionally to be interpreted as including D/A. The verbs *mettre* and *donner* may also be interpreted as including D/A. In this case, there is no particular specification of the content of D/A, that is, there is no specification of direction, up, away, or otherwise, and no specification of aspect. Instead, there is a vaguer default value for D/A, so that *donner* can mean "give away" or "give up," with an implicit goal or telic interpretation, and *mettre* can mean "put on," "put up," or "put away," with a similarly vague D/A interpretation. (These verbs may still require a PP [RELP] in French in some circumstances).

Thus, the general difference between English and French with respect to verbs of motion is that D/A can be included in the lexical representations of verbs in French, but is not (in general) be included in English.

Finally, our mapping principles lead to an explanation of the problem of how we can represent the difference between French and English verbs such as *enter* and *entrer* (examples [41] and [42]). Recall that the problem here is that D/A seems to be conflated into the verb in English as well as in French, although principle (44) suggests that this conceptual category usually does not map into the verb. As it is put in Talmy (1985), conflation of direction into a verb is quite limited in English. So why may it occur in these verbs?

We propose that the crucial fact is that the French and English verbs do not take the same form of complement: the French ones take a PP, while the English ones take an NP. This indicates that while the French verbs conflate only D/A, the English counterpart actually conflate the entire content of the preposition — including REL and SF. That is, verbs such as *enter* actually conflate the entire semantic content of a preposition. Incorporating REL actually changes the argument structure of the verb, allowing the locational object of the preposition to become the direct argument of the verb (cf. Baker 1985 on incorporation of prepositions).[21]

This type of example actually reinforces our view of the essential difference between English and French with regard to directed motion: French can only represent D/A in Vs, and English usually expresses D/A in prepositions. But there are cases in which the entire content of a preposition is incorporated into a verb at the lexical level.

At this juncture, we would like to mention another researcher, Talmy (1985, 1991), whose work is in the same spirit as the present study. This work is set within a quite different framework, which does not assume the same ideas about syntactic structure, but is nevertheless comparable. However, we believe that our emphasis on the nature of categories, and specifically the category preposition and the associated conceptual categories, is essential to understanding the link between the behavior of lexical verbs and the rest of the grammatical system.

Examples such as those in section 3 and also in section 6 were discussed in Talmy (1985), which compares primarily English and Spanish. Talmy refers to them as differences in "Lexicalization Patterns"; he proposes that parts of meaning, such as "Direction of Motion" and "Fact of Motion," are conflated in a single morpheme,[22] and that these patterns differ regularly cross-linguistically. He observes the following patterns in the Romance languages and English:

(46) Romance: Fact-of-Motion + Direction-of-Motion
               *Fact-of-Motion + Manner-of-Motion

     English: Fact-of-Motion + Manner-of-Motion
               Fact-of-Motion + Direction-of-Motion
                    (not the norm)

The first pattern, for Romance languages, is exemplified by our examples (27), (29), (31), (34b), and (35b) above; in all these examples, the meaning of the verb includes linear motion and the direction of that motion. That the pattern conflating motion and manner does not exist in French is illustrated in (60b) in section 6, while (60a) shows that this pattern does exist in English. And although Talmy claims that verbs conflating direction and motion are scarce in English, he takes verbs such as *enter* and *exit* (examples [41] and [42]) to be verbs of this type; he suggests that since these verbs are borrowings from Latin, they are able to display Lexicalization Patterns more typical of Romance languages.

Talmy (1985) also relates the existence of verb-particle to these facts. He proposes that particles are grammatical elements he calls "satellites," which in English include particles and other non-argument complements of the verb. In Talmy (1985), he lists examples of satellites in various languages, which include English verb particles, German verb prefixes, Latin and Russian verb prefixes, Chinese verb complements, Lahu "versatile verbs," Caddo incorporated nouns, and Atsugewi polysynthetic affixes.

Satellites combine with the verb into what he calls a "verb complex" (what we call a complex predicate). In Talmy (1991), he elaborates greatly on this idea, saying that the main event (the schematic core of the framing event) is conveyed by different constituents, depending on the language. In English-type languages, which, according to Talmy, include the Slavic languages, Chinese, Finno-Ugric, and many others, satellites carry the main predication. In French-type languages, which include the Romance languages, Semitic, Japanese, Tamil, and many Bantu languages, among others, the main predication must be carried by the verb.

Talmy (1985) captures many of the generalizations we have tried to account for, and of course that paper was very influential to the present study. However, concentrating on the lexicalization patterns of verbs alone does not take into account how cross-linguistic differences in other categories may influence differences in verbs. We see as crucial that there is a trade-off between what is expressed in verbs, or conflated as part of their meaning, and what is expressed by another category. Thus, in English, the existence of directional particles and the directional component of prepositions allows the option of simpler verbs, while in French, the lack of directional particles and of a directional component in prepositions forces direction to be expressed in the verb. In fact, in Talmy (1991), it is recognized that variation in the syntactic category that corresponds to the core event of a clause is responsible for major differences between languages. Still, we claim that the lexical and morphological properties of minor categories should be put at the forefront of such investigations.

Thus, a major consequence of our approach is that a cross-linguistic theory of lexicalization patterns and verbal alternations must take into account the inventory of minor (closed-class, functional) categories found in each language, and of their properties. A theory of lexical semantics of verbs can not be undertaken in isolation from the rest of the grammar, especially from the consideration of functional categories.

5. THE INTERNAL STRUCTURE OF PREPOSITIONS

Let us now consider the structure of a prepositional phrase, given that we have said that it corresponds to three separate categories in conceptual structure.

We assume there is X-bar structure at LCS, and that the operation of "conflation" is just head movement at this level, following Hale and Keyser (1990).

First, consider the properties of SF. It is obviously [+N], since when it occurs alone it has a nominal interpretation and can be equated to nominals. It is a semantic functor on NPs (DPs; sometimes CPs), which yields a [+N] projection.

(47)

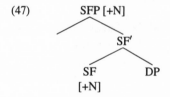

REL must have the properties usually ascribed to P, traditionally. It is assumed that REL, like the traditional P, has an internal argument, usually SFP, DP, or CP. We will also assume that it has an external argument in its Theta-grid that is usually not satisfied within the PP, although this point is controversial;[23] in any event, this assumption does not make much difference for the present discussion. Recall that examples of REL alone are *at, to, with, from,* and so on.

(48)

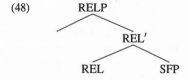

The LCS of forms that conflate SF and REL, such as *in, under,* and so on, involves head-movement of SF to REL:

(49)

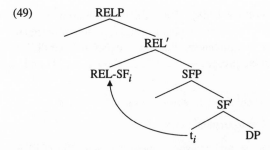

Determining the position and characteristics of D/A is more difficult, because of the mixed behavior of the syntactic category that best corresponds to it: the prepositional particle. It is clear that it is highest in the hierarchy of the "prepositional" categories: when it is expressed separately in a series of prepositions (for instance, *out from under*, in example [22] above), it always occurs first. In French, although it is never expressed separately in syntax, we must also assume that it is adjacent to the verb at CS, and thus higher in hierarchy than REL or SF, because in order to conflate with the verb there must be no barrier to head movement. We will see further evidence in sections 6 and 7 that particles must be able to incorporate with the verb at LF in English.

Semantically, D/A must be close to the verb, too. As we claim in section 6, D/A is a category, and perhaps a set of features, that is conceptually tied to the verb. This is natural, because the event expressed by verbs inherently has aspectual and directional properties. Almost all verbs are associated with aspectual properties such as duration, iterativeness, and telicity, and a D/A element can modify those properties. Spatial verbs, that is, verbs whose semantics involves spatial concepts, also have inherent spatial properties, including direction; thus, with these verbs only, D/A can optionally express direction. (Even with these verbs, a non-directional interpretation is possible.)

We can posit the following structure:

(50)

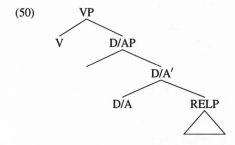

This is actually very similar to structures proposed by van Riemsdijk (1978), Jackendoff (1977), and Rooryck (1993) that take particles to be the specifier of P. The essential difference (other than the fact that we are separating prepositional components and renaming the central prepositional component "REL") is that D/A is projected as a functional head, with its own X-bar projection. However, many elements that were treated traditionally as specifiers in the system, following the X-bar scheme of Jackendoff (1977), are now considered independent functional categories (cf. Abney 1987, Pollock 1988). Thus, the configuration in (50) is a modern version of older proposals about the position and function of particles.

We must also admit, for completeness, that there exists the possibility of having multiple PPs or particles present in the VP, as shown in (24) and (25) (repeated here).

(24)   Joey walked from his school down the street to his grandma's house.

(25)   Go on over along the river to Grandma's house!

Particles can certainly occur alone, and can sometimes occur with PPs (RELPs or D/APs) in the following structure:[24]

(51)

This assumes that D/A, or D/AP, may sometimes occur alone in complement position of the verb. This is true, and must be allowed. We can see particles as intransitive prepositions, as Emonds (1985). However, with our finer-grained account of the category preposition, this amounts to saying that D/A may take a complement, but it is not obligatory.

To summarize, our hypotheses predict various possibilities for conflation (incorporation at LCS) of "prepositional" categories, assuming the following structure at LCS (which is present universally):

(52)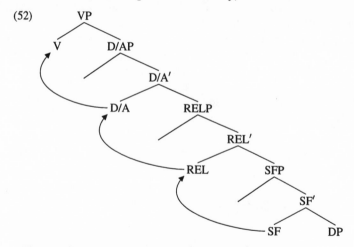

The possible conflations of categories are then:

SF into REL	(French and English)
REL (and SF) into D/A	(English only)
D/A into V	(French)
All into V	(English, at least)

These possibilities account for the data presented so far; the obligatoriness in French for conflating D/A into V, and the lack of a separate morpheme for it account for the non-existence of particles in this language.

6. PREPOSITION-STRANDING AND PSEUDOPASSIVES

Our proposals also shed light on another major difference between prepositions in English and French: the ability to appear in preposition-stranding and pseudopassive constructions.[25] Examples (53) and (54) illustrate these constructions in English; (55) and (56) illustrate the impossibility of a similar construction in French.

(53)   a.   Which chair did you sit on?
      b.   Which box did you put the book in?
      c.   Which candidate did you vote for?

(54)   a.   This chair has been sat on.
      b.   That candidate was voted for by 48 percent of the people.

(55)   a.   *Quelle chaise est-il assis sur?
         which-fem chair is-he seated on
         "Which chair did you sit on?"
      b.   *Quelle boîte a tu mis le livre dans?
         which-fem box have you put the book in
         "Which box did you put the book in?"
      c.*/? Quel candidat as-tu voté pour?[26]
         which candidate have-you voted for
         "Which candidate did you vote for?"

(56)   a.   *Cette chaise a été assise sur/dessus.
      b.   *Ce candidat a été voté pour.
         "This candidate has been voted for."

We will follow many researchers, including Hornstein and Weinberg (1981), Kayne (1983), and Baker (1988), in taking preposition-stranding to depend on the possibility of reanalysis between the verb and preposition. English allows this kind of reanalysis, and French does not.

The question, then, is what allows reanalysis between preposition and verb.

According to Kayne (1983), it is not reanalysis per se that is forbidden in French, for French has verb-verb reanalysis, especially with the verb *faire*. Rather, it is V-P reanalysis specifically that is not allowed. Kayne proposes that the difference lies in the way the categories govern: in English prepositions can govern structurally; in French they cannot. Verbs, he says, govern structurally. He then claims that reanalysis is only allowed between categories that govern in the same way, thus ruling out V-P reanalysis in French but not in English.

Our proposal that D/A is encoded in a prepositional element in English but not in French allows a quite different solution to this question, although one that still hinges on a difference in the category preposition in the two languages. We may say, quite simply, that it is the presence of D/A in the English preposition that allows it to reanalyze with the verb. We follow Baker (1985) in taking this reanalysis to be incorporation of P into V at LF. In these terms, we propose that:

(57)   D/A must incorporate into V (at or before LF).

Notice that this statement is valid for French as well; since D/A conflates with the verb, that is, it incorporates into it at LCS, this condition is met automatically prior to syntax.

What motivation can we give for (57) to be true? Put another way, what licenses this incorporation, and what requires it? The answer lies in the semantic nature of the category D/A. We have said that D/A expresses concepts of direction or aspect (or, as discussed in section 9, something common to both). These concepts are inherent to the internal structure of an event, or *aktionsart*; an event of motion inherently has a direction, and many other types of events have inherent aspectual properties such as duration, repetitiveness of subevents, or boundedness. The verb is the element that expresses the core of the event in a clause. Thus, since the Direction/Aspect concepts are inherently part of the internal structure of the event, they must be composed with the verb that introduces this event at the level of semantic processing, which is LF. We can see (57) as a requirement on the well-formedness of the event: the event is only well-formed if all information about its *aktionsart* is included with it. The Direction/Aspect concepts expressed must not only be composed with the verb, but also be semantically compatible with the *aktionsart* of the verb; verification of this compatibility might be accomplished by feature checking at LF, which would also force D/A to move to V. (More on features in section 8.)

Thus, what licenses and in fact requires that D/A move to V is the fact that it inherently expresses properties of the event, together with the idea that the various parts of the event must form a complex at LF (cf. Klipple 1991 on the licensing of elements such as arguments and internal modifiers in event structure). Another way to state this might be to say that D/A is composed of inherently verbal features, which must be checked with the verb.

There is another possibility in the formation of questions and relative clauses in English, that of pied-piping the preposition, as illustrated in (58); this is the only way to apply wh-movement to the PP in French. This suggests that V-P reanalysis is optional in English.

(58)   In which box did you put the book?

This poses a problem, since in the framework of Chomsky (1992), optional movement is not permitted. A way to capture this optionality would be to say that speakers can understand the preposition to include D/A or not, as they choose; since there is no morphological signal, they have this choice. Then we can hypothesize that D/A always incorporates into the verb at LF (or before); in cases of pied-piping, D/A is simply not present in the preposition. This is supported by the fact that pied-piping is not acceptable when a particle is present, if we assume, as above, that a particle is an instantiation of D/A:[27]

(59)   *Up on which shelf did you put the book?
       (from: I put the book up on that shelf)

Actually, pied-piping is only marginally acceptable in the idiolect of the present author; I prefer preposition-stranding in most cases, even when it is supposed to be stylistically incorrect. I suspect that almost all speakers have a preference for one or the other form, and that the purported optionality of preposition-stranding is really a choice between dialects, or at least between registers.

One difficulty remains. Preposition-stranding and the pseudopassive are apparently quite rare across languages. If their existence in a language depended only on the presence of D/A in prepositions, we would expect a larger number of languages to exhibit these constructions. However, it is more likely that the possibility for these constructions depends on a combination of factors. They could be precluded by a number of different factors cross-linguistically, especially when overt case systems are involved, in which REL might be inseparable from the NP for morphological reasons. Another case is languages such as Chinese, in which we would expect a verb-like preposition to be strandable. However, in this language there is no wh-movement, so the question is difficult to test.

7. GOALS AND RESULTATIVES

The mapping differences between French and English can be extended to explain other regular differences between the two languages, this time with respect to complexes of V + PP and V + Adj. English allows these constructions, with a goal or resultative meaning; we assume that in both cases these are complex predicate constructions. French does not permit such complex predicate constructions, but allows only V + V complex predicates. This, as we will see, is related to the mapping differences we have discussed above.

Example (60) illustrates a regular difference between verbs of manner of motion in English and French (from Carter 1984):

(60)   a.   The bottle floated under the bridge.
       b.   La bouteille a flotté sous le pont.
            the bottle has floated under the bridge
            "The bottle floated under the bridge."

Example (60a) is ambiguous; it can mean either that the bottle is located under the bridge, floating around, or that the floating bottle was moving toward the bridge so that it came to be under it (and may or may not have continued down the river). Example (60b), on the other hand, is unambiguous; only the stationary reading, in which the action of floating occurs under the bridge, is found.

This difference in interpretation holds for a large number of motion verbs, including *walk/marcher*, *swim/nager*, and so on,[28] as illustrated by (61a) and (61b):

(61)   a.   Benny walked to the store.
       b.   Benny a marché au magasin.
            Benny has walked at-the store
            "Benny walked at (around in) the store"

In this case, the English sentence is unambiguous, because *to* can only indicate the endpoint of the event—so it means "get to the store by walking." On the other hand, (61b) is also unambiguous, but it can only mean "walk (around) at the store"—that is, be at the store, and then walk.[29] As in the case of (60b), it is impossible to interpret the PP as the goal of the motion.

This difference in the interpretation of V + PP combinations parallels another, the possibility for V + adjective resultative constructions. The examples in (62) illustrate this construction; those in (63) show that corresponding examples do not exist in French (see also Levin and Rapoport 1988):

(62) a. John hammered the metal flat.
      b. Mary wiped the table clean.
      c. Jane combed her hair smooth.
      d. Bob ironed the shirt flat.
      e. I shot him dead.
      f. Bill squashed the bug flat.
      g. I bleached the blouse white.

(63) a. *Jean a martelé le cuivre plat.
          Jean hammered the copper flat
      b. *J'ai cuit la viande sèche.
          I cooked the meat dry
      c. *J'ai cuit la viande en cendres.
          I cooked the meat to cinders
      d. *Marie a repassé la blouse plate.
          Marie ironed the blouse flat
      e. *J'ai javellisé la blouse blanche.
          I bleached the blouse white

We take the V + PP with a resultative reading to be the same structure as the adjectival resultative constructions. Both are licensed by event licensing, that is, because they function semantically as parts of the internal aspectual structure of the event (see Klipple 1991, 1993; Levin and Rapoport 1988 also show that there must be an additional type of licensing to allow this type of construction.)

The fact that this construction is allowed in English but not in French follows from our hypotheses about the instantiation of the category D/A. Resultative constructions in English are cases in which an adjective is indicating the telicity of the event; that is, it provides telic aspect. Telic aspect is one of the concepts represented by D/A. Then, in a certain sense, we can say that the adjective in these constructions includes (or conflates) D/A in English.

There is nothing in the principles proposed in the previous sections that prohibits D/A from being included in adjectives in English. All that is said is that D/A can be encoded outside of the verb. Furthermore, the adjectives in these constructions certainly have the appropriate aspectual relationship to the verb to function as D/A.

Still, there is something odd about saying the category D/A is represented in the adjective when it has the appropriate function and position in the VP. The problem here lies in how to delineate the notions of a functional category — the function it performs and the position in which it occurs. In current theory, most functional categories have only one possible base position in a clause, and that position can only be filled by that functional category. For many functional categories, perhaps, the distinction does not make much difference. However, in the present case, although we have proposed a category — the prepositional particles — that does encompass a group of morphemes with syntactic properties different from any others, it may also be joined with a lexical category, depending on the particularities of the language.

It is interesting to note that Talmy (1985) faces a dilemma similar to ours in whether to treat his "satellites" as a separate category, or as a separate "grammatical function" (which could be translated into a separate, special position in a configurational theory of grammar). He actually argues at one point that satellite must be a grammatical function, and then continues to refer to it as a grammatical category. In Talmy (1991), he again treats satellite as a grammatical category.

We will maintain our proposal that D/A should be treated as a conceptual category, which is probably constituted of grammatical features, as we discuss in section 8. The resolution of the problem will have to wait for a more complete understanding of the relations of functional categories to their functions and positions.

8. CONCEPTUAL CATEGORIES AS DISTINCTIVE FEATURES

Let us now turn briefly to the question of how conceptual categories might be treated as a group of grammatical features.

We take grammatical distinctive features, like distinctive features in phonology, to be the encoding of the distinctions that language pays attention to.[30] These features operate at the interface of conceptual/intentional system and the grammar; the conceptual system allows many semantic distinctions, but the grammar is not sensitive to most.

A conceptual category, then, is a feature bundle (or structured hierarchy of features) at the interface of conceptual/intentional system and the grammatical system (this interface is LF in Chomsky 1993, Di Sciullo 1993).

We assume that grammatical features must be binary, because they encode a distinction between having a property and not having it. There may be more features in syntax than in phonology, since the conceptual space is probably larger.

Finding the actual inventory of features is, of course, the most difficult problem, and the present study cannot propose a set of them. We assume that they should include phi-features that have been proposed (such as [±wh]); various case features and tense features; quantifier, number, and gender features — in short, features to form all functional categories. They also should encompass features proper to lexical categories, including [+N] and perhaps [+V]; however, see Muysken and van Riemsdijk (1986) and Abney (1987) for criticisms of using the features [±N, ±V] to distinguish lexical categories (N, V, A, P).

The features underlying D/A must encode event properties such as direction, duration, telicity, iteration, and intensity. Differences between spatial functor (SF) concepts might also be distinguished by features, although this might instead be treated as lexical content that is not relevant to the grammar, that is, the content that the grammatical component of the language does not "pay attention to."

Understanding categories as features or groups of features clarifies our proposal that the syntactic category preposition corresponds to a set of conceptual categories that varies from language to language. With a feature theory, we can rephrase the proposal as saying that features or groups of features may be divided up differently in different languages — something that is generally assumed in feature theories already.

Many linguists hold that functional categories are made up of grammatical features (cf. Abney 1987, Speas 1990, Reuland 1985, and the authors represented in Muysken and van Riemsdijk 1985). This is a view we adopt here; we argue that conceptual categories are actually distinctive features at the interface with the C/I system.

However, it is often implied that lexical categories cannot include the full range of functional features (although they do have the features ±N, ±V). One consequence of our analysis will be that lexical categories can encode at least some of these conceptual distinctive features. It may be that lexical categories are in fact distinguished by the property that they can have semantic or descriptive content *in addition to* features; that is, they have semantic properties that are not featurized, that are not grammatically distinctive.

Our analysis entails that a category, even a "minor" category such as a preposition, can be a conflation of several categorial features. Moreover, a major lexical category can include (have conflated into it) grammatical features, and which features are included varies cross-linguistically. Conversely, a grammatical feature may be included in, or conflated into, a number of different categories, language-dependently.

There is debate over whether prepositions should be considered to be lexical or functional categories. They exhibit properties of both. This is a question that cannot be resolved by the present study, for it would require delving into the properties of all functional and lexical categories. However, we can make a few comments on the situation.

In many current theories of grammar, prepositions are grouped with the "lexical" categories. Chomsky (1986) lists the lexical categories as N, V, A, and P, and this grouping is generally assumed in recent work on the distinction between functional and lexical categories. It is interesting to note, however, that earlier, in Chomsky (1980), P is stated not to be a lexical category. Abney (1987) suggests that P should be unspecified for his feature [±Functional]. It seems that prepositions are just on the border of this distinction. How we should treat them hinges on what "lexical" category means. Prepositions seem to be where the distinction between the two breaks down.

Abney (1987) lists several properties of functional categories that differentiate them from lexical categories. According to him, the most important property of functional categories is that they lack "descriptive content"; they "mark grammatical or relational features, rather that picking out a class of objects" (Abney 1987, p. 65). Other properties of functional categories are that they are (1) generally closed class elements; (2) are phonologically and morphologically dependent; (3) permit only one, non-argument complement; and (4) are inseparable from their complement.

Prepositions seem to be split in these properties: they are closed-class, often unstressed, and have only one complement, but one that is usually thought of as an argument. Neither do prepositions seem to have as much descriptive content as other "lexical" categories, Abney's principal distinguishing property. They pick out a class of relations, including spatial, temporal, and thematic ones, but it is a rather small class. They certainly do not have the variety and scope of meaning that nouns and verbs have. On the other hand, it could be argued that the conceptual space in which prepositional concepts exist is simply smaller; it includes only the differences possible in three-dimensional space or on a temporal line, and a few other non-spatio-temporal relations.

Some syntactic properties have been claimed to hinge on the difference between lexical and functional categories. In Chomsky (1986), an important property of lexical categories is that they L-mark the constituents they govern, and thus can properly govern; functional categories cannot do this. Kayne (1983) argues that prepositions can differ in this property; in English, they are proper governors, and in French they are not (see section 6).

Another property, cited by Speas (1990), is that lexical categories can take a variety of types of complements, which are restricted by theta-marking but not by syntactic category. In older theories, only lexical categories can have specifiers, and only they have X-bar structure.[31] Once again, PPs seem to have hybrid properties; PPs have less complex structures than other lexical categories, but more than functional categories (cf. van Riemsdijk 1978, Jackendoff 1977 for discussion).

The resolution of whether prepositions are functional or lexical categories will have to wait until the determining factors for this distinction are clarified. This may hinge on how much extralinguistic semantic content they have — that is, on what the grammar "pays attention to" in the semantic content.

9. THE NON-SPATIAL SEMANTICS OF PREPOSITIONS AND PARTICLES

In previous sections, we have claimed that the semantics of prepositions is not basically spatial but abstract and common to many domains. We see them as semantically aspectual in nature; that is, they modify temporal, spatial, and scalar properties of the element to which they are attached. This implies that we see aspect as subsuming a group of related abstract properties, rather than only temporal properties.

By aspectual structure, we mean not only the temporal properties of events, but also more abstract properties involving what Pustejovsky (1988) calls the "geometry of the event." We use the definitions in (64), from Di Sciullo and Klipple (1994).

(64)   *Aspectual structure*: The temporal, spatial, and scalar vectors in the geometry of the event.
       Vector: A quantity having direction as well as magnitude, denoted by a line drawn from its original to its final position. (*Oxford English Dictionary*)

Traditionally, aspect is often taken to deal with only the temporal structure of an event. The aspectual structure of the event associated with a verb, or *aktionsart*, comprises properties such as telicity or delimitedness (whether or not the event has an endpoint), duration, and stativity.

We hold that these are not only temporal properties, but have spatial and abstract correlates as well. As argued in Klipple (1991) (adapting ideas of Hale 1985 and Kipka 1990), we take aspect to be based on a more abstract system of measure, that of delimitation of vectors, which may be spelled out more concretely in the temporal, spatial, or scalar domain. The spatial structure of an event is aspectual, particularly with verbs of motion, in which spatial and physical properties are relevant; whether the event has a goal (which is the natural endpoint), whether it has a path and is therefore extended over space, and whether it is a directed event, are all notions that correlate with temporal aspectual notions. Other properties can also be aspectual; for instance, the notions of measuring out on a scale, and of amount. It was argued in Tenny (1987) that the direct argument has an aspectual role because it measures out and delimits the event. Other researchers, including Heinrichs (1985), have drawn parallels between aspectual relations and the mass/count distinction in NPs.

Determining the semantic properties of prepositional elements is complicated by the fact that their interpretation depends on the other constituents with which they occur. They vary in interpretation according to both their complements (usually an NP) and to the elements they complement or modify. In order to achieve this type of varying interpretation, prepositions and particles must be underspecified in meaning (cf. Di Sciullo and Klipple 1994).[32]

We claim, again following Di Sciullo and Klipple (1994), that the semantics of prepositional elements varies for the most part with what is called the "semantic field" of the constituent they modify or predicate of — specifically, in the constructions we are considering, the verb.

The notion of semantic field is used by many linguists, including Gruber (1965), Jackendoff (1983), Talmy (1985), and Hale (1985). A wide variety of lexical items may share an abstract semantic element; this element has a common meaning abstracted away from the context inherent in a specific lexical item. This inherent lexical context is what is called the semantic field of the expression.

A semantic field is a sort of conceptual pseudospace; we consider semantic fields to be part of the human Conceptual-Intentional system. They form a mathematical space, which can be instantiated as a three-dimensional grid (as in the case of physical space) or a directed line (as in the case of temporal or scalar dimensions).

Then, we take prepositional elements to have an underspecified, aspectual function that takes on a fuller interpretation in combination with a semantic field. Another constituent, say, the verb in a V + PP construction, sets up a conceptual pseudospace (semantic field) containing points, shapes, or vectors. The preposition, as an aspectual modifier, specifies some component of these points, shapes, or vectors. The preposition itself does not belong to any semantic field, but takes on a different interpretation in each field.

For illustration, consider examples (65) through (68). The prepositions in (65) have a spatial interpretation; those in (66), an abstract possessional use; those in (67), a temporal interpretation; and those in (68), some other abstract relational interpretation.

(65)   a.   Bill went/walked/skipped to the market.
      b.   The river goes to the sea.
      c.   The book is on the table.

    d.   Mary is at school.
    e.   Fluffy is in the box.

(66)   Bob sent the letter to Bill.

(67)   a.   He read the book in three hours.
        b.   John went skiing on Saturday.
        c.   Bill received calls throughout the day.
        d.   The swearing-in occurred at noon.

(68)   a.   We left her in a state of exhaustion.
        b.   She achieved internal peace through meditation.
        c.   They live in poverty.

Particles have the same kind of variety of interpretation, as illustrated the spatial uses in (20), and by the aspectual uses in (37), both repeated here:

(20)   a.   The balloon went up.
        b.   The lion ran away.
        c.   Lily climbed down.

(37)   a.   finish up
        b.   work away
        c.   calm down
        d.   eat up
        e.   chill out (relax)
        f.   think through
        g.   read over
        h.   do over

Furthermore, the semantics of prepositions can vary in even more specific ways with an NP they modify, or on their internal argument. Even their spatial relation component is not fully specified (Herskowits 1986, Vandeloise 1991). Consider the spatial relations covered by the preposition *in* in (69):

(69)   a.   The water in the vase
        b.   The flowers in the vase
        c.   The crack in the vase

This type of variation in interpretation complicates the semantics of prepositions even further. However, it is not clear that it is a problem that concerns study of the grammar, that is, it does not seem to have any effect on structure; this problem is most likely in the domain of conceptualization of spatial relations.

Of course, in earlier sections we have argued that "prepositional elements" are in fact conflations of three different conceptual categories, so it is fair to ask which of these categories are to be attributed this sort of underspecified semantics. We think it likely that all of these categories should be. Particles, which we have taken to be instantiations of D/A, certainly vary in interpretation between spatial and aspectual uses. Prepositions such as *at*, *to*, and *with*, which may consist only of REL, also display quite a variety of interpretations, depending on their linguistic context. Since SFs rarely occur separately from RELs in the languages we are considering, it is more difficult to analyze them; but they certainly display the types of variation found in (69), and also have different spatial, temporal, and abstract uses.

This is not to say that the three categories do not differ in their LCS entries; they still are bundles or structures of different features, and have different structures and complements. It is just that we can treat the very limited semantic content of the categories in a similar way.

We suspect, in fact, that this is the way to understand the semantics of functional categories in general: as functors with very sparse lexical entries, consisting perhaps only of features, with their interpretation in a context determined in large measure by the semantic specifications of other constituents.

10. CONCLUSION

Our analysis has rested on the hypothesis that the grammar is modular in structure: it is composed of different levels of structure, syntax, morphology, and LCS, which are differentiated by the types of elements are combined at each level — full words, bound morphemes, or abstract elements. All are subject to principles of grammar, and all have an X-bar structure. The ability of the model to capture generalizations across all levels is strong support for this approach.

We have argued that the notion of category is pertinent to all levels of grammar, but these categories are relativized to each level. Specifically, conceptual categories exist at the level of LCS; we assume these categories to be universal. The structures of LCS and syntax are then parallel, and there is a mapping from one to the other; however, they are not identical.

We propose that much of the variation across languages results from language-particular differences in this mapping, in keeping with theories such as those of Chomsky (1992) and Di Sciullo (1993), in which it is argued that cross-linguistic variation reduces to variation in properties of individual morphemes.

We argue specifically that several syntactic differences between English and French, including the existence of prepositional particles, the interaction of verbs and prepositions, the possibility of preposition-stranding and the pseudopassive, and the possibility of V + P and V + Adj reanalysis all result from a difference in the mapping of the conceptual category Direction/Aspect to syntactic categories. We claim that D/A maps into the verb in French, and outside of the verb in English. D/A is a conceptual category that is inherently related to the event, which is carried by the verb; it combines with the verb universally for semantic processing at LF.

Many of our examples are treated in the literature under the rubric of lexical alternations of verbs. We claim that more attention should be paid to the behavior of prepositions and other categories that interact with the verb when researching questions of verbal alternations and lexicalization patterns.

Categories are understood as groupings of features, following the general point of view of Muysken and van Riemsdijk (1985). Features are what language "pays attention to" at the interface with the Conceptual-Intentional system. The conceptual categories we have dealt with are all taken to be aspectual in nature, and semantically underspecified.

NOTES

This essay is a development of Klipple (1992). I would like to thank Anna-Maria Di Sciullo, Jeff Gruber, John Lumsden, and Mireille Tremblay for their helpful comments on this work.

This study was supported by Social Sciences and Humanities Research Council of Canada grant 411-92-0012 (to Anna-Maria Di Sciullo), FCAR grant 94 ER 0401 (to Anna-Maria Di Sciullo, Monique Lemieux, and Marie-Thérèse Vinet), and a grant from the Fonds Institutionnels de Recherche de l'UQAM (to Anna-Maria Di Sciullo).

1. In the framework of Chomsky (1981) and theories that followed, these principles included Binding theory, Case theory, Government theory, Theta theory, and so on. This approach was modular in that each sub-theory of the grammar operated independently on the structure. Recent approaches such as Chomsky (1993), however, have rethought each of these principles, and emphasis has been put on the checking of features and on individual morphemes that bear these features. Although it is clear that the principles that exist operate in an independent and modular fashion, there is less a consensus at present as to what these principles are.

2. Curme (1905) lists approximately 180 prepositions in German and 320 in English, in Curme (1931). However, his lists include many that are morphologically (*northwards*) or syntactically complex (such as *for the benefit of* and *in conformity with*), and others that seem more like adverbs (such as *halbwegs*, "halfway"), so we can assume that the lists are quite inflated. No matter what the precise number should be for any particular language, it is clear that the category preposition is quite different from the categories noun, verb, and adjective, whose members number in the thousands.

3. I have discussed the reasons for this departure from Jackendoff at length in Klipple (1991). Briefly, although the intuition that there is a path associated with every event of motion has a lot of merit, his use of the Path argument treats the following notions on a par: AT, TO, TOWARDS, FROM, and AWAY-FROM. Yet, these have very different semantic and syntactic properties. Aspectually, AT is stative, TO and FROM are telic, and TOWARDS and AWAY-FROM are atelic. The first three can be predicates, but this does not seem to be true for TOWARDS and AWAY-FROM. Moreover, the syntactic behavior of the corresponding prepositions is not the same, especially in a language such as Chinese; see Klipple (1991) for details.

4. According to Li and Thompson (1981), most of the current prepositions of this type in Chinese are historically derived from verbs.

5. The question of whether a language has pre- or postpositions was linked to many other properties of language by Greenberg (1961). The facts about Chinese, and also the arguments presented here about the several categories underlying prepositions, suggest that a finer-grained approach to the question of language universals is needed. Careful consideration must be made when identifying elements as the same category cross-linguistically; their function must be taken into account, as well as their interaction with other categories. To do this properly would, of course, be a massive amount of work, and proposals such as Greenberg's are certainly a good beginning.

6. Data is from Fortescue (1984).

7. On the other hand, the instantiation of REL seems to be quite different, if we are right in hypothesizing that it is indicated by oblique Case-markers. An investigation of this will have to wait for further research.

8. There is another interpretation marginally possible for these sentences, in which the place is somewhere at the zoo and the spot is somewhere under the table; this interpretation

is a case of a relational PP (including REL and SF nodes) in a structure of Locative Inversion. This interpretation is the only one possible in *under the table is a spoon*, but it is not the favored interpretation here.

9. Furthermore, I do not accept that the conceptual primitives that Jackendoff calls "path-functions" should be lumped into one class; there is a residue, which includes TOWARDS and AWAY-FROM. I take these to be functions taking a place and yielding a direction.

10. For the moment, I will not take a stand on the direction of Particle Movement, that is, on where the particle originates.

11. We would then have to argue that REL or SF (probably REL) contain features that block Case-assignment; or, instead, that D/A alone can combine (reanalyze) with the verb in a way that REL cannot; or that it is the presence of the NP complement, not the prepositional element itself, that blocks Case.

12. These are not the same as aspectual inflections such as progressive or perfect. Following Klipple (1991), we assume that these inflections operate at a higher level, and select for the *aktionsart* of the VP but do not change it.

13. Things are further complicated by the use of the verbs *qu*, "go," and *lai*, "come," as directional or aspectual particles. These elements retain the normal indexical use of *go* and *come* (directionally away from or toward speaker), although they do not serve as main verb. Note that *come* and *go* in English can serve a similar function, as in *come sit with me* or *go visit Grandma*. These also lose the syntactic properties of a main verb (cf. Pollock 1989), although they do not necessarily correspond exactly to their Chinese correlates.

14. This is bad on the intended reading; there is another possible reading in which Edwidge throws her shoes around randomly, perhaps up in the air.

15. Actually, there is a set of prepositional prefixes in French, discussed in Di Sciullo and Klipple (1994), that do seem to have the same sorts of directional and aspectual functions as English particles. It seems that prepositional elements can encode the D/A function in morphology in French; perhaps the constraint needed to explain the data here must prevent D/A from being encoded separately from the verb at the level of syntax.

16. Some speakers find it grammatical to use a preposition with *enter*, as in

    i. OK/*Enter into the room

For such speakers, though, there is a meaning change; the sentence means something like "make an entrance," with the implication that the room is somehow affected by the action of entering. The author does not find such examples acceptable, although in examples with abstract semantics, such as *enter into a discussion*, the preposition is always permissible.

17. Rose-Marie Déchaine (p.c.) has objected that the prefixes in Vs such as *emporter*, *soulever*, and so on, are directional particles. They may have a directional meaning, but they do not necessarily serve the same function as the English particles discussed here. Still, they bear a great resemblance to particles on various counts; see Di Sciullo and Klipple (1994) for discussion of these prefixes. For present purposes, it is important to note that in any case these elements are not separate from the verb *at the syntactic level*, although they might be separable at the morphological level. It is in the syntactic behavior of prepositions that English and French show many differences.

18. The statement that such elements exist as separate elements in syntactic structure does not preclude their existence in morphological structure. In Di Sciullo and Klipple (1994), it was argued that there is a class of prepositional prefixes whose function and semantic contribution is very close to that of D/A particles in English. However, even if these are correctly analyzed as D/A, they do not conflict with the principle, if we

assume, following Di Sciullo, that such affixes are combined with the verb at a level of Morphological Form, and that at syntactic structure (LF) they are within the verb.

19. It may seem stipulative to just treat these verbs as exceptions, but it is clear that *put* and *give* do obligatorily select for complements that are usually optional. Perhaps this is due to the fact that these verbs do not have much semantic content to begin with, and sometimes serve as light verbs.

20. *Put* has other properties that distinguish it from motion verbs; for instance, it cannot occur with the preposition *to*:

    i. *I put the book to the table.

Actually, *to* does occasionally occur with this preposition, as in *put your ear to the ground*. However, in this case, *to* is being used with an unusual positional meaning; note that one can also say *his ear is to the ground*. (Cf. Klipple 1992 for more discussion.)

21. We could strengthen the principle in (44) to say that in English, D/A must be expressed outside of the verb in syntax. However, this is probably too strong a statement.

22. Talmy (1985) was the originator of the term *conflation* for this process, but it is important to note that he did not understand this as incorporation at LCS, for he works in a different framework.

23. We assume that PPs (or RELPs, here) usually satisfy their external argument positions through one of several structures in which they are predicates: either through predication with a copula, through forming a complex predicate with the verb (with Theta-identification of the external arguments of the P with one of the arguments of the verb), or as a modifier (which we take to be predication of the E-position of a verb or R-position of a noun). In this they are very similar to adjectives. In languages such as English or French, they cannot predicate more directly of their external arguments, although in languages such as Chinese they can, acting as verbs.

24. It might also be possible to represent this in a VP-shell structure like that of Larson (1988). What is important is that several particles or "PPs" are allowed to occur in sequence, as we saw in (24) and (25), and not as part of the same constituent.

25. Preposition-stranding does not have the same restrictions as pseudopassive. They cannot be exactly the same phenomenon. The D/A features may still be important in preposition-stranding, since they are inherently verbal modifiers. However, there is no complex predicate formed, so reanalysis cannot occur in preposition-stranding. Preposition-stranding involves wh-movement, pseudopassive involves NP-movement.

26. This sentence is actually permissible for many speakers of Quebec French. However, even for these speakers, preposition-stranding is not possible in general.

It is also possible in this dialect to have the "stranded" preposition present with no corresponding wh-moved NP:

    i. Je sors avec.
    ii. J'ai voté pour.

It thus seems unlikely that this should be treated as preposition-stranding.

27. Pied-piping is not in fact allowed, even if the particle is left behind:

    i. *On which shelf did you put the book up?

If we say that D/A is a functional category that selects RELP, then extraction of the RELP would be prohibited for the same reason that extraction of NP from DP is not allowed.

28. Noteable exceptions are *aller*, "go," and *courir*, "run," which do take PPs with goal interpretations.

29. Actually, some French speakers do not accept this sentence on any interpretation.

30. These features will be unlike phonological features in that they are at a totally different interface than the phonological system. We may expect that the number of features, inventory of features, interrelations between them (if any), and relations to the structure will be not necessarily be similar to what we find in phonology.

31. Of course, functional categories are now hypothesized to have X-bar projections. We may ask what has happened to the criterion of having a "specifier" in the old sense, and to other distinctions of early X-bar theory.

32. In Di Sciullo and Klipple (1994) it is argued that preposition-like prefixes on verbs in French have a similar function to that of particles, and have the same sort of underspecification as prepositions and prefixes. The semantic fields we isolate there are Static spatial (physical), Directional (dynamic spatial), Stative (abstract space), Scalar (measure; directional stative). These can be considered subfields of some of Jackendoff's fields; the list is not meant to be exhaustive.

These prefixes at least sometimes seem to have a Direction/Aspect function. They are separate from the verb morphologically in French; but note that they are not separate from it in syntax, and so do not contradict the principle in (43). This is another way that variation can occur at the mapping between levels of grammar; the mapping between LCS and morphology differs just as it does between LCS and syntax and morphology and syntax.

REFERENCES

Abney, Steven. 1987. "The English noun phrase in its sentential aspect." Doctoral diss., MIT, Cambridge Mass.

Baker, Marc. 1986. "A Theory of Grammatical Function Changing." Doctoral diss., MIT, Cambridge Mass.

Carter, Richard. 1988. "On linking: Papers by Richard Carter." *Lexicon Project Working-Papers* 25. Center for Cognitive Science, MIT, Cambridge Mass.

Chomsky, Noam. 1992. A minimalist program for linguistic theory. *MIT Occasional Papers in Linguistics* 1. Department of Linguistics and Philosophy, MIT, Cambridge, Mass.

———. 1986. *Barriers*. Linguistic Inquiry Monograph 13. Cambridge, Mass.: MIT Press.

———. 1981. *Lectures on government and binding*. Dordrecht: Foris.

Comrie, Bernard. 1976. *Aspect*. Cambridge, Mass.: Cambridge University Press.

Curme, G. 1905. *A grammar of the German language*. New York: Frederick Ungar.

———. 1931. *A grammar of the English language*. Essex, Conn.: Verbatim (reprint, 1977).

Di Sciullo, Anna-Maria. 1993. "Modularity and the mapping from the lexicon to the syntax." *Probus* 2:257–290.

Di Sciullo, Anna-Maria, and Elizabeth Klipple. 1994. "Modifying Affixes." *Proceedings of the Western Conference on Linguistics XXIII*. University of Washington.

Dowty, David. 1979. *Word meaning and montague grammar*. Dordrecht: Reidel.

Emonds, Joseph. 1985. *A unified theory of syntactic categories*. Dordrecht: Foris.

Ernst, T. 1987. "Theta-theory and the syntax of Chinese PPs. Ms. Ohio State University, Columbus.

Fortescue, M. 1984. *West Greenlandic*. Croom Helm Descriptive Grammars. London: Croom Helm.

Greenberg, J. H. 1966. "Some universals of grammar with particular reference to the order of meaningful elements." In *Universals of language*, 2d ed., ed. J. H. Greenberg, 73–113. Cambridge, Mass.: MIT Press.

Gruber, Jeffrey S. 1965. "Studies in lexical relations." Doctoral diss., MIT, Cambridge, Mass. In *Lexical structures in syntax and semantics*, Part I, Amsterdam: North Holland, 1976; and *MIT Working Papers in Linguistics*, Department of Linguistics and Philosophy, MIT, Cambridge, Mass.

Hale, Kenneth. 1985. "Notes on world view and semantic categories: Some Warlpiri examples." In *Features and Projections*, ed. Peter Muysken and Henk van Riemsdijk, 233–245. Dordrecht: Foris.

Hale, Kenneth, and Jay Keyser. 1991. "On the syntax of argument structure." Ms. MIT, Cambridge, Mass.

Heinrichs, E. 1985. "A compositional semantics for aktionsarten and NP reference in English." Doctoral diss., Ohio State University, Columbus.

Herskowits, A. 1986. *Language and spatial cognition*. Cambridge: Cambridge University Press.

Higginbotham, James. 1985. "On semantics." *Linguistic Inquiry* 16/4:547–594.

Hoekstra, Teun, and Rene Mulder. 1989. "Unergatives as copular verbs: Locational and existential predication." Ms. University of Leiden, Leiden, Holland.

Hornstein, Norbert, and Amy Weinberg. 1981. "Case theory and preposition stranding." *Linguistic Inquiry* 12/1:55–91.

Jackendoff, Ray. 1977. *X-bar syntax*. Linguistic Inquiry Monograph 2. Cambridge, Mass.: MIT Press.

———. 1983, *Semantics and cognition*. Cambridge, Mass.: MIT Press.

Kayne, Richard. 1983. *Connectedness and binary branching*. Dordrecht: Foris.

Keyser, Samuel Jay, and Tom Roeper. 1990. "Re-: The abstract clitic hypothesis." Ms. MIT, Cambridge, Mass.

Kipka, Peter. 1990. "Slavic aspect and its implications." Doctoral diss., MIT, Cambridge, Mass.

Klipple, Elizabeth. 1993. "Towards a theory of oblique arguments." *Proceedings of the Annual Meeting of the Canadian Linguistic Society*. Toronto Working Papers in Linguistics. University of Toronto.

———. 1992. "The lexicalization of direction in French and English." *Actes de l'Atelier Lexique-Syntaxe* (Cahiers Linguistiques de l'UQAM 1).

———. 1992. "Resultative predicates and resultative modifiers." Paper presented at Annual Meeting of the Canadian Linguistics Association, University of Prince Edward Island.

———. 1991. "The aspectual nature of thematic relations." Doctoral diss., MIT, Cambridge, Mass.

Larson, Richard. 1988. "On the double object construction." *Linguistic Inquiry* 19/3:335–391.

Levin, Beth, and Tova, Rapoport. 1988. "Lexical subordination." In *Papers from the XXIV Regional Meeting*, 275–289. Chicago Linguistic Society, University of Chicago, Chicago, Ill.

Li, C., and S. Thompson 1981. *Mandarin Chinese: A functional reference grammar*. Berkeley, Calif.: University of California Press.

Li, Yafei. 1990. "On V-V compounds in Chinese." *Natural Language and Linguistic Theory* 8:177–207.

Muysken, Peter, and Henk van Riemsdijk. 1985. "Projecting features and featuring projections." In *Features and Projections*, ed. Peter Muysken and Henk van Riemsdijk, 1–30. Dordrecht: Foris.

Pollock, Jean-Yves. 1989. "Verb movement, universal grammar and the structure of IP." *Linguistic Inquiry* 20:365–424.

Pustejovsky, James. 1988. "The geometry of events." In *Studies in generative approaches to aspect*, ed. Carol Tenny, *Lexicon Project Working Papers* 24, Center for Cognitive Science, MIT, Cambridge, Mass., 19–39.

Reuland, Eric. 1985. "A feature system for the set of categorial heads." In *Features and Projections*, ed. Peter Muysken and Henk van Riemsdijk, 41–89. Dordrecht: Foris.

Rooryck, Johan. 1993. "On the functional projection of prepositions." Talk given at Université du Québec à Montréal, June 1993.

Ruwet, Nicolas. 1982. "À propos des prépositions de lieu en français." In *Grammaire des insultes et autres études*, 317–340. Paris: Seuil.

Speas, Margareth. 1990. *Phrase structure in natural language*. Dordrecht: Kluwer.

Talmy, Leonard. 1991. "Path to realization: A typology of event conflation." Unpublished ms.

———. 1985. "Lexicalization patterns: Semantic structure in lexical forms." In *Language Typology and Syntactic Description* 3, ed. T. Shopen, 37–149. Cambridge: Cambridge University Press.

Thomason, Richemond, and Robert Stalnaker. 1973. "A semantic theory of adverbs." *Linguistic Inquiry* 4:195–220.

Vandeloise, Claude. 1991. *Spatial prepositions: A case study from French*. Chicago: University of Chicago Press.

Van Riemsdijk, Henk. 1978. *A case study in syntactic markedness: The binding nature of prepositional phrases*. Lisse: Peter de Ridder.

FIVE

On the Modularity of Case Theory:
A Case against the Visibility Hypothesis

MIREILLE TREMBLAY

1. MODULARITY VERSUS VISIBILITY

The system of grammar put forth in Chomsky (1981, 1986, 1993) is modular in the sense that "the full complexity of observed phenomena is traced to the inter-action of partially independent subtheories, each with its own abstract structure" (Chomsky 1981:135). Within such a framework, we expect subtheories to interact at specific levels of representation (or at interfaces in the Minimalist Program [Chomsky 1993]). Any principle or well-formedness condition making reference to more than one subtheory is highly suspicious.

This chapter is concerned with two questions: To what extent are subtheo-ries independent modules and should the interaction between those modules be allowed to be encoded formally in the theory of grammar, or should it be restricted to interaction on linguistic expressions, as has been proposed for the passive con-struction (see Chomsky 1981)? We argue in favor of a theory of grammar in which subtheories are completely independent and interact only at the interface. These issues are addressed with respect to Case and Theta theory.

According to the Visibility Hypothesis, the function of Case is to make an argument visible for Theta-marking (a proposal attributed to J. Aoun). The Visibility Hypothesis is motivated on theoretical grounds: it is an attempt to subsume Case theory under Theta theory. In this paper, we reconsider the theory-internal and empirical motivations for postulating that Case theory is to be included under Theta theory. Underlying the Visibility Hypothesis is the assumption that Case and Theta theory are closely interconnected and that the class of Case and Theta-assignees is the same. However, it will be argued that the Case Filter and the Theta Criterion do not apply to the same class of categories. In particular, while the Theta Criterion applies only to arguments, the Case Filter must apply to any element bearing the feature [+N], whether they be predicates (nominal and adjectival) or expletives. If the Case Filter applies to both predicates and expletives, then the function of Case cannot be limited to making an argument visible for Theta-marking. This is because, by definition, predicates and expletives do not receive a Theta-role. This constitutes a strong argument against Visibility.

The discussion will be organized as follows. Section 2 reviews theoretical claims that have been made with respect to Case and Theta theory and the Visibility Hypothesis. Section 3 provides empirical evidence against the Visibility Hypothesis. Finally, section 4 addresses the question of a Case theory in a truly modular grammar, focusing on such issues as feature checking and agreement.

2. INTERACTION BETWEEN CASE AND THETA THEORY

2.1. Case Theory

Case theory regulates the distribution of NPs within sentences. Every phonetically realized NP must bear Case, or be part of a Case-marked chain. The presence of lexically realized non-Case-marked NPs is ruled out by the Case Filter.

(1)   *Case Filter*
       *NP, if NP has phonetic content and has no Case. (Chomsky 1981:49)

In Chomsky (1981), Case is assumed to be assigned under government by a Case-assigning head. In languages such as English and French, only the [−N] categories (verbs and prepositions), and INFL, are Case-assigners.[1]

2.2. The Visibility Hypothesis

Originally, Case theory was proposed to account for the fact that infinitival clauses with subjects could only appear after a preposition or a verb, which are Case-assigners, but not after a noun or an adjective, which are not Case-assigners. This theory of abstract Case (Vergnaud 1982, Chomsky 1981) stated that every lexically realized NP must be assigned abstract Case for morphological reasons. However, Lasnik and Freidin (1981) argued that the Case Filter applies to *wh*-traces, thereby removing the morphological motivation for the Case Filter.

Chomsky (1981), following a proposal by Joseph Aoun, proposed the Visibility Hypothesis, according to which the Case Filter is a condition on argumenthood. According to the Visibility Hypothesis, the function of Case is to make an argument chain visible for Theta-marking.[2] Case is thus a necessary condition for Theta-role assignment.

The literature mentions at least two problems with the Visibility Hypothesis: the fact that argument PRO is not Case-marked and the fact that expletives are subject to the Case Filter but are non-arguments.

Chomsky and Lasnik (1993) consider the fact that PRO appears in non-Case-positions and propose to incorporate PRO into the structural Case system by assuming that PRO does have Case, but of a different kind. They argue that PRO bears null Case, and that this null Case is the realization of the Spec-head relation, in which the head INFL lacks tense and agreement features. They thus eliminate the disjunction from the Visibility condition (the fact that all arguments but PRO need Case) by assuming that PRO also bears Case.

This analysis of PRO takes care of one counterexample to the Visibility Hypothesis and, if correct, is compatible with the claim that arguments need Case. It does not address the main question we are asking here: Are arguments the only elements that require Case?

To refute the Visibility Hypothesis, one needs to compare the set of Case-assignees to the set of Theta-assignees. Are there elements that bear a Theta-role but no Case; are there categories that bear Case but are Theta-assigners? If it can be shown that the Case Filter and the Theta Criterion do not apply to the same class of categories, then we have evidence against Visibility.

According to Case theory (Chomsky 1981), only [+N, −V] argumental categories are subject to the Case Filter. In the next section, we argue that the Case Filter applies to all [+N] categories independently of their argumental status, thereby providing empirical motivation for not subsuming Case theory under Theta theory. Evidence will come from the study of copular and existential sentences in languages with an overt Case system and from *avoir*, "have," constructions: section 3.1 focuses on nominal predicates, while sections 3.2 and 3.3 deal with expletives and adjectives, respectively.

3. AGAINST THE VISIBILITY HYPOTHESIS

3.1. Nominal Predicates and Case

We mentioned that expletives offer a possible counterexample to the Visibility Hypothesis, since they are non-arguments with Case. This section considers another type of NP that is subject to the Case Filter but does not receive a Theta-role, namely, nominal predicates. We consider two types of constructions: section 3.1.1 deals with constructions such as (2), in which the nominal predicate *une bonne étudiante* and its subject *Marie* bear the same Case, while section 3.1.2 focuses on less studied constructions, such as (3), in which the nominal predicate *du charme* and its subject *Marie* bear different Cases.

(2)   NP   NP   Marie est une bonne étudiante
        subject predicate Marie is a   good student
        [α Case] [α Case]

(3)   NP   NP   Marie a   du   charme
        subject predicate Marie has IND charm
        [α Case] [β Case]

3.1.1. *Nominal Predicates in Copular Sentences and Small Clauses*

Nominal predicates that bear the same Case as their subjects are found in two constructions: those in which the nominal predicate and its subject are used with *être*, "be," as in (4), and those in which the predicate and its subject form a Small Clause (SC), as in (5). In both (4) and (5), *Anne* is the subject and *une bonne étudiante* is the predicate.

(4) Je considère que [Anne est une bonne étudiante].
     I   consider that Anne is a   good student

(5) Je considère [Anne une bonne étudiante].
     I   consider Anne a   good student

Tremblay (1991) and Moro (1990) have both argued, based on independent evidence, that predicate nominals in copular sentences are subject to the Case Filter; that the subject NP and the predicative NP do not have a distinct reference and are coindexed (NP_i be NP_i); and that the subject transmits its Case to the predicate. Thus, in an example such as (4), repeated in (6), *Anne* and *une bonne étudiante* are coindexed, and both bear nominative Case.

(6) Je considère que [[Anne]$_i$ est [une bonne étudiante]$_i$]
                         +NOM   +NOM

Evidence in favor of such a proposal is provided by Latin and Old French, two historically related languages with morphological case. In these languages, nominal predicates used with *be* bear the same morphological Case as their subject. When the subject bears nominative Case, the predicate also appears with nominative Case, as illustrated in (7).

(7) a. Caesar dux   est.   LATIN
         Caesar master is   (= Moro [33a])
         +NOM +NOM

     b. Je   sui ses fieus, il   est mes pere.   OLD FRENCH
         I   am his son, he   is my father
         +NOM   +NOM +NOM   +NOM

When the subject bears accusative Case (by Exceptional Case-marking), then the predicate also bears accusative Case.

(8) dicunt   Caesarem ducem esse   LATIN
     say-they Caesar   general to-be   (= Moro [33b])
              +ACC   +ACC

Note that this is also true of predicates used without the copula (i.e., in Small Clauses). In (9), the attribute of the complement bears the same case as the complement, namely, accusative Case.

(9) a. Pater filium suum IPHICLEM vocavit.   LATIN
         Father son   his Iphiclès called   (Gal 1960:100)
                +ACC   +ACC
         "The father called his son Iphiclès."

     b. Romani Ciceronem consulem creaverunt.   (Gal 1960:100)
         Romans Ciceron   consul   named
                 +ACC   +ACC
         "The Romans named Ciceron consul."

In passive constructions, the direct object becomes a subject and the predicate also bears nominative case, since it is now predicated of the subject.

(10) Filius a patre Iphicles vocatur.   (Gal 1960:100)
      Son   by father Iphicles been-named
      +NOM   +NOM
      "The son was named Iphicles by his father."

According to Moro, the fact that predicative NPs in copular constructions require Case does not indicate that the Visibility Hypothesis is not well founded. Rather, Moro proposes "to reformulate the 'case criterion' as affecting argumental chains rather than lexical NPs." "Given that a predicate and a subject do not instantiate different argumental chains, we can conclude that case assignment to argumental chains is still a necessary condition for visibility" (Moro 1990:9). Thus, for Moro, the fact that predicates in *be* sentences need Case is not a valid argument against visibility.

In copular sentences with *be*, the nominal predicate receives Case from another NP, possibly under agreement (see section 4.2 for discussion). In such cases, the two NPs bear the same Case.

(11) NP   NP
      [α Case] [α Case]

This allows Moro to maintain the visibility condition on Theta-assignment: the predicate and its subject are part of the same argumental chain, and the Case Filter applies to argumental chains.

We believe, however, that Moro's claim concerning the Visibility Condition on argument chains does not account for all cases in which a nominal predicate needs Case. The next section introduces a different class of copular constructions in which the subject NP and the predicate NP do not bear the same Case:

(12) NP   NP
      [α Case] [β Case]

In such cases, there is no coreference between the subject and the predicate, and thus they cannot share Case. Given that such predicates do not share the Case of another NP, the fact that they require Case cannot be attributed to a Case requirement on some other NP. They must receive Case directly from a Case-assigning head, and this constitutes an argument against the Visibility Condition.

3.1.2. *Nominal Predicates in Avoir and Epistemic Constructions*

In this section, we consider cases in which the predicate does not share the Case features of another NP, and must therefore receive its own Case from a Case-assigning head.

(13)   H   NP
         ⤷
        Case

We discuss two cases: constructions with *avoir*, "have," in which a predicate receives Case from *avoir*, and epistemic constructions, in which a predicate in a Small Clause receives Case from the verb which governs the Small Clause.

3.1.2.1. *Avoir constructions*   In Tremblay (1991/1992), I argued that French (and English) have two copulas: *avoir*, "have," and *être*, "be," whose distribution is syntactically conditioned. *Avoir* and *être* are copulas in that neither contributes meaning. They are similar in that neither is a Theta-assigner (as in Guéron 1986), but they differ crucially in that only *avoir* can assign accusative Case.

(14)   AVOIR: $[-\theta, +ACC]$
        ÊTRE: $[-\theta, -ACC]$

This proposal accounts for the fact that semantically equivalent predicates such as *charmante* and *du charme* in (15) occur with *être* and *avoir*, respectively.

(15)   a.   Marie est charmante.
              Marie is charming.
        b.   Marie a   du   charme.
              Marie has IND charm.

In such constructions, neither *avoir* nor *être* are Theta-assigners, and in both cases the subject *Marie* is a derived subject. Both constructions involve a small clause in which a predicate assigns a Theta-role to its subject. In (15), both *charmante* and *du charme* Theta-mark their subject NP *Marie*,[3] as shown in (16). *Marie* then moves to the subject position, where it can receive nominative Case.

(16)   a.   e INFL être [$_{SC}$ [Marie] [charmante]]
                           θ

        b.   e INFL avoir [$_{SC}$ [du charme] [Marie]]
                           θ

It is the categorial status of the predicate that triggers the choice of copula. In (15a), *Marie est charmante*, the predicate is an adjective and, as such, can (and must) agree in Case (as well as gender and number) with the NP it modifies: the subject *Marie*. In French, only gender and number features are overt; the Case feature has no phonological reflex.

(17)   Marie   est charmante
        +NOM   +NOM

We will see in section 3.3 that in languages with an overt Case system, such as Latin, adjectives in similar copular constructions bear nominative Case, just like nominal predicates.

(18)   Rosa   est pulchra
        +NOM   +NOM

In (15b), *Marie a du charme*, the predicate is a noun that is also subject to the Case Filter. This NP, however, does not bear the same referential index as the subject NP.

(19)   Marie$_i$ a du charme$_j$.

Thus, nominative Case cannot be transmitted to the predicate *du charme*, which must therefore get Case from the Case-assigning copula, *avoir*.[4]

(20) Marie$_i$ a du charme$_j$
     +NOM +ACC

Avoir constructions thus provide evidence that, contrary to what is currently assumed in Case theory and the Visibility Hypothesis, nominal predicates require Case. This Case requirement on nominal predicates is an argument against the Visibility Hypothesis. The data discussed in the next section provide further evidence to that effect.

3.1.2.2. *Epistemic constructions* Ruwet (1982) has noted that epistemic verbs such as *trouver*, "find," can take two types of complements. These are illustrated in (21) and (22). In one case, *trouver* can take a sentential complement with the copula *être*, as in (21a), or an ordinary Small Clause (SC), as in (21b). When *trouver* takes a SC complement, it assigns accusative Case to the subject of the SC, as shown by the presence of the accusative clitic in (21c).

être/accusative alternation
(21) a. Jean trouve que Marie est charmante.
       Jean finds that Marie is charming
    b. Jean trouve Marie charmante.
       Jean finds Marie charming
    c. Jean la   trouve charmante.
       Jean HER-ACC finds charming

What Ruwet noted is that epistemic verbs can take another type of complement. In such cases, we have either a sentential complement with *avoir*, as in (22a), or a SC with a dative NP, as in (22b) and (22c).

avoir/dative alternation
(22) a. Jean trouve que Marie a du charme.
       Jean finds that Marie has IND charm
    b. Jean trouve du charme à Marie.
       Jean finds IND charm DAT Marie
    c. Jean lui   trouve du charme.
       Jean HER-DAT finds IND charm

Why does *être* alternate with the accusative construction, while *avoir* alternates with the dative construction?

The account of the *être*/accusative alternation is straightforward, since under most analyses of such constructions both alternants involve an SC in which the adjectival predicate assigns a Theta-role to its subject, as we saw in (16a).

(23) [$_{SC}$ [$_{NP}$ Marie] [$_{AP}$ charmante]]
                θ

When the SC is used with *être* (21a), *Marie* can get its Case from INFL and transmit it to the predicate *charmante*. In other cases (21b), the subject of the SC gets accusative Case from the main verb, and then transmits it to the adjectival predicate, as we saw in section 3.1.

(24)   a.   ... [$_{CP}$ que [Marie] est [$_{SC}$ [$_{NP}$ t$_i$] [$_{AP}$ charmante]]]
                                    +NOM   +NOM

        b.   ... trouve [$_{SC}$ [$_{NP}$ Marie] [$_{AP}$ charmante]]
                                    +ACC   +ACC

The *avoir*/dative alternation is somewhat different, since in this case the SC involves the presence of two Case-requiring NPs that cannot be coindexed and thus share Case. In such cases, the predicate precedes the subject. We can tell that this is the D-structure order because it is the order we find in the SC embedded under *trouver*, as in (22b).

(25)   [$_{SC}$ [$_{NP}$ du charme] [$_{NP}$ Marie]]
                                    θ

In constructions such as (22b), the main verb *trouver* assigns accusative Case to the first NP, *du charme*, and the second NP bears the default Case: dative.[5]

(26)   Jean trouve [$_{SC}$ [$_{NP}$ du charme] [$_{NP}$ Marie]]
                                    +ACC   +DAT

On the other hand, in sentential constructions such as (22a), the main verb can no longer assign accusative Case to the NP (just as it could not in [21a]). In such cases, the copula *avoir* is required to assign accusative Case to the NP *du charme*, and the second NP can now be raised to receive nominative Case.

(27)   ... [$_{CP}$ que Marie$_i$ a [$_{SC}$ [$_{NP}$ du charme] [$_{NP}$ t$_i$]]]
                        +NOM   +ACC

The existence of the dative/*avoir* alternation in epistemic constructions is important for a number of reasons: first, the fact that *avoir* can be omitted shows that it does not contribute meaning; second, the close relationship between *avoir* and dative Case highlights the role of *avoir* as a dummy Case-assigner; finally, this data shows that nominal predicates such as *du charme* need Case, and that they require a Case different from that of their subject. We have only discussed the construction *avoir du charme*, but we believe that the same analysis also applies to constructions such as *avoir les yeux bleus*, "to have blue eyes," *avoir peur*, "to be afraid," *avoir sa fille de malade*, "to have one's daughter sick," and so on. The next section discusses another type of Case-requiring non-Theta-receiving NP: expletives.

3.2. The Case of Expletives

Expletives pose a different problem for the Visibility Hypothesis since they are a different type of non-argument with Case. A number of proposals have been made in the literature to answer this dilemma, including Safir's (1982) account in terms of Case transmission, and Chomsky's (1991) Expletive Replacement Hypothesis. In this section, we argue that French expletives provide evidence that at least some expletives require Case for themselves, thereby arguing against the Visibility Hypothesis.

Safir (1982) proposes an account in terms of Case transmission: in sentences such as (31), the expletive *there* does not need to receive Case for itself, it needs Case for the NP *a man*. Thus, there is chain formation between *there* and *a man*.

(28) There is a man in the garden.

Under such an approach, the Visibility Condition is assumed to apply to argumental chains rather than individual NPs: A chain is Case-marked if it contains one Case-marked position and a position in a Case-marked chain is visible for Theta-marking.

Subsequently, in order to account for the fact that expletive-argument pairs have the same locality properties as NP movement chains (as noted in Burzio 1986), Chomsky (1986) argued that such pairs involve NP-movement of the object NP to the subject position at LF. According to the Expletive Replacement Hypothesis (Chomsky 1986), expletives are not visible or legitimate objects at the level of the semantic interpretation, so they must be substituted by their associate at LF. *There* is thus eliminated by LF-substitution.

(29) a. There arrived a man.
 b. A man$_i$ arrived t$_i$.

Since the expletive occupies an A-position at S-structure (SPEC of IP), the LF-movement forming the amalgamated expletive is A-movement. This explains the fact that the expletive-argument pair seems to meet the conditions on A-movement.

Chomsky (1991) subsequently proposed to treat *there* as an LF-affix, and argued that this movement rule is not a substitution rule, as in (29b), but an adjunction rule. Since *there* has specific features, it is undeletable, by the condition of recoverability of deletion. Since *there* lacks inherent phi-features (including number) or category, these features will "percolate" from its associate on usual assumptions. If agreement is checked at LF, then it will already have to have been established at S-structure, yielding the overt agreement.

According to Chomsky, *there* must be in a Case-marked position, by the chain condition, which requires that an LF chain be headed by a Case-marked position, and Case must be assigned to the associate NP independently. There cannot be a process of Case transmission, for that process would allow a sentence such as (30) to satisfy the Case Filter.

(30) *there seems a man to be in the room

Therefore, Chomsky assumes that Case must be assigned at S-structure to the associate NP, much in the line of Lasnik (1989),[6] who made a similar proposal based on examples such as (31).

(31) I consider there *(to be) a solution.

In (31), *be* assigns Case directly to *a solution* and *there* also receives Case (from *consider*). So there is no S-structure process transmitting Case from the expletive there to its associate. Chomsky thus argues that the notion of LF-adjunction eliminates much of the motivation for Case-transmission theories.

The assumption that *be* is a Case-assigner reintroduces the problem that expletives constitute for the Visibility Hypothesis: given that the associate NP can receive Case from *be*, the fact that expletive *there* requires Case can no longer be attributed to the Case requirement on the associate NP. The Case requirement on expletive *there* would thus seem like an argument against Visibility.

However, we have argued in section 3.1.2.1 that *être* and *be* are not Case-assigners and that they involve a process of Case transmission. The fact that in languages with overt Case nominal predicates used with *be* bear nominative Case (as we saw in section 3.1.1) constitutes a strong argument against the claim that *be* is a Case-assigner.

A comparative discussion of existential constructions in English and French provides further evidence in favor of Case transmission and the claim that at least some expletives need Case.

Unlike English, which has existential constructions with *be*, French has existential constructions with *avoir*.

(32) a. There is a book on the table.
      b. Il   y a   un livre sur la table.
          EXP Y has a   book on the table

Chomsky (1991) mentions that expletive *there* has 3 salient properties: (1) it requires an associate NP (the associate NP licenses the expletive); (2) number agreement is not with *there* but with the associate; and (3) there is an alternate form with the associate in the subject position after overt raising. French expletive *il* in existential constructions does not share two of these properties: first, there is no agreement with the associate NP, as shown in (33); and second, there is no alternative form with the associate in subject position. Raising of the associate NP triggers a change in the choice of copula (*être*, "be," rather than *avoir*, "have").

(33) Il   y a   trois livres sur la table.
      EXP Y has three books on the table

(34) Trois livres sont sur la table.
      Three books are on the table

Under the present analysis, the difference between the two languages would have to be attributed to the properties of the expletives. The presence of *avoir* in French indicates that the NP adjacent to it (*trois livres*, in this case) requires Case. The fact that *trois livres* needs Case shows that it cannot get Case via a Case-transmission process. This indicates that *il* cannot transmit Case (see Pollock 1981 for a similar proposal). The presence of *be* in English indicates that *three books* can receive Case from there.

The difference is corroborated by the observation that in French the subject does not agree in number with the object, while in English it does.

(35) a. Il   y a   trois livres sur la table.
          EXP Y has three books on the table
      b. There are three books on the table.

This shows that we have chain formation in English but not in French. We have argued in section 3.1.1 that agreement is conditional on coindexing and that Case transmission is part of a general process of agreement. Even though we may have an explanation for the fact that English *there* needs Case, we still need an explanation for the fact that French *il* needs Case too. In French, the Case requirement on expletives cannot be linked to a Case-transmission or chain-formation process. We thus believe that French existential constructions provide a further argument against Visibility, since they involve Case-marked non-arguments.

The following data from Old French provides empirical evidence in favor of the proposed Case distinction between *have* and *be* existential contructions. Old French allowed for both *have* and *be* existential sentences. As predicted by our analysis, in existential sentences with *have*, the associated NP appears with accusative Case, while in existential sentences with *be*, the associated NP appears with nominative Case (data from Dufresne, Dupuis, and Tremblay 1995).

(36)   i jacinthes (+NOM) clers   i   *est* il   od le cristal et od le beril.
       the ruby   sparkling CL is   IL with the crystal and the beryl
       "There is the sparkling ruby with the crystal and the beryl."

                                                                        (Brandan, p. 3)

(37)   ... dont il   n'   i   *avoit* nul   qu'on ne tenist a preudome et a bon chevalier.
                  EXP NEG Y had   none (ACC)
       "... and there was none ...

                                                                        (Artu, 066 005)

3.3. Adjectival Predicates

We have seen that the Case Filter applies not only to argumental NPs, but also to predicative NPs and expletives. In this section, we argue that the Case Filter also applies to adjectival predicates.

In Latin, adjectival modifiers and predicates agree in Case, gender, and number with the noun they modify, as shown in (38) and (39).

(38)   a.   Pulchra rosa   est in tabula.
            Pretty rose   is on table
            +NOM +NOM

       b.   Pulchram rosam amamus.
            Pretty   rose   we-like
            +ACC   +ACC

(39)   a.   Rosa   est pulchra.
            Rose   is pretty
            +NOM   +NOM

       b.   Rosae   sunt pulchrae.
            Roses   are pretty
            +NOM   +NOM

Moreover, there are languages in which adjectives can bear a Case different from the Case of their subject (just like nominal predicates). Neidle (1988:11) mentions that, in Russian, both nominal and adjectival predicates embedded under verbs such as *consider* occur in the instrumental Case. The following illustrates adjectives bearing instrumental Case.

(40) a. On   ee   ščital   krasivoj.
          He   her   considered pretty
          +NOM +ACC   +INST
          "He considered her pretty."

      b. On   ee   našel umnoj.
          He (NOM) her (ACC) found clever (INST)
          "He found her clever."

Such predicates can occur in no other case, except when there is an emphatic modifier.

Furthermore, adjectives occurring in second predicate position of ordinary short sentences may either (a) agree in case with the noun they modify, or (b) occur in the instrumental case. (Examples cited in Neidle 1988:124 but attributed to Comrie 1974.)

(41) a. Ivan   vernulsja ugrjumyj/ugrjumym.
          Ivan   returned gloomy.
          (+NOM)   (+NOM)/(+INSTR)

      b. Mne   nužno   bylo streljat' pervomu/pervym
          (for)me necessary was to shoot first.
          (+DAT)   (+DAT)/(+INSTR)

These data seem to indicate that adjectives need Case independently from the noun of which they are predicated. Given that all adjectives are predicates (or modifiers), this shows that the Case Filter applies to all adjectives, and since all nouns are subject to the Case Filter (as we saw in sections 3.1.1 and 3.1.2), this shows that the Case Filter applies to any [+N] category. I believe that the phenomenon of auxiliary selection can be explained similarly.

3.4. Past Participles as Adjectives: A Case-theoretic Account of Auxiliary Selection

We have argued that French has two copulas *avoir* and *être*. Neither of these verbs contributes meaning. It is this characteristic that allows them to function either as copulas or auxiliaries. We have explained the phenomenon of copula selection in terms of agreement, coindexation, and Case: *être* is selected when the subject and the predicate can be coindexed, yielding to agreement and Case transmission, and *avoir* is selected when there is no coindexation, no agreement, and no Case transmission. Extending this analysis to auxiliary selection means that we will also provide an explanation in terms of agreement, coindexation, and Case.

This approach is promising since we observe a link between coindexation and selection of auxiliary *être*, as shown in (42). *Avoir* is selected (42a) when the subject and the clitic are not coindexed, and *être* is selected (42b) when the subject and the clitic are coindexed.

(42) a. Marie$_i$ les$_j$ a   vus.
          Marie them AVOIR saw.
          "Marie saw them."

    b. Marie$_i$ s$_i$' est vue.
       Marie SELF ÊTRE saw.
       "Marie saw herself."

The data in (43) shows that there is also a link between agreement of the past participle and auxiliary selection.

(43) a. Marie est arrivée.
        Marie ÊTRE arrived-FS
        "Marie has arrived."
     b. Marie a mangé.
        Marie AVOIR eaten
        "Marie has eaten."

It thus seems that auxiliaries *avoir* and *être* are subject to the same conditions on selection as copulas *avoir* and *être*, which would justify a unified analysis.

This suggests that auxiliary selection, just like copula selection, is to be linked to Case theory, and thus that auxiliary *avoir* is selected when (accusative) Case is required. There is historical evidence in favor of this proposal. Dupuis (1989) has argued that auxiliary *avoir* comes from main verb *avoir* (copula *avoir*, in our terms), and that this verb has the ability to assign accusative Case, as shown in (44), in which both the past participle and the direct object bear accusative Case.

(44) ... se tu eusses toutes ces vertuz sauvees en toi.
       if you had all these virtues saved in you
          +ACC   +ACC

The claim that auxiliary *avoir* is selected when (accusative) Case is required leads us to the conclusion that there is no distinction between active and passive past participles: both are adjectives and require Case. Past participles, just like nominal predicates, can receive Case from a Case-assigning head, *avoir*, or under agreement, in which case auxiliary *être* will be selected. We can thus explain the fact that past participles used with *être* agree with the subject, while past participles used with *avoir* do not.

(45) a. Marie a du charme.   NOMINAL PREDICATE
        +NOM +ACC
     b. Marie a couru.   PAST PARTICIPLE
        +NOM +ACC

(46) a. Marie est une bonne étudiante.   NOMINAL PREDICATE
        +NOM   +NOM
     b. Marie est charmante.   ADJECTIVAL PREDICATE
        +NOM   +NOM
     c. Marie est tombée.   PAST PARTICIPLE
        +NOM   +NOM

This analysis is motivated historically. Foulet (1963) notes that in Old French the past participle used with *avoir* bears accusative Case, even when no object is present, while past participles used with *être* bear nominative Case. Benoit (1991) notes that this is true of both passive and ergative past participles.

(47)   ... que il n'eüst   parlé à moi et   que ge ne   l'eüsse conneü.
         that he NEG has talked to me and that I   NEG him had known
                                                        +ACC

PASSIVE
(48)   ... n   'i   avoit un seul qui ne   fust morz par armes.
         NEG CL- has   one only who NEG was killed by arms.
                                                   +NOM
         "There was none who didn't die by arms."

ERGATIVE
(49)   ... si dist au   chevalier qui estoit venuz avec lui.
         too said to-the knight   who was   came with him.
                                                   +NOM
         "... said to the knight had come with him."

When there is a direct object, it receives its Case from the auxiliary. Thus, we can explain the requirement that transitive verbs always select auxiliary *avoir*.

(50)   Marie a mangé une pomme.

Our account of auxiliary selection thus explains the link between agreement on the past participle, auxiliary selection, and the position of the subject at D-structure.

3.5. Summary

We have argued that the Case requirements on nominal and adjectival predicates and on expletives provide a strong case against the Visibility Hypothesis.

The rejection of the Visibility Hypothesis is problematic since it deprives Case theory of its Theta-theoretic motivations, and thus excludes Case theory from the realm of semantic relations. The function of Case theory must be recast and its role within grammar redefined. Given that there are strong links between Case theory and grammatical relations, we believe that an association between Case theory and X-bar theory would be a better lead (as proposed, for example, in Bittner and Hale 1993).

4. CASE THEORY IN A MODULAR GRAMMAR

What are the theoretical consequences of our proposal for Case theory and Agreement theory? Chomsky's (1981) model has undergone major changes. The Government and Binding framework has been abandoned in favor of the Minimalist Program. The subtheories that have been most affected by the change are Case theory and Agreement theory, which have been unified in terms of X-bar theory.

4.1. Recent Developments in Case Theory

Case theory is now seen as a theory of feature-checking: across languages, both subjects and objects must raise and check Case features in the Spec-Head relationship with an appropriate functional head, in which the appropriate functional heads are the heads of the Agreement Phrases (AgrP). In Chomsky (1993), structural Case is taken to be solely the reflection of a particular relationship, that of a head to its specifier (Spec, Head). Head government plays no role in this framework.[7] Both agreement and structural Case are then seen as manifestations of the Spec-head relation (NP, AGR).

Nominative Case, being a function of finiteness, is checked via the Agreement Phrase immediately dominating Tense (T): AgrS. The inflectional heads, T and Agr, each have two features: verbal features and nominal features. The verbal features check the corresponding inflectional properties of the verb and the nominal features check the properties of NPs. The derivation is convergent if, for any given inflectional head, the N- and V-features are properly paired, that is, matched. T raises to AgrS and the subject NP raises to Spec AgrSP.

(51)

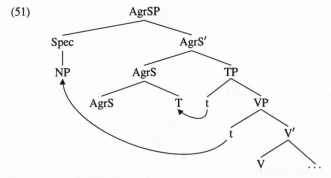

Accusative Case is checked via the Agr-phrase immediately dominating the verb: AgrO. The object must thus raise to Spec AgrOP. Verbs may or may not have the ability to assign structural Case. If V has the feature [+Case], then, after raising of the verb in AgrOP, the complex [AgrO-V] will also have this feature and will check accusative Case in the position [Spec AgrO]. In this case, the V-features are checked by the raising of the verb into AgrO, and the N-features are checked by raising the object NP in Spec AgrOP.

(52)

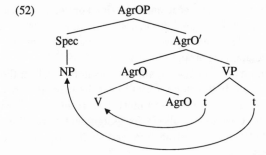

If V has [−Case] (that is, is unaccusative), an NP in Spec AgrO will not have its Case checked, and will therefore have to move to Spec AgrS.

Chomsky and Lasnik (1993) unifies the notions of agreement and morphological Case under the label "abstract Case": "Case is a relation of XP to H, H an

X⁰ head that assigns or checks the Case of XP." When the feature appears in both XP and H, they call the relation "agreement"; when it appears only on XP, they call it "Case." Both types of relations involve a head and a maximal projection.

(53)   Agreement: H   XP
                      +Case   +Case

(54)   Case: H   XP
                      −Case   +Case

This formulation of Agreement and Case thus allows a Case-assigner to bear Case-features. We believe that this approach is problematic because it goes against Stowell's (1981) Case Resistance Principle, according to which a Case-assigner cannot receive Case.

(55)   *Case Resistance Principle*
        Case may not be assigned to a category bearing a Case-assigning feature. (Stowell 1981:146)

4.2. Case Theory and Agreement Theory

The theory of Case we have outlined in section 3 is compatible to a certain extent with that of Chomsky (1993) and Chomsky and Lasnik (1993). We have argued that a [+N] category may receive Case under government (by a V, or P, or INFL), or under agreement (with another Case-bearing element). We can now rephrase Chomsky and Lasnik's dichotomy between agreement and Case in our terms: Case can appear on both XP and YP, if both are [+N] categories, and Case appears on XP only when H is [−N].

(56)   a.   Case transmission: XP   YP
              (agreement)   [+N]   [+N]
                                   +Case   +Case
        b.   Case assignment: H   XP
                                   [−N]   [+N]
                                   −Case   +Case

Case assignment is a relation between a head and a maximal projection; Case is assigned by a [−N] head to a [+N] maximal projection. Note that we are not claiming that Case assignment is done under government. Case assignment may proceed through a Spec-head relation, as proposed in Chomsky (1993).

Case transmission is a relation between two maximal projections that bear the feature [+N]. In Case transmission, both categories will bear the Case features. In order to transmit its Case, a maximal projection must have received it from a Case-assigning head [−N]. So Case theory allows for assignment of the Case feature by a [−N] head to a [+N] maximal projection, and sharing of the Case feature between [+N] categories.

This extension of the scope of Case theory allows for a real dichotomy between Case-assigning categories [−N] and Case-receiving categories [+N]. A [+N] category cannot assign Case, it can only share it, and it can only share a Case it has received from a Case assigner, that is, a [−N] head.

Chomsky's (1993) discussion of predicate adjectives may offer a formal explanation for how agreement may proceed. Chomsky argues that both kinds of structural relations with a predicate (verb, adjective) involve Agr: Agr alone, for agreement relations; the element T or V alone (raising to Agr) for Case relations. Predicate adjectives involve a Small Clause in which the AP is dominated by an AgrP, as shown in (49). Raising of the subject of the predicate to Spec AgrP and raising of A to AgrA creates the structure for NP-adjective agreement internal to the predicate phrase.

(57)

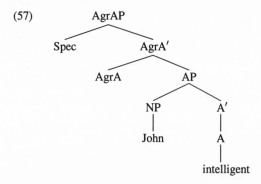

When the Small Clause is the object of a verb such as *consider*, the subject of the predicate (*John* in [59]) raises to [Spec-AgrO] at LF to receive accusative Case. When the Small Clause occurs after a verb such as *be*, the subject (of the adjectival predicate) raises overtly to receive nominative Case and verb agreement. In such cases, the subject NP (*John*) enters into three relations: (i) a case relation with [T AgrS]; (ii) an agreement relation with AgrS; and (iii) an agreement relation with AgrA.

We propose to extend this analysis to nominal predicates, since we have argued that nominal predicates may also receive Case through agreement.

(58)

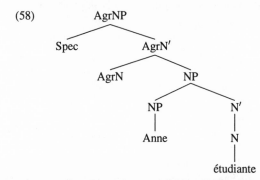

This analysis is supported by the fact that nominal predicates also share gender and number features with their subject. In (59), the determiner, the nominal predicate, and its adjectival modifier all bear the feminine feature.

(59)   Anne est une bonne étudiante.
       Anne is a   good student

5. CONCLUSION

This chapter provided arguments against Visibility. We have argued that Case theory cannot be subsumed under Theta theory, since the Case Filter applies to categories that do not receive a Theta-role, namely nominal and adjectival predicates and expletives. Such categories can get Case from a Case-assigning head (via a Spec-head relation with Agr) or under agreement with another [+N] category.

As far as nominal predicates are concerned, we have considered two types of copular sentences: copular sentences with *être* (*be*), in which the nominal predicate gets Case under agreement with another Case-bearing nominal, and copular sentences with *avoir* (*have*), in which the nominal predicate gets Case directly from a Case-assigning head. We have also considered a third class of constructions in which the nominal predicate gets Case from a main verb. Finally, we have argued that French expletives provide an additional argument against Visibility.

As for adjectival predicates, we have seen that in most cases, the adjectival predicate gets Case under agreement with the nominal to which it is related. We have also argued that such predicates can get Case independently, as in the Russian instrumental examples, or from a Case-assigning head, as in past-participle constructions.

We have thus extended the Case Filter so that it applies to all categories bearing the feature [+N]. The distinction between the Case-assigning categories and Case-requiring categories can now be expressed in terms of the feature [±N].

Implicit in our reformulation of Case theory is the claim that Case theory must be distinguished from Agreement theory, just as Case theory was distinct from Government Theory in earlier studies. In general, Case features do not appear on Case assigners. For example, nominative Case appears on subjects only, while subject agreement appears on both INFL and the subject. Similarly, accusative Case appears on objects only (and maybe past participles), but never on the accusative assigning verb. Agreement between objects and past participles occurs under special circumstances, but never involves the verb (although in some languages obligatory cliticization may look like agreement).

To conclude, our discussion provided an argument in favor of the modularity of grammar. Subtheories are independent modules and must remain independent in the theory of grammar.

NOTES

This research was supported by the SSHRC grant #411-92-0012 (La modularité de la grammaire: arguments, projections et variations) attributed to Anna-Maria Di Sciullo, by the FCAR grant #94ER0401 (Interfaces, invariants et relativisation) attributed to Anna-Maria Di Sciullo, Monique Lemieux, and Marie-Thérèse Vinet, and by the Fonds institutionnel de recherche (UQAM) to Anna-Maria Di Sciullo. The author wishes to thank the members of these projects, especially Anna-Maria Di Sciullo and Aimé Avolonto, for their helpful comments.

1. Chomsky (1986) revises Case theory and introduces a distinction between two types of Case: inherent and structural. Structural Cases (nominative and objective) are assigned in terms of S-structure position, independently of Theta-marking, while inherent Cases (oblique and genitive) are assigned at D-structure by a head if and only if this head also Theta-marks the NP. This distinction was proposed to account for the fact that sentences such as (ia) cannot be saved by *of*-insertion, as in (ib).

  i. a. *the belief [John to be the winner]
   b. *the belief [of John to be the winner]

Chomsky argues that (ib) is ungrammatical since at D-structure the noun *belief* does not govern and Theta-mark the subject of the embedded clause and cannot therefore assign inherent Case to it. See section 4.1 for a discussion of more recent developments in Case theory.

2. Theta theory is concerned with the thematic relations between lexical heads and their arguments. It also includes a well-formedness condition, the Theta Criterion, whose role is to ensure that all Theta-roles (thematic roles) have been assigned properly.

> *Theta Criterion*
> Each argument bears one and only one Theta-role and each Theta-role is assigned to one and only one argument. (Chomsky 1981:36)

3. The relative order of the subject and the predicate will be discussed in section 3.1.2.2.

4. To illustrate this, consider the two sentences in (i).

  i. a. Marie est une fille.
    Marie is a girl.
   b. Marie a une fille.
    Marie has a girl.

If neither *avoir* nor *être* has semantic content, how can we account for the difference in meaning between (ia) and (ib)? As discussed in section 3.1.1, we will assume that the two NPs that occur with the copula *être* in (ia) do not have a distinct reference. If we assume that predicates denote a set of individuals that bear the property denoted by the predicate, this would mean that in *Marie est une fille*, *Marie* belongs to the set of individuals denoted by the predicate *une fille*. This set has a referential index and *Marie*, being a member of that set, is coindexed with it. Being coindexed with the subject, the predicate can form a Case-chain with the subject. Consequently, the two NPs will be nominative.

  ii. [Marie]$_i$ est [une fille]$_i$
    +NOM   +NOM

In (ib) however, *Marie* does not belong to the set of individuals denoted by the predicate *une fille*. Therefore, the predicate cannot be coindexed with the subject and cannot form a (Case)-chain, and must be assigned Case independently.

  iii. [Marie]$_i$ a [une fille]$_i$
    +NOM   +NOM

Thus, the main idea is that the difference in meaning between (ia) and (ib) is a direct consequence of the different coindexing, and the choice of copula follows as a mere Case consequence of the different coindexing.

5. Dative Case is the default Case, as we can see from causative constructions.

i. a. Jean a   fait   manger Marie.
Jean AUX made eat   Marie
"Jean made Marie eat."
ii. b. Jean a   fait   manger une pomme à   Marie.
Jean AUX made eat   an   apple DAT Marie
"Jean made Marie eat an apple."

6. As noted in Lasnik (1989), the Case transmission hypothesis presupposes that *a man* cannot receive Case from *be*. However, if *be* is a Case-assigner, then the expletive need not transmit its Case to its associate NP, and we no longer have an explanation for the fact that expletives need Case. Lasnik argues that *be* is a Case-assigner and thus that there is no Case transmission between *there* and *a man*. Lasnik then proposes to extend Visibility in such a way as to make it not only a condition on Theta-marking, but also on movement: to be visible as a target for movement, an NP position must have Case, if in principle it could have Case. In Lasnik's system, then, expletives and their associate NP must be assigned Case independently. The expletive bears nominative Case and the associate NP bears partitive Case.

7. In Chomsky and Lasnik (1993), the distinction between structural and inherent Case is maintained in two structurally different positions: structural Case is assigned under a Spec-head relation with AgrO, while inherent Case is still assigned under governement by a head.

REFERENCES

Benoit, Anne-Marie. 1991. "La mort d'un prédicat en ancien français." Toronto Working Papers in Linguistics, University of Toronto.
Bittner, Maria, and Ken Hale. 1993. "Ergativity: Towards a theory of a heteregeneous class." Ms. Rutgers and MIT.
Brecht, Richard D., and Catherine V. Chvany, eds. 1974. *Slavic transformational syntax.* Ann Arbor: Michigan Slavic Publications, University of Michigan.
Burzio, Luigi. 1986. *Italian syntax: A government and binding approach.* Dordrecht: Reidel.
Chomsky, Noam. 1981. *Lectures on government and binding.* Dordrecht: Foris.
——. 1986. *Knowledge of language.* New York: Praeger.
——. 1991. "Some notes on the economy of derivation and representation." In *Principles and parameters in comparative grammar*, ed. Robert Freidin, 417–454. Cambridge, Mass.: MIT Press.
——. 1993. "A minimalist program for linguistic theory." In *The view from Building 20: Essays in linguistics in honor of Sylvain Bromberger*, ed. Ken Hale and Samuel Jay Keyser, 1–52. Cambridge, Mass.: MIT Press.
Chomsky, Noam, and Howard Lasnik. 1993. "Principles and parameters theory." In *Syntax: An international handbook of contemporary research*, ed. J. Jacobs, A. von Stechow, W. Sternefeld, and T. Vennemann, 506–569. Berlin: Walter de Gruyter.
Comrie, Bernard. 1974. "The second dative: A transformational approach." In *Slavic transformational syntax*, ed. Richard D. Brecht and Catherine V. Chvany, 123–150. Ann Arbor: Michigan Slavic Publications, University of Michigan.
Dufresne, Monique, Fernande Dupuis, and Mireille Tremblay. 1995. "Expletives and change in French: A case in favor of a morphological approach to diachronic syntax." Ms. Université du Québec à Montréal, Montréal.
Dupuis, Fernande. 1989. "L'expression du sujet dans les subordonnées en ancien français." Doctoral diss., Université de Montréal.

Foulet, Lucien. 1963. *Petite syntaxe de l'ancien français*. Paris: Champion.

Gal, Roger. 1960. *Manuel de latin, liber primus*. Paris: Les Éditions O.C.D.L.

Guéron, Jacqueline. 1986. "Le verbe avoir." In *Recherches linguistiques de Vincennes* 14.

Lasnik, Howard. 1989. "Case and expletives." Ms. University of Connecticut, Storrs, Conn.

Lasnik, Howard, and Robert Friedin. 1981. "Core grammar, case theory, and markedness." In *Theory of markedness in generative grammar*, ed. A. Belletti et al. Pisa.

Moro, Andrea. 1990. "The raising of predicates: Copula, expletives and existence." Ms. Università di Venezia, Venice, Italy, and MIT, Cambridge, Mass.

Neidle, Carol. 1988. *The Role of Case in Russian Syntax*. Dordrecht: Kluwer.

Pollock, Jean-Yves. 1983. "On Case and impersonal constructions." In *Levels of Syntactic Representation*, ed. Robert May and Jan Koster. Dordrecht: Foris.

Ruwet, Nicolas. 1982. "Le datif épistémique en français et la condition d'opacité de Chomsky." In *Grammaire des insultes et autres études*. Paris: Seuil.

Stowell, Timothy. 1981. "Origins of phrase structure." Doctoral diss., MIT, Cambridge, Mass.

Safir, Ken. 1982. "Syntactic chains and the definiteness effect." Doctoral diss., MIT, Cambridge, Mass.

Tremblay, Mireille. 1991. "Possession and datives: Binary branching from the lexicon to syntax." Doctoral diss., McGill University, Montréal, Québec.

———. 1992. "Avoir ou être." *Revue québécoise de linguistique* 22/1:145–164.

Vergnaud, Jean-Roger. 1982. "Dépendances et niveaux de représentation en syntaxe." Doctoral diss., Université de Paris VII.

SIX

Argument Projection, Thematic Configurationality, and Case Theory

JEFFREY S. GRUBER
& CHRIS COLLINS

1. OBJECTIVES

The main objective of this chapter is to eliminate Theta-role assignment as an independent theoretic module determining correspondence between arguments in a syntactic structure and thematic roles in a structure apart from syntax, for example, in a Theta-grid (Stowell 1981), independent "argument structure" (Williams 1984), or autonomous conceptual or semantic structure (Jackendoff 1983, 1990; Gruber 1990, 1992a, b). Concomitantly, this entails the determination of the wide variety of primitive thematic relations configurationally, as well as the derivation of overt forms from them through the operation of principles of syntax. We will assume the general framework of Chomsky's (1993) Minimalist program, in which derivations are constrained by principles of economy and conditions on the syntactic interfaces, PF (Phonological Form) and LF (Logical Form).

Our objectives are in spirit similar to those put forth by Hale and Keyser (1993) in seeking a configurational Theta theory in which projection results from principles of syntax. We aim at overcoming a limitation in the basic syntactic configurations currently proposed in their model: the fact that they admit the projection of only two arguments.

In our account, overt argument projection is the movement of a noun phrase into a Case-marking position. The account thus gives indirect evidence for the theory of Case-assignment as movement into the specifier of an agreement phrase.

The theory will also provide a framework for capturing the difference between serializing and non-serializing languages, as well as the variation found among verb-serializing languages. On our account, all languages are serializing in underlying form. Differences between languages reduce to the stage in the derivation at which "conflation" of the serial form takes place.

The plan of our chapter is this. In section 2, the basic data that we will account for are described. In section 3, we explicate our syntactic approach to thematic structure. A detailed account of the conditions on argument projection based on this model is given in section 4. In section 5, its further justification is demonstrated by its natural description of serial verb constructions, providing an account of language variation in the syntax of complex events.

2. COMPLEX THEMATIC STRUCTURES

The meaning of a sentence may be commonly described as a relation among elementary events or situations. In the following sentence,

(1)   The stone knocked the ball into the road.

two events are related, meaning "the stone hit the ball, and the ball went into the road." These events are in a relation of consequence, with the first event resulting in the second.

Elementary events in turn may be described as consisting of elemental relations among event participants. In "the ball went into the road," *the ball* relates to *the road* as a figure relates to its location or ground (Talmy 1976). In this case, it is its final location. Participants so related are termed Theme and Goal respectively (Gruber 1965, 1976), and such relations are termed thematic relations or roles.

Thematic roles may be viewed as relations among variables, which when given values express elementary events or situations. Sets of thematic relations then constitute thematic functions (Jackendoff 1976, 1990). "The ball went into the road" is described by a "Motional" function expressing a change of position. This function consists of the thematic relations of Theme, Source, and Goal. Like Goal, Source relates to the Theme as its location, but its initial one. In the given sentence, Source is implicit, but may be explicit, as in *the yard* in "the ball went out of the yard into the road."

A Motional function may then be represented by the triple

(2)   *Motional function*: $< \Theta, \Sigma, \Gamma >$

where Θ, Σ, and Γ are thematic (Theta-) role variables for Theme, Source, and Goal, respectively. A two-variable function involving only the roles Theme and Location we may term a Locational function, as in:

(3)   The stone is in the yard.

in which *the stone* is Theme and *the yard* is Location. A Locational function therefore corresponds to the pair

(4)   *Locational function*: $<\Theta, \Lambda>$

in which Λ is a Theta-role variable for Location.

When a function is present, all its thematic roles are present, either implicitly or explicitly. Conversely, thematic roles cannot appear apart from their existence in thematic functions.[1]

The other elemental event in (1), "the stone hit the ball," is described by a Motional thematic function expressing coming into contact. Here *stone* is Theme, *ball* is Goal, and Source is implicit. The two functions are distinguished by semantic field or dimension, namely, Position and Contact, respectively. Thematic roles generalize over such dimensions, and many others. This phenomenon has been called "cross-field generalization" (Jackendoff 1976).

Sentence (1), then, expresses a relation of consequence between Contact and Positional thematic functions. This may be represented somewhat formally in the following "functional" notation. This notation is useful for providing a clear overall picture of complex thematic relationships:

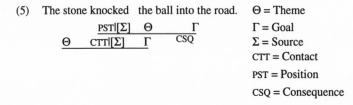

(5) The stone knocked the ball into the road.   Θ = Theme

           PST|[Σ] Θ   Γ   Γ = Goal

   Θ   CTT|[Σ] Γ   CSQ   Σ = Source

                              CTT = Contact

                              PST = Position

                              CSQ = Consequence

In representations such as (5), stemming from work with Ogwueleka (1987), horizontal lines represent Theta-functions, labeled with conceptual dimension, for example, PST (Positional) or CTT (Contact). Arguments are labeled with Theta-roles below them. Brackets indicate implicit Theta-roles. A vertical stroke identifies the category said to be "assigning" the Theta-roles of the function, namely, the head verb *"knocked"* in the example. In (5), both the Goal of the Contact function, Γ(CTT), and Theme of the Positional function, Θ(PST), may be said to be "assigned" or "linked" to *the ball*. We will refer to this as Γ; Θ colinking.

The relation of consequence between the functions is represented by placing one function above the other. The Contact function, describing the initial event in this relation, is termed the precedent function. The Positional function, describing the final or resulting event, is termed the consequent function. The precedent function is represented below the consequent one. (See Jackendoff [1990] for a comparable but distinct treatment.[2]) A conceptual dimension, Consequence CSQ, distinguishes the relation between functions here from other sorts of sequence.

On a deeper analysis, a Motional function would be a relation of temporal sequence between two Locational functions. Thus (6a) is equivalent to (6b) in which temporal sequence is represented in a way similar to consequence:

(6) a. The stone went out of the yard into the road.

          Θ PST| Σ   Γ

    b. The stone went out of the yard into the road.

          Θ PST| Λ (= Γ)

          Θ PST| Λ (= Σ)   TMP   TMP = Temporal

The "precedent" and "consequent" Locations Λ(PST)s are identified as Source Σ(PST) and Goal Γ(PST), respectively. This shows the essential relational or configurational nature of thematic roles.

Theta-roles are distinguished with respect to thematic function in these representations. However, the order in which they appear in the representation of each function is not significant and does not identify them. This relational aspect of Theta-roles is accomplished in a syntactic configurational representation. The functional representation (as in [6]) is nevertheless lucid in stating the Theta-structure of an utterance, and will in fact turn out to be more or less homomorphic with the configurational one we will propose. In the following, it will be used to exemplify generalizations in argument projection.

2.1. Direct Object Projection

Example (5), repeated below as (7a), differs from (7b) in that $\Theta; \Theta$ colinking occurs instead of $\Gamma; \Theta$ (notation of the dimension of Consequence is omitted for simplicity of presentation).

(7) a.   The stone knocked the ball into the road.

PST|[Σ]	Θ	Γ
Θ CTT|[Σ]	Γ	

   b.   The stone knocked against the wall into the road.

Θ PST|[Σ]	Γ
Θ CTT|[Σ] Γ	

Example (7b) means "the stone hit the wall and (the stone) went into the road." Examples (7a) and (b) express the same function types, namely, Motional <CTT> and <PST>. Also the same head word determining or assigning the roles of these functions occurs in each, namely, *knock*. They differ however in colinking. They also differ in syntactic form, namely, with direct object noun-phrase *the ball* versus prepositional-phrase complement, *against the wall*.

The two sentences are, in a sense, minimal pairs, contrasting syntactically and semantically. Switching the colinking patterns between them yields unacceptable correspondences of form and meaning:

(8) a.   *The stone knocked the wall into the road.

Θ STE|[Σ]	Γ
Θ CTT|[Σ] Γ	

      (* = The stone hit the wall and went into the road.)

   b.   *The stone knocked against the ball into the road.

STE|[Σ]	Θ	Γ
Θ CTT|[Σ] Γ		

      (* = The stone hit the ball and the ball went into the road.)

The generalizations needed to capture the distinctions in (7) and (8) are conditions on the assignment of a Theta-role to a direct object, involving the notions of "most consequent function" and "most consequent Theta-role," as follows:

(9)   *Internal θ-Role Projection Condition*
      A θ-role $\rho(\delta)$ of θ-function δ is projected as an NP complement (= object) of a head X^0 only if:
      A. The θ-function is the most consequent θ-function of the head X^0;
      B. The θ-role $\rho(\delta)$ is the most consequent θ-role of the complement NP.

A function of X^0 means a function specified in X'. In (7a), as in (7) and (8) generally, the most consequent Theta-function of the head *knocked* is <PST>. Since the most consequent Theta-role of the direct object *the ball* in (7a) is Θ(PST), A and B of (9) are satisfied. Hence the projection condition correctly describes the form-meaning correspondence in (7a) as acceptable.

On the other hand, the thematic structure in (8a) is unacceptable with a direct object. Here the most consequent role of the direct object *the wall* would be Γ(CTT). However the most consequent function of *knocked* is <PST>. Therefore Γ(CTT) cannot be the Theta-role projected as direct argument here, and the form-meaning correspondence in (8a) is unacceptable.

We can explain the sentences of (7, 8b) with prepositional phrase complements in *against* in terms of the internal projection condition in the following way. Consider the most consequent functions and roles within the PP. Prepositions such as *against* specify their object to bear a certain Theta-role assigned by the head verb, here Γ(CTT). Technically, we may assume the verb assigns the role to its prepositional-phrase complement. The preposition, assigning no role of its own, then transmits this role to its object. Hence, in (7b), Γ(CTT) is assigned to *the wall* by its head, the preposition *against*, and is its most consequent role. The most consequent function of the preposition is that of the Theta-role it specifies, namely, <CTT>. Hence in (7b) the projection conditions are satisfied within the prepositional phrase.

In (8b), however, Θ(CTT) is assigned, by hypothesis, to the prepositional phrase, and therefore transmitted to its object. Hence the most consequent role of *the ball* within the PP is Θ(PST). But the most consequent function of the preposition *against* is the specified function <CTT>, as before, and so *the ball* cannot be projected as Θ(PST). The form-meaning correspondence in (8b) is therefore not acceptable.

2.2. Inadequacy of a Minimal C-Command Condition

The internal projection condition is based on thematic structure. One may argue that a condition based on overt syntax is sufficient, such as one based on minimal c-command: a resultative predicate has as its subject the direct object if there is one, otherwise the subject is the subject of the sentence. However, note that the same conditions hold in the case of a complex thematic structure even when there is no overt resultative predicate. The paradigm with the verb *smash* in (10) parallels that with *knock*.

(10)   a.   The stone smashed the cup.
$$\text{STE} |[\Sigma, \Gamma] \quad \Theta$$
$$\Theta \quad \text{CTT} |[\Sigma] \quad \Gamma$$
   (= The stone hit the cup and the cup broke.)

   b.   The cup smashed   against the stone.
$$\Theta \quad \text{STE} |[\Sigma, \Gamma]$$
$$\Theta \quad \text{CTT} |[\Sigma] \quad \Gamma$$
   (= The cup hit the stone and [the cup] broke.)

(11)   a. *The cup smashed   the stone.

  Θ   STE|[Σ, Γ]
  Θ   CTT|[Σ]   Γ

  (* = The cup hit the stone and [the cup] broke.)

   b. *The stone smashed against the cup.

  STE|[Σ, Γ]   Θ
  Θ   CTT|[Σ]   Γ

  (* = The stone hit the cup and the cup broke.)

Here <CTT> and <STE> functions stand in a relation of consequence. Γ(STE) is implicit, but can be explicit, as in *apart* in "the stone smashed the cup apart." The projection conditions based on thematic structure apply whether a resultative predicate such as *apart* is overt or not.

Furthermore, secondary predicates of the subject are possible even when there is an overt direct object. Therefore a principle of minimal c-command is not sufficient, as we see in examples such as the following:

(12)   a. They evacuated the city into the countryside.

  STE|[Σ, Γ]   Θ
  Θ   PST| Σ   Γ

   b. Water   filled up the bucket from the tap.

  STE|[Σ]   Γ   Θ
  Θ PST| Γ   Σ

Example (12a) means "they went out of the city into the countryside <PST>, and the city became empty <STE>." The predicate *into the countryside* expressing Γ(PST) has as its "subject" *they* Θ(PST), despite the presence of the direct object *the city*. Here we understand "subject" of a secondary predicate as the argument projecting a Theta-role, especially the Theme, of the same function as the predicate. The most consequent role of *the city* is Θ(STE), so that the internal projection condition is satisfied.

Example (12b) means "the water went into the bucket out of the tap <PST>, and the bucket became full <STE>." Here the predicate *out of the tap* Σ(PST) has as its subject *the water* Θ(PST). The most consequent role of the direct object *the bucket* is, again, Θ(STE), and the projection condition is satisfied.

In the examples of (12), the secondary predicates in question do not project a role of the most consequent function. Therefore one may not view them as fully "resultative." Nevertheless, they are not depictive predicates. Therefore we conclude that examples such as (12) are counterexamples to a simple, minimal c-command condition.

Secondary predicates whose "subjects" are prepositional phrases are also possible, so that c-command is not even a necessary condition. Consider the following:

(13)   John   filled the tank half-full with gasoline/it out of the pump.

  STE|[Σ]   Θ   Γ
  PST| Γ   Θ   Σ
  Θ   CST|[Σ: = Θ]   Γ

Given this thematic structure, since Θ(PST) is not of the most consequent function in each, it cannot be projected as direct object. Θ(PST) is, however, projectable by a preposition so specified, namely, *with*, in (13). The secondary predicate expressing Σ(PST) of the same function has, accordingly, the expression of Θ(PST) as its "subject." These are subjects in the thematic sense, despite the absence of c-command. In fact, since the projection conditions determine that Θ(STE), of a function other than the most consequent one, will be projected by a preposition, a lack of c-command is predicted for such predicates.

The condition on direct object projection has the character of a principle of syntax involving a locality relation. The projection of a Theta-role as a direct complement of a verb only from its most consequent function suggests that this function is closer to the place of projection, for example, a structural Case-position, than others. The internal projection conditions then need to be explained in a configurational or syntactic model of thematic representation, as will be shown in sections 3 and 4.

2.3. Subject Projection

Another projection condition is involved in determining the subject Theta-role. The following sentences with *knock* have the thematic structures of (7), with either Γ; Θ or Θ; Θ colinkings. Although the thematic structures of these sentences also do not violate the internal projection conditions (9) of the previous section, they are nevertheless unacceptable:

(14)   a. *The ball   knocked   into the road with the stone.

$$\frac{\Theta \qquad \text{PST}|[\Sigma] \qquad \qquad \Gamma}{\Gamma \quad \text{CTT}|[\Sigma] \qquad \qquad \qquad \qquad \qquad \Theta}$$

(* = The stone hit the ball and the ball went into the road.)

b. *The wall knocked the stone into the road.

$$\frac{\text{PST}|[\Sigma] \qquad \Theta \qquad \qquad \Gamma}{\Gamma \quad \text{CTT}|[\Sigma] \qquad \quad \Theta}$$

(* = The stone hit the wall and [the stone] went into the road.)

c. *The road knocked the ball with the stone.

$$\frac{\Gamma \quad \text{PST}|[\Sigma] \quad \Theta}{\text{CTT}| \qquad \quad \Gamma \qquad \Theta}$$

(* = The stone hit the ball and the ball went into the road.)

d. *The road knocked the stone against the wall.

$$\frac{\Gamma \quad \text{PST}| \qquad \Theta}{\text{CTT}| \qquad \Theta \qquad \qquad \Gamma}$$

(* = The stone hit the wall and [the stone] went into the road.)

In (a, b), Goal of the precedent function is assigned to the subject position. In (c, d), Goal of the consequent function is so assigned. These sentences show that the most precedent role of the subject cannot be Goal.

Here a form of the so-called thematic hierarchy (Jackendoff 1976, 1990; Grimshaw 1990) seems to be at work determining the Theta-role of the subject. A condition based on the relation of precedence/consequence may be proposed:

(15)   *External Projection Condition*
        The Theme of the most precedent Theta-function is projected externally.

Condition (15) is an approximation[3] and is in a sense opposite to the internal projection condition (9), which refers to the most consequent Theta-function. The condition is plainly violated in (14a–d). In all previously given examples, Theme of the most precedent function appears as subject.

Example (13b) with *soak* satisfies the external projection condition by means of Θ(CTT) in the most precedent function assigned to the subject. Similarly, a verb such as *repel* satisfies the condition with a precedent function of the "Causational" dimension <CST>, denoting "affect," that is, contact of an abstract sort:

(16)   The vapor repelled the insects.   CST = Causational

$$\begin{array}{ccc} \Sigma & \text{PST}|[\Gamma] & \Theta \\ \hline \Theta & \text{CST}|[\Sigma] & \Gamma \end{array}$$

Thematic structure involving the Causational function should correspond to Jackendoff's (1990) "action tier." It seems that *do to/with* entails this precedent <CTT> or <CST> function, with $\Gamma; \Theta$ colinking to a consequent function, not necessarily agency:

(17)   a.   What did the sponge do to the water?
            — it soaked it up full.
       b.   What did the vapor do to the insects?
            — it repelled them.

As in the case of *soak* (13b) and *repel* (16), non-Theme roles may appear in the subject if they are not the most precedent role assigned there. This is a common occurrence among agentive verbs, in which Θ(CST) is the most precedent role assigned to subject, satisfying the projection condition.

(18)   John   took the   book from Bill.   PSS = Possessional

$$\begin{array}{ccc} \Gamma & \text{PSS}| & \Theta & \Sigma \\ \hline \Theta & \text{CST}|[\Sigma: = \Theta] & \Gamma \end{array}$$

Take assigns Goal of Possession to the subject in the most consequent function, but Θ(CST), namely, Agent, in the most precedent function.

3. CONFIGURATIONAL REPRESENTATION OF THEMATIC STRUCTURE

In its original conception a fundamental aim of the theory of thematic relations (Gruber 1965, 1976) was to achieve syntactic and semantic explanation on the basis of Theta-functions and Theta-roles determined entirely configurationally.[4] This distinguished thematic relations from the system of semantic roles of Fillmore (1968), for example. Thus, Theta-roles did not occur except as part of complete elemental Theta-functions, in which they were defined relationally. An attempt was made to distinguish Theta-roles configurationally in a "prelexical" structure (McCawley 1971). Conditions on lexical insertion led to syntactic form and its variation. The structural relation defining Theme and distinguishing it from Location, Source or Goal was a "subject" position, while Location, Source, and Goal corresponded to "complement" positions. Location was determined as a sole complement, while Source and Goal were determined as a complement pair, with Source distinguished from Goal by a (non-configurational) feature of negativity.

The idea of determining thematic roles in a syntactic structure finds expression today in certain hypotheses and frameworks. The Unaccusative Hypothesis (Perlmutter 1978, Burzio 1986), associates certain Themes with underlying, that is, D-structure, object positions. The Uniformity of Theta-role Assignment Hypothesis (UTAH, Baker, 1988) supposes that, in principle, all Theta-roles correspond to particular D-structure syntactic relations, although not all Theta-roles need be syntactically distinguished from one another. The lexical relational structure of Hale and Keyser (1993) employs configurations of Larson (1988), maintaining binary branching in "unambiguous paths" (Kayne 1984). In this framework, a VP at the lexical relational level encodes a predication between specifier and complement. A minimal predication in our terms is the elemental relation of Theme and Locational role (for example, Location, Source, or Goal), that is, an elemental Theta-function.

Thus simple thematic configurations can, in part, be represented as in the example that follows, in which Theta-role labels are mnemonic only:

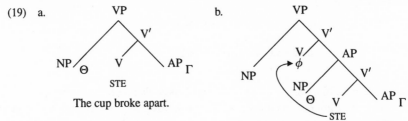

(19) a. VP ... The cup broke apart.   b. VP ... John/the stone broke the cup apart.

In (19a) the VP specifies Theta-roles, representing an elemental thematic predication. Example (19b) is a VP shell (Larson 1988), in which the lower VP specifies Theta-roles. The head of the upper VP is a null, "light" verb, canonically entailing causation or agency, said to "implicate" the thematic predication of the lower VP. Conflation between the verbs is necessary, the lower incorporating into the upper.

In a fully configurational theory of thematic relations, all Theta-roles are distinctively represented syntactically. The VP shell permits the distinct relational representation of only two Theta-roles in the lower thematic VP, generally the Theme and a Locational role. Thus all distinctions of Theta-role within a single function, such as Theme, Location, Source and Goal, cannot be represented. Furthermore, there is no possibility of representing distinctions of Theta-roles among different functions. Hence, none of the generalizations discussed in the previous section, which crucially depend on the representation of multi-functional thematic structures, can be described.

For example, except in the case of unaccusatives, whatever Theta-role is assigned to subject cannot be represented. In addition, other roles, such as Source and Instrument, cannot be represented along with the Theme and Goal. Yet these roles cannot be regarded as adjuncts. So-called Instrument is Theme of a nonmost consequent function, usually $\Theta(\text{CTT})$ or an intermediate $\Theta(\text{CST})$. Thus in the transitive use of "*knock*," $\Theta(\text{CTT})$ appears as subject, as in (7a) and (20a). In its causative form, $\Theta(\text{CTT})$ can appear as direct object (20b) or as an oblique Instrument (20c).

(20) a. The stone knocked the wall apart.

        STEI[Σ]   Θ   Γ

   Θ CTTI[Σ]   Γ

   b. John   knocked the stone against the wall.

        CTTI[Σ]   Θ   Γ

    Θ CSTI[Σ: = Θ] Γ

   c. John   knocked the wall apart with the stone.

          STEI[Σ]   Θ Γ

          CTTI[Σ]   Γ   Θ

      Θ CSTI[Σ: = Θ]   Γ

The fact that *the stone* appears as direct object in (20b) shows that Instrument cannot be an adjunct and must be thematic. But a simple VP shell cannot uniformly represent the three or four Theta-roles in (20b) and (20c). In particular, the thematic identity of *the stone* as Θ(CTT) among the three sentences cannot be structurally represented.

The intransitive use of *knock*, as in (7b) and (21a), as well as its causative counterpart (21b), is particularly problematic.

(21) a. The stone knocked apart against the wall.

       Θ   STEI[Σ] Γ

       Θ   CTTI[Σ]   Γ

   b. John knocked the stone apart against the wall.

        STEI[Σ]   Θ   Γ

     Σ   CTTI   Θ   Γ

    Θ CSTI[Σ: = Θ] Γ

In these examples, there are two Theta-functions, apart from that involved in agency (<CST>), with Θ; Θ colinking between them. The VP shell can accommodate only one such predication or function, however. Nor can the Theta-roles in this set be related systematically to those in (20).

3.1. X-bar Theory and Asymmetric Conjunction

An adequate configurational or syntactic model of thematic relations requires that structures have unambiguous thematic significance. As noted, the Hale and Keyser model can accommodate in this respect the simple thematic relation between Theme and Locational Theta-role. They assume, as also adopted by Chomsky (1993), that the head-complement relation has the fundamental significance of implicating some relationship. The NP in the specifier is connected to this relationship via predication. We may say then that the specifier and complement relate to each other as roles in an elemental predication or thematic function.

That is, we identify thematic roles in X-bar structure as in (22).

(22) *Thematic Roles*

Thematic labels within the X-bar structure are entirely mnemonic, as roles would be determined purely by the configuration. The head, V^0, contains the content of the conceptual dimension σ.

Thus a minimal base-generated VP has the significance of the simple Locational function of Theme and Location, as in (23).

(23)   The stone is in the yard

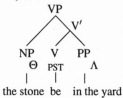

the stone be   in the yard

Let us then consider how relations of precedence/consequence or sequence may be represented. Such relations are overtly expressed by a form of conjunction:

(24)   a.   John went to the store and bought some cheese (there).
      b.   John took a stone and broke the window (with it).

These sentences are ambiguous, having either the sense of a conjunction of two unrelated events or events related by logical and/or temporal sequence. There is evidence to suppose that conjunction is asymmetric, framed on the X-bar pattern (Collins 1989), as in (25a), rather than symmetric, as in (25b), and that this X-bar structure has thematic significance when expressing event sequences.

(25)   a.   CjP (=S_0)   b. S_0

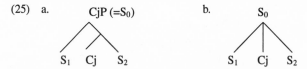

We assume that CjP (Conjunction Phrase), like conjunction, has the property of being in some respect categorially identical to its conjuncts, which must be similar in some way to each other.

Conjuncts expressing event sequences have the property that extraction is possible, at least from the second conjunct. This is evidence for the X-bar structure proposed for asymmetric conjunction, and, in the case of event sequences, that the head of CjP L-marks its "complement" conjunct, thereby permitting extraction (Chomsky 1986). That is, conjunction expressing event sequences has thematic significance:

(26)   a.   The cheese which John went to the store and bought.
      b.   The window which John took a stone and broke.

(27)   a.   ?The store to which John went and bought some cheese.
      b.   ?The stone which John took and broke the window.

This possibility disappears in the case of conjunction expressing separate events, where, presumably, the conjunction creates a barrier for extraction, since neither clause is L-marked:

(28)   a.   *The cake which John went to the store and bought from the church.

b. *The window which John took a stone and broke with a hammer.

In (28), the sense is that of unconnected events, and extraction is not possible.

3.2. Complex Thematic Relations

We propose the extension to the Hale and Keyser model of admitting asymmetric conjunction between VPs, and that this is configurationally identified with the notions of sequence and consequence within complex predicates.

Suppose the head of CjP conjoining VPs can specify a conceptual dimension of consequential distance (CSQ), determining a relation of consequence between subevents. These subevents, corresponding to thematic functions, would constitute a complex event, corresponding to a complex thematic structure. A configurational thematic representation for a complex structure such as that of (21a) would then be as in (29) (X' nodes will generally not be labeled).

(29)   The stone knocked the wall apart.

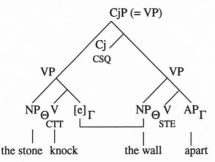

Example (29) represents a complex thematic structure involving <CTT> and <STE> functions in a relation of consequence. VP in the specifier of Cj-CSQ represents the precedent function, while VP in its complement represents the consequent function. Note that CjP with VPs in both specifier and complement is itself categorially VP. Thematic labels of role and conceptual dimension are mnemonic, although the distinction between Locational roles is ignored. Heads without lexical item are presumed to be phonologically null, but lexical and specified with conceptual dimension.

"Colinked" thematic positions are indicated by "⌊...⌋." When coreferential Θ-positions are ultimately represented by a single argument, that is, colinked, we will hypothesize that one of them is null [e]. Material support for this supposition is given in section 4.3. In this case, we presume, in accordance with the object projection conditions, it is the relatively consequent one that is projected as object, while the other is null.

The structure must be subject to "conflation" or incorporation into a single, or at least fewer, verbal heads. This matter will be considered in the next section, 3.3, and also in the context of serial verbs in section 5.

Now consider along these lines a possible, perhaps partial, representation of the causative/agentive use of *knock* involving Instrument. Example (20c) would be as in (30).

(30)   John knocked the wall apart with the stone.

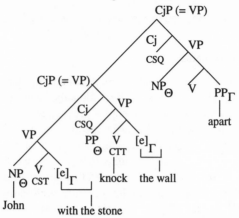

Between this causative structure and in the noncausative (29), the UTAH is directly satisfied: thematic roles and thematic functions correspond to particular syntactic positions. Further, a range of Theta-roles are simply represented, so that, as hypothesized, all thematic distinctions correspond to syntactic ones.

3.3. Head-incorporation

As shown in Hale and Keyser (1993), the derivation of surface form in English involves conflation or incorporation of verbal heads. We surmise that this is driven by a universal requirement that incorporation of verbal heads under a single clausal tense phrase, TP, is obligatory at LF. All such verbal heads must incorporate in order to check a tense feature.

In example (34), the CTT head must incorporate into the STE and CSQ heads. We assume the CTT head to be non-null, while the others are null, since the <CTT> function is specified by *knock* in its lexical sense.[5] Unlike the Hale-Keyser model, however, we require this incorporation to include the possibility of movement out of a specifier into the head. This seems to violate the Head Movement Constraint, said to derive from the Empty Category Principle, whereby the trace of movement must be properly governed (cf. Chomsky 1981, Travis 1984, Baker 1988): a head may move only out of a complement into the head that governs it.

Pesetsky (1991) argues that head movement out of specifiers must be allowed just in case movement into the head from a complement position has previously taken place. This is necessary for connectedness in Chains that license parasitic gaps, and to account for such paradigms of compound formation as in (31).

(31)   a.   shooting of deer
        b.   deer-shooting
        c.   *hunter-shooting (of deer)   (* = hunters shoot (deer))
        d.   hunter-[deer-shooting]   (= hunters shoot deer)

Incorporation of the subject, that is, the head of the specifier, is permitted just in case incorporation of the object, that is, the head of the complement, has taken place. This is illustrated in (32).

(32)   a.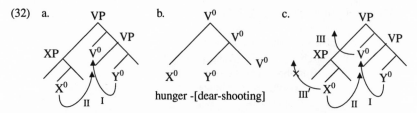

hunger -[dear-shooting]

The head V^0 must semantically compose with its complement head Y^0 (I), before composing with its specifier head X^0 (II), as in (32a). Given, then, that conflation must accord with semantic composition, the resultant derived form is thus (32b) exemplified by (32c). The N-head of the specifier, for example, the subject in (31), can incorporate into the V (I in [32a]) if the N-head of the complement does (II), producing a structure as in (32b). The composite V-head may then move across Spec VP (III in [32c]).

Note that this order implies that raising out of a specifier to a higher V^0, as in step III' of (32c), crucially does not occur. For example, a raised object cannot be incorporated into the higher verb, although thematic objects in the presence of complements can:

(33)   a.   *peace-predicting to come (* = predicting peace to come)
       b.   child-coaxing to eat vegetables

Similarly, in CjP, the V-head of the complement VP moves to Cj, then the V-head of the specifier VP. Only thereafter does the composite Cj-head move across Spec CjP. The order is crucially not directly from the head of the specifier to a head outside CjP. As will be explained in section 4.1, this order of head movement derivationally determines minimality domains in which XP-movement is possible, in the sense of Chomsky (1993), producing the asymmetries in subject and object projection conditions.

Incorporation proceeds accordingly in (34). The null V-STE head incorporates into Cj-CSQ, with which the non-null V-CTT head is then able to incorporate, producing the compound head:

(34)   [[CTT:knock]$_V$ [[STE:*null*]$_V$ [CSQ:*null*]$_{Cj}$]$_{Cj}$]$_{Cj}$

Although not morphologically evident in English single-verb heads, in which all but one head is null, conflation of verbal elements is clear in languages with compound verb constructions, where two or more heads are non-null. In Igbo, for example, (20a) would be rendered as in the example that follows, in which CTT and STE verbal heads are visibly merged:

(35)   ùkwúte kù-jì-rì   ája.   (Igbo) [JSG]
       stone   hit-break-AFF wall
       "The stone smashed the wall."

In a serial verb construction, on the other hand, CTT and STE verbal heads remain unconflated at S-structure, or before Spell-out in Chomsky's (1993) Minimalist terms. In such a construction in Yoruba the equivalent of (20a) would then be as in (36a).

(36) a. i. òkúta gbá ògiri fọ́.   (Yoruba) [JSG]
          stone hit wall break
          "The stone smashed the wall."
      ii. gbi-gbá-fọ́   ni òkúta gbá ògiri fọ́.
          NOM-hit-break FOC stone hit wall break
          "It was hitting and breaking that the stone did to the wall."
   b. i. ó   gbá òkúta mu   ògiri.
          3Sg hit stone go-against wall
          "He hit the stone against the wall."
      ii. *mu   ògiri ni ó   gbá òkúta.
          go.against wall FOC 3Sg hit stone
          (* = It was against the wall that he hit the stone.)
   c.   ó   bà kèkéè-mi   jẹ́.   (Abraham 1958)
          3Sg spoil bicycle-1Sg [spoil]
          S/he spoiled my bicycle.

Nevertheless, incorporation at LF must occur in the case of serial verbs. This is materially supported by the possible appearance of deverbal compound nominals in predicate clefting over serial verb constructions in Yoruba, as in (36a). Finally, further evidence of LF serial verb incorporation appears in the phenomenon of "splitting verbs" (Awoboluyi 1978), as in (36c). These consist of elements with no independent significance: *bà-jẹ́*, "spoil," must be interpreted as a lexical unit. It must therefore be a conflated form at LF. Indeed, that a serial verb construction is conflated at LF accords with its sense as a single event, not different in sense from a single- or compound-verb construction, and that single-eventedness is associated with incorporation into a single tense-operator.

The parameter determining incorporation or non-incorporation at S-structure, supposing it obligatory at LF, is considered further in section 5.

4. CONFIGURATIONAL ACCOUNT OF PROJECTION CONDITIONS

4.1. XP-movement and Minimal Domains

Part A of the internal projection condition for direct objects (9) requires that they be projected only from the most consequent function. The external projection condition for subjects (15) requires that they be projected only from the theme position of the most precedent function. Given the configurational representation of consequence above, these conditions now follow straightforwardly from the theory of case assignment as movement to the specifier position of an agreement phrase (AgrP) (Chomsky 1991).

Suppose AgrOP, in which structural Case is assigned to direct objects is outside the asymmetric conjunction complex. That is, the relevant AgrOP is associated with CjP, not with the individual VPs. This accords with categorial identity of CjP conjoining VPs as a VP. We also assume that AgrSP, in which structural Case may be assigned to subjects, is associated with the tense phrase TP (Chomsky 1991). The relevant structure of (20a) would then be as in (37).

(37)   The stone knocked the wall apart.

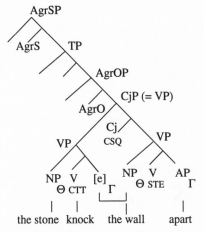

Direct object and subject projection requires movement of an NP into some Spec AgrP, either overtly, or covertly at LF. This requires movement to a position outside CjP. It is evident that this is possible only from an NP in the most consequent function (an object) or from the position of Theme in the most precedent one (a subject). This follows the conception that filled specifier positions present minimality barriers to movement, and that these are obviated by head-movement, the path of which is crucial.

On the basis of principles of Relativized Minimality (Rizzi 1990) and Chomsky's (1993) Minimalist program, a filled specifier blocks XP-movement across it because it is a potentially closer target. In addition Chomsky (1993) postulates the following "minimal link" condition:

(38)   Distances to positions within the same minimal domain are equivalent.

Head-movement thus creates a head-Chain with an extended minimal domain, which may include both a filled specifier position and an empty one beyond it. Since these positions are then equidistant targets of movement, such head movement obviates the "barrier" of the filled position.

4.2. Projection of Objects and Subjects

Consider first movement from the Theme position in the most consequent function, represented by VP-STE in (56). The filled Spec CjP, namely, VP-CTT, blocks movement of the NP Θ(STE) to Spec AgrOP. However, head movement occurs, covertly in English at LF, creating the head-Chain [[AgrO Cj], [Cj]$_t$], whose minimal domain includes both Spec-CjP and Spec-AgrOP. Movement of NP Θ(STE) in Spec VP-STE to Spec AgrOP is now permitted, there being no shorter potential target. The NP Θ(STE), we may say, is then projectable as object from the most consequent function represented by VP-STE. Similarly, a Goal in the most consequent function should also be projectable, but requiring possibilities not elaborated here.[6]

Consider now projection from the Theme position of the most precedent function, namely, the subject. This is the position of Spec VP-CTT in (37). Nothing presents itself as a minimality barrier to its movement to Spec AgrSP. We assume that AgrO (or TP) L-marks CjP = VP, and, recursively, its VP specifier. (See Chomsky 1986a on the L-marking of specifiers.) Hence, movement out of the VP specifier is not in principle prevented. Therefore Theme of the most precedent function may move to Spec AgrSP to receive Case and be projected as subject.

The Theme, that is, specifier position of the VP representing the most precedent function, is homologous to that of a VP-internal subject (Kuroda 1985) in a single VP or VP-shell model. An NP in the VP representing the most consequent function is in the position of an internal complement NP. The former moves to Spec AgrSP to get Case, while the latter moves to Spec AgrOP, and not vice versa. In the model presented here, this follows for the same reasons given by Chomsky (1992) for the VP shell. Should the VP-internal subject, namely, the Theme of the most precedent function, move to Spec AgrOP, this filled position, as a potential closer target, will block movement of the complement NP to Spec AgrSP. Consequently, the Theme position of the VP representing the most precedent function will be projected as subject, while an NP of the most consequent function will be projected as object. Thus derivation proceeds as in (39a).

(39)   a.   The stone knocked the wall apart.

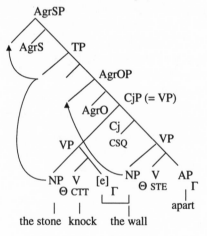

(39)   b.   The stone knocked apart against the wall.

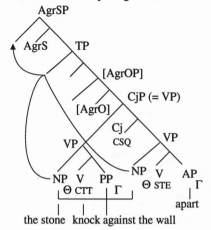

Similarly, projection in an unaccusative form consists of the licit movement of both colinked Themes "across the board," to Spec AgrSP, disregarding (inactive) AgrOP, as in (39b). Projection, and hence movement out of CjP from other positions, must be prevented however. In (37/39) consider the position of Γ(CTT) in the precedent function, which can be projected neither as object nor subject. See examples such as (8a) and (14a, b). The filled specifier NP Θ(CTT) blocks movement as a potential closer target. This minimality barrier would be obviated if there could be head-movement across it, creating the Chain [[AgrOP V-CTT], [V-CTT]ₜ]. However, this movement is impossible. Crucially, as discussed, the path of incorporation must be V-CTT to Cj to AgrO/T. Thus XP-movement can cross the specifier (VP) of CjP from the complement (consequent function), but cannot cross the specifier (NP) of the specifier of CjP (precedent function). Hence a role of the precedent function cannot be projected as object (8a), nor can a precedent Goal be projected as subject (14b), as shown in (40a, b).

(40)   a.   *The stone knocked the wall apart.
             (* = The stone hit the wall and the stone broke.)

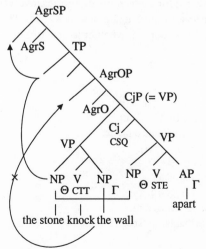

(40)   b.   *The wall knocked the stone apart.
         (* = The stone hit the wall and the stone broke.)

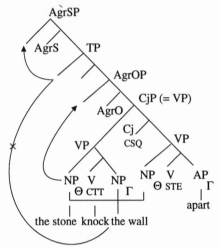

Such illicit head-movement would be required to project from any position in the configurations presented other than one in the VP representing the most consequent function or the Theme of the most precedent function. This, then, derives Part A of the condition on the projection of direct objects and the condition on the projection of subjects in complex thematic structures from syntactic principles applied in a configurational thematic representation.

5. SERIAL VERBS

5.1. Colinking and Null Representation of Arguments

As we have noted, colinking is mediated by empty categories. That is, among thematically colinked elements, all but one is a null category. Our configurational thematic representation requires the presence of such empty categories.

Collins (1993) gives evidence for such empty categories involved in colinking in Ewe serial verb constructions, through examples such (41). The clitic *yi* (CL) doubles XPs not structurally Case-marked, whether lexical or null.

(41)   a.   i.   Kofi fo Yao (*yi).   (Ewe: Collins 1992)
                  K.   hit Y. CL
                  "Kofi hit Yao."
            ii. Kofi kpa   ati-e[7]   tati   (yi).
                  K.   carved stick-DEF pestle CL
                  "Kofi carved the stick into a pestle."
            iii. Kofi zo   fie-to   (yi).
                  K.   walked king-like CL
                  "Kofi walked king-like."
        b.   Fie-to$_i$ e   wo zo [t$_i$] (yi).
                  king-like FOC he walked CL
                  "It is king-like that he walked."

c.   me nya   qdevi-e$_i$ [e$_i$] dzo   (yi).
     I   chased child-DEF   leave CL
                    [Θ$_i$] PST|[Σ, Γ]
     Θ APL|[Σ]   Γ$_i$
     "I chased the child away."

Example (41a) shows the use of *yi* as a clitic pronoun (CL) doubling an overt NP. It is not usable in (41a.i), in which the direct object has accusative case, but may appear in (41a.ii) and (41a.iii), in which a resultative nominal complement does not require structural Case. Example (41b) shows that *yi* can mark a trace [t$_i$] of A-bar movement of the focused NP *fie-to*, "king-like"; that is, it can mark an empty category. Example (41c) shows a serial verb with a partial representation of its thematic structure, in which colinking is indicated by coindexing of coreferential Theta-roles. *Yi* in (41c) doubles the empty category [e$_i$] Theme of *dzo*, "leave," "colinked" — that is, coreferential with — the lexical NP *devi-e*, "the child," object of *nya*, "chase."

5.2. The Serial Verb "Parameter"

From the standpoint of the syntactic structure we have developed for complex thematic relations, the salient fact about serial verbs is that they represent this structure in a relatively unconflated form. We have postulated that incorporation of the heads of asymmetrically conjoined thematic VPs is obligatory at LF. That is, incorporation of verbal heads under a single clausal T is necessary to check the tense features of the verbs.

Chomsky (1993) proposes that operations at LF are less costly than in overt syntax, before S-structure, that is, Spell-out. Given that derivations proceed in the most economical way, conflation, that is, head incorporation, will wait to LF unless forced. The serial-verb versus single-head parameter then amounts to conditions under which verbal incorporation may and must occur before Spell-out.

Thus we postulate the following parameters of language variation, distinguishing languages that have serial verb constructions (SVCs) from those that do not:

(42)   *SVC Languages:*   Verbs incorporate into TMP at LF.
       Non-SVC Languages: Verbs incorporate into TMP/CSQ before Spell-out.

Igbo represents a mixed case. As already mentioned, some thematic structures discussed earlier in serial form appear as compounds in Igbo, repeated in (43) in functional representation.

(43)   a.   Ùkwúte kù̀-jì-rì   ája.   (Igbo [JSG])
            stone   hit-break-AFF wall
                    STE|[Σ, Γ]   Θ
            Θ   CTT|[Σ]   Γ CSQ
            "The stone smashed the wall."

    b.   Òkúta gbá ògiri   f<u>ó</u>   (Yoruba [JSG])

         stone hit wall   break

                [Θ]   STE|[Σ, Γ]

       Θ CTT|[Σ] Γ CSQ

       "The stone hit the wall and the wall broke."

The types in (44), however, are serial in both Igbo and Yoruba:

  (44) a. O jì   mmà bhá-a   jí.   (Déchaine 1991)

         3Sg hold knife peel-ASP yam

                 STE|[Σ, Γ] Θ

         [Θ]   CTT|[Σ]   Γ TMP

         A CTT| Θ   A = Accompaniment

         Θ CST| Γ

         "S/he peeled yam with a knife."

    b. Ngozi sì   Enugu gá   Lagos.   (Uyanne 1990)

         N. go.from E.   go.to L.

         Θ   PST| Γ

         Θ   PST| Σ TMP

         "Ngozi went from Enugu to Lagos."

    c. Adha si-ri   an<u>u</u>   ri-e.   (Peter Ihionu, p.c.)

         A.   cook-AFF meat eat-ASP

         Γ   [Θ] CMP|[Σ]

         STE|[Σ, Γ]   Θ TMP   CMP = Compositional

         Θ CST|[Σ]   Γ

         "Ada cooked meat and ate it."

As the lexical item *jì*, "hold," suggests, Instrument here includes an Accompaniment role A(CTT) assigned to subject. Besides Instrument, expressions of Accompaniment and of Source appear as serial verb constructions in Igbo (44b). Source, as already noted, and Accompaniment are both expressions of Locational relations involved in Motional functions, and are related to each other by thematic asymmetric conjunction of a Temporal dimension. In (44c), a serial verb construction exhibiting characteristic "object-sharing," expresses a single event comprising a sequence of subevents. These also are related to each other by temporal sequence rather than consequence, and hence asymmetric conjunction of a Temporal dimension.

    Expressions that are serial in Igbo appear, then, to be those involving asymmetric conjunction of the Temporal dimension TMP, in contrast to those that involve consequence CSQ, which become compound. We can describe this in the following way:

  (45) *Igbo SVCs*:
      Incorporation of verbs into CSQ occurs before Spell-out.
      Incorporation of verbs into TMP occurs at LF.

Thus our configurational account of thematic structure and argument projection provides a direct basis for an account of language variation in the forms in which thematic heads may appear: single-headed, compound, or serial verb.

    In sum, we have shown that a configurational Theta theory is possible in which the range of thematic relations can be represented, while the projection of thematic heads and arguments results from principles of syntactic derivation. The theory involves the minimalist conception of X^0-incorporation and XP-movement to satisfy morphological properties at the interfaces (tense features and Case), thus accounting for thematic head patterns and argument projection conditions. It necessitates the elaboration of VP-shell representation of thematic structure by asymmetric conjunction, and the colinking of Theta-roles between subevents by the mediation of empty categories.

NOTES

The work of Jeffrey S. Gruber was supported by the Social Sciences and Humanities Research Council of Canada grant no. 411-92-0012: "La Modularité de la Grammaire: Arguments, Projections, et Variations" and Fonds Institutionnel de Recherche (Université du Québec à Montréal) to Anna-Maria Di Sciullo.

1. The Theta-functional nature of roles of Accompaniment (e.g., "along with ... ") and Path (e.g., "across ... ") will not be considered in this chapter.

2. The relation of consequence in cases such as this appear to be represented in Jackendoff (1990) as one of modification: the consequent event is modified by a *by*-function whose argument is another event. Events (and states) are represented as two-argument thematic functions, in which the first argument may generally be identified as Theme. On the other hand, a tier structure is used in Jackendoff to represent the relation between what he distinguishes as the thematic part of the event and the "action tier" involving Agent and Patient. An action tier is associated with every thematic tier in the structure of an event, a distinct conception worthy of scrutiny. It appears, however, that the relation between the action tier and the thematic tier may also be described as one of consequence. Moreover, in Jackendoff, a rather large variety of one- and two-argument thematic functions are distinguished categorially. From the standpoint of our program, since thematic functions comprise sets of Theta-roles defined relationally, such functions themselves need ultimately to be distinguished only configurationally, apart from distinctions of conceptual dimension.

3. The condition stated here is appropriate for the level of detail of event-structure discussed in this chapter, which seeks to present the basis for a theory of thematic configurationality. The condition only applies in the domain of resultative structures involving Theme and Goal, which is the extent of the detail in the configurational representations in section 4 demonstrating the projection conditions here. Looking further, however, Source, but not Goal, is also projectable as subject from the most precedent function., the role of Agent being a prime example. Moreover, any precedent role colinked with a consequent Theme can be projected as subject under certain aspectual conditions (e.g., *fill with/empty of*). Also, verbs expressing simple non-resultative Locational or Motional thematic structures, such as *contain* and *own*, with Location as subject; *drop* and *lose* with a Source subject; or *acquire*, with an apparent Goal subject, exhibit other asymmetries. An account of these facts requiring a more complete representation of event structure is the focus of Gruber (1994) and chapter 7 in this volume.

4. Thematic roles are to a certain extent represented configurationally in the conceptual structure of Jackendoff (1990). Conceptual structure, however, is autonomous of grammatical syntax, with which it presumably interfaces at LF. The aim of our program here is to explore not only the configurational nature of thematic structure, but also to represent it in grammatical syntax. Its correspondence with elements in a conceptual structure at LF will therefore be that much more direct.

5. But this is inessential. The verb *break* would specify an STE head, so that substituting *break* for *knock* in (34) would have the consequent head as lexical and the precedent one as null. Similarly, see the instances of compound and serial verb constructions below, in which both heads are lexical.

6. Projection from the Goal- or other Locational-role position of the most consequent function, including that in the derivation of double-object constructions, is possible, although probably under marked conditions of some sort.

7. We adopt the convention of Yoruba and Igbo here in representing the Advanced Tongue Root (ATR) feature with an underdot or underscore: *o̱, e̱*.

REFERENCES

Abraham, R.C. 1958. *Dictionary of modern Yoruba*. London: University of London Press.

Awoboluyi, Oladele. 1978. *Essentials of Yoruba grammar*. Ibadan, Nigeria: Oxford University Press.

Baker, Mark C. 1988. *Incorporation: A theory of grammatical function changing*. Chicago: University of Chicago Press.

———. 1989. "Object sharing and projection in serial verb constructions." *Linguistic Inquiry* 20:513–533.

Burzio, Luigi. 1986. *Italian syntax*. Dordrecht: Reidel.

Chomsky, Noam. 1972. *Studies on semantics in generative grammar*. The Hague: Mouton.

———. 1981. *Lectures on government and binding*. Dordrecht: Foris.

———. 1986a. *Barriers*. Cambridge, Mass.: MIT Press.

———. 1986b. *Knowledge of language: Its nature, origin, and use*. New York: Praeger.

———. 1991. "Some notes on economy of derivation and representation." In *Principles and parameters in comparative grammar*, ed. R. Freiden. Cambridge, Mass.: MIT Press.

———. 1993. "A minimalist program for linguistic theory." In *The view from Building 20: Essays in linguistics in honor of Sylvain Bromberger*, ed. Kenneth Hale and Samuel Jay Keyser. Cambridge, Mass.: MIT Press.

Collins, Chris. 1989. "Conjunction adverbs." Ms. MIT, Cambridge, Mass.

———. 1992. "Case in Ewe and Yoruba." *Proceedings of the Kwa Comparative Syntax Workshop*, MIT, 1992, *MIT Working papers in linguistics* 17:53–70. Department of Linguistics and Philosophy, MIT, Cambridge, Mass.

———. 1993a. "Topics in Ewe syntax." Doctoral diss., MIT, Cambridge, Mass.

Déchaine, R. 1991. "Serial verb constructions." Ms. University of Massachusetts, Amherst, Mass.

Fillmore, Charles. 1968. "The case for case.' In *Universals of linguistic theory*, ed. Emmon Bach and Robert T. Harms. New York: Holt, Rinehart and Winston.

Fodor, Jerry A. 1970. "Three reasons for not deriving 'kill' from 'cause to die.' " *Linguistic Inquiry* 1:429–438.

Giorgi, Alessandra, and F. Pianesi. 1991. "Toward a syntax of temporal representation." *Probus* 3.2:1–27.

Grimshaw, Jane. 1990. *Argument structure*. Cambridge, Mass: MIT Press..

Gruber, Jeffrey S. 1965. "Studies in lexical relations." Doctoral diss., MIT, Cambridge, Mass. In *Lexical structures in syntax and semantics*, Part I, Amsterdam: North-Holland, 1976; and *MIT Working Papers in Linguistics*, Department of Linguistics and Philosophy, MIT, Cambridge, Mass.

———. 1990. "Complex Θ-structures." Ms. MIT Lexicon Project seminar, October, MIT, Cambridge, Mass.

———. 1992a. "Proper argument projection in Igbo and Yoruba." *Proceedings of the Kwa Comparative Syntax Workshop*, January, 1992, *MIT working papers in linguistics* 17, Department of Linguistics and Philosophy, MIT, Cambridge, Mass.

———. 1992b. "Thematic configurational constraints in serial verb constructions." Presented at the 23rd Annual Conference on African Linguistics, University of Michigan, Ann Arbor.

———. 1994. "Principles of a configurational Θ-theory. In *A festschrift for Dong-Whee Yang: Explorations in generative grammar*, 69–111. Kookmin University, Seoul, Korea.

Hale, Kenneth, and Samuel J. Keyser. 1993. On argument structure and the lexical expression of syntactic relations. In *The view from Building 20*, ed. Kenneth Hale and Samuel Jay Keyser, 1–52. Cambridge, Mass.: MIT Press.

Jackendoff, Ray. 1972. *Semantic interpretation in generative grammar*. MIT Press, Cambridge, Mass.

———. 1976. "Toward an explanatory semantic representation." *Linguistic Inquiry* 7:89–150.

———. 1983. *Semantics and cognition*. Cambridge, Mass.: MIT Press.

———. 1990. *Semantic structures*. Cambridge, Mass.: MIT Press.

Kayne, Richard S. 1984. "Unambiguous paths." In *Connectedness and binary branching, Studies in generative grammar* 16. Dordrecht: Foris.

Kuroda, S.-Y. 1985. "Whether you agree or not: Rough ideas about the comparative grammar of English and Japanese." Ms. UCSD.

Larson, Richard. 1988. "On the double object construction." *Linguistic Inquiry* 19:335–391.

Li, Yafei. 1990. "On X^0-binding and verb incorporation." *Linguistic Inquiry* 21:399–426.

McCawley, James. 1971. "Prelexical syntax." In *Linguistic developments of the Sixties — Viewpoints for the Seventies*. Monograph Series on Languages and Linguistics 24, ed. R. O'Brian, 19–33. Georgetown University.

Ogwueleka, O. Samuel. 1987. "Thematic roles and syntactic processes in Igbo." Doctoral diss., Obafemi Owolowo University, Ile-Ife, Nigeria.

Perlmutter, David. 1978. "Impersonal passive and the unaccusative hypothesis." *Proceedings of the Berkeley Linguistic Society*, ed. J. Jaeger et al., 4:157–189.

Pesetsky, David. 1995. *Zero syntax*. Cambridge, Mass.: MIT Press.

Pinker, Steven. 1989. *Learnability and cognition: The acquisition of argument structure*. Cambridge, Mass.: MIT Press.

Pollock, Jean-Yves. 1989. "Verb movement, universal grammar, and the structure of IP." *Linguistic Inquiry* 20:365–424.

Poletto, Cecilia. 1991. "The aspect projection: An analysis of the 'passé surcomposé.'" Ms. Università di Padova, Padova, Italy.

Rizzi, Luigi. 1990. *Relativized minimality*. Cambridge, Mass.: MIT Press.

Stowell, Tim. 1980. "Origins of phrase structure." Doctoral diss., MIT, Cambridge, Mass.

Talmy, Leonard. 1976. "Semantic causative types." In *Syntax and semantics*, vol. 6: *The grammar of causative constructions*, ed. M. Shibatani, 57–149. Cambridge, UK: Cambridge University Press.

———. 1978. "Figure and ground in complex sentences." In *Universals of human language: Syntax* (vol. 4), ed. J. Greenberg. Stanford, Calif.: Stanford University Press.

Tenny, Carol. 1989. "The aspectual interface hypothesis." *Lexicon Project working papers* 31, Center for Cognitive Sciences, MIT, Cambridge, Mass.

Travis, Lisa. 1984. "Parameters and effects of word order." Doctoral diss., MIT, Cambridge, Mass.

Uyanne, C. Grace. 1990. "Constraints on semantic relations/syntactic structure in Igbo SVCs." B.S. Thesis, University of Benin, Benin City, Nigeria.

Williams, Edwin. 1984. Grammatical relations. *Linguistics Inquiry* 15:639–674.

SEVEN

Modularity in a Configurational Theta Theory

JEFFREY S. GRUBER

1. SIGNIFICANCE

1.1. Thematic Configurationality

The event structures expressed by sentences consist of relations among subevents and their participant roles, called thematic roles or relations. We will say that a theory of the thematic structure of sentences is strictly configurational if every thematic role distinction is represented by a configurationally distinct position in this structure. Strict Thematic Configurationality therefore implies an isomorphism between thematic relations and equivalence classes of positions in syntactic structures.[1] Thus, given this principle, thematic or event-structural aspects of semantics must be purely syntactic. More specifically, meaning or interpretation in respect to these aspects must be a function of category type (functional properties) and configuration (purely formal structural/syntactic relations) only. There can be no representation of thematic relations as substantive categories or features. The syntactic forms representing thematic structure may or may not be identified with those of a component of grammatical syntax. However, a minimalist conception of Strict Thematic Configurationality would seem to require that they are: that there is no autonomous system of thematic relations apart from grammatical syntax.

Strict Thematic Configurationality in grammatical syntax constitutes the general conceptual underpinnings of the theory of thematic relations in Gruber (1965, 1976). As shown in Gruber and Collins (chapter 6 in this volume), the minimalist program of Chomsky (1989, 1993) now appears to provide means for the significant attainment of such a theory. In the framework of this program, utterances are the result of optimal derivations to obtain objects interpretable at the interfaces.

155

Thematic configurationality in this context means that interpretability depends on interaction between the proper discharge of the functional properties of categories and the basic (thematically interpreted) configurations in which they appear.

The principle of Strict Thematic Configurationality relates to both grammatical syntax and semantics. In grammatical syntax, the Uniformity of Theta Assignment Hypothesis (UTAH) (Baker 1988), is less strong than Strict Thematic Configurationality. This principle implies that similar syntactic structures are subject to uniform thematic interpretation. Under the UTAH, it is therefore possible for certain thematic distinctions to form an equivalence class by which they have indistinguishable configurational representation in syntax. For example, Source and Goal may have the same configurational representations, being distinguished by substantive semantic content or feature. The work of Hale and Keyser (1993) in principle seeks thematic configurationality, at least to the degree of the UTAH, but, due to limitations in the VP shell analysis they adopt, allows such many-to-one thematic-syntactic correspondences. This means that certain thematic relations must be regarded as essentially substantive or represented in a conceptual structure apart from syntax. In respect to the principle of Strict Thematic Configurationality, such syntactic analyses are insufficiently semantic, in the sense that there is less than complete interpretability of thematic relations from syntactic relations alone.

However, from the standpoint of this principle, it is also the case that many semantic accounts are insufficiently syntactic, in that thematic relations are represented in ways that are less than completely relational or configurational. For example, a certain thematic role may be taken as determined by an independent primitive predicate. Rather, Strict Thematic Configurationality requires that thematic relations themselves constitute the sole basis for determining the argument content of possible semantic predicates. Decompositional analyses such as those of Jackendoff (1972, 1983, 1990) and Talmy (1976, 1985) seek thematic configurationality, but permit independent primitive predicate distinctions, such as that between Source and Goal.

In Gruber (1965, 1976) a completely configurational distinction between Source and Goal was not attained. In this chapter, we provide a configurational representation in syntax of this distinction, as adumbrated in Gruber and Collins, together with an account of asymmetries in argument projection based on it. (See also Gruber 1994a, b; 1995b, c.)

Strict Thematic Configurationality in syntax forces the representational and correspondence problems of thematic structure — that is, the problems of representing thematic structure semantically and its correspondence with syntactic predicate-argument structure — to be regarded with equal centrality. Work in syntax focusing on satisfying conditions posed by the argument projection problem may have relative disregard for the representational problem, taking it to be peripheral or relegating it to another domain. In contrast, work in semantics may focus on problems of representation with less attention to the argument projection problem, leaving it for further research. The adoption of Strict Thematic Configurationality, however, puts a far heavier condition on theoretic adequacy, since it requires simultaneous solution of both problems.

1.2. Theoretic Approach

In this chapter, we develop a theory of thematic structure and argument projection adhering to the principle of Strict Thematic Configurationality in grammatical syntax. We state the principle as follows:

(1) *Strict Thematic Configurationality in Syntax*
Every thematic relational distinction is distinctively represented configurationally in syntax.

In Gruber and Collins, the basis for such a configurational Theta theory is developed. Thematic roles are configurationally determined in a VP shell-like structure, as in Hale and Keyser (1993), following Larson (1988), while the theory of Case as movement into specifiers of agreement phrases (Chomsky 1992) is adopted. Thus "argument projection" is not a matter of assignment of Theta-roles specified and projected from the lexicon, as in Stowell (1981), Williams (1984), and Gruber (1990, 1992a, b), but is understood as movement into a Case-position from a basic thematic position. Such a conception is implicit in the minimalist theory of Chomsky (1993). Essential also is the concept of economy of derivation involving movement constrained in minimal domains, that is, the Minimal Link Condition of Chomsky (1993). In order to accommodate representation of the relation of sequence or precedence-consequence in event structure, the VP-shell concept is elaborated in Gruber and Collins to include asymmetric conjunction phrases (CjP). Colinking among thematic roles is obligatory in such structures, and this is mediated by empty categories. Constraints on movement within this structure predict conditions relating argument projection and thematic relations.

In this chapter, a full approach to a strictly configurational thematic theory is made. This is done with the addition of one theoretic element: the uniform inclusion of extended phrasal projections in event representations. Each VP in a shell or more elaborate structure is extended by a TP (tense phrase) and a (potentially active) agreement phrase (Demuth and Gruber 1993). Conceptually, for every occurrence of a lexical phrasal projection, such as a VP representing the thematic structure of an elementary event, a TP is necessitated to constitute it with reference-related properties (just as NP necessitates a determiner phrase DP); this is then extended by an agreement phrase that functions in the projection of predicate-argument structure. Extensions of thematic lexical phrases by aspectual phrases in event structure is also necessitated.

The need to characterize relations between syntax and inner aspect or *aktionsart* (Vendler 1967; Dowty 1979) by identifying or including functional and aspectual structure within event (VP-shell) representations has been recognized in the literature (Collins and Thráinsson 1993; Gruber 1967; Pustejovsky 1988; Tenny 1987, 1989; Travis 1992; Verkuyl 1972, 1993). In Demuth and Gruber (1993), the basic phrasal projection sequence of agreement phrase, tense phrase, and lexical phrase is found to characterize syntactic structures at the level of overt inflectional morphology. The presence of these sequences naturally and necessarily extends to covert representations of event structure. Possible structures are thus strongly constrained in respect to phrasal sequence types, although they may be quite elaborate in repetition of these types.

The theoretic addition of functional phrasal projections in event representations provides a framework in which the possibilities of movement for argument projection from basic thematic positions predicts generalizations and asymmetries. Besides the Minimal Link Condition, a principle of economy of derivation in Chain formation operates in predicting these asymmetries: a Chain is formed as late as possible in a derivation. Thus, arguments are projected with structural Case in the highest position attainable.

Since functional phrasal projections, including agreement phrases, are present in all subevent representations, a uniform account of semantic and structural Case by movement is possible (Rooryck 1994). The efficacy of such a uniform mechanism for Case is evident in the determination of argument projection patterns in general. A strictly configurational analysis of the Source/Goal distinction can be provided, while yielding an account of argument projection asymmetries involving Source and Goal. In principle, thematic hierarchies (Jackendoff 1972, 1990; Grimshaw 1990) are epiphenomenal on movement effects in event structure configurations. Finally, event-structure uniformly elaborated with functional projections permits a configurational account of obligatory thematic colinking,[2] or Theta-identification (Higgenbotham 1985). In particular, movement into a "local topic" position in subevent structure determines thematic colinking. The requirement for colinking between Theta-roles of subevents in complex structures reflects the need for their identification as relative local topics at LF. There is also the suggestion of configurational effects involving positions in which aspectual relations between subevents are determined.

1.3. Modularity

We briefly review here implications of the configurational Theta theory for the concept of modularity in grammar, sketching the plan of presentation in this paper. A minimalist view of Strict Thematic Configurationality implies that "Theta Theory" as an independent module reduces to the licensing of X-bar structures at the syntactic-conceptual interface, say, at Logical Form (LF), by their interpretation as elemental thematic relations, that is, Theme/Locational-role relations.[3] X-bar theoretic structures at LF therefore constitute the configurational thematic representation. There is no module of Theta-role assignment as such. Rather, the interpretation of all so-called Theta-roles depends solely on X-bar configurations among lexical phrasal projections.

The configurational representation of Theta-roles in event structures and their projection as arguments have certain implications for the nature of constraints on the composition of X-bar theoretic structures. Uniform extensions of functional and lexical phrasal projections must form an iterating pattern of phrasal sequences for each subevent. Although elaborate, an overall simplicity in the fractal-like repetition of these patterns may be recognized. Thus, X-bar sequences are constrained with respect to type, with concomitant multiplicity of unit sequences. The general form of event structure in this conception is developed in section 2.

Argument projection is accomplished by the interaction of Case theory, colinking, and aspect at the LF interface. These interact in a modular fashion by movement through the X-bar theoretic event representations. While A-movement is driven only by the need for Case, they share a formal similarity in that they all license expressions at LF by movement into configurationally distinctive functional phrasal projections, differing only in the properties of the categories involved. Asymmetries of argument projection are thus predicted with respect to the configurational distinctions between Theme and Location, Source and Goal, and precedent and consequent subevents. Modular accounts of these asymmetries as they appear in simple event structural types are given in rest of the chapter.

Among these asymmetries are the Location/Theme Subject/Object and Source/Goal Subject/Object Asymmetries (see sections 3, 5.1), which state that, for simple event structures, Location, Source, and Theme may be projected as subject, and Goal and Theme as object, but not vice versa except by special means. This condition more accurately covers the ground of the External Theta-role Projection Condition in Gruber and Collins. The Complement Role Projection Condition, part B of the Internal Theta-role Projection Condition described but not accounted for in Gruber and Collins, states that a Theta-role in the complement must be Case-marked with respect to its most consequent role. This is now explained through modular interactions (section 4): colinking blocks Case-marking with respect to the precedent role. In addition, we account for an asymmetry in resultative constructions: the Theme of a precedent subevent may be Case-marked in English by *of* or *with*, depending on whether it is a Source or a Goal of that subevent that is colinked (Talmy 1985). This is the Source/Goal Oblique Theme Asymmetry (section 5.2).

2. CONFIGURATIONAL EVENT STRUCTURE

We consider first the general form of configurational event structure representations, which are necessary for both thematic representation and argument projection. In these structures, phrasal projections that are purely thematic are extended by both aspectual and functional phrases, forming iterating sequences of constrained patterns.

2.1. Time Adverbs and Inner Aspect

A correlation exists between thematic structure and the stative/active aspectual distinction, as revealed in the use of temporal adverbs. A stative or Locational verb such as *stand/stay*, with roles of Theme and Location, contrasts thematically with a Motional or active verb,[4] such as *go/roll*, with Theme and at least implicit Source and Goal roles. The thematic distinction correlates with an aspectual one. Both can take temporal adverbs in *until/for*, but only the latter can take an adverb in *by/in*:

(2) a. The dog stood/stayed in the yard (until/for T; *by/in T).
     b. The stone was rolling/rolled out of the yard into the road (until/for T; by/in T).

In Motional verbs, there is an additional Theta-role, namely two Locational roles, Source and Goal. Similarly, in Motional verbs, there is an additional temporal adverbial possible. This suggests a configurational correlation. The event structure of a Motional verb is an elaboration of that of a Locational verb, providing configurational distinctions for the additional Theta-role and temporal adverb. In particular the Theta-role of Source seems to be associated with the *by/in* phrase.

As in Hale and Keyser (1993) and Chomsky (1993), we take a VP, or any lexical phrasal projection composed according to X-bar theory to be licensed by its interpretation as an elementary predication. Suppose the elemental predicational relation is that between Theme and Location, represented in the specifier and complement positions of a lexical phrasal projection. In Hale and Keyser (1993), Chomsky (1993), and Gruber and Collins (chapter 6 this volume), the specifier is associated with Theme and the complement with Location. We will show, however, that it is essential in a complete representation of event structure to reverse this as the basic interpretation of thematic positions.

Asymmetric conjunction CjP representing the precedence-consequence relation, as in Gruber and Collins, naturally extends to representing the sequential relation of Source and Goal. The latter is at the level of conjoining Locational events, that is, simple VPs, each representing a Theme-Location relation. The asymmetries in argument projection in resultatives discussed in Gruber and Collins show that the consequent subevent must be represented in the complement of CjP, while the precedent subevent is represented in the specifier of CjP. If simple VPs are conjoined, the Location in the "precedent" VP in relation to that in the "consequent" VP[5] naturally corresponds to the Source-Goal relation. A Location in the VP complement of CjP is a Goal, while a Location in the VP specifier of CjP is a Source.

Suppose further that each VP or CjP can be associated with a quantitative aspectual phrase AqP, in which temporal adverbs, for example, denoting an extent or a point of time, are generated. In this way, any elaboration of thematic structure will correspond to an elaboration of inner aspectual structure. Approximate event structure representations for (2a) and (2b) are given respectively in (3a) and (3b).

(3)   a.   b.

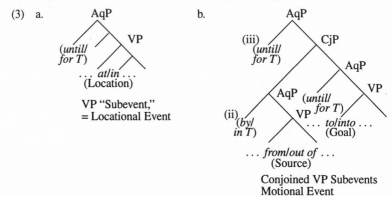

Time adverbials denoting temporal extent (*until/for T, by/in T*) are indicated. Adverbials denoting a point of time (*at T*) also may occur. *For T* or *in T* denotes the temporal extent of a subevent, while *until T* or *by T* denotes its temporal endpoint.[6]

There is but one such subevent in the Locational event (3a). In the Motional event (3b), however, there are three, that is, the Source subevent, the Goal subevent, and the event as a whole. The use of *until/for* is ambiguous. It may be associated with the Motional event as a whole (iii), hence denoting the time spent rolling into the road.[7] Or it may be associated with just the Goal subevent (i), denoting the time in the road after arrival. In contrast, *by/in* denotes the time before entering the road.[8] Thus, *for/until* temporal adverbs are distinguished from *by/in* temporal adverbs configurationally, paralleling the distinctions between Location or Goal, namely, *at/in* or *to/into*, and Source, namely, *from/out of*, respectively — the latter distinguished by being in the specifier of CjP.

The uniform presence of AqPs in relative positions in event structure seems to have the potential of providing an account for the range of possibilities of inner aspect or *aktionsart* distinctions, as well as their relation to thematic structure. This could be determined by the content of various AqPs, whether or not lexically specific or overtly expressed by a temporal adverb.[9] AqP in relation to VP is thus comparable to a number phrase in relation to NP (or DP). As has been observed (cf. Jackendoff 1990), differences of iterativity, durativity, and punctuality of VPs are semantically similar to differences of plurality, countability, and singularity of NPs. The consistent and uniform presence of AqP in association with VP has consequences necessary for the account of argument projection and various asymmetries, as we shall see.

2.2. Basic Thematic Radical

Let us consider now the basic positions in the VP radical that determine the Theme-Locational role relation. We have shown that precedent subevent representations and Source are identified with the specifier of CjP, while consequent subevent representations and Goal are identified with the complement of CjP. The interpretation of the relation between the specifier and complement of CjP must be similar to that between the specifier and complement of VP, although differing in functional respects. This means that we would expect a similarity between the precedent-consequent subevent relation and the Source-Goal relation, that is, the specifier-complement of CjP, on the one hand, and either the Theme-Location or Location-Theme relation, on the other.

It is, in fact, the Location-Theme relation that is similar to the Source-Goal or precedence-consequence relation. This can be seen in approximate equivalences such as the following:

(4) a. A implies B.   b. A leads to B.
         ... entails...   B stems from A.
         ... involves...   Things proceed from A to B.
         ... includes...

These verbs express relations in a conceptual dimension (Circumstantial; cf. Jackendoff 1976) in which the thematic roles denote events. Thus the specifier and complement positions of a Circumstantial VP express a Location-Theme relationship in (a). Asymmetric conjunction CjP also expresses a relation between events, namely, the subevent VPs it conjoins. Thus the specifier and complement VPs of CjP in (b) express a Motional event between Source and Goal subevents. An equivalence is then possible in certain respects between the relations determined by CjP and a Circumstantial VP. This equivalence implies the configurational determinations of thematic relations in (5).

(5) a.   b.

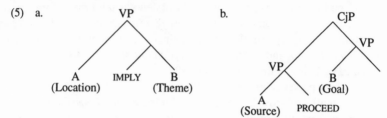

Since Source and Goal are in relative specifier-complement positions of CjP (5b), so must be Location and Theme. Location is therefore in the relative specifier position of VP, so that Source and Goal, also Locational roles in relation to their Themes, must be VP specifier positions.

We therefore establish the basic thematic radicals in (6a), as in a Locational event, which combine in the precedence-consequence relation of a Motional event (6b), denoting Temporal sequence (TMP).[10]

(6) a. *Locational relation (Theme-Location relation)*

$$
\begin{array}{l}
\text{VP} \quad\rule{1cm}{0.4pt}\; \Theta \\
\quad\; |\quad \text{PST} \qquad < \Theta, \Lambda > \\
\Lambda
\end{array}
\qquad
\begin{array}{l}
\Lambda = \text{Location} \\
\Theta = \text{Theme} \\
\text{PST} = \text{Positional}
\end{array}
$$

The tree stood in the yard.

b. *Motional relation (precedence-consequence/Source-Goal relation)*

$$
\begin{array}{l}
\text{CjP} \quad \text{VP} \rule{1cm}{0.4pt}\; \Theta \\
\quad | \qquad |_{\Gamma}\; \text{PST} \\
\quad \text{TMP} \\
\quad \text{VP} \rule{0.5cm}{0.4pt}\; \Theta \qquad \text{(Consequent subevent)} \\
\quad |\quad \text{PST} \qquad\qquad\quad < \Theta, \Gamma > \\
\quad \Sigma \qquad\qquad \text{(Precedent subevent)} \\
\qquad\qquad\quad < \Theta, \Sigma >
\end{array}
\qquad
\begin{array}{l}
\text{CjP} = \text{Conjunction Phrase} \\
\text{TMP} = \text{Temporal sequence} \\
\Gamma = \text{Goal} \\
\Sigma = \text{Source}
\end{array}
$$

Go from the bush to the tree.

As we shall see, these relative positions of thematic relations in the VP radical (Location and Theme) and in CjP (Source and Goal) are essential in accounting for argument projection effects and asymmetries.

2.3. Phrasal Projection Sequences

Argument projection as movement into agreement phrases requires extensions of the VP by functional phrasal projections. In Demuth and Gruber (1993), overt evidence in Bantu languages is found that the basic extended phrasal projection unit is AgreementP-ReferentialP-LexicalP. For example, in Setswana, a "compound" or periphrastic auxiliary verb construction shows heads of these types in each word of the construction:

(7) lo-kwal-o lo-n-e   lo-ka-bo lo-fed-ile   (Cole 1955)
     11-book-? 11-past-be 11-pot-be 11-end-perf
     Agr-N-?D Agr-V-T   Agr-T-V   Agr-V-T
     "The book might have ended."

We take it as the minimal assumption that this extended projection unit, called a Basic Projection Sequence, is always present. In particular, it is covertly present in inner event structure, including extensions of VPs within VP shells or more elaborate event structures.

Conceptually, the extension of every VP by TP is similar to that of the extension of every NP by DP. Every lexical projection (NP, VP, AqP, CjP) must be extended by a functional projection (DP,TP) imparting referential properties (Di Sciullo and Williams 1987). The DP/TP is further extended by an agreement phrase functioning for the projection of predicate-argument structure. A Basic Projection Sequence for an extended thematic VP is exemplified in (8).

(8)   AgrP   TP   VP
       ⌐ ⌐ ⌐ ⌐ ⌐⌐ ⌐──── Θ
                    PST
                  Λ
       The tree stood in the yard.

The thematic relation in the example is of the Positional (PST) conceptual dimension or field (Gruber 1965, 1976, 1990; Jackendoff 1972, 1976, 1990). Conceptual dimensions are associated with thematic heads, for example, VP-PST (cf. Gruber and Collins).

In Demuth and Gruber (1993), Basic Projection Sequences combine to form Lexical Projection Sequences. In these sequences, the last or lowest lexical phrasal projection is thematic, while the rest are non-thematic, containing a light or dummy verbal head ("be"). Thus, the complex auxiliary construction in the Setswana example is a lexical phrasal projection sequence in which the first two (auxiliary) words denote tense and modality only while the last denotes aspect and the thematic verb.

If argument projection or Case-assignment uniformly results from movement into an agreement phrase, then to project two Theta-roles as arguments, as in a Locational sentence with a single thematic VP radical such as above, at least two basic projection sequences, each with its AgrP, must constitute the lexical phrasal projection sequence associated with a thematic VP. Indeed, this is already provided, given that every thematic VP radical is associated with a quantificational aspectual phrase AqP. That is, with every thematic radical, we have a lexical phrasal projection sequence as exemplified in (9).

(9)   AgrP TP   AqP AgrP TP   VP
       ⌐ ⌐ ⌐ ⌐ ⌐   ⌐ ⌐ ⌐ ⌐ ⌐ ⌐ ⌐ ⌐──── Θ
                                    PST
                                  Λ
       The tree stood in the yard.

This extended phrasal projection sequence constitutes the basic unit of subevent structure. The salience of the unit embodies functional necessity and architectural simplicity: functional phrases necessitated for each lexical phrasal projection appear in similar patterns repetitively. The unit is overtly evidenced in languages such as Bantu. It is also evident in the inner aspect associated with each subevent representation. The repetitive appearance of these units accords with the spirit of Strict Thematic Configurationality applied to general event structure: similar relations are represented similarly at each level of structure. We turn now to how event structure in this form is necessitated in argument projection.

3. BASIC ARGUMENT PROJECTION PATTERNS AND ASYMMETRIES

3.1. Simple Locational Event Structures

A sentence expressing a simple Locational thematic relation would also be the simplest in respect to event structure. Its representation in terms of extended phrasal projection sequences through which thematic elements move for Case accounts for the range of argument projection patterns and asymmetries relative to thematic roles.

A uniform mechanism for argument projection or Case assignment is the simplest assumption. In particular, argument projection effected by movement into agreement phrases, as in structural Case, should be extended to all kinds of Case. This would include then projection of oblique and/or semantically Case-marked arguments, in English typically marked by a preposition.[11] Event-structure representations in the form of repetitive extended phrasal projection units permits such a uniform treatment. This is because of the association of AgrPs with aspectual or thematic phrasal projections throughout the structure.

The phrasal projection sequence containing AqP and VP includes two AgrPs. Case or argument projection in the AgrP associated with the VP captures the notion of semantic Case. The distinctive characteristic of semantic Case is that it is thematically specific; it is also typically associated with Locational roles rather than with Theme. If both the Theme and the Location must move for Case, the Location, but not the Theme, may be Case-marked in the agreement phrase specifically associated with the thematic VP radical, for example, AgrP-TP-VP-PST in (10).

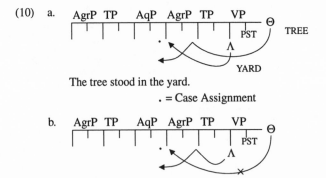

(10) a.

The tree stood in the yard.

. = Case Assignment

b.

AgrP-VP-PST is thematically specific; that is, only the element identified as the Location may move into it. Hence, it is the position of semantic Case-marking of Location, as shown in (10a). The A-movements of Theme and Location to achieve this, crossing one specifier each, are possible because the minimal domain of each head is extended by head incorporation of one into the next (Chomsky 1993). The element in the Theme position may not be Case-marked in AgrP-VP-PST, however, as such movement would require movement across a minimal domain, namely, across two specifier positions, as shown in (10b).

Note that the Theme must always move into TP-VP, or it will never be able to move into a Case position higher in the event structure. Thus, Theme always reverses its c-command relation with Location by its movement into TP before its Case-assignment. In this configuration, the position of Theme corresponds to that of the "internal Theta-role" or object that moves to subject in accordance with the Unaccusative hypothesis (Perlmutter 1978).

This asymmetry in movement and Case assignment between Location and Theme corroborates the interpretation of the basic positions of specifier and complement as Location and Theme, as well as the sequence of functional phrasal projections in the order agreement phrase, referential phrase (TP), and lexical/thematic phrase (VP).

The presence of TPs in inner event structure is not necessary merely as a landing site, however. Evidence shows that it has consistent reference-related function in argument identification. In respect to Case and argument projection, just as TP associated with substantive tense in clauses distinctively assigns nominative Case, inner TPs must serve functionally in providing distinctive Case-features to be discharged in their associated AgrPs. Inner TPs also serve functionally for obligatory thematic colinking or Theta-identification between subevents, and seem implicated also in relative aspectual phenomena between subevents.

The foregoing implies that the projection of Theme as argument, that is, its Case-marking, will always be structural, that is, not semantic in a thematically specific position, although it may be oblique (prepositional, for example, marked by *with* or *of*), rather than direct.[12] In the simple event structure described earlier this may be in AgrP-AqP. However, it is necessary to distinguish a full clause containing substantive tense from a form, such as a nominal, which does not. The presence of substantive tense in a clause implies an additional basic projection sequence headed by its own (aspectual) lexical phrasal projection, which we will label AtP. TP-AtP assigns nominative Case in its associated AgrP.

The derivation of a sentence expressing a simple Locational event with Theme as nominative subject and Location as semantically Case-marked complement, an "unaccusative" configuration, will then be as in (11a).

(11)   a.

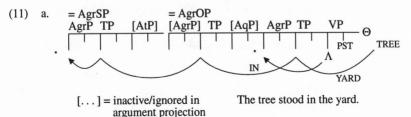

[. . .] = inactive/ignored in   The tree stood in the yard.
argument projection

b.

(the presence of the tree in the yard)

As in Gruber and Collins, all functional and lexical heads incorporate or conflate by LF for the checking of Event/T-features (cf. Pollock 1989, Higginbotham 1985, Chomsky 1993).

A comparable (deverbal) nominal form (11b) without substantive tense (TP-AtP) could Case-mark Theme in AgrP-AqP. This position appears to be that of oblique Case marked by *of* in English. The position is the same as that of AgrOP (= AgrP-AqP) with AgrSP (= AgrP-AtP) absent. We surmise that Case here is oblique in nominals (genitive) rather than direct (accusative), as in verbs, because it lies below the point of conflation of highest thematic head, here that of the NP.[13] This distinction plays a role in determining the oblique Case of Theme in the Source/Goal Oblique Theme Asymmetry discussed in section 5.2.

Note that in the clause (11a), argument projection of the subject is in the highest possible AgrP. This reflects a principle of economy of derivation in Chain formation, perhaps an instance of "procrastinate" (Chomsky 1993), which we postulate as follows:

(12)   *Optimality of Chain Formation*
A Chain is formed as late as possible in a derivation.

Here, for an A-Chain, this means argument projection is effected in the highest position attainable for structural Case.

Chomsky's (1993) Form Chain is an "all-at-once" operation that amalgamates links into a Chain, so that numerous links do not lessen optimality. Argument projection under Strict Thematic Configurationality indicates further that Form Chain is in fact optimal if it applies latest, that is, highest, in the derivation, resulting thereby in a maximal number of links. This effects an optimality opposite in a sense to that in single-link movement, which must be as short as possible, namely, the Minimal Link Condition. Semantic Case, in a position achieved by one "link," does not involve the operation of Chain formation. Therefore Case will either be structural in the highest possible position, or it will be semantic, in the lowest position. But intermediate relevant positions will not function for argument projection if an interpretable result is possible with argument projection in a higher position. The necessity for this economy principle will be further evident in its effects in the derivations to follow.

AgrPs, as well as aspectual phrases, that are inactive for predicate-argument projection (indicated in square brackets above) do not provide argument positions and so are ignored in the A-movement involved in argument projection. That is, minimality is relativized (Rizzi 1990), so that they do not enter into the computation of minimality domains. This fact plays no role when Location is semantically Case-marked, as in (11). However, Location in a simple Locational event structure may be structurally and directly Case-marked as subject, as in (13).

(13)

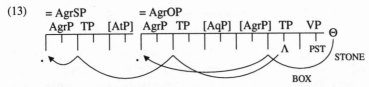

The box contained the stone.

The lexical distinction between a verb such as *stand*, with semantically Case-marked Location, and a verb such as *contain*, in which Location is projected as subject, amounts to the inactivity of the agreement phrase associated with the VP, AgrP-VP.[14] For *contain*, it is inactive or absent. The lexical distinction could be a specification resulting in the need for the Case-feature of TP-VP-PST to be undischarged (or unchecked) in AgrP at LF. A-movements for Case would then result in argument projection of Location as subject, in AgrP-AtP (= AgrSP), and Theme as object, in AgrP-AqP (= AgrOP). In this "transitive" configuration, the position of Location as specifier of VP corresponds to that of subject, in accordance with the Internal Subject hypothesis (Kuroda 1985).

Note that AtP and its extension is necessary in the projection of the arguments of a verb such as *contain* because both its two roles, Theme and Location, must be structurally Case-marked. That is, since Location is not semantically Case-marked, in other words, since AgrP-VP is inactive for Case, two AgrPs active for Case associated with aspectual phrasal projections are required.

The precise number of active phrasal projections is crucial in determining where Theta-roles are projected as arguments. In the simplest Locational event structure, expressed in a clause whose main verb is like *stand* or *contain*, there are just the three basic phrasal projection sequences above: that of AtP, AqP, and VP. All simple Locational event structures must contain these three—no more, no less. If this is the case, it is predicted that the opposite argument projection to that of *contain*, as shown in (14), is impossible for simple Locational event structures, since it would violate minimality of movement.

(14)   = AgrSP   = AgrOP
         AgrP TP   [AtP] AgrP TP   [AqP] [AgrP] TP   VP Θ
                                                          Λ   PST

3.2. The Location/Theme Subject/Object Asymmetry

From the foregoing, we see that the configurational Theta theory with Strict Thematic Configurationality predicts that in unmarked circumstances a simple Locational event-structure cannot result in the argument projection of Location as direct object in AgrP-AqP while Theme is projected as subject in AgrP-AtP. That is, the following asymmetry is predicted:

(15)   *The Location / Theme Subject/Object Asymmetry*
       In a simple event structure expressing a Locational thematic relation, either:

a.   The subject is Theme and the Location is an oblique complement, or
b.   The direct object is Theme, with Location as subject.

Thus Theme subject with oblique Location, or Location subject with Theme object should be simple and relatively unmarked Locational types, while (apparent) Theme subject with (apparent) Location object will be different or marked in some way. Only Location subject/Theme object forms can be both truly transitive and express a truly simple event structure. The object of a true transitive is projected as an argument or Case-marked in AgrOP, that is, in the highest AgrP-AqP in the above configuration. In a passive form, the object moves further to AgrSP as subject. Thus, the true object of a transitive will generally reveal itself by the possibility of its being the subject in a passive.

The object in a simple event structure represents a Theta-role of a subevent that is not a result or in consequence of some other subevent: the Theme of a resultant or consequent subevent colinked with a Locational role of a precedent subevent is the configuration of an "affected" object. In other words, "affected" objects are generally Themes of such resultant subevents, accounting for many of the cases described by Tenny (1987, 1989). Thus, an object in a truly simple event structure shows up as being "unaffected." In general, then, the Location/Theme Subject/Object asymmetry predicted by the configurational Theta theory is that, among verbs expressing Locational events, only Location subject/Theme object forms can have objects that are both passivizable and unaffected.

Consider the list of verb types in Table 7.1. Verbs apparently expressing a simple Locational event may be unmarked with Theme subject and oblique Location (a), or with Location subject and Theme object (b). The appearance of a Theme as subject and a Location as direct object occurs only if the event structure is complex, that is, if it is a resultative structure (c), or if the apparent direct Location object is actually implicitly oblique (d), or if it is not in fact a Locational event but a Motional[15] one (e), another relatively unmarked type in which the object can be a Goal (Γ), Accompaniment (A), or Path (Π) (see sections 3.4 and 4.2).

Passive is possible only if a true direct object is present, namely, one Case-marked in AgrOP, that is, in these configurations, AgrP-AqP. This is not so when the object is explicitly oblique, as in (a) of Table 7.1 or example (16a), and so also would not be expected when the object is implicitly oblique. We would presume this to be the case in (d), in which the preposition or other Case-marker is presumed to have incorporated with the verb in Phonological Form (PF), not affecting LF (for example, merged or fused in Spell-out, see Halle and Marantz 1993). Passive is possible, however, in the actual Location subject/Theme object case $< \Lambda, \Theta >$ of a simple Locational event (b), as well as in cases that actually involve a Motional event with Goal object (e), and in which there is a complex structure in which the Location object is colinked with the Theme of a consequent subevent (c). In this last case, the object is Case-marked with respect to the consequent Theme, as described in Gruber and Collins and further in section 4.2, and is an "affected" object, which distinguishes the object in (c) from all the other cases.

Table 7.1. Verbs Showing the Location/Theme Subject/Object Asymmetry

		Thematic Structure		*Passive/ Affected Object*
a.	Simple Locational	$< \Theta,^0\Lambda >$ subject Θ,oblique Λ	*be, stand, lie, stay, belong (to)*	no passive unaffected complement (explicit oblique Case)
b.	Simple Locational	$< \Lambda, \Theta >$ subject Λ,object Θ	*contain, own,* * *hold, include, involve, entail, imply, mean*	passive unaffected object
c.	Complex Resultative	$< \Theta, [\Lambda; \Theta] >$ subject Θ,object Λ (Λ is colinked with Θ of a consequent subevent)	*occupy, inhabit, cover*	passive affected object
d.	Simple Locational	$< \Theta,^{(0)}\Lambda >$ subject Θ, object Λ (object is an implicit oblique complement)	*touch, abut, adjoin*	no passive unaffected object
e.	Simple Motional	$< \Theta, \Gamma/A/\Pi >$ subject Θ, object Γ, Accompaniment A or Path P	*touch, hit, see, reach, attain; precede, follow, accompany; straddle, cross, surround, cover*	passive unaffected object

*Have, which may express a simple Locational event with apparent Location subject, is exceptional and does not have a passive form.

(16) a. i. The book belongs to John./*John is belonged to by the book.
       ii. How is the book affected?/What is happening to the book?
          * — It belongs to John.
     b. i. John owns the book./The book is owned by John.
       ii. How is the book affected?/What is happening to the book?
          * — John owns it.
     c. i. They occupy the house./The house is occupied by them.
       ii. How is the house affected?/What is happening to the house?
          — They occupy/are occupying it.
     d. i. The branch touches the wall./*The wall is touched by the branch.
       ii. How is the wall affected?/What is happening to the wall?
          * — The branch touches it.
     e. i. The branch is touching the wall./The wall is being touched by the branch.
       ii. How is the wall being affected?/What is happening to the wall?
          * — The branch is touching it.

Note that *touch* in (16d) is a Locational verb with Location complement, as indicated by the simple present tense form, and so the Location must be an implicit semantically Case-marked complement $< \Theta,^{(0)}\Lambda >$. In (16e), however, *touch* is a Motional verb with Goal complement, as indicated by the present progressive form; accordingly, the Goal may be a direct object. The argument pattern Theme subject/Goal object $< \Theta, \Gamma >$ is an unmarked form for simple Motional sentences, as will be discussed in the following section.

3.3. Simple Motional Event Structures

As we have seen, the representation of the precedence-consequence relation by asymmetric conjunction naturally applies to the representation of simple Motional events, as temporally sequential relations between two Locational subevents. Completing the subevent representations shown in (3b) with functional phrasal projection sequences, a simple Motional sentence would have the basic structure in (17).

(17)

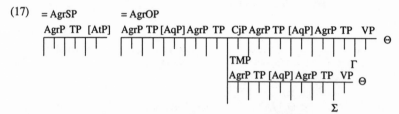

The structure is simple in its iteration of similar phrasal sequence patterns for each subevent representation, conforming to the principle of Strict Thematic Configurationality. As will be seen presently, complete phrasal projection sequences, including AqPs and their functional extensions, are necessary in each subevent representation, and affect argument projection in a precise manner. Note in particular that CjP, which has thematic properties in determining a precedence-consequence relation between subevents — here that of temporal sequence (TMP) — has its own functional extensions, in this case those of the event or clause as a whole.

Argument projection of thematic roles in an unaccusative intransitive form, in which the subject is Theme, and Source and Goal are semantically or obliquely Case-marked, is straightforward, as shown in (18).

(18)

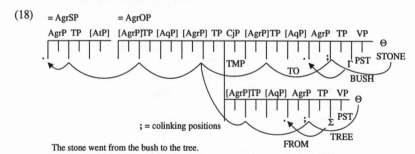

The stone went from the bush to the tree.

For the proper derivation of argument projection patterns, it is essential that all thematic elements always be Case-marked. In this instance of an unaccusative form, Source and Goal must be Case-marked in the local AgrP-VP, even if the resultant oblique argument is implicit, as it often may be. As previously seen, the Themes of the Locational subevent representations, also driven to obtain Case, then must always move into TP-VP. Obligatory colinking between Locational subevent representations joined by asymmetric conjunction CjP to form a Motional event occurs only between the Themes of the subevents. Obligatory colinking, in fact, seems to occur just in virtue of the Themes both necessarily appearing in TP-VP of their respective subevent representations.

Thematic colinking, or Theta-identification between subevent representations seems to be necessary to license conjunction between them, possibly when heads of the subevents are incorporated or conflated at LF. Intuitively, intimately conjoined subevents describe "paths" in some abstract sense. Obligatory colinking would then be an expression of the necessity that intimately conjoined paths be of the same entity. That is, the local topic of the subevents must be identified with each other. Such obligatory identification, as well as simultaneous Case-assignment, occurs between subjects in the realm of sequential clausal conjunction.

(19)   John$_i$ took a hammer and (*Mary/*he$_i$) broke the window.

It appears, then, that TP-VP, or in general the TP immediately associated with a thematic phrasal projection, functions to determine local topicality, and hence identity between them in an asymmetric conjunction configuration. We will refer to the element in Spec TP of a thematic phrase as the local thematic topic of the subevent. We therefore postulate the following condition for obligatory thematic colinking:[16]

(20)   *Obligatory Thematic Colinking Condition*
Local thematic topics of conjoined subevent representations are identified.

The implications and necessity for this condition will become apparent in the discussion to follow.

In a cross-modular fashion, then, elements from basic Theme positions in a Motional event structure are driven by the need for Case, but move into positions of obligatory colinking. Obligatory thematic colinking interacts specifically with Case: elements from basic thematic positions that are obligatorily colinked are not Case-marked independently, but Case is assigned only once among such colinked elements. This follows from economy of derivation. Since obligatory thematic colinking or identification occurs derivationally prior to argument projection or Case-assignment, the colinked "sub-argumental" elements must form a single A-Chain. A-Chains are Case-marked just once. Movement for Case, in the configuration above (18), is optimal if both Theme elements move "across the board." The same process would account for the necessarily null subject in the second of sequentially conjoined clauses in (19). Further effects of the interaction between colinking and Case will be seen in the analysis of resultative structures in section 4.

As discussed in Gruber and Collins, movement out of the highest position in the specifier of CjP is not blocked by the crossing of any minimality domain in structures like (18); that is, the position is effectively "L-marked" (Chomsky 1986), so that both Themes move across CjP. Source and Goal are Case-marked locally, that is, semantically in their respective AgrP-VPs. The colinked Themes move optimally to the highest structural Case position, AgrP-AtP, that is, AgrSP, as subject. Optimality of Chain formation demands that AgrOP, the highest AgrP-AqP, be inactive, as is AgrP-CjP, resulting in a typical unaccusative configuration, with the Theme — the internal "object"-role — projected as subject.

As in the case of simple Locational event structures, transitive Motional forms involve the inactivity of thematically local AgrPs for Case, namely, AgrP-VP of the Goal or Source subevent representation. If these agreement phrases are inactive for Case, then Goal or Source must move for structural Case — here, either as subject or object. Since Goal and Source are configurationally determined, these thematic elements move from different positions. This results in asymmetries of argument projection for transitive forms with respect to these thematic roles.

The derivation of a transitive sentences expressing a simple Motional event structure is given in (21).

(21)

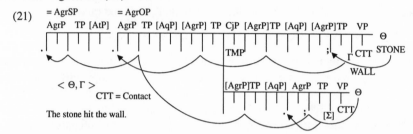

The derivation here for a verb (for example, *hit*) of the conceptual dimension of Contact (CTT) yields the pattern of Theme subject with Goal object. AgrP-VP-Γ(CTT) is inactive for Case, so that Goal moves to TP-AqP-VP and then across CjP through TP-CjP. Note that the presence of the aspectual phrase AqP-VP, and in particular its TP extension, provides a necessary landing site for the Goal, which would otherwise be blocked from movement across the specifiers of both TP-VP, filled by Theme, and CjP. That is, no derivation with Goal object would be possible without AqP-VP-Γ(CTT).

(22)

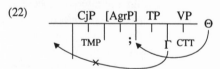

Source is implicitly Case-marked in AgrP-VP-Σ(CTT) in (21). Since Goal is in TP-CjP, it is impossible for the Theme of the Goal subevent representation to move across CjP. Rather, the Theme must move from the Source subevent representation. Since the Themes are colinked, the movement for Case of just one of them is necessary and, in this case, optimal. The Theme in the Goal subevent representation then stops at the colinking position TP-VP-Γ(CTT), while the Theme from the Source subevent representation moves out of CjP to TP-AqP-CjP.

The configuration is now effectively that of the Internal Subject Hypothesis for transitive sentences. The Goal moves out of the complement of CjP to be projected as direct object in AgrP-AqP-CjP, while Source moves out of the specifier of CjP to subject position in AgrP-AtP (= AgrSP). Note that the presence of AtP and AqP-CjP and their functional extensions is again essential for argument projection in the Theme subject/Goal object < Θ, Γ > construction.

The derivation of a transitive sentence expressing a simple Motional event with Source structurally Case-marked is similarly straightforward. In this case, Source is projected as subject and Theme as direct object ($< \Sigma, \Theta >$), as shown in (23) for a verb of the Positional (PST) conceptual dimension.

(23)

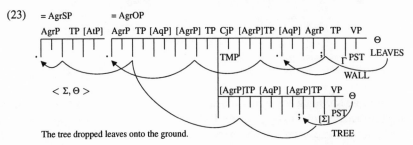

The tree dropped leaves onto the ground.

Here the local agreement phrase in the Source subevent representation is inactive for Case, so that Source must move for structural Case. Concomitantly, it is the Theme in the Goal subevent representation that also moves for Case, while the Theme of the Source subevent representation stops at the colinking position. The Goal is semantically Case-marked in AgrP-VP-Γ(PST). The configuration is similar to that in which Theme is projected as subject and Goal as object (21), again mirroring the position of internal arguments in the Internal Subject Hypothesis. Here Source moves out of the specifier of CjP into subject position, while Theme moves out of the complement of CP into the object position. We thus derive the acceptable Source subject/Theme object $< \Sigma, \Theta >$ Motional transitive.

As in the case of the Locational sentence, the modular interactions of basic X-bar theoretic structure, Case, movement, and, here, colinking result in the possibility of only a limited number of argument structure types for simple event structures. Thus it is impossible to derive for a simple Motional event structure a true transitive sentence with Goal subject and Theme object, $*< \Gamma, \Theta >$, or with Theme subject and Goal object, $*< \Theta, \Sigma >$. The structures that seem to exemplify these forms must in fact be marked or different in some way; that is, they do not represent simple Motional event structures.

Example (24) shows impossible derivations for simple $< \Gamma, \Theta >$ and $< \Theta, \Sigma >$ types.

(24)   a.

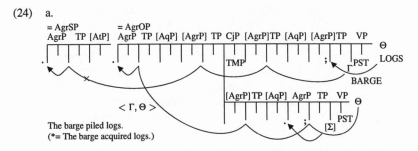

The barge piled logs.
(*= The barge acquired logs.)

b.

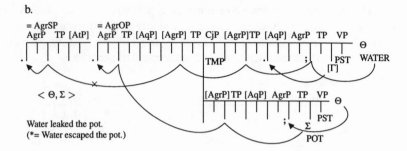

Water leaked the pot.
(*= Water escaped the pot.)

For a simple Motional configuration, movement of Θ to be Case-marked as object blocks movement of Γ to be Case-marked as subject (a). Similarly, movement of Σ to be Case-marked as object blocks movement of Θ to be Case-marked as subject.

3.4. The Source/Goal Subject/Object Asymmetry

From what has been shown, the configurational Theta theory predicts the following Source/Goal asymmetry in argument structure:

(25)   *The Source/Goal Subject/Object Asymmetry*
   In a sentence expressing a simple Motional event structure, either:

   a.   The subject is Theme and the Source and Goal are oblique, or
   b.   The direct object is Theme, with Source as subject, or
   c.   The direct object is Goal, with Theme as subject.

The asymmetry implies that the only simple Motional event structures will have the forms $< \Theta, {}^0\Sigma, {}^0\Gamma >$, $< \Theta, \Gamma >$, and $< \Sigma, \Theta >$. Other structures either will not be simple Motional event structures or will not be true transitives. This is evidenced in the case of Locational event structures by whether the object/complement can be passive or affected. In particular, only true transitive simple Motional event structures will have objects that can be both "unaffected" and subjects of a passive. Consider, then, the verbs, organized according to type, in Table 7.2.

(26)   a.   i.   The ball rolled to the tree./(*)The tree was rolled to by the ball.
          ii.   *What happened to the tree? — The ball rolled to it.
      b.   i.   The stone struck the wall./The wall was struck by the stone.
          ii.   ?What happened to the wall? — The stone struck it.
      c.   i.   The tree dropped leaves./Leaves were dropped by the tree.
          ii.   *What happened to the leaves? — The tree dropped them.
      d.   i.   They abandoned the house./The house was abandoned by them.
          ii.   What happened to the house? — They abandoned it.
      e.   i.   The train left the station./*The station was left by the train.
          ii.   *What happened to the station? — The train left it.
      f.   i.   They fled the city./The city was fled by them.
          ii.   *What happened to the city? — They fled it.
      g.   i.   They obtained the book./The book was obtained by them.
          ii.   What happened to the book? — They obtained it.

Table 7.2. Verbs Showing the Source/Goal Subject/Object Asymmetry

		Thematic *Structure*		*Passive/* *Affected Object*
a.	Simple Motional	$< \Theta, ^{0}\Sigma, ^{0}\Gamma >$ subject Θ, oblique Σ/Γ	*go, roll*	no passive unaffected oblique complement
b.	Simple Motional	$< \Theta, \Gamma >$ subject Θ, object Γ	*hit, strike, slap,* *kick, rub, touch,* *see*	passive unaffected object
c.	Unmarked Motional	$< \Sigma, \Theta >$ subject Σ, object Θ	*drop, leak, gush,* *sprout, emit,* *produce, cause*	passive unaffected object
d.	Complex Resultative	$< \Theta, [\Gamma/\Sigma; \Theta] >$ subject Θ, object Γ/Σ (Γ/Σ is colinked with Θ of consequent subevent)	*smash, penetrate,* *invade, abandon*	passive affected object
e.	Simple Motional	$< \Theta, ^{(0)}\Gamma/\Sigma >$ subject Θ, object Γ/Σ (object is implicit oblique complement)	*enter, leave,* *depart, escape*	no passive unaffected object
f.	Simple Motional	$< \Theta, \Pi >$ subject Θ, object not Γ/Σ, but Direction or Path Π	*approach;* *avoid, flee,* *escape**	passive unaffected object
g.	Complex Motional	$< [\Sigma/\Theta; \Gamma], \Theta >$ (subject role, e.g. Γ, is colinked with Agent (Σ) (i) or Θ (ii) of precedent subevent)	*(i) obtain, buy;* *(ii) gather, collect,* *catch, soak up,†* *absorb*	passive affected object
h.	Possessional Motional	$< \Gamma, \Theta >$ (subject Γ marked, similar to object Γ in double object construction)	*acquire, inherit* *(cf. give, sell),* *receive, get* *(cf. send),* *hear, perceive* *(cf. show), learn,* *understand* *(cf. tell, teach)*	passive unaffected object

*Escape is polysemous exemplifying (e) with Source (i) or (f) with Direction object (ii):
   i. The convict escaped the prison./*The prison was escaped by the convict.
   ii. The felon was not convicted and so escaped prison/. . . and so prison was escaped/avoided by him.

†These alternate with forms without the precedent subevent, in which the Theme is subject:
   i. The table collected dust./The dust collected on the table.
   ii. The bush caught the ball./The ball caught in the bush.

      h. i.   They received the letter./The letter was received by them.
          ii. *What happened to the letter? — They received it.

Row (a) of Table 7.2 and example (26a) consists of unaccusative intransitive
types expressing a simple Motional event; passive is not ordinarily possible, and

the complement is unaffected. Rows (b) and (c) are verbs expressing simple Motional events with either Theme subject and Goal object or Source subject and Theme object, respectively: these are true transitives with directly Case-marked objects that are passivizable, while the object is "unaffected," since the event structure is simple. Locational roles colinked with the Theme of a consequent subevent form complex event structures in (d), which do not fit the pattern of the Source/Goal Subject/Object Asymmetry, since we do not have a simple event structure: in these cases, the object is "affected," while passive is natural. In (e), the object appears as various locational roles ($\Omega = \Lambda, \Sigma, \Gamma$), which actually have implicitly semantically/obliquely Case-marked complements, and passive is unnatural. Row (f) at first looks like verbs with Goal or Source objects, but in fact does not entail these objects necessarily being at the Source or Goal at any time. In (g), a Goal, or other role, as subject is licensed by its colinking with an Agent (i) or a precedent Theme (ii) that can appear as subject; here, passive is generally possible and the object is generally affected.

In both Table 7.2 and example (26) (h) is problematic: a Goal appears in the subject with Theme object, but the verb is not agentive and the object is passivizable and unaffected; however, these verbs generally require a Goal subject that is animate, or the inalienable Possessor of the Theme. This seems to relate them to verbs that show double object constructions (in parentheses in Table 7.2), in which the Goal is similarly constrained (Grimshaw 1987, Tremblay, 1990, 1991):

(27) a. Give/roll the dog the bone.
 b. *Give/roll the tree the stone.
 c. Give/?roll/fix the house a new roof.

(28) a. The dog got the bone.
 b. *The tree got the stone.
 c. The house got a new roof.

This could mean that Goal subject verbs, as well as double object constructions, involve Possessor raising (see Gruber 1995c). For example, a Possessor of the Theme, colinked with the Goal, could raise out of the Source-subevent representation to subject in a derivation configurationally similar to that of the $< \Sigma, \Theta >$ construction, but yielding the apparent $< \Gamma, \Theta >$ construction. If the Goal object in a double object construction, such as (29a), were similarly derived by raising a Possessor from a Source subevent representation, it would also explain why a similar animate Goal object is not licensed in a non-causative form when the subject is Theme (b), since that derivation would be configurationally similar to the excluded $< \Theta, \Sigma >$ construction. Rather, the non-causative counterpart to the double object construction is just the $< \Gamma, \Theta >$ form (c) in question.

(29) a. John passed the book to Bill/... Bill the book.
 b. *The book passed *(to) Bill from John.
 c. Bill received the book from John.

Lexically unmarked options exist for verbs representing simple Motional event structures. These options are just those predicted by the asymmetries, given that the lexicon does not specify for these verbs whether the agreement phrase for semantic Case AgrP-VP is active or not. The verb may then be used in any of

Table 7.3. Lexical Alternations in Accord with the Source/Goal
Subject/Object Asymmetry

a.	$< \Theta, {}^0\Gamma >, < \Theta, \Gamma >$	*hit, strike, slap, kick, rub, ... :*	i.	It hit the wall.
			ii.	It hit against the wall.
b.	$< \Theta, {}^0\Sigma >, < \Sigma, \Theta >$	*drop, drip, leak, gush, sprout, radiate, exude, ... :*	i.	Leaves dropped from the tree.
			ii.	The tree dropped leaves.
c.	$< \Theta, {}^0\Sigma >, < \Sigma, \Theta >$	Cause: Σ(CST):	i.	John died from pneumonia.
			ii.	Pneumonia killed John.
d.	$< \Theta, {}^0\Omega >,$ $< \{\Omega; \Theta\}, {}^0\Theta >$	*pile, load, spread (over), stack, drip, trickle, leak*	i.	*The barge piled logs.
			ii.	The barge piled high with logs.
			iii.	Logs piled onto the barge.
			i'.	The bucket dripped water.
			ii'.	The bucked dripped empty of water.
			iii'.	Water dripped out of the bucket.

the unmarked ways. Thus, if the verb is of the conceptual dimension of Contact (Table 7.3a), the Goal may be a direct unaffected object (i) or may appear obliquely (ii). Similarly, there is a class of verbs of the Positional conceptual dimension (b) in which the subject may be either Theme with oblique Source complement (i) or Source with Theme direct object (ii).[17] Causes, which are Sources of the Causational conceptual dimension (CST), may similarly appear (c) either as an oblique complement or adjunct (i) or as subject (ii). In (d), options are between simple and complex event structures: for example, *pile* cannot be used, in accord with the asymmetry, with a Goal subject and Theme object in a simple Motional event structure (i), but if the Goal is colinked with the Theme of a resultant or consequent event, Goal can appear as subject (ii); on the other hand, Theme can appear as subject with Goal oblique (iii). All three structures are possible, however, with Source as subject (i', ii', iii'), as accords with the asymmetry.

The impossibility of (d.i.) in Table 7.3 arises out of a Source/Goal asymmetry pertinent to resultative structures, which will be discussed in section 5.1. Thus, constraints on argument projection and patterns result not from Theta-role/argument-position specification, but from basic configuration and movement.

4. RESULTATIVE EVENT STRUCTURES

4.1. Inner Aspect

A resultative event structure consists of Motional subevent representations in a precedence-consequence relation. Each of these contains additional aspectual possibilities, reflecting the general property of event structure to include aspectual phrasal projections in each subevent representation:

(30)

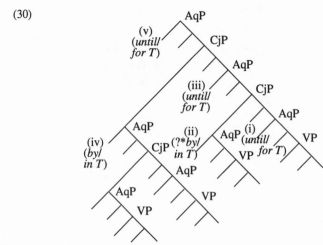

For example, in

(31)   The wind was blowing/blew the sand out of the yard into the road (until/for T;
by/in T).

for/until T, in position (v), has scope over the entire resultative event, meaning the
time sand was blowing into the road; if it occurs in position (iii), it has scope over
just the consequent Motional subevent, meaning the time the sand was entering the
road; in position (i), it has scope over just the consequent Goal subevent, meaning
the time the sand is in the road after entering. *By/in T* in position (ii) has scope
over the consequent Source subevent, and denotes the time the sand was in the
yard, and after leaving and before entering the road; if in position (iv), it has scope
over the precedent Motional subevent and denotes the time the wind was blowing
before sand entered the road.[18]

The conjunction phrase representing a resultative event expresses consequence (CSQ), not just temporal sequence (TMP), as in the case of a Motional
event. Extending each lexical phrasal projection by the functional sequence associated with it, we have the general structure in (32) for a resultative event (CjP-CSQ)
between two Motional subevents (CjP-TMP), for example, one of Contact (CTT)
and one of change of State (STE).[19]

(32)

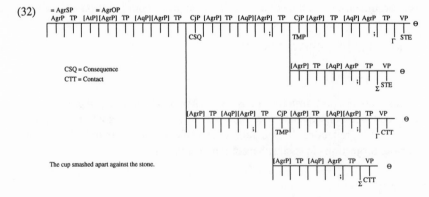

Note that similar phrasal sequences and structures appear at each level of event representation. This reflects the spirit of Strict Thematic Configurationality in that similar relations must be represented in the same way at each level of structure.

We turn next to considerations of argument projection in resultative structures.

4.2. Object/Complement Projection Conditions

It is straightforward to derive the Internal Theta-role Projection Condition presented in Gruber and Collins for complex event structures representing resultatives. An essential additional consideration is the modular interaction of principles of colinking with those of thematic interpretation of X-bar theoretic event structure, Case, and movement.

Colinking is determined configurationally by movement into the local topic positions of relevant subevent representations relative to CjP. The local topic position is the Spec TP associated with the thematic phrasal projection, VP (or CjP). In a resultative event representation, each CjP-TMP requires colinking between the Source and Goal subevents conjoined by it, which is determined in the respective TP-VPs. As we have seen, since only Theme moves into these positions, Motional subevents involve Θ; Θ colinking between Locational subevents only.

For the resultative construction as a whole, it is CjP-CSQ which requires colinking between the Motional subevents conjoined by it. The local topic of the precedent Motional subevent in the precedent TP-CjP-TMP must therefore be identified with the topic of the consequent subevent in the TP-CjP-TMP associated with that subevent. Thus the Theta-role of whatever element moves into the precedent TP-CjP-TMP is colinked with that in the consequent one. For example, in (32), the thematic element that moves into TP-CjP-VP-CTT, which may be the precedent Theme, Source, or Goal, is colinked with the element in TP-CjP-VP-STE, which is normally Theme.[20] These colinking positions play a crucial role in modular interactions and argument projection.

In Gruber and Collins, the Internal Theta-role Projection Condition is described and partially accounted for. It may be restated in the form of the conditions in (33), exemplified in (34).

(33) *Internal Theta-role Projection Conditions*
    a.   Object Role Condition: Only a role of the most consequent subevent may be projected as direct object.
    b.   Complement Role Condition: A complement argument is Case-marked with respect to its most consequent colinked role.

(34) a. The cup smashed against the stone.   (Γ; Θ colinking in object)
        (= The cup hit the stone and the cup broke.)
    b. The stone smashed the cup.   (Θ; Θ colinking in subject)
        (= The stone hit the cup and the cup broke.)
    c. *The stone smashed against the cup.   (*= Γ; Θ colinking)
        (*= The stone hit the cup and the cup broke.)
    d. *The cup smashed the stone.   (*= Θ; Θ colinking)
        (*= The cup hit the stone and the cup broke.)

The Object Role Condition (33a), as explained in Gruber and Collins, follows from the CjP configuration and conditions on movement for Case in minimal domains. Let us consider the derivation of this condition in the present framework. Suppose subject SBJ and object OBJ as in (35), are defined as the XPs that move into Spec AgrSP and AgrOP, respectively. Example (33a) states that if a role is projected as object, it must be of the most consequent subevent, that is, out of the complement of CjP, as in (35a), not out of the specifier. Suppose OBJ is in Spec CjP, that is, it is a role of the precedent subevent. If SBJ c-commands OBJ in the precedent subevent (b), then, as in Gruber and Collins, SBJ blocks OBJ to AgrOP movement, since the minimal domain determined by X^0-movement is not over the specifier of the specifier of CjP. On the other hand, if OBJ c-commands SBJ in the precedent subevent (c), OBJ to AgrOP movement blocks SBJ to AgrSP movement, even if SBJ is colinked in the consequent subevent. Therefore, OBJ is always from the complement of CjP, and hence of a consequent subevent (a).

(35)   a.   b.   c.

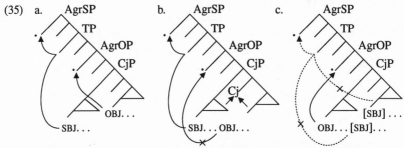

The Complement Role Condition (33b) corresponds to part B of the Internal Theta-role Projection Condition of Gruber and Collins. It derives from the interaction of event structure, Case, and movement, as before, and, in addition, of colinking. In Gruber and Collins, sufficient structure is not provided in event representations for the colinking positions necessarily involved in an account of the Complement Role Condition. With the more complete articulation of event structure here, however, a straightforward account is possible.

As we have stated, NP movement is driven by the need for Case, not colinking. Consider (36). Suppose in (a) the consequent role α is colinked with the precedent role β in local topic positions.

(36)   a.   b.

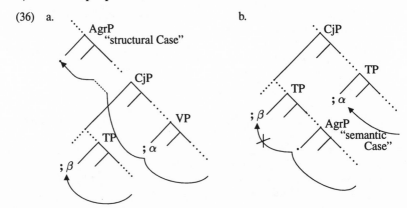

In this configuration, the structural Case position of the consequent role is higher and attained derivationally later than its colinking position. Hence, a thematic element must move further for structural Case than its colinking position. The semantic Case position of the precedent role, however, is derivationally prior to its colinking position (b). If it is semantically Case-marked, it cannot move further for colinking, since movement is driven only by Case. Optimality of Chain formation also implies that there can be no intermediate structural Case positions for the precedent role. Therefore, Case will always be in respect to the consequent colinked role, deriving the Complement Role Condition.

In brief, the Complement Role Condition follows from the fact that a precedent colinked element cannot be Case-marked locally because it cannot move thereafter to its c-commanding colinking position.[21] Thus, the interaction of movements for Case and colinking is essential in deriving the condition.

4.3. Derivations of Form/Meaning Patterns

In the following sections, we review the mechanisms of possible and illicit or blocked derivations in the paradigm of (34), showing the operation of modular interaction in effecting the Object/Complement Role Projection Conditions (33).

In the complex unaccusative construction of (34a), there is just one direct Case assigned. Within a resultative event structure such as shown in (37b), a Theta-role originating in the complement of CjP-CSQ is of the consequent subevent, while a Theta-role in the specifier of CjP-CSQ is of the precedent subevent. The thematic functional representation (a) roughly describes (b), with the precedent subevent represented below the consequent one, and Theta-roles indicated under the arguments expressing them (cf. Gruber and Collins).

(37)   a.   The cup smashed (apart) against the stone.

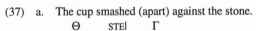

b.

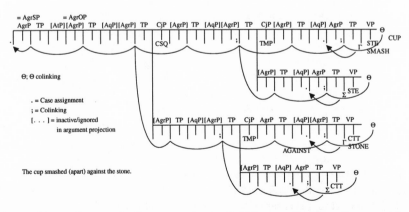

The positions of semantic Case, namely, AgrP-VPs, are all active, Case-marking Source and Goal of both Motional subevents, which may all be implicit.[22] The

Themes of the Locational subevents within the each Motional subevent are colinked, as are the Themes of the Motional subevents themselves. Form Chain optimality requires "across-the-board" movement of the colinked Themes to the highest structural Case position in AgrSP (= AgrP-AtP).

The derivation of the transitive construction (34b) with two structural Cases is similarly straightforward, as shown in (38). Given, again, the resultative event structure representation of (32), the most consequent Theta-role of the object is the Theme Θ(STE) of the most consequent Motional subevent, originating in the complement of CjP. It moves in the normal fashion for Case as direct object to AgrOP (= AgrP-AqP-CjP-CSQ). The subject Theta-role is the Theme of the precedent Motional subevent Θ(CTT), originating in the specifier of CjP-CSQ. It moves out of CjP-TMP-VP-CTT from the Source subevent without blocking to be Case-marked as subject in AgrSP (= AgrP-AtP), crossing the Goal of the precedent Motional subevent Γ(CTT) in the colinking position:

(38)   a.   The stone smashed the cup (apart).

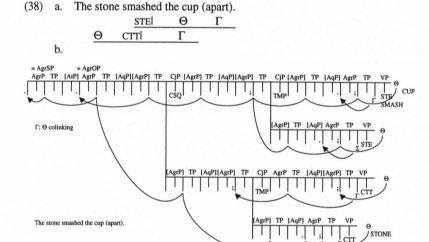

b.

In the precedent Motional subevent, the Goal is colinked rather than semantically Case-marked. This means that AgrP-VP-Γ(CTT) is inactive for Case. Γ(CTT) then moves for structural Case, passing into TP-CjP-VP-CTT, where it is colinked with the consequent Θ(STE) in TP-VP-STE. Because it is colinked, it forms an effective A-Chain with Θ(STE) and therefore need not, and hence must not, move independently for Case. It therefore does not move further.

The unacceptable form/meaning patterns are particularly revealing of the necessary modular interactions involved in derivations. The form in (34c) violates the Complement Role Condition on argument projection (34b). As shown in (36a), the consequent Theta-role Θ(STE) is colinked with the precedent role Γ(CTT). This cannot be Case-marked semantically in respect to the precedent colinked role. As seen in (36b), the precedent role Γ(CTT) is colinked in virtue of its movement into TP-CjP-VP-CTT. If it is semantically Case-marked at AgrP-VP-CTT, however, its further movement, after Case-assignment, into the colinking position would not be driven and hence would be impossible, as shown in (39).

(39) a. *The stone smashed against the cup (apart).

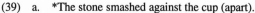

(*= The stone smashed the cup apart.)

b.

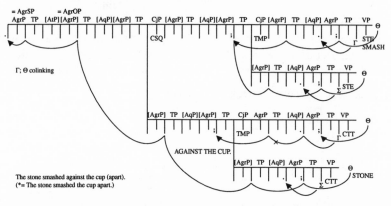

Example (34d) violates the Object Role Condition (33a). The Goal of the precedent Motional subevent Γ(CTT) cannot be projected as direct object. Since the precedent Θ(CTT) is colinked, it moves into TP-CjP-VP-CTT. If Γ(CTT) is direct object, it must pass through TP-AqP-CjP-VP-CTT. That is, it cannot cross CjP-CSQ, except from the highest position, as shown in (35b), deriving the Object Role Condition. From this position, in order to end up at AgrOP, it must pass through TP-CjP-CSQ. But this blocks Θ(CTT) and/or Θ(STE) moving to subject, as shown in (35c), deriving the Object Role Condition. In addition, Γ(CTT) is blocked by Θ(CTT) in TP-CjP-VP-CTT. This is shown in (40).

(40) a. *The cup smashed the stone.

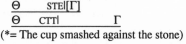

(*= The cup smashed against the stone)

b.

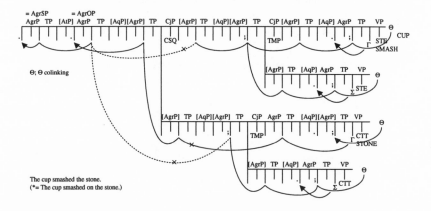

As noted, the Object Role Condition reflects the Internal Subject Hypothesis, predicting that in a transitive form only the subject may proceed from the precedent subevent, represented in the specifier of CjP/VP.

4.4. Further Derivations: Precedent Source and Theme Arguments

A Source or Theme of the precedent subevent is, like a Goal, blocked in resultative structures from being projected as direct object. Thus the Object Role Condition applies in respect to the Source and Theme, as well as the Goal. Consider the acceptable unaccusative form in (41), in which Source is Case-marked obliquely.

(41)   a.   The water drained free from the bottle.

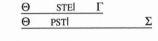

   b.

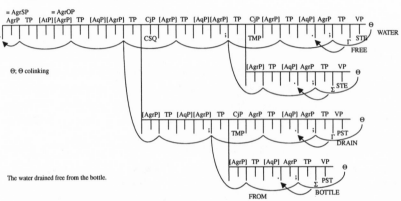

As in the previous unaccusative example, (37), all AgrP-VPs are active, and semantically Case-mark all Sources and Goals, at least implicitly. Accordingly, the Themes are all colinked and move for structural Case "across the board" to subject as the sole direct argument.

Reflecting the Object Role Condition (33a), the Source of the precedent Motional subevent cannot be projected as direct object. Thus (42) is unacceptable.

(42)   a.   *The water drained the bottle free.

$$\begin{array}{lll} \Theta & \text{STE|} & \Gamma \\ \Theta & \text{PST|} & \Sigma \end{array}$$

(*= The water drained free from the bottle.)

b.

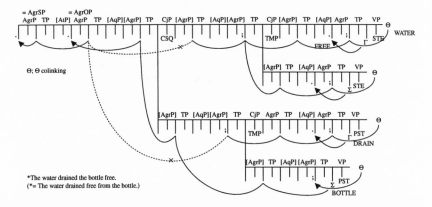

Θ; Θ colinking

*The water drained the bottle free.
(*= The water drained free from the bottle.)

If the precedent Source is structurally Case-marked, its semantic Case position AgrP-VP-Σ(PST) is inactive. It would then move through TP-CjP-CSQ c-commanding the subject Θ(PST/STE). However, this blocks movement of subject out of CjP-CSQ, as before. Note, however, that this example of blocking precedent Source as object reveals the Object Role Condition more purely than the Goal example. The precedent Σ(PST) is not blocked in its movement to object position by the colinked Θ(PST) at TP-CjP-VP-PST. Rather the subject is blocked by the object, as shown in (c) deriving the Object Role Condition.

The Object Role Condition also pertains to Themes of the precedent subevent, which are similarly blocked from appearing as direct object. In (43), an acceptable form with Goal colinked with Theme in the subject and oblique Theme in the object is shown, with its derivation in (b).

(43) a. The bottle filled   with water.

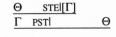

   b.

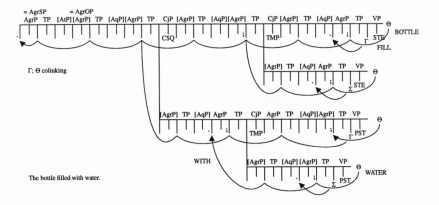

Γ; Θ colinking

The bottle filled with water.

Since Γ(PST) is colinked, AgrP-VP-Γ(PST) is inactive for semantic Case, and Γ(PST) moves for structural Case into the colinking position TP-CjP-VP-PST. The precedent Θ(PST) then moves out of the Source subevent for structural Case, but does not move to subject. Instead the precedent AgrP-CjP-VP-PST is active and Case-marks Θ(PST) obliquely, marked by *with*. The position AgrP-CjP is also relevant for morphologically similar comitative (Accompaniment) Case, also marked by *with* in English, as will be discussed below.[23] By Form-Chain optimality Γ(PST) moves with colinked Θ(STE) across the board for direct Case as subject.

The precedent Theme, however, cannot be projected as direct object. Thus (44) is unacceptable.

(44)　a.　*The bottle filled　water.

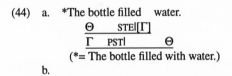

　　　　　(*= The bottle filled with water.)

　　　b.

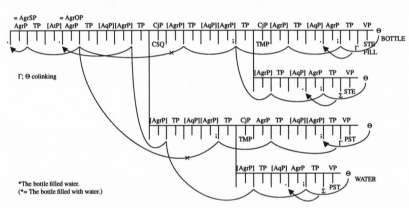

For the colinking of Goal here, the precedent AgrP-CjP-VP-Γ(PST) must be inactive as Γ(PST) moves for structural Case through TP-CjP-VP-PST, where it is colinked. If Θ(PST) moves beyond for structural Case as object, into TP-CjP-CSQ, it blocks movement of the subject Γ(PST);Θ(STE). In the case of an (unacceptable) precedent Theme object, the precedent Theme, here Θ(PST), is again not itself blocked by the colinked Γ(PST);Θ(STE), but blocks the latter from moving to subject.

5. SOURCE/GOAL ASYMMETRIES IN RESULTATIVES

Resultative constructions also exhibit Source/Goal argument projection asymmetries, which reflect the basic configurationality of these roles. The Source/Goal Subject/Object Asymmetry in Resultatives involves the possibilities of projection of the Source or Goal of the precedent subevent as subject or object. The Source/Goal Oblique Theme Asymmetry involves the precedent Theme projected as an oblique argument, as in example (43), exhibiting an asymmetry in its Case, or the form of its Case-marker, that correlates with whether Source or Goal is colinked.

We will show that these again reflect the configurational determination of Source and Goal and the interactive modular theory of argument projection presented here involving Case, colinking and movement. In addition, the Source/Goal Oblique Theme Asymmetry shows the configurational determination of specific Cases. Just as Theta-roles are determined configurationally in the initial positions of elements in a base-generated structure, distinctive Cases or argument types are determined configurationally in positions of agreement phrases accessible by movement of the thematic elements.

5.1. The Source/Goal Subject/Object Asymmetry in Resultatives

An asymmetry among resultative sentences similar to that for simple Motional sentences, concerning where the Locational role, that is, Source or Goal, of the precedent subevent may be projected as an argument, is shown in the examples of (45) of acceptable or unacceptable form/meaning correspondences:

(45) a. i. The stone smashed the cup apart.

$$\frac{\text{STE}|\qquad \Theta \qquad \Gamma}{\Theta \quad \text{CTT}|\qquad \Gamma}$$

(= The stone knocked against the cup and the cup broke apart.)

   ii. *The apple dropped the branch bare.

$$\frac{\text{STE}|\qquad \Theta \qquad \Gamma}{\Theta \quad \text{PST}|\qquad \Sigma}$$

(*= The apple dropped from the branch, and the branch became bare.)

   b. i. The branch dropped the apple free.

$$\frac{\text{STE}|\qquad \Theta \qquad \Gamma}{\Sigma \quad \text{PST}|\qquad \Theta}$$

(= The apple dropped from the branch and the apple became free.)

   ii. *The stone smashed the cup apart.

$$\frac{\text{STE}|\qquad \Theta \qquad \Gamma}{\Gamma \quad \text{CTT}|\qquad \Theta}$$

(*= The cup knocked against the stone and the cup broke apart.)

In all the examples in (45) there is colinking in the object. In (a) either the precedent Goal (i) or the precedent Source (ii) is colinked. Example (a.i.), with precedent colinked Goal, is acceptable, and is identical to (34b) in the paradigm for the Internal Theta-role Projection Conditions (33). Example (a.ii.), however, with precedent colinked Source, but otherwise configurationally the same as (a.i.), is unacceptable.

In (b), Θ; Θ colinking appears in the object, while either the precedent Source (i) or the precedent Goal (ii) appears uncolinked in the subject. Example (b.i.), with bare Source subject, is here acceptable, while (b.ii.), with bare Goal subject but otherwise configurationally the same, is unacceptable with this thematic configuration and meaning.

The generalization shown in these examples may be stated as the following asymmetry:

(46)   *The Source/Goal Subject/Object Asymmetry in Resultatives*
    When Theta-roles are colinked in the object, then:

    a.   The role of the precedent subevent in the object can be a Goal, but not a Source.

    b.   The role of the precedent subevent in the subject can be a Source, but not a Goal.

The asymmetry necessarily pertains in cases in which there is colinking in the object. It may be regarded as an instance of the similar asymmetry for simple non-resultative Motional event structures, but for resultatives the asymmetry is neutralized when a Source or Goal is colinked in the subject: both precedent Source and Goal colinked in the subject may form an acceptable derivation, as is clear from the examples presented for the Source/Goal Oblique Theme Asymmetry in section 5.2. The asymmetry also shows the External Theta-role Projection condition in Gruber and Collins to be inaccurate when Source is involved; thus (45a.ii.) is unacceptable with a precedent colinked Source, although a precedent Theme is subject; however, (45b.i.), with bare Source subject, is acceptable.

The Source/Goal Subject/Object Asymmetry in Resultatives reflects modular interaction in derivations among conditions of movement for Case, colinking, and thematically interpreted X-bar theoretic configurations. In particular, movement of elements to subject for Case is blocked by elements in colinking positions. Base configurations determining the thematic roles of elements distinguish what movements may be possible among them.

In general, a precedent Locational role (Source or Goal) colinked in the object will block the precedent Theme from moving to subject for Case unless the Theme comes out of the specifier of the precedent CjP-TMP, that is, the Source subevent. In that case, the Locational role would come out of the complement of the precedent CjP-TMP, that is, the Goal subevent, so that it would be a Goal that is colinked, not a Source. On the other hand, a Theme colinked in the object means that any precedent role moving to subject must come out of the specifier, not the complement, of the precedent CjP-TMP, that is, out of the Source subevent. Hence, it would be Source, and not Goal, that can be projected as bare subject.

Consider first the cases in which the precedent Source or Goal is colinked in the object, (45a.i.) and (ii). The acceptability of (45a.i.) has already been shown (cf. [38]).

Suppose, however, the precedent colinked role is Σ, as in (45a.ii.) and (47).

(47)

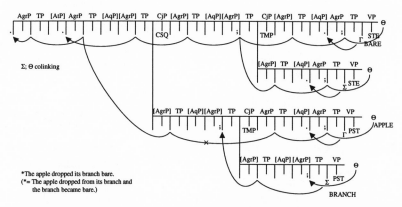

*The apple dropped its branch bare.
(*= The apple dropped from its branch and
the branch became bare.)

The precedent Source must reach the colinking position TP-CjP-VP-PST out of the Source subevent in the specifier of CjP-VP-PST. The precedent Theme then would move for Case to subject out of the Goal subevent in the complement of CjP-VP-PST. The precedent Source, however, blocks its movement to subject.

Consider now instances in which the precedent Theme is colinked in the object and the subject is either the precedent Source or Goal, as in (45b). This constitutes a possible derivation if the subject is a Source, but not if it is a Goal. The derivation of (45b.i.) with Source subject is shown in (48).

(48)

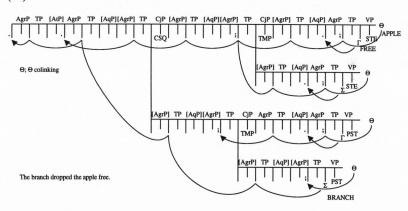

The branch dropped the apple free.

With Θ; Θ colinking, the precedent Θ(PST) must be in TP-CjP-VP-PST. It can move to this position out of the Goal subevent representation in the complement of CjP-VP-PST. The precedent Source Σ(PST) can then move for Case to subject out of the Source subevent representation in the specifier of CjP-VP-PST, without blocking.

An optimal derivation cannot result if the subject is a bare Goal, however, as in (45b.ii.) and (49).

(49)

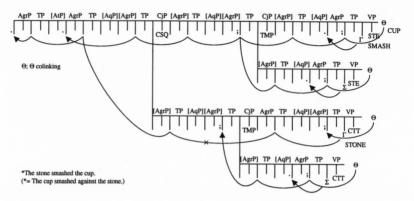

A subject element must move out of the specifier of CjP-CSQ from TP-AqP-CjP, which can be reached by the Source, as in (45b.i.) and (48). A Goal subject, however, must come out of the Goal subevent representation in the complement of CjP-VP-CTT. But if the precedent Theme Θ(CTT) is colinked with the object in TP-CjP-VP-PST, Γ(CTT) cannot cross it, as in (45b.ii.) and (49).

5.2. The Source/Goal Oblique Theme Asymmetry

An asymmetry in the oblique Case-marking of a precedent Theme depending on whether the precedent Source or Goal is colinked in the subject is shown in example (50).

(50) a. The barge piled high with/*of the logs.

$$\begin{array}{ccc} \Theta & \text{STE}| & \Gamma \\ \hline \Gamma & \text{PST}| & \Theta \end{array}$$

b. The bottle drained (empty) of/*with the water.

$$\begin{array}{ccc} \Theta & \text{STE}| & \Gamma \\ \hline \Sigma & \text{PST}| & \Theta \end{array}$$

The generalization can be stated as follows:

(51) *The Source/Goal Oblique Theme Asymmetry*
      In a resultative structure, the Case of the precedent Theme differs depending on whether there is Γ; Θ or Σ; Θ colinking.

      a. With Γ; Θ colinking, the Case is similar to that of comitatives or Instruments (*with*).

      b. With Σ; Θ colinking, the Case is similar to that of the genitive object of DPs (*of*).

The configurational Theta theory accounts for the asymmetry. To show this, we provide below a derivation of the possible sentences in (50) and demonstrate the impossibility of derivation of the corresponding sentences with opposite Case marking on the Theme. The thematic structure of (50a) and its derivation in (52) are precisely similar to that of (43):

(52)

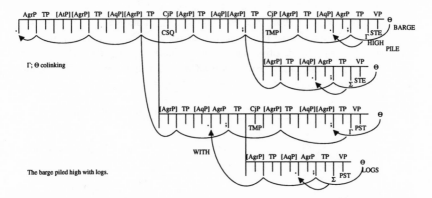

The precedent Γ(PST) moves out of the Goal subevent representation in the complement of CjP-VP-PST for structural Case to TP-CjP, in which it is colinked with the consequent Θ(STE). Γ(PST) and Θ(STE) then optimally move together for structural Case to subject. The precedent Θ(PST) must then move out of the Source subevent representation in the Spec CjP-VP-PST for Case, which it obtains in AgrP-CjP. This is structural oblique Case, *with*, in English.[24] We show later the relation of the Case-marking of the oblique Theme here with other uses of *with*.

Consider now the derivation of (50b) as shown in (53), in which a precedent Source rather than a Goal is colinked. Because of the configurational difference of Source from Goal, the Theme must be Case-marked in a different position if it is the Source that is colinked, resulting in a difference in Case.

(53)

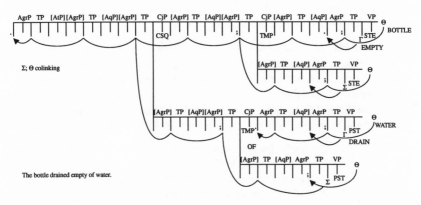

Here Σ(PST) moves out of the Source subevent representation in the specifier of CjP-VP-PST for structural Case into TP-CjP, in which it is colinked with Θ(STE). The precedent Θ(PST) then must move out of the Goal subevent representation in the complement of CjP-VP-PST. But the presence of Σ(PST) in TP-CjP blocks Θ(PST) from moving out. It is therefore optimal for it to get oblique structural Case within Spec CjP-VP-PST, hence at AgrP-AqP. This Case is distinctively marked *of* in English. As will be shown, this Case position is configurationally similar to that of the genitive marking of the object in a deverbal noun.

The opposite Case-markings are impossible, as shown in (54). On the one hand, the precedent Theme Case-marked at AgrP-CjP is blocked in the case of Σ; Θ colinking (a). On the other hand, Theme Case-marked at AgrP-AqP-VP-PST is blocked in Γ; Θ colinking (b) by Form-Chain optimality, since the Theme can move further for structural Case, namely, to AgrP-CjP-tmp.

(54) a.

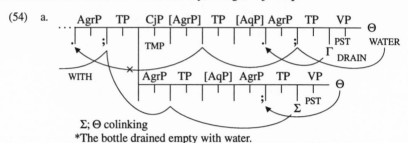

Σ; Θ colinking
*The bottle drained empty with water.

b.

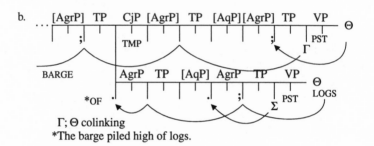

Γ; Θ colinking
*The barge piled high of logs.

5.3. Configurational Case Determination

An account can be made of the overt forms (*with* or *of*) of oblique Case assigned to the Theme in these constructions by relating these to an analysis for comitative (*with*) or genitive Object (*of*) Case positions, showing that these positions are configurationally similar.

The oblique Theme in a resultative with Γ; Θ colinking is consistently Case-marked by *with* in examples such as in (55a); in AgrP-CjP, as in (b).

(55) a. i.   The bottle slowly filled with water.
         ii. John loaded the truck with logs.
         iii. John supplied the students with books.
         iv. John adorned the table with flowers.

      b. :

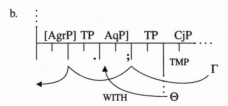

For oblique Theme, the Goal colinked at TP-CjP-TMP moves for Case through TP-AqP to be projected as subject (or as object, in causatives). The Theme, then, coming from the Source subevent representation, is blocked from movement for Case beyond AgrP-CjP.

A blocking similar to that of Theme by a Goal of the same subevent occurs in a similar configuration for a comitative or Accompaniment Theme role blocked by the main Theme of a Motional event. Accompaniment Theme is consistently Case-marked by comitative *with* in examples such as in (56a), which could be in configurations as in (b).

(56)   a.   i.   The pad is on the table with the pen.
            ii. The stone rolled down the hill with the log.
            iii. John threw the ball over the fence with the bat.
            iv. John took the book (with him) into the room.

   b.
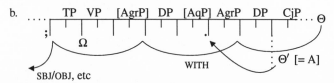

An Accompaniment role is represented by asymmetric conjunction of DPs in Theme position, yielding a main Theme Θ in the complement of CjP, and a secondary Theme $\Theta' = A$ (Accompaniment) in the specifier of CjP. Instead of DP-CjP moving as a unit as a conjoined DP for Case, both receive Case separately. The Accompaniment element A must then move out of Spec CjP to AgrP-CjP, the configuration of comitative *with*. Θ raises through DP and crosses Locational role W in VP, becoming configurationally identical to a sole Theme, and moves for Case normally as Theme.[25]

The position of Case-marking of the oblique Theme in the $\Sigma; \Theta$ colinking construction is likewise configurationally similar to that of the genitive object of deverbal nouns marked by *of*. The oblique Theme in a resultative with $\Sigma; \Theta$ colinking is consistently Case-marked by *of* in examples such as in (57a); in AgrP-AqP, as in (b).

(57)   a.   i.   The bottle emptied of water.
            ii. John drained the tub of water.
            iii. They robbed the peasants of their land.
            iv. John washed the cloth of stains.

   b.
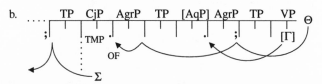

The precedent Source out of the Source subevent representation is colinked at TP-CjP. The precedent Theme is therefore from the Goal subevent representation, hence blocked from movement for Case beyond AgrP-CjP, and so Case-marked in AgrP-AqP.

A similar blocking occurs in deverbal nouns, resulting in the necessity to Case-mark an "object" obliquely as genitive *of* in a configurationally similar position relative to the verb from which the noun derives. The object of a deverbal noun is consistently Case-marked by genitive *of* in examples such as in (58a), which could be in configurations as in (58b) (cf. 11b).

(58)   a.   i.   The shooting of the deer by the hunters.
             ii. The destruction of the city by the enemy.
             iii. The hitting of the wall by the stone.
             iv. The dropping of fruit by the tree.

       b.   ... DP$_i$ ...

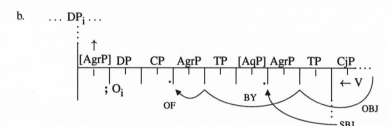

A deverbal noun is represented as a clausal structure CP embedded in a DP. The CP contains an operator (like a wh-operator) that identifies the event denoted in the clause, or an argument of the event, to the nominal head. If there is no Tense, there is no AtP or its functional extension.

The OBJ argument out of the complement of CjP of the event representation, moves for Case to AgrP-AqP. The SBJ argument out of the specifier of CjP moves for Case to AgrP-CjP. Movement for Case of these internal arguments is blocked beyond AgrP-AqP by the CP structure containing the operator O linking elements of the verbal structure to nominal head.[26] Case is therefore oblique or prepositional, since it is in positions below that in which the thematic head incorporates into a word. Oblique genitive Case marked by *of* in English is assigned in AgrP-AqP. Thus the oblique Theme in resultatives with $\Sigma; \Theta$ colinking is Case-marked in a position configurationally similar to that of the object in deverbal nouns, and is marked similarly by *of*.

Note that the configuration for *by*- and *with*-Cases are similar (AgrP-CjP) and often morphologically the same.[27]

The configurational determination of Case-types as positions in event structure representations, as indicated here for two types of oblique Case, as well as for the distinctions of direct and oblique Case, and structural and semantic Cases, accords with the general program for argument projection in a configurational Theta theory. Event structure representations, conforming to the principle of Strict Thematic Configurationality, involve the iteration of similar functional and lexical phrasal projection sequences for each subevent. Within this structure derivations of sentences result from modular interactions involved in movement from configurationally distinguished thematic positions to configurationally distinguished positions of colinking, inner aspect, and Case. We have here focused on an account of asymmetries of argument projection reflecting configurational distinctions in the relatively non-complex structures of simple and resultative events.

The configurational Theta theory we have approached, however, is intended to account for the full range of thematic roles and argument projection patterns of more complex structures.

NOTES

This work was supported by the Social Sciences and Humanities Research Council of Canada grant no. 411-92-0012: "La Modularité de la Grammaire: Arguments, Projections, et Variation" and Fonds Institutionnel de Recherche (Université du Québec à Montréal) to Anna-Maria Di Sciullo.

1. Strict Thematic Configurationally does not necessarily imply that each syntactic relation has a unique thematic interpretation. There could be equivalence classes of syntactic relations such that each class has a unique thematic interpretation. In that case, every thematic relational distinction would be distinctively represented by an equivalence class of syntactic structures.

2. The phenomena is also to be identified with that of object sharing in serial verbal constructions (Baker 1989), as shown in Gruber (1992b, 1995a).

3. Or figure-ground (Talmy 1976). Identifying the Theme-Location relation with figure-ground developed in work with Pierre Pica (Gruber and Pica 1992).

4. We will use the terms "Locational" and "Motional" to refer to thematically distinct event structures (cf. Gruber and Collins), in contrast with the terms "stative" and "active" which refer to kinds of aspect. *Stand* is Locational, involving the roles Theme and Location, but may be aspectually "active," as in "they are standing there"; *Extend* is Motional in an abstract sense, involving the roles Theme, Source, and Goal, but is aspectually "stative," in "it extends from here to there."

5. We will continue to use the contrastive terms "precedent' and "consequent" to refer to relations of simple sequence as well as actual consequence.

6. Actually a Temporal Goal, indicating the existence of further elaboration of structure within AqP.

7. Concomitantly, the Positional Goal must have an iterative sense (as with *beat*) or the sense of a Path (*toward*). This is because a temporal adverbial denoting an extent implies the effective iteration or duration of the subevent representation over which it has scope, that is, it is non-telic. A temporal adverbial denoting a point of time implies no such iteration, as in change from green to red at noon, a punctual event. (See notes 8 and 9.)

8. That is, it is associated with iterations of the Source subevent representation (ii) before reaching the Goal. If it is a Motional subevent, its iteration means a fractal-like succession of usually implicit (possibly infinite) Sources and Goals. This can be explicit (*the ball rolled [[[from the bush to the tree] to the wall] to the river]*). The temporal adverbial at (ii) has scope over this iteration excluding the final Goal, and so covers positions in and after leaving the initial Source. These considerations underline the configurational connection between aspect and thematic structure. I have benefited from discussions on these topics with Elizabeth Klipple. See also Verkuyl (1993).

9. See note 8 above. For example, among Locational verbs, the temporal adverbial for stay, which may be implicit, must entail a duration (*stay until/for/*at T*), while for *stand*, it may denote a point in time. Among Motional verbs, the temporal adverbial at T(ii) (= time of arriving at the tree) for a verbal expression such as *roll* or *go to* (achievement verb) may not denote a point (*roll to the tree *at T*), whereas for a verb such as *reach* or *get to* (accomplishment verb) it must do so (*reach the tree at/*forT*) (see note 18).

10. To conserve space in large representations, here and henceforth trees are drawn with complement branches extended horizontally to the right. X^0 and X-bar categorial labels of nodes are also generally omitted.

11. Beyond this assumption, we do not here investigate the nature of prepositions. But see note 13.

12. We will describe Case according to two distinct dimensions: semantic versus structural and oblique versus direct. Semantic Case is thematically specific and is assigned in the agreement phrase directly associated with a thematic phrasal projection, particularly that of a VP (or NP). Structural Case is elsewhere, particularly in an agreement phrase associated with an aspectual phrasal projection. See note 27. Oblique Case is strongly marked morphologically, perhaps by a preposition, and is not associated with agreement, while direct Case is often associated with agreement and is less strongly marked. It seems that direct Case is assigned in a position relatively local to the point of highest conflation of the thematic heads at Spell-out, that is, at the point of entering computation for phonological form (PF) (cf. Chomsky 1993). Oblique Case would be remote from this domain in some sense. See Demuth and Gruber (1993), Giorgi and Pianesi (1991), Poletto (1991) for the association of agreement, and hence direct Case, with the termination of head conflation. Semantic Case is necessarily oblique in a language such as English, but could be direct in a language with serial constructions in which the position of semantic Case is local to the point of conflation of a verbal head at Spell-out (cf. Gruber and Collins).

13. Case marked *'s* in English nominals, reserved for subjects and parallel to nominative in clauses, but oblique (genitive) in nominals for the same reason, could be in an agreement phrase corresponding to AgrP-AtP.

14. Argumentally "active" aspectual phrases may play a role in forcing alternative projection pattern types, such as ergativity, by blocking otherwise possible movements.

15. Abstract "Motional" is also included, for example, extension over space, as in verbs such as *extend*, *cover*, and *surround*.

16. This conception of colinking has benefited from discussions with Pierre Pica.

17. For discussion of these or related alternations, see Levin (1993).

18. For a telic verb, that is, an accomplishment or achievement verb, such as *roll to* or *reach*, respectively (cf. notes 8 and 9), AqP at position (v) may not be an extent, while (iv) may be (*roll to/reach the tree in/*forT*).

19. Positions of obligatory colinking ";" are indicated for future reference.

20. Between the precedent and consequent Motional subevents only three patterns of obligatory colinking normally occur: Θ; Θ; Σ; Θ; and Γ; Θ only (cf. Gruber 1992b, 1995a). Evidently, the topics of the Locational subevents percolate to be that of the consequent Motional subevent as a whole. This means that the Themes of these subevents must also always move into the consequent TP-CjP-TMP. Hence only the colinked Theme can be projected with structural Case from the consequent Motional subevent of a resultative. This seems to be so: for example, the tree, a Goal in (i), cannot be a direct object, although it can be oblique, as in (ii).

    i. *the ball hit the tree against the wall

      (*= the ball hit the wall and bounced against the tree)

    ii. the ball rolled into the yard against the wall

      (= the ball hit the wall and bounced into the yard)

Such a Theme would be an "affected Theme," so that many instances of the condition that a direct object must be "affected" (Tenny 1987, 1989) may result from the interaction of argument projection and colinking.

21. The Complement Role Condition implies that unergative intransitives cannot result from the semantic Case-marking of a precedent role colinked with an "object" role, which then moves to subject. Rather, an unergative must result from implicitly Case-marking object in AgrOP. That is, an unergative is an implicit transitive.

22. Note that it is essential that adverbial or adjectival particles that bear Theta-roles, such as *apart*, move for Case, as all thematic elements do. They would in fact be lexically specified with semantic Case, so that they can only move to a semantic Case position to legitimize this specification.

23. The similar configuration for a verb such as *smash* is blocked for aspectual reasons:

> *The cup smashed with the stone.

In particular, if it moves to subject, the colinked precedent Goal Γ(CTT) must pass through TP-AqP. This appears to have a particular interpretation, namely that the precedent event can be multistaged with respect to the consequent subevent. This contrasts *fill* with *smash*. For *smash*, the precedent Θ(CTT) moves to subject through TP-AqP, so that the colinked role cannot appear there, with the interpretation that the precedent subevent is single-staged relative to the consequent subevent. Thus there is further modular interaction between colinking and Case with inner aspect. (See note 24.) This interaction is characterized and embodied in the Aspectual Colinking Subject/Object Asymmetry developed and accounted for in Gruber (1994b).

24. Optimally, Θ(PST) moves to subject, but here cannot as the colinked role Γ(PST) must move to TP-AqP for aspectual reasons:

> *Logs piled the barge high.

Pile necessarily expresses a multistaged precedent subevent in relation to the consequent Motional subevent, in contrast to *smash* (see note 23), for which the precedent subevent must be single-staged, and the colinked Γ(CTT) must not be in TP-AqP.

25. The CjP configuration, together with $\Theta; \Theta$ colinking in Motional event representations results in the sense of an Accompaniment relation between Θ and Θ'=A. A, as well as Θ, relates as Theme to both Σ and Γ, namely, as specifier to complement, and hence as Theme to Locational role or figure to ground. The relation of Θ to A is also that of Theme to Locational role. Hence, Accompaniment A has properties of both Theme and Locational role.

26. The presence of an operator in derivational morphology arose in discussions with A.-M. Di Sciullo and is developed in Di Sciullo (1993).

27. *By*-Case, that of passive, and perhaps ergative, when direct, would be more inclusive than the AgrP-CjP assigning *with*-Case. Since CjP is thematic in certain respects, Case in AgrP-CjP may have some properties of semantic Case. The lower it is in event-structure the more thematically specific it is. (See note 12.)

REFERENCES

Baker, Mark C. 1988. *Incorporation: A theory of grammatical function changing*. Chicago: University of Chicago Press.

————. 1989. "Object sharing and projection in serial verb constructions." *Linguistic Inquiry* 20:513–533.

Chomsky, Noam. 1986. *Knowledge of language: Its nature, origin, and use*. New York: Praeger.

————. 1989. "Some notes on economy of derivation." In *MIT working papers in linguistics* 10, ed. I. Laka and A. Mohajan. Department of Linguistics and Philosophy, MIT, Cambridge, Mass.

————. 1993. "A minimalist program for linguistic theory." In *The view from Building 20: Essays in linguistics in honor of Sylvain Bromberger*, ed. Kenneth Hale and Samuel Jay Keyser, 1–52. Cambridge, Mass.: MIT Press.

Chomsky, Noam, and Howard Lasnik. 1992. "Principles and parameters theory." In *Syntax: An international handbook of contemporary syntax*, ed. J. Jacobs, A. van Stechow, W. Sternefeld, and T. Vennemann. Berlin: de Gruyter.

Cole, Desmond T. 1955. *An introduction to Tswana grammar*. Johannesburg: Longmans, Green and Co.

Collins, Chris and Höskuldur Thráinsson. 1993. "Object shift, double object constructions and the theory of Case." In *Papers on Case and agreement II, MIT working papers in linguistics* 19, ed. Colin Phillips. Department of Linguistics and Philosophy, MIT, Cambridge, Mass.

Di Sciullo, Anna-Maria. 1993. "The complement domain of a head at morphological form." *Probus* 5:95–125.

Di Sciullo, Anna-Maria, and Edwin Williams. 1987. *On the definition of word*. Cambridge, Mass: MIT Press.

Demuth, Katherine, and Jeffrey S. Gruber. 1993. "Constraining XP Sequences." Paper presented at the Sixth Niger-Congo Syntax and Semantics Workshop, 1993, Boston University. In *Niger-Congo syntax and semantics* 6, ed. Victor Manfredi and K. Reynolds, Boston University African Studies Centre, Boston, Mass., 1995]

Dowty, David. 1979. *Word meaning and Montague grammar*. Dordrecht: Reidel.

Giorgi, Alessandra, and Fabio Pianesi. 1991. "Toward a syntax of temporal representation." *Probus* 3/2:1–27.

Grimshaw, Jane. 1987. "Getting the dative alternation." *MIT working papers in linguistics* 10. Department of Linguistics and Philosophy, MIT, Cambridge, Mass.

————. 1990. *Argument structure*. Cambridge, Mass.: MIT Press.

Gruber, Jeffrey S. 1965. "Studies in lexical relations." Doctoral diss., MIT, Cambridge, Mass. In *Lexical structures in syntax and semantics*, Part I, Amsterdam: North-Holland, 1976; and *MIT working papers in linguistics*, Department of Linguistics and Philosophy, MIT, Cambridge, Mass.

————. 1967. "Look and see." *Language* 43/4:937–947.

————. 1990. "Complex Θ-Structures." Ms. MIT Lexicon Project seminar, October, MIT, Cambridge, Mass.

————. 1992a. "Proper argument projection in Igbo and Yoruba." *Proceedings of the Kwa Comparative Syntax Workshop*, January *MIT working papers in linguistics* 17, Department of Linguistics and Philosophy, MIT, Cambridge, Mass.

————. 1992b. "Thematic configurational constraints in serial verb constructions." Paper presented at the twenty-third Annual Conference on African Linguistics, University of Michigan.

————. 1994a. "Principles of a configurational Theta-Theory." In *A festschrift for Dong-Whee Yang: Explorations in generative grammar*, Kookmin University, Seoul, Korea.

————. 1994b. "Configurational Θ-theory and argument projection asymmetries." Paper presented at the Configurations conference, University of Quebec at Montreal, October. To appear in *Configurationality in linguistic theory*, ed. Anna-Maria Di Sciullo, forthcoming.

————. 1995a. "Thematic configurationality and serial verb constructions." In *Issues in African languages and linguistics: A tribute to Professor Kay Williamson*, ed. E.N. Emenanjo and Ozo-Mekuri Ndimele. Aba, Nigeria: National Institute for Nigerian Languages.

————. 1995b. "Thematic configurations and syntactic structure." Paper presented at the conference Linguistics by the End of the Twentieth Century: Achievements and Perspectives, Lomonosov State University of Moscow, February.

————. 1995c. "Configurational accounts of thematic linking regularities: The Possessional/Spatial Asymmetry." To appear in *Configurations*, ed. Anna-Maria Di Sciullo, Somerville, Mass.: Cornell Cascadilla Press.

Gruber, Jeffrey S., and Pierre Pica. 1992. "Structure thématique, structure conceptuelle et représentations mentales: Quelques réflexions sur les rapports langue-vision." Ms. Université du Québec à Montréal, and MIT, Cambridge, Mass.

Hale, Kenneth, and Samuel J. Keyser. 1993. "On argument structure and the lexical expression of syntactic relations." In *The view from Building 20: Essays in linguistics in honor of Sylvain Bromberger*, ed. Kenneth Hale and Samuel Jay Keyser, 1–52. Cambridge, Mass.: MIT Press.

Halle, Morris, and Alec Marantz. 1993. "Distributed Morphology and the pieces of inflection." In *The view from Building 20: Essays in linguistics in honor of Sylvain Bromberger*, ed. Kenneth Hale and Samuel Jay Keyser, 1–52. Cambridge, Mass.: MIT Press.

Higginbotham, James. 1985. "On semantics." *Linguistic Inquiry* 16:547–593.

Jackendoff, Ray. 1972. *Semantic interpretation in generative grammar*. Cambridge, Mass.: MIT Press.

————. 1976. "Toward an explanatory semantic representation." *Linguistic Inquiry* 7:89–150.

————. 1983. *Semantics and cognition*. Cambridge, Mass.: MIT Press.

————. 1990. *Semantic structures*. Cambridge, Mass.: MIT Press.

Kuroda, S.-Y. 1985. "Whether you agree or not: Rough ideas about the comparative grammar of English and Japanese." Ms. UCSD.

Larson, Richard. 1988. "On the double object construction." *Linguistic Inquiry* 19:335–391.

Levin, Beth. 1993. *English verb classes and alternations: A preliminary investigation*. Chicago: University of Chicago Press.

Perlmutter, David. 1978. "Impersonal passive and the Unaccusative Hypothesis." In *Proceedings of the Berkeley Linguistic Society* ed. J. Jaeger et al., 4:157–189.

Poletto, Cecilia. 1991. "The aspect projection: An analysis of the 'passé surcomposé.'" Ms. Università di Padova, Padova, Italy.

Pollock, Jean-Yves. 1989. "Verb movement, universal grammar, and the structure of IP." *Linguistic Inquiry* 20:365–424.

Pustejovsky, James. 1988. "The geometry of events." In *Studies in generative approaches to aspect*, ed. Carol Tenny, *Lexicon Project Working Papers* 24, Center for Cognitive Science, MIT, Cambridge, Mass., 19–39.

Rizzi, Luigi. 1990. *Relativized minimality*. Cambridge, Mass.: MIT Press.

Rooryck, Johan. 1994. "Prepositions, functional projections, and minimalist Case-assignment." Presented at the Comparative Germanic Syntax Workshop 9, January 5–6, Harvard University, Cambridge, Mass.

Stowell, Tim. 1980. "Origins of phrase structure." Doctoral diss., MIT, Cambridge, Mass.

Talmy, Leonard. 1976. "Semantic causative types." In *Syntax and semantics*, vol. 6: *The grammar of causative constructions*, ed. M. Shibatani, 43–116. Cambridge, U.K.: Cambridge University Press.

———. 1978. "Figure and ground in complex sentences." In *Universals of human language: Syntax* (vol. 4), ed. Joseph Greenberg. Stanford, Calif.: Stanford University Press.

———. 1985. "Lexicalization patterns — Semantic structure in lexical forms." In *Language typology and syntactic description*, ed. Timothy Shopen, 57–149. Cambridge, U.K.: Cambridge University Press.

Tenny, Carol. 1987. "Grammaticalizing aspect and affectedness." Doctoral diss., MIT, Cambridge, Mass.

———. 1989. "The Aspectual Interface Hypothesis." *Lexicon Project working papers* 31, Center for Cognitive Sciences, MIT.

Travis, Lisa. 1992. "Inner aspect and the structure of VP." *Cahiers de Linguistique de l'UQAM*, 1/1:130–147.

Tremblay, Mireille. 1990. "An argument sharing approach to ditransitive constructions." *Proceedings of the West Coast Conference on Formal Linguistics* 9, 549–563. Stanford Linguistics Association, Stanford University, Stanford Calif.

———. 1991. "Possession and datives." Doctoral diss., McGill University, Montreal, Quebec.

Vendler, Zeno. 1967. *Linguistics in philosophy*. Ithaca, N.Y.: Cornell University Press.

Verkuyl, Henk J. 1972. "On the compositional nature of aspects." *Foundations of Language*, Supplementary Series 15. Dordrecht: Reidel.

———. 1993. *A theory of aspectuality: The interaction between temporal and atemporal structure*. Cambridge, U.K.: Cambridge University Press.

Williams, Edwin. 1984. "Grammatical relations." *Linguistic Inquiry* 15:639–674.

EIGHT

On Passive as Partitive Quantification

JOHAN ROORYCK

1. THE MODULAR ACCOUNT OF PASSIVE

In the modular framework of generative grammar, passive is reduced to the inter-action of various principles involving Case theory, movement, and Theta theory (Chomsky 1981). Movement of the object to subject position is dependent on the thematic vacuousness of this subject position, which in turn is obtained by the "absorption" of the external thematic role by the passive morphology transmit-ting this thematic role to the *by*-phrase (Jaeggli 1986; Baker, Johnson, and Roberts 1989). Movement is triggered as a consequence of Burzio's (1986) generalization: a verb without an external Theta-role has no accusative Case to assign. Since no accusative Case is available for the object NP in the postverbal position (or in Spec AgrOP, in the minimalist framework), the object NP moves to subject position, where nominative Case is available. If the object stays in object position, it can only do so if provided with inherent partitive Case, yielding impersonal passives (1c) with necessarily indefinite (partitive) NPs in object position (Belletti 1988).

(1) a. Murasaki played the zithern.
     b. The zithern was played by Murasaki.
     c. There were various instruments played by the musicians.

As a result, there is no rule in the grammar referring to the label "passive." Passive arises through the interaction of various syntactic modules that are independently motivated.

2. EMPIRICAL ADEQUACY

Although this modular picture of passive is appealing, it is well known that it is empirically inadequate as it stands. Simply put, the theory overgenerates. It predicts that any transitive verb should be able to enter a passive configuration, irrespectively of its thematic structure. Nevertheless, verbs with a direct object expressing Location, but not only those, display various restrictions on passive (see Lamiroy 1993 for an overview):

(2) a. This box contains twelve bottles of Meursault.
     b. *Twelve bottles of Meursault are contained by this box.
     c. Ce livre comporte cinq chapitres.
         "That book comprises five chapters."
     d. *Cinq chapitres sont comportés par ce livre.
         "Five chapters are comprised by that book."

(3) a. Eugénie/everyone knows Eustache.
     b. Eustache is known by *Eugénie/everyone.
     c. Gonzague/neuf millions de personnes habite(nt) Paris.
         "Gonzague/nine million people live in Paris."
     d. Paris est habité par *Gonzague/neuf millions de personnes.
         "Paris is lived in by Gonzague/nine million people."

It is therefore a simple and crucial empirical fact that passive diathesis is more restrictive than active diathesis. Why should this be the case? Before the days of modular syntax, when rules like passive were still around, some of these "exceptions" to passive were explained by a thematic hierarchy: the Location object in (3c) is too low on the hierarchy to be promoted to subject position as in (3d), and cannot be projected higher than the Agent of *habiter*, "live in" (Jackendoff 1972). Note that the application of this hierarchy must be directly linked to a specific type of movement, such as passive. In present-day Generative Grammar, establishing such a link cannot be considered in any way an explanation for the facts. At best, it would express a descriptive generalization. The question would immediately arise as to why the hierarchy applies to passive or A-movement, but not to *wh-* or A-bar movement. Moreover, even if such a generalization were possible, we would still be left in the dark with respect to the intermediate status of examples such as (3d), where the quantification of the *by-* phrase seems to matter in some way. The constraint cannot be stated as one on stative verbs, either: various stative verbs allow for passive:

(4) a. Ceci implique cela.
         "This implies that."
     b. Cela est impliqué.
         "That is implied."
     c. Sept chapitres constituent ce livre.
         "Seven chapters constitute this book.
     d. Ce livre est constitué de sept chapitres.
         "This book is constituted of seven chapters."

Ideally, the explanation for the constraints noted above would not merely establish a descriptive link between passive and the thematic or aspectual structure of the verbs concerned. A stipulation to the effect that Location objects cannot raise to an empty Spec IP position is one that simply cannot be made to follow from the interactions that yield passive in the generally accepted modular account we sketched above.

It seems, however, that the constraint might be stated inappropriately. Indeed, the very formulation of the constraint as one on Location objects might be entirely false. This much is suggested by the intermediate status of the examples in (3). Jackendoff's (1972) attempt to explain the Locative constraint on passive through the interaction of passive and a universal thematic hierarchy applying to the output of a passive rule not only fails on the basis of these examples, but it also reveals a more important methodological point. A thematic account of the Locative constraint views passive morphology as semantically inert: the passive morphology itself cannot be responsible for the effects of the Locative constraint. The same is true in present-day accounts of passive: passive involves a syntactic configuration that is shared by raising contexts, movement of the object NP to subject position is "blind" to the thematic contents of the object, and passive morphology is tied only to the "neutralization" ("absorption") of the external argument of the verb. Crucially, passive morphology is not linked to the thematic role of the object. It seems, then, that even in the modular account of passive sketched above, we can do no better than stipulating the limitation on passive in terms of the type of NP objects that can be moved to subject position. At the same time, there seems to be nothing in the syntax forcing us to assume that the thematic structure of a verb should have an influence on passive morphology. We may therefore conclude that stating the Locative constraint in thematic terms is a descriptive artifact that not only fails to adequately describe the problem at hand in the light of the examples in (3), but also leads to a theoretically unappealing stipulation. This means that we have to look outside of Theta theory for an explanation of the limitations on passive illustrated above.

In this chapter, the limitations on passive illustrated in (2) and (3) will be derived from nonthematic properties. It will be argued that passive morphology, and especially the role of the copula, should be taken seriously if a modular account of these limitations is to be achieved (see also D'Hulst 1992). I will try to show that passive is even more modular than has been assumed before, and that this modularity offers an elegant and flexible solution to the problem of overgeneration of passives.

3. PARTIVITY: *BE* AND Q_P

I would like to argue that the constraints on passive noted above are most crucially determined by partitive properties of the verb *be/être* that is used as a passive auxiliary. More specifically, the limitations on passive will be related to the following alternation:[1]

(5) a. The whole is its/a number of/*the parts.
   (be = hold, contain)
   b. The parts are *their/*the/a whole.
   (be = constitute)

The sentence (5a) shows that *be* can be equivalent to "hold" or "contain': the whole "contains" a number of parts. In the sentences in (5b), this part-whole relation is reversed. The only grammatical combination in (5b) involves an indefinite NP in the predicate, and has a meaning closer to "constitute." The sentences (5b), in which the predicate involves a definite NP, are ungrammatical because they are incompatible with both the "constitute" and the "contain" meaning of *be*. Assuming that a part-whole relation is a form of quantification, the "contain' meaning of *be* could be called the quantificational use of *be*. I would like to distinguish this quantificational use of *be* both from the "constitute" meaning in (5b) and from its predicational use, illustrated in (6):[2]

(6) a. Polycarpe is sick // in his hometown // his usual self // their/the/a director.
     b. The parts are available // in their/the/a box.

Following Déchaine (1994), I will assume that the different uses of *be* should not be attributed to the inherent polysemy of *be*. Rather, the different uses of *be*, which does not itself have an intrinsic meaning, are triggered by the syntactic context in which this word is inserted (Déchaine 1994; see also Postma 1993).

What is the nature of the alternation in (5)? It seems that quantificational properties are the key to understanding what is going on. Descriptively speaking, (5a) is characterized by a part-whole relation between the subject NP and the predicated NP. The predicated NP has to entertain a partitive relationship with the subject. The definite determiner is excluded because it does not allow for such a partitive reading.

This description can be formally implemented through the licensing of the predicated NP by a partitive operator Q_p. Let us assume that this partitive operator is a functional projection that yields the quantificational reading when it appears in the context of *be*. When Q_p is not present, the predicational reading follows.[3] This is the reading of (6) but also of (5b): since a partitive reading cannot be licensed for the predicative NP, only the predicational reading is available. This analysis of quantificational *be* versus predicational *be* can be formalized along the lines of Kayne's (1993) and Hoekstra's (1993) theory of auxiliary selection, in which the notion of selection has been modularly eliminated.

Kayne (1993) analyzes "possessive" *be* with a dative possessor like Latin *esse*, "be," and English *have*, in essentially the same way. The structure of *have/be* includes a DP, the D^0 head of which can assign dative case. In Kayne's (1993) analysis, the D^0 either does not incorporate and assigns dative case to the possessor (Hungarian, Latin), or it incorporates and does not assign case to the possessor, which ends up as the subject of *have* (English). The structure in (8a) is a simplified version of the structure Kayne assumes for *be* in Hungarian, which has a dative possessive construction like the one illustrated here for Latin. The structure (8b) represents Kayne's analysis of English *have*, which corresponds to *be* with an incorporated D^0.

(7) a. Sunt nobis mitia poma.
         Are us$_{DAT}$ many apples$_{NOM}$
         "We have many apples."
     b. sunt [$_{DP}$ nobis [D^0_{DAT}] mitia poma]

(8) a. e   be $[_{DP}$ we $D^0{}_{DAT}$ $[_{DP}$ many apples]]

　　b. We have $_{be+D^0\text{-}DAT}$ $[_{DP}$ $^tD^0\text{-}DAT$ $[_{DP}$ many apples]]
　　　　　　⤴_____⌐

Kayne's (1993) analysis of *have* in (8) can now be extended to quantificational *be* in (5a):

(9) The whole is$_{be+Q_p{}^0}$ $[_{Q_pP}$ $^tQ_p{}^0$ $[_{DP}$ its parts]]
　　　　　　　　⤴_____⌐

As in Kayne's (1993) analysis, the A-bar position of Spec Q_p is turned into an A-position by incorporation of $Q_p{}^0$. It is easy to see that the sentence (5a), with the structure in (9), can be considered a partitive *be* variant of the *have* sentence in (10a), which has the dative structure proposed by Kayne (1993) as in (10b). For the most part, partitive (5a–9) and dative (10a, b) are equivalent.

(10) a. The whole has (its) parts.
　　　　　(have = contain, have as a property)

　　　b. The whole has$_{be+D^0\text{-}DAT}$ $[_{DP}$ $^tD^0\text{-}DAT$ $[_{DP}$ (its) parts]]
　　　　　　　　　　⤴_____⌐

　　　c. *The parts have the/a whole.
　　　　　(have = contain, have as a property)

In other words, the interpretation that quantificational *be* (= *be*+Q_p) establishes between the whole and its parts should be viewed as a relation between quantifier and quantified. We may then assume that adequate interpretive paraphrases for (5a–9), repeated here as (11a), are as in (11b). The sentence (5b), repeated as (11c), cannot be paraphrased in the same way.

(11) a. The whole is its parts.
　　　b. The whole has/contains parts as a defining or intrinsic property.
　　　c. *The parts are the whole.
　　　d. *The parts have/contain the whole as a defining or intrinsic property.

The interpretive paraphrases in (11) can be viewed as a way of spelling out the partitive syntactic structure behind (11a), which is exemplified in (9). The importance of these paraphrases will become clear as the passive auxiliary *be* is discussed in section 3.

There is independent evidence for the existence of partitive Q_p. Latin has a construction in which *esse*, "be" is constructed with a genitive. The subject of *esse*, "be" expresses a partitive property of the NP marked with genitive:

(12) a. est　　　　adulescentis　　maiores natu　vereri.
　　　　is$_{3rd\ p.sg.}$ of-young-person elders by-birth to respect
　　　　To respect his elders is (should be) one the properties of a young person.
　　　　"It behooves a young person to respect his elders."

　　　b. est　　　　sapientiae　maiores natu　vereri.
　　　　is$_{3rd\ p.sg.}$ of-wisdom elders by-birth to respect
　　　　"It testifies to (is a property of) wisdom to respect one's elders."

In the framework developed by Kayne (1993), which we adopt here, the genitive case assigned by *esse*, "be" must be viewed as a partitive case licensed by Q_p. Kayne's (1993) dative structure for Latin possessive *be* in (7) can now be extended to the partitive construction (12b), as in (13a).[4] The Small-Clause construction of which *sapientia* is the DS subject is motivated by an analysis of *be* as an unaccusative verb (e.g. Heggie 1988, Moro 1990). In this way, there is a minimal contrast between (13a) and the predicational (13b):

(13)   a.   est $[_{Q_pP}$ sapientiae$_i$ $[Q_{\text{part-GEN}}]$ $[_{SC}$ t$_i$ [maiores natu vereri]]]

   is$_{\text{3rd p.sg.}}$ of-wisdom   elders by-birth to respect

   "It testifies to (is a property of) wisdom to respect one's elders."

   b.   sapientia est $[_{SC}$ t$_i$ [maiores natu vereri]]

   "Wisdom is to respect your elders."

It might be the case that the partitive construction (13a) and the dative construction (7) can be reduced to two sides of the same coin. The trouble is that it is unclear what the coin would be. Importantly, the dative construction can only be used for animate possessors, and indicates alienable possession: the possessor has the object at his disposal (Kühner and Stegmann 1955:I.307). There are no examples of the type **libro sunt multa folia*, "The book has many leaves." The genitive construction applies to both animate and inanimate[5] NPs, and can refer to intrinsic possession, an inalienable quality: wisdom *includes* the intrinsic property, which is to respect your elders. The partitive reading takes the NP marked with genitive on its property reading; the dative NP seems to be treated as an individual. It might very well be the case, then, that the dative/partitive alternation, which is overtly realized in Latin, should be defined as an alternation between expressing possession of properties (inclusion, inalienable, partitivity) and possession characterizing an individual (non-inclusion, alienable, comitative).

We can tentatively conclude that the verb *be* can be constructed with two types of possessive-like complements: a quantificational Q_pP complement, and a determinative DP complement. In both cases, the D^0 and the Q_p^0 head can either incorporate into *be*, respectively yielding possessive *have* (8) and partitive *be* (9), or they can remain unincorporated, respectively triggering dative (7) and partitive (13a) case on NP.

4. PASSIVE AS *BE*+Q_P: THE INFORMAL EFFECTS OF FORMAL PARTITIVE QUANTIFICATION

The claim of this essay is that the passive auxiliary *be/être* involves the quantificational reading of *be*, or rather, the combination of *be* and Q_p. How should this be interpreted? Simply put, it means that passive *be* relates the surface subject to the participial predicate in such a way that the participial predicate is interpreted as a partitive property of the surface subject. This means that the auxiliary *be*, which is traditionally viewed as a fairly neutral part of the passive morphology, compositionally contributes to the meaning of the entire passive configuration. A passive sentence such as *The Aztec empire is destroyed by Cortéz* then receives a structure as in (14a), similar to (11). In the same way as (13a), (14a) can be paraphrased as (14b):

(14) a. The Aztec empire is$_{be+Q_p^0}$ [$_{Q_pP}$ t$_{pQ_p^0}$ [destroyed by Cortéz]]

   b. "The Aztec empire has as a defining property the fact that it is destroyed by Cortéz"

This means that we interpret passive as a way of defining an intrinsic property of the internal argument DP moved to subject position. The function of *be* is limited to being a support for passive in the sense that *be* functions as an element incorporating the passive morpheme Q_p. Passive *be* is syntactically complex, since it comes with a Q_p attached to it that confers a partitive, "inalienable" reading to the participial predicate when relating this predicate to the surface subject. The relevant configuration for passive is identical to the one proposed by Kayne for *have* as *be* with an incorporated D^0. Instead of an incorporated D^0, passive *be* incorporates a partitive Q^0, and can be represented as in (15b):

(15) a. DP$_i$ BE+D^0 [$_{DP}$ e$_i$ t$_{D^0}$ [... [$_{VP}$ e$_i$ V DP]]]
      (= Kayne 1993 for HAVE)
   b. DP$_i$ BE+Q$_p^0$ [$_{Q_pP}$ e$_i$ t$_{Q_p^0}$ [... [$_{VP}$ e V e$_i$]]]
      (passive BE)

In this way, the configuration for passive is identical to that of both the partitive and the dative possessive construction with *esse*, "be," in Latin. In the passive configuration, the Q_p incorporated into *be* establishes a partitive quantificational relation between the surface subject and the predicate: by incorporating into *be*, the complex X^0 *be*+Q$_p^0$ functions as a partitive operator binding the trace of Q_p, and hence the entire Q_pP, which is viewed as a "defining part of" the subject DP.

Clearly, for sentences such as (14a), or any other run-of-the-mill passive, the elaborate paraphrase in (14b) does not make any difference. However, we now want to show that both the partitive structure in (14a) and the paraphrase in (14b) can adequately explain the ungrammaticality of the passive sentences in examples (2) and (3) above.

First of all, there is a set of verbs in which quantification of the NP contained in the *by*-phrase has an influence on the acceptability of the passive. The paraphrase *have as an intrinsic or defining property* makes it clear that, in this case, partitivity does play a role. Someone can have the socially defining property that everybody knows him or her: this can be viewed as a defining, partitive property of that person. It is much more difficult to imagine that the fact that someone is known by a particular person constitutes a defining property carried by that person. Similarly, Paris cannot be intrinsically defined by Gonzague's living there, although it is intrinsically defined by the fact that nine million people live there. Note that if Paris were to be depopulated by some catastrophic event, with a single person surviving, (3d) would be acceptable in the same way the sentence *Cette maison est habitée par Louis*, "that house is inhabited by Louis," is acceptable: a house, or a depopulated Paris, can be intrinsically defined by the fact that one person lives there.

(16) a. Eugénie/everyone knows Eustache.
   b. Eustache is known by *Eugénie/everyone.

    c. Eustache has as a defining or intrinsic property the fact that *?Eugénie knows him/everybody knows him.

(17) a. Gonzague/neuf millions de personnes habite(nt) Paris.
        "Gonzague/nine million people live in Paris."
     b. Paris est habité par *Gonzague/neuf millions de personnes.
        "Paris is lived in by Gonzague/nine million people."
     c. Paris has as a defining or intrinsic property the fact that nine million people live there/*that Gonzague lives there.

(18) a. Joséphine/tous les habitants a/ont quitté ce village.
        "Joséphine/all the inhabitants left that town."
     b. Ce village a été quitté *par Joséphine/par tous les habitants.
        "That village was left by Joséphine/by all its inhabitants."
     c. This village has as a defining or intrinsic property the fact that all inhabitants left it/*that Joséphine left it.

In these cases, the pluralization of the *by*-phrase allows for the participial predicate of passive *être*, "be," to be turned into an intrinsic property of the surface subject. Note that these meaning effects cannot be reduced to pragmatics or knowledge of the world: our knowledge of the world only allows us to build interpretations for getting around the specifically syntactic constraints passive sets up. What counts as a distinctive, defining, or intrinsic property thus is often defined with respect to a context that involves knowledge of the world. This is not to be considered a drawback of the analysis; quite the contrary. The quantificational part-whole relation established by passive between the subject NP and the predicate functions as an interpretation algorithm that can be satisfied by various "real world" situations as long as these situations conform to the part-whole structure set up by syntax. Context and "real world" knowledge, then, simply allow us to linguistically "fit in" situations in such a way that they conform to the basic syntactico-semantic part-whole requirement. If the syntactic partitive structure and the interpretation of the sentence do not match, the sentence is ungrammatical.

The hypothesis developed here is not entirely new. In fact, it was developed in a pragmatic framework by Cureton (1979). Cureton (1979) suggested that a passive sentence expresses something pragmatically "significant" about the surface subject. The problem with this kind of pragmatic analysis is that it is very hard to determine objectively what is "significant." Nevertheless, I think Cureton's (1979) intuition is fundamentally correct. In the framework developed here, Cureton's (1979) notion of "pragmatically significant" is viewed as a mere effect of the specific syntactico-semantic partitive constraints imposed by passive.

Let us now take a look at the more difficult nut to crack for this analysis of passive. Verbs such as *contain* and *comporter*, "contain" never enter a passive configuration:[6]

(19) a. This fine wooden box contains twelve bottles of Meursault.
     b. *Twelve bottles of Meursault are contained by this fine wooden box.
     c. *Twelve bottles of Meursault have as a defining or intrinsic property the fact that this fine wooden box contains them.

No amount of contextual fiddling yields a grammatical passive in these cases. The interpretive paraphrase in (19c), which is only a paraphrase for the quantificational property expressed by $be+Q_p$, explains why: the "container" property can never be construed as an intrinsic, inalienable property of twelve bottles of wine. Importantly, the fact that good bottles of wine are usually sold by the dozen in a wooden box is not enough to license an inherent relation between the box and the bottles: this remains an "accidental" alienable property of the bottles. However, this is not always true. The following example suggests that in some cases the paraphrase lets us down:

(20) a. Ce livre comporte cinq chapitres.
          "The book comprises five chapters."
     b. *Cinq chapitres sont comportés par ce livre.
          "Five chapters are comprised by this book."
     c. Five chapters have as a defining or intrinsic property the fact that this book contains them.

Since chapters usually occur in books, the chapters could be said to be inherently defined by the book. However, the fact that paraphrase (20c) is quite good is due to independent factors. First of all, there is the necessarily approximative nature of the paraphrase. In fact, *have*, in "have as a defining or intrinsic property," should be interpreted as *contain, comprise,* or *hold.* The reason I have not used these verbs in the paraphrase has to do with the fact that it is difficult to say of persons and closely related "groups of persons" such as cities, villages (cf. supra [16–18]) that they "hold" a property. Nevertheless, it is this more restrictive meaning of *have* that is intended in the paraphrase. Now, if we change the paraphrase in the case of the inanimate subjects in (20c) to *comprise/hold*, the paraphrase becomes much worse:

(21) *Five chapters comprise/hold the defining or intrinsic property that this book contains them.

The second reason (20c) is so good has to do with the fact that *chapter* is a relational noun in the same way as nouns such as *sister, toe,* and so on. Since chapters are intrinsically related to books, the paraphrase in (20c) with *have* starts functioning as an explicitation of this relational property, and not of the partitive property of passive.

Let us now come back to the complete ungrammaticality of passives of "container" verbs such as *contain* and *comprise.* The fact that *have as an intrinsic property* has to be restrictively interpreted as *contain as an intrinsic property* now yields an explanation for this ungrammaticality. It is impossible to establish a partitive relation between a subject (whole) and a predicate that has to denote an intrinsic property "contained" by that subject, if the predicate expresses the property of "containing" the subject itself. In other words, it is impossible for the interpretive containee (*the chapters*), which is the subject of the passive sentence, to syntactically function as a container-whole with respect to a (partitive) predicate (*to be comprised by the book*) that can only be interpreted as the container of the subject (*the chapters*). Something cannot contain an object and at the same time be contained in this object.

This view of the part-whole relation as an intrinsic or defining container-contained relation can also explain a number of differences between passives of "container" verbs that involve the animacy of the external argument:

(22) a. This bottle holds five gallons.
     b. *Five gallons are held by this bottle.

(23) a. The terrorists hold five hostages.
     b. Five hostages are held by the terrorists.

A bottle holds five gallons in the sense that it contains five gallons. As a result, five gallons cannot be defined by the passive $be+Q_p$ as a container/whole entertaining a partitive relation with respect to a predicate which expresses the quality of containing the gallons. Terrorists, however, do not usually hold hostages by containing them inside themselves. As a result, the hostages can be described as having/"containing" the defining property of being held prisoner, making possible the passive in (23b).

We now have to check whether this analysis can also explain more delicate cases of ungrammatical passives. A first case is exemplified in (24).

(24) a. Bill was seen *(by Sue/in the company of Derek).
     b. (There is a social context in which) Bill has the defining or intrinsic property *that someone saw him/that someone saw him in the company of Derek/that Sue saw him.

In (24a), the presence of any complement is necessary to allow for an interpretation of *seen* as a defining or intrinsic property of the subject. It is important to point out that in this case, the notion of defining property is related to a context. Whether a predicate can be viewed as a defining property "contained" by the subject is a factor of the backdrop provided. In (24a), the context provided to allow for a "defining" property is a social one. Within a social context, Bill can be viewed as being defined by the fact that he is seen with Derek, or by Sue, but it is impossible to define Bill socially by the fact that some unspecified person saw him. In more formal terms, the passive part-whole relation serves as a quantificational format for interpretation, and it can only be interpreted if contexts that allow for such a partitive relation are projected onto it. The social context is such a context.

This brings us to another set of cases in which what I will call the "casual character" of the participial predicate that prevents successful passives.

(25) a. Les troupes irakiennes ont abandonné/quitté la ville de Koweit.
        "The Iraqi troops have abandoned/left the city of Koweit." (Lamiroy 1993:18)
     b. La ville de Koweit a été abandonnée/*quittée par les troupes irakiennes.
        "The city of Koweit was abandoned/left by the Iraqi troops." (Lamiroy 1993:18)

There is only a subtle difference between *quitter*, "leave" and *abandonner*, "abandon": dictionaries define *abandonner* as leave permanently. *Quitter*, on the other hand can be interpreted as a more "casual" leaving: you may still come back. If I leave the city today, I may come back tomorrow, but if I abandon the city today, the implication is that I will not return at all. In short, the sentence (25b) is acceptable with *abandonner*, "abandon," because a predicate with permanent qualities can be construed as an inherent, defining property of the city of Koweit. However, *quitter*, "leave," in (25b) is a predicate with a more "casual" quality of leaving for now, and as such cannot be construed as an inherent, defining property of the city of Koweit.

Let us take an even closer look at a verb such as *quitter*, "leave." With animate direct objects, *quitter*, "leave," can have an additional meaning to the "casual" meaning just discussed. More in particular, *quitter*, "leave" can also have the meaning of "separate from one's partner," clearly a more permanent and defining quality.

(26) a. Léontine a quitté son collègue à six heures précises.
          "Léontine left her colleague at six o'clock sharp."
     b. Amélie a finalement quitté Alphonse après 20 ans de mariage.
          "Amélie finally left Alphonse after 20 years of marriage."

In the passive, the only meaning remaining is the more permanent one:

(27) a. *Ce collègue a été quitté par Léontine à six heures précises.
          "That colleague was left by Leontine at six o'clock sharp."
     b. Alphonse a finalement été quitté par Amélie après 20 ans de mariage.
          "Alphonse was finally left by Amélie after 20 years of marriage."

Again, this difference can only be explained if it is accepted that passive *be*+Q_p imposes a partitive interpretation on the subject-predicate relation, in which the predicate must denote an inherent, defining property of the subject. In (27b), the husband Alphonse can be inherently defined by the property that his wife has permanently left him. In the sentence (27a), the colleague cannot be easily defined by the "casual" fact that Léontine left him at six. It is no doubt possible to construe a context in which the colleague would be inherently defined by this fact, but my point is clear.

One more example of the "casual constraint" also involves a verb with a "Location" direct object. A verb such as *rencontrer*, "meet" can be opposed to the verb *recevoir*, "receive," in a passive sentence:

(28) a. Plusieurs personnes ont rencontré/reçu Madeleine à cette réception.
          "Several people have met/received Madeleine at that reception."
     b. Madeleine a été *rencontrée/reçue par plusieurs personnes à cette réception.
          "Madeleine was met/received by several people at that reception."
     c. It is a defining property of Madeleine that several people *met/received her at that reception.

Whence this contrast? The verb *rencontrer*, "meet," does not imply any social definition: people meet people everywhere without necessarily controlling who they meet. If you say *I met a crook, a thief, and an attorney at the party*, they are not socially defined by your meeting them. However, if you say *I received a crook, a thief, and an attorney at the party*, there is a sense in which these people are defined by your receiving them. Receiving, then, confers a more socially "defining" property to the direct object than the more "casual" *rencontrer*, "meet." Note, crucially, that the social quality attributed to the subject is defining, but not permanent. The permanent quality of a predicate, as in the case of *abandonner*, "leave," is a sufficient but not a necessary condition for the construal of a successful passive. Coming back to the *rencontrer/recevoir* contrast, for the sentence (28b), we can say that Madeleine is socially defined with respect to the reception by the fact that she is received by many people. However, the casual quality of *rencontrer*, "meet," cannot be construed as a predicate inherently defining Madeleine in the context of the reception.

Another case that gets a natural explanation in the analysis of passive as a partitive construction is the passive of verbs like *sleep*. It is often observed that these verbs can be passivized, but that the *by*-phrase is somehow restricted to V.I.P.s:

(29)   This bed was slept in by *Joe Sixpack/Napoleon/Bolívar/Babe Ruth.

Surely, this cannot be a property of beds or of the predicate *sleep* by themselves. However, we have assumed that passive is such that it imposes a partitive quantificational structure in which the predicate *slept* has to become a defining, inherent property for *the bed* in subject position. The only way in which this can be achieved in (29) is to have the predicate denote an important enough event that allows to define the bed as something special. The "V.I.P. constraint" on the *by* phrase of *sleep* then has exactly the same function as the plurality constraint on the *by* phrase of the sentences in (3) with *habiter*, "live," and *connaître*, "know."

Context plays an important role in the acceptability of these sentences, since it provides the interpretive backdrop against which the partitive relation between subject and predicate is to be understood.

(30)   a.   Quand nous avons vu Sophie et Gérard de l'autre côté de la rivière,
              *le pont de Jambes a été traversé pour les rejoindre/
              plusieurs signes ont été échangés pour les inviter à nous rejoindre.
              "When we saw Sophie and Gérard on the other side of the river,
              the bridge was crossed to go and meet them/
              several signs were exchanged to invite them to join us."
         b.   Quand les troupes ennemies ont cessé le feu de l'autre côté de la rivière,
              le pont de Jambes a été traversé pour encercler leur 3ième division de cy-
              clistes.
              "When the enemy troops had ceased fire on the other side of the river, the
              bridge was crossed to encircle their 3rd division of cyclists."

In the context of a meeting between friends, the bridge cannot be defined by the property of our crossing it with a fairly innocent "casual" purpose. In the context of war, the bridge is inherently defined by our property of crossing it with an "important" or defining purpose.

The paraphrase "be an inherent/defining/inalienable property of" is only an approximation of the interpretation algorithm provided by $be+Q_p$. Discourse factors improve the sentence to the extent that they bring it closer to an interpretation in which the predicate can be interpreted as an inherent property of the surface subject. The following sentences, which are a slight adaptation of Lamiroy (1993:31), show that a number of factors can be used to establish a partitive property reading for the subject of a passive sentence:

(31)   a.   La rivière traverse la ville.
              "The river goes across the city."

    b.   La ville est traversée par la rivière.
        "The city is crossed by the river."

(32)   a.   Ce taxi traverse la ville en dix minutes.
           That cab goes across the city in ten minutes."
      b.*?La ville est traversée par ce taxi en dix minutes.
           "The city is crossed by that cab in ten minutes."
      c.   La ville a été traversée par ce taxi en dix minutes.
           "The city has been crossed by that cab in ten minutes."
      d.   La ville peut être traversée par un bon taxi en dix minutes.
           "The city can be crossed by a good cab in ten minutes."

In (31b), it is simply an intrinsic quality of the city that a river runs through it, and therefore the passive is fine. In (32b), the city can in no way be intrinsically defined by one particular cab crossing it in ten minutes. In (32c), the perfective morphology of *être*, "be," presents the predicate as an event that is closed off. This aspectually "closed" character of the event turns the predicate into a defining property of the city: the fact that the city has been crossed in ten minutes might be a "new" or exceptional property for the city. The difference between (32b) and (32c) is that in (32b), the predicate cannot be construed as a property, whereas the perfective morphology on the passive auxiliary in (32c) does construe the predicate as a characteristic. In (32d), the generic reading of the sentence, enhanced by the modal, makes the city into one of those cities that have the intrinsic property that they can be crossed in ten minutes by any cab. Finally, this view of passive also explains the particularities of certain passives that have no equivalent active counterpart (33a) (Postma 1994), or certain passives which allow for a *by*-phrase without having an active counterpart (33b, c). In this context, it is also important to note that in (33b), the meaning of *possess*, "own," is changed into a psychological one: the passive participle receives an inalienable property (see Postma 1994). This is not an accidental property of passive participles, but quite a productive one across languages: stative passive participles with new "psychological" meanings can be coined from existing nouns that bear no transparent semantic relation with the psychological meaning of the participial predicate such as *suiker*, "sugar," *muts*, "cap" in Dutch (33d, e), or *lune*, "moon" in French (33f).

(33)   a.   Jan is breedgeschouderd. (Postma 1994)
           Jan is broadshouldered.
           "Jan has broad shoulders."
      b.   Sophie is possessed by the devil.
      c.   *The devil possesses Sophie.
      d.   Die man was HELEMAAL gesuikerd. (nonstandard)
           That man was entirely sugared (speech of a Dutch colleague)
           "That man was completely crazy."
      e.   I hoop dat de professoren goedgemutst zijn die dag.
           "I hope that the professors well capped are that day."
      f.   J'espère que les profs seront bien lunés ce jour-là.
           I-hope that the professors will-be well mooned that day there
           "I hope the professors will be well disposed that day."

In any case, it is clear that the various passives in (33) are used to express an inherent, inalienable, defining property of the animate subject. If it is accepted that inalienability is a special form of partitivity, the analysis presented here can at least partially derive this meaning as a consequence of the syntactic configuration that imposes a partitive structure. A prediction of this analysis is that all cases of nonstative passives that do not have an active counterpart should involve a partitive relation between subject and predicate, in the sense that the predicate expresses an inherent, defining property of the subject. In this way, the productive process of the formation of inalienable predicates can be viewed as the result of a purely syntactic configuration.

5. IMPERSONAL PASSIVES

The analysis presented here immediately raises the question as to how the impersonal construction is to be conceived of. How can Q_p establish a partitive relation between an empty subject and a predicate? The impersonal configuration should be thought of as in (34b). The only difference with passive (34a) is that the Q_p^0 head of Q_pP has not incorporated into *be*. As a result, the impersonal configuration does not partitively relate the surface subject to the predicate, contrary to the passive configuration. The internal argument moves to Spec Q_pP at LF to check partitive case: this is the only function of Q_pP in the impersonal construction. If we compare the impersonal and the passive configuration, there are only two ways in which Q_p^0 can satisfy its properties. First, Q_p^0 can incorporate into BE, yielding a "partitive" passive construction in which the Q_pP containing the passive construction is predicated as a defining part of the surface subject (34a). In that case, the Q_p incorporated into *be* enables a partitive quantificational relation between the surface subject and the predicate: by incorporating into *be*, the complex X^0 *be*+Q_p^0 functions as a partitive operator binding the trace of Q_p and hence the entire Q_pP, which is viewed as a "defining part of" the subject DP. The second way for Q_p^0 to satisfy its properties is to stay in its base-generated position checking partitive case at LF producing the impersonal construction (34b).[7] In this way, Belletti's (1988) analysis of partitive "inherent" case in impersonal constructions is simply reformulated as a property of structural case.[8] As in Belletti's (1988) analysis, partitive case accounts for the indefiniteness effect on the internal argument.

(34)　a.　[L'empire]ᵢ a été+Q_p^0　[Q_pP t'ᵢ Q_p^0　[... [vp détruit tᵢ]]]

　　　　"The empire has been　　　　　　destroyed"

　　　b.　Il　　　a été [Q_pP e Q_p^0　　[... [vp détruit [plusieurs empires]]]]

　　　　　　　　　　　　　　　　　　LF-movement

　　　　"There　have been　　　　　destroyed various empires"

Following Kayne's analysis, the A′ position of SpecQ_p is not turned into an A position in (34b), since Q_p^0 does not incorporate. As a result, the partitive DP will be prevented from moving further than SpecQ_p at LF.

The analysis proposed here is not entirely new. Lasnik (1994) has suggested that the partitive case in impersonal constructions is checked by a passive functional head. The novelty of the approach presented here resides in the claim that passive constructions generally include a partitive functional head that can incorporate (34a) or not (34b). The effects of this partitive quantificational head are quite different in both cases: in the impersonal construction, the partitive head Q_p^0 licenses partitive case on NPs in its Spec by Spec-head agreement. When incorporated into *be*, however, the head Q_p^0 establishes a partitive relation that is more predicational in nature, partitively relating the entire Q_pP complement to the NP subject of the passive sentence.

Lasnik (1994) explains the difference between Romance and Dutch, where the impersonal passive is very productive, and English, where it is not,[9] as the result of the fact that Romance (c.q. Dutch) passive checks partitive case, while the English passive does not.

(35) a. È stato messo un libro sul tavolo.
          has been put a book on the table.
      b. *There has been put a book on the table.

In Lasnik's (1994) approach, the question is left open as to how this difference arises. Lasnik (1994) suggests that some optionality in Case-checking must be involved in order to permit the nominative derived subject in personal passives as (35a). In other words: how does the partitive case get out of the way? In the proposal outlined above, the difference between English on the one hand and Romance/Dutch on the other is due to the fact that the Q_p^0 head obligatorily incorporates in English, yielding passives as in (34a), while in Romance and Dutch the Q_p^0 head optionally incorporates, yielding both personal and impersonal passives. The incorporation of the partitive Agr head is, however, not without consequences: a partitive relation between predicate and subject results, triggering the effects that have been described in the previous section. Unlike Chomsky and Lasnik's (1993) and Lasnik's (1992) analyses, the approach advocated here does not invoke further LF adjunction of the indefinite object DP to *there*. Chomsky and Lasnik (1993) propose this adjunction in order to account for the fact that the verb always agrees with the internal argument in English. Nevertheless, this type of adjunction is suspect on principled grounds, since it is not clear why XP adjunction to elements in Spec position should be limited to *there*.[10] Moreover, it remains unclear why in languages such as French the verb never agrees with the internal argument, but always takes "default" singular agreement. The structure (34b) allows for a simpler account of the facts. In French, impersonal *il*, "it," is of the category NP and therefore triggers third-person agreement of *be* by Spec-head agreement. In English, *there* is of the category P and cannot trigger Spec-head agreement on *be*. Since *be* belongs to the same extended projection as Q_pP, only head-head agreement can ensure the "checking" of agreement features for *be* in AgrSP. As a result, *be* in $AgrS^0$ must have the same features as Q_p^0, which gets the features of the internal argument DP by movement of this DP at LF and its subsequent Spec-head agreement.

As it stands, however, the configurational analysis advanced in generative analyses predicts that personal and impersonal passives should cover the same set of data, apart from case considerations and the "partitivity constraint" outlined above. However, it seems that the impersonal passive is constrained in a way that is completely different from personal passives. Strikingly, most of the passives discussed above that become acceptable if a contextual partitive relation is projected onto them are completely ungrammatical in the impersonal construction. Constructions with "container" verbs, which are always ungrammatical in a passive configuration, are equally ungrammatical in an impersonal configuration.

(36)   *Il a été possédé plusieurs personnes par le diable.
        *Er waren verschillende mensen door de duivel bezeten.
        "There were many people possessed by the devil."

(37)   *Il a été contenu du vin dans cette bouteille.
        "There was contained wine in that bottle."

(38)   a.   *Il a été traversé plusieurs villes par cette rivière.
              "There were crossed many cities by that river."
        b.   ?Il avait déjà été traversé plusieurs contrées merveilleuses (par Sinbad le marin).
              "There had already been crossed several marvelous regions (by Sinbad the sailor)."

(39)   a.   Il *est/a été dormi dans mon lit.
              "There was slept in my bed."
        b.   *Il a été dormi dans plusieurs lits par Napoléon pendant la campagne de Russie.
              "There has been slept in several beds by Napoleon during the campagne de Russie."

(40)   a.   Plusieurs épouses ont déjà été quittées par ce salaud de Jean-Pierre.
              "Several spouses have already been left by that asshole of a Jean-Pierre."
        b.   *Il a déjà été quitté plusieurs épouses par ce salaud de Jean-Pierre.
              "It has been left many spouses by that asshole of a Jean-Pierre."

(41)   a.   Il a déjà été *quitté/évacué/abandonné plusieurs villes par les Irakiens dans le territoire kurde.
              "There have already been left/evacuated/abandoned several cities by the Iraqis in Kurdish territory."
        b.   *Il a été rencontré plusieurs personnes par le ministre.
              "There have been met several persons by the minister."

(42)   *À partir de la seconde moitié du 20ième siècle, il a été habité de plus en plus de grandes villes par des millions d'habitants.
        "Ever since the second half of the twentieth century, there have been inhabited more and more cities by several million inhabitants."

(43)   *Il est connu plusieurs personnes par tout le monde.
        "There are known several people by everyone."

(44)   Il a été vu plusieurs objets étranges dans le ciel nocturne.
        "There were seen various strange objects in the night sky."

It is clear that the impersonal construction is more restricted than passive is. This is due to the well-known fact that the impersonal construction is aspectually constrained to verbs expressing events that include definite bounds, either accomplishments (*build*), achievements (*find*), but also processes that can be viewed as a repetition of bounded subevents (*discuss*). Stative verbs such as *love, know, like,* and *hold* are excluded, as well as the stative Location verbs such as *habiter,* "inhabit" in (42). Similarly, unbounded processes or states such as *amuse* or *love* are generally excluded. Nevertheless, a Stative verb such as *aimer,* "love" can be used in an impersonal passive if the interpretation of the sentence involves several "countable" instances of the state: (45b) is well-formed because the interpretation of the sentence involves several "cases" or instances of love on this old planet. The multiplicity of states is a factor which overcomes the lexically unbounded aspectual property of the stative verb *aimer,* "love," since it allows for the sentence to be interpreted as involving at least a certain number of stative situations that are "closed off" or bounded: the interpretation of (45b) involves a set of "closed off" situations involving love. Such an interpretation is not available in (45a).

(45) a. *Il a été aimé/amusé/connu un des linguistes par les enfants.
          "There were liked/amused/known one of the linguists by the children."
      b. Il a été aimé sur cette vieille terre depuis que le monde est monde.
          "There has been loved on this old planet ever since the world existed."

Exactly the same factor is argued by Lamiroy (1987) to be relevant for stative verbs complementing aspectual verbs: an aspectual verb such as *begin* can only be followed by a stative verb if there is a multiplication of stative situations:

(46) a. *Cet ouvrier a commencé à posséder une maison.
          "That worker began to possess a house."
      b. Après la seconde Guerre, les ouvriers ont commencé à posséder des maisons.
          "After the second World War, workers began to possess houses."

In both the impersonal passive and in aspectual complementation, the "countability" of situations allows the structure to overcome an aspectual restriction. In aspectual complementation, the "countability" of the sentence allows for enough aspectual structure so as to allow for an inchoative interpretation. In the impersonal passive, the "countability" of the sentence enables the unbounded lexical aspect expressed by the verb to be interpreted as "closed off" or bounded in the sense that the sentence (45b) refers to "countable" instances of a state.

This aspectual constraint on impersonal passives also extends to grammatical aspect: the process inherent in accomplishments needs to be "closed off" by perfective aspect, and cannot be modified by durative adverbs such as *for an hour.*

(47) a. Il *est construit/a été construit une belle maison près du Parc Monceau.
          "There *is/has been built a beautiful house next to the Parc Monceau."
      b. Il a été lu plusieurs livres (*pendant une heure.)
          "There have been read several books (*for an hour)."

Similarly, some Process-like verbs such as *dormir,* "sleep," can only be used in the impersonal construction with perfective aspect as illustrated in (39a). At the same time, however, (39b) shows that perfective aspect is not sufficient to consider a Process event as "bounded." In (39a), there is a single event of sleeping in my bed, and as a result the Process event can be considered to have been "closed off." In (39b), however, the beds Napoleon slept in are undefined, and as a result the amount of sleeping events in undefined, hence undelimited, not bound. Notice that this is not the case in (47b), in which the Accomplishment verb *read* licenses a bounded reading event including an undefined number of books. The sentences in (39) and (47b) are therefore very illustrative of the fact that the "bounded" aspect of the sentence has to be calculated on the basis of the lexical and syntactic properties of the sentence (Verkuyl 1972). This aspectual constraint excludes the examples (6, 36, 39, 40, 42, 44) that include stative verbs, as well as all "container" verbs, since these are never "bounded." It also explains the contrast in (37) between "stative" and "dynamic reading of *traverser*, "cross." The sentence (38a) involves a permanent property of the river that has no bounds, while the "dynamic" reading of *traverser*, "cross," in (38b) is aspectually bound, yielding an acceptable impersonal sentence. Note that in the example (44), *voir*, "see," is interpreted with the "bounded" reading of "perceive." The ungrammaticality of the examples (40) through (41) can also be attributed to the "boundedness" restriction on the impersonal configuration. This may come as a surprise, since *quitter*, "leave" and *rencontrer*, "meet" seem to be temporally bounded in the same way as *trouver*, "find" and *découvrir*, "discover": all of these verbs are Achievements. Nevertheless, *trouver*, "find" and *découvrir*, "discover," allow for impersonal constructions, while *quitter*, "leave," and *rencontrer*, "meet," in (40) through (41) do not.

> (48)   a.   Il a été trouvé plusieurs complexes de temples par Jones.
>   "There were found/discovered several temple complexes by Jones."
>   b.   *Il a été quitté plusieurs épouses par Jones.
>   "There were left/met several spouses by Jones."

Why is this the case? Importantly, *meet* and *leave* only specify the starting point of the event, whereas for verbs such as *find* and *discover*, there is a starting point and an endpoint of the event, which coincide most of the time.[11] This property can be checked by the fact that *meet* and *leave*, but not *find* and *discover*, allow for durative adverbs despite their traditional Vendlerian classification as Achievements.

> (49)   a.   Sally met/left Archibald for an hour.
>   b.   Sally found/discovered a nickel (*for an hour).[12]

Within the class of Achievements, there is a distinction between verbs that can be modified by *for an hour* and verbs that cannot be so modified. The verbs *meet* and *leave* seem to be inherently "open-ended": they do not impose a lower temporal bound. The impersonal construction requires precisely such a lower bound for the event. As a result, impersonal constructions with *rencontrer*, "meet," and *quitter*, "leave," are ruled out by virtue of the temporal boundedness restriction.

Clearly, the determination of what constitutes a bounded event is determined by both lexical and inflectional aspect.[13] Despite its complexity, it is a formal property that has precise consequences in impersonal constructions. The question now arises as to whether this "boundedness" restriction is a property that can be derived in the framework proposed here. I would like to suggest that the "eventive/bounded" aspectual constraint derives from the syntactic configuration be+Q_pP which is present in both the impersonal and the passive construction.

In the configuration outlined in (34b), impersonal *il*, "there," is not at all coindexed with the internal argument DP, but rather with the entire QP complement. The function of *be* in the impersonal construction is to indicate the existence of the predicate. The predicate therefore functions as the only argument of *be*. In contexts in which *be* does not relate a DP subject to a predicate, but is itself the only predicate of the subject, *be* takes on the meaning of "exist," as in *the universe simply is*. Whatever the syntactic-semantic reasons for this meaning, we would like to suggest that this same meaning is also present in the impersonal construction: *be* simply indicates that its Q_pP complement "exists" or "is the case." This meaning is responsible for the aspectual restrictions on the Q_pP complement: although *be* or *exist* are themselves purely stative verbs, they require from their argument that it has somehow "come into existence." This can be seen when *be* or *exist* are predicated of abstract nouns such as *beauty* or *circularity*: sentences such as *Beauty/Circularity exists* or *Real beauty simply is (it cannot be described)* only refer to specific cases of beautiful objects or circular arguments, that are (countable) *instantiations* of the abstract nouns. This "specific" interpretation does not arise when *be* relates a referential subject to a predicate: *Beauty is undefinable*. If *be* selects a single sentence-like complement as in the impersonal construction, it does not relate a referential subject to a predicate. As a result, *be* requires that this complement be a (countable) *instantiation*. A sentence-like complement can only be interpreted as a (countable) instantiation if it does not refer to a state or an otherwise unbounded process. Only bounded events are (countable) instantiations. Therefore, for the impersonal construction to be predicated of *be*, Q_pP needs to be aspectually "closed off." This analysis formalizes those functionalist analyses that ascribe an "existential (Martin 1979) or a "presentational" (Vet 1980) character to the impersonal subject *il*, "there," in French, and view the impersonal subject as an *image de la situation repère*, "an image of the situation referred to." In this analysis, the impersonal subject is indeed a syntactic "image" of the event in Q_pP, since it is coindexed with it. The careful reader will have noticed that the analysis presented here entails a view of both passive and the impersonal passive construction as a special case of complementation (cf. also Hoekstra 1993). We will make an attempt to flesh out this idea in the next section.

6. *BE*+Q_p AND RAISING

We have seen in section 4 that context builds an interpretation for the syntactico-semantic "partitive" property of passive. Passive *be*+Q_p should be viewed as compositional: the Q_pP projection requires an interpretation in which the selected participle is viewed as an inherent, constitutive property of the internal argument NP moved to subject position of *be*. The function of *be* is only to provide the subject-predicate structure for the relation between the NP and the participle: in a sense, it provides *be* support. The meaning of some verbs does not allow them to be construed as such a property, and in other cases, only certain contexts allow for the predicate to be construed as an inherent property of the surface subject.

In an active sentence, there is no partitive relation between the participle and the subject: in *John destroyed his bike*, John is not intrinsically characterized by his destroying the bike. In *the bike is destroyed by John*, there is an intrinsic relation between the bike and its being destroyed: its destroyed nature is presented as part of the bike.

Importantly, *be*+Q_p has a semantic content, and hence should be considered a "real" raising verb, such as *seem*, *appear*, and the aspectual verbs, such as *begin*, *continue*, *stop*, and so on. Ter Meulen (1990) has shown that a quantificational analysis of aspectual verbs yields far-reaching insights in the way they are related to each other. In a sense, ter Meulen (1990) treats aspectual raising verbs as quantifiers over events. For other raising verbs such as deontic and epistemic modals, quantificational properties are also an essential ingredient (see Hoekstra 1993, Barbiers 1993 for a recent analysis). *Be*+Q_p now is similar to raising verbs in that it does not have a thematic structure of its own, and adds a quantificational relation to the sentence. The difference is, of course, that aspectual verbs only modify (quantify) the event interpretation of the IP complement they select, whereas passive *be*+Q_p establishes a part-whole relation between the NP moved to subject position and the predicate.

The question now arises as to why the raising verb *be*+Q_p is correlated with a participial predicate in which the external argument is realized obliquely. Why couldn't this raising verb select a full-fledged infinitive? This might have to do with the target variables of the quantifiers involved: *be*+Q_p has no scope over events but relates NPs to predicates in a partitive sense. *Bona fide* raising verbs such as aspectual and modal verbs do take events as their variables (ter Meulen 1990, Barbiers 1993). Therefore, it simply follows that aspectual and modal raising verbs should appear in a context where there is something for them to have scope over, namely the functional projection associated with temporally specified events TP. This has nothing to do with selectional restrictions *per se* but with satisfaction of scopal properties: the modal or aspectual verb needs to be in a sufficiently local context with respect to the appropriate event variable. Since passive *be* does not have the same scope as aspectual and modal raising verbs, the requirement to select an AgrSP-TP not only does not apply to passive *be*, AgrSP-TP complementation would prevent *be* from exercising its scopal properties on the participial projection, since that participial projection (*in casu* Q_pP) would not be sufficiently close to *be*: Q_pP must be directly in the context of *be* to allow for incorporation of $Q_p{}^0$ into *be* and to allow the resulting *be*+Q_p to quantify over Q_pP.

If this general line of reasoning is correct, we are led to a number of conclusions with respect to Burzio's generalization. Chomsky (1992) admits that PRO has (abstract) Case in infinitival CPs (see Vanden Wyngaerd 1993 for extensive arguments to this effect). Now it was generally assumed in the LGB framework that precisely lack of Case, which was related to the [−tense] character of the infinitive, triggers movement of the infinitival subject to the Spec AgrSP position of the matrix verb in raising contexts. If PRO has Case, or, more generally, if infinitives can assign Case to NP subjects, there is no trigger for movement of the infinitival NP subject to the matrix Spec AgrSP of the tensed raising verb. In other words, we would expect structures of the type *It seems John to have a bike* to be perfectly fine, since the infinitival tense can assign Case to the subject in the minimalist framework.[14] The fact that these sentences are ungrammatical, and that the subject needs to move to the subject position of the raising verb, suggests that there is some additional mechanism that removes or suppresses the (abstract) Case normally assigned by an infinitival AgrSP. The same is true in passive configurations: in some way or another, the accusative case of AgrOP needs to be removed. Notice that if Chomsky (1992) is right in claiming that AgrSP and AgrOP are identical, and only differ in labeling as a handy mnemonic device, we would indeed expect that both AgrSP in raising contexts and AgrOP in passive contexts are subject to Case removal.

Now let us simply assume that AgrSP and AgrOP are never "neutralized," but that "neutralized," "Case-defective" AgrS/OP simply *is* (a specific type of) Q_pP.[15] Simply put, Q_pP is the defective form of AgrOP sitting on top of the passive participle. This should be less surprising than it seems: Agr projections clearly have very elementary quantificational properties, as they convey features such as person and number. The idea proposed here, then, is that Agr can host more than just [person, number, gender] agreement and nominative/accusative Case. For passive, we suggest that AgrOP hosts a partitive quantifier, which assigns partitive case if it is not incorporated as in impersonal passives. If the partitive quantifier incorporates, as in passive, the AgrOP hosting Q_pP will be "Case-defective."

The passive and impersonal configuration arise as they do because *be*, being unaccusative, does not provide an "active" AgrO that could assign accusative. This now seems to be in line with Hoekstra's (1984, 1993) proposals regarding the auxiliary *have* as identical to *be*, with the only difference that *have* does have an AgrOP projection that can license accusative Case. *Have* "adds on" to the participle what has been "lost" by the participial "defective" AgrOP/Q_pP projection, namely an AgrOP that can provide accusative Case (Hoekstra 1993).

How does Q_pP manifest itself in the context of raising verbs? Recall we suggest that AgrSP in raising verbs also needs to be "neutralized," since for raising to occur, the infinitival AgrSP should not have a case to assign to its subject. In the terms of the analysis presented here, AgrSP needs to be a Q_pP. It seems that there is some evidence for this radical position. In modal raising verbs in French, Q_pP can be made visible. More in particular, modal verbs in French can co-occur with the adverb *bien* in the "weak" epistemic interpretation, in which *pouvoir*, "can," and *devoir*, "must," do not have the interpretation of "strong" necessity or possibility, but of "weak" probability/eventuality.

(50) Il doit/pourrait (bien) pleuvoir un de ces jours.
      "It should/might very well rain one of these days."

This "adverb" *bien* has a concessive meaning close to "very well" in the English gloss. In combination with the modal, it indicates that the "strong" epistemic meaning of *pouvoir*, "can/*devoir*, "must" is "weakened" in the sense that the opinion of the speaker is taken into account, yielding the meaning of probability/eventuality instead of the stronger necessity/possibility. The overt appearance of *bien* is not required to obtain the "weak" epistemic reading, but when it is present, no other reading can obtain. This suggests that *bien* has a zero allomorph, and that the morpheme corresponding to *bien/∅* is responsible for the "weak" epistemic meaning of *pouvoir*, "can/*devoir*, "must."

Importantly, *bien* also functions as a quantifier translating a subjective amount that is considered to be high from the point of view of the speaker.

> (51)   Elle connaît bien des personnes./Il a mangé bien des pommes.
>   "She knows quite some people."/"He ate quite a few apples."

In both the modal and the nominal context, then, *bien* quantifies in an identical way: in the modal context, it specifies that the probability/eventuality is high with respect to the position of the speaker, whereas in the nominal context, it specifies quantity with respect to the position of the speaker. It is my contention now that *bien* in a modal context is the head of a Q_pP projection that incorporates into the modal. Independent evidence for incorporation of *bien* comes from other verbs, the meaning of which changes in the presence of *bien*. *Bien vouloir* does not mean *vouloir*, "want," but something more close to "admit," *aimer bien*, means "like," not "love," as *aimer* does. By themselves, these changes in meaning, which all have a vaguely "concessive" or "speaker-related" flavor, do not constitute evidence for incorporation. However, in some cases the meaning change has syntactic correlates:[16]

> (52)   Voilà une façon de laquelle Delphine aime *(bien) que Louis prépare le faisan.
>   "This is a way in which Delphine (rather) likes that Louis prepares pheasant."

Aimer, "love" is normally a factive verb, and *bien* seems to have the property of suspending factivity. Now, if factivity is a lexical property that is manifested through selectional restrictions of the verb on the embedded C^0 (cf. Rooryck 1992), *bien* can only suspend the factive property of *aimer*, "love," if it incorporates into that verb. If *bien* simply were an adverb modifying the verb, it would be very hard to explain how this adverb would be capable of changing the selectional properties exercised by a verb.

This Q_pP projection, which is overtly present as *bien*, can be considered to play the role of "Case-defective" AgrSP in the infinitival complement of the modal raising verbs *pouvoir*, "can," and *devoir*, "must."[17]

> (53) Il_i doit/pourrait bien $[_{AGR\text{-}S\text{-}P} t_i [_{AGR\text{-}S^0} t_{bien}] [_{VP}$ pleuvoir un de ces jours]]

Both passives and modals then have "Case-defective" Agr projections that can be identified as quantifiers.[18]

The very same idea can now be extended to aspectual raising verbs. Aspectual verbs have been described by ter Meulen (1990) as Generalized Quantifiers. The relations among aspectual verbs can be represented in a three-dimensional square of oppositions:

(54)   *Three-dimensional square of aspectual quantifiers* (ter Meulen 1990)

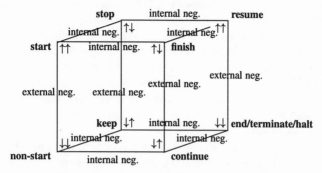

This representation relates the logical squares of oppositions inherent in aspectual verbs. It allows for an explanation of various semantic properties of aspectual verbs such as monotonicity and negation. For instance, the "internal negation" line relating *start* and *stop* translates the idea that *stop doing something* is equivalent to *start not doing something*. Similarly, *keep doing something* is equivalent to *not stop doing something*, the external negation of *stop doing something*.[19]

From a syntactic point of view, the quantificational properties described by ter Meulen (1990) for each aspectual raising verb might correspond to as many different Q_pPs occurring in the complement AgrSP/Q_pP position of these raising verbs. In all of these cases, it might be proposed that the Q_p head of this Q_pP incorporates into the aspectual verb. The quantificational properties of aspectual verbs might now be viewed as a result of incorporation of a quantifier into a verbal host (*be*) deriving the corresponding aspectual raising verb. Every raising verb has its own $Q_p{}^0$.

In all of these cases, it might be claimed that the Q_p head of this Q_pP incorporates into the aspectual verb. In its most extreme form, this hypothesis would entail that every raising verb basically involves *be* followed by a Q_pP. Each Q_pP would have a specific quantificational property corresponding to it, and each incorporated Q^0 head would be responsible for the eventual surface manifestation of the raising verb. Alternatively, and less radically, we might say that modal and aspectual verbs are lexically inserted with their quantifiers already incorporated, and that these quantifiers select an AgrSP whose head is such that it can function as a variable for the quantifier inside the raising verb. This analysis has the same effects as the incorporation analysis: in both cases, the head Q_p of Q_pP is bound by the quantificational operator.

This analysis of raising verbs would offer the start for an explanation of an otherwise curious property of French raising verbs. Raising verbs in French can express Tense (*aller/venir de/risquer/avoir failli*), Mood (*pouvoir/devoir*), and Aspect (*tarder, commencer, être en train de, arrêter* ...).[20] Unlike inflectional elements expressing Tense, Mood, and Aspect, raising verbs expressing Tense, Mood, and Aspect always are accompanied by a quantificational property. For modal verbs, the operators of necessity and possibility, this may be a trivial observation. Similarly, we have already noted that ter Meulen's analysis provides a framework for describing the quantificational properties of aspectual raising verbs. The quantificational properties of raising verbs are, however, especially striking and rather unexpected in the case of raising verbs expressing future and past tense: these raising verbs always have a modal property of possibility (*risquer, avoir failli*), necessity (*aller, venir de*) or a generic/habitual reading (*avoir tendance à*, "have a tendency to") associated with them. If this observation is correct, it needs to be explained since a priori there is no reason why raising verbs could not simply express Tenses of the same type as those expressed by inflectional elements, without a modal property.

We would like to briefly illustrate these modal properties of raising verbs expressing Tense, since they may not be immediately obvious.

(55)   En Alaska, il a tendance à neiger quand on s'y attend le moins.
       In Alaska, it has tendency to snow when one self to-it it expects the least.
       "In Alaska, it generally snows when it is least expected."

(56)   Il risque de pleuvoir.
       It risks to rain.
       "It is possible that it will rain."

(57)   Il a failli pleuvoir.
       It has barely-escaped to rain.
       "There was a possibility of rain/it almost rained."

(58)   a.   Elle va avoir un enfant.
            "She is going to have a baby."
       b.   Elle aura un enfant.
            "She will have a baby."

(59)   Elle vient d'arriver à Bruxelles.
       "She comes from to-arrive in Brussels."
       She just arrived in Brussels.

Generic or habitual interpretations have been often described as involving some sort of universal quantification (see Krifka 1988). A similar analysis should apply to (55). The epistemic modal "possibility" reading of *risquer* and *avoir failli* is sufficiently clear from the glosses and translations in (56). The necessity reading of the so-called "futur proche" *aller* can be deduced by comparing the contextual implications of the inflectional future in (58b) with those of the periphrastic future *aller* in (58a): (58a), but not (58b), implies that one is pregnant. Example (58b) can be said of a seven-year-old (she will have a baby when she is a grownup), but saying (58a) referring to a seven-year-old would be distinctly odd under normal assumptions about child-bearing age. This shows that *aller* carries the meaning of an "inescapable" future. This interpretation, and the implication in (56a) triggered by it, should be viewed as a result of the epistemic modal necessity inherent in *aller*: If *aller* in (58a) carries not only the meaning of future but also that of necessity, a situation that states the future necessity of having a baby contextually licenses the implication of pregnancy.[21] Interpretive notions such as "inescapable" future and the traditional term *futur proche* then follow from the combination of the modal and the temporal characteristics yielding a property of "future necessity" inherent in *aller*.

Another indication that modal necessity is involved in *aller* is that as a raising verb, *aller* cannot be used with a perfective aspect (60). This is unexpected because inflectional future tense and the "possible" periphrastic future *risquer* can co-occur with perfective aspect (60): if *aller* simply expressed a future, it should be combinable with perfective aspect, expressing a future perfective.[22]

(60) *Il est allé pleuvoir (demain matin).
       It is gone to rain (tomorrow morning).
       "It went to rain (tomorrow morning)."

(61) Il aura plu (demain matin).
       "It will have rained (tomorrow morning).

(62) Hier soir, il a risqué de pleuvoir à un moment donné.
       "Yesterday evening, there was a risk of rain for a moment."

Now, it is generally the case that objective epistemic necessity is incompatible with perfective aspect. In (63), the necessity of a raining event can only involve objective epistemic necessity,[23] and perfective aspect is excluded:

(63) Il doit absolument/*a absolument dû pleuvoir pour assurer les besoins en eau potable.
       It must absolutely/have must absolutely to-rain in-order-to ensure the needs in water drinkable.
       "Rain is/was necessary to ensure the needs for drinking water."

(64) La pluie a été nécessaire pour assurer les besoins en eau potable.
       "The rain has been necessary to ensure the needs for drinking water."

The sentence (64) shows that objective epistemic necessity is not intrinsically incompatible with perfective aspect. Therefore, it is not clear to us why there is this aspectual constraint on objective epistemic necessity expressed by *devoir*, "must." What is clear, however, is that the restriction that is responsible for ruling out the combination of *devoir*, "must," and perfective aspect can also be invoked to rule out the combination of *aller* and perfective aspect, if it is assumed that *aller* involves a modal epistemic operator of necessity.

The modal epistemic nature of *aller* also shows up in other Romance languages. In Italian, *andare*, "go," can be used as a passive auxiliary with the meaning of epistemic necessity. In the same way as the French raising verb *aller*, *andare* cannot be used with a perfect tense and is restricted to third person and generic contexts (see D'Hulst 1992 for further discussion):

(65) Questi problemi vanno/*sono andati ulteriormente esaminati.
       "Those problems must be examined later."

The relation between raising verbs and passive that we have assumed in this essay might allow for a way of configurationally relating the passive and the raising construction: *aller/andare* license complementation involving a quantification-like head that does not assign Case.[24] Finally, coming back to the recent past *venir de* in (59), we would like to suggest that it involves past necessity in the same way *aller* involves future necessity. The argument for this analysis is harder to make than for *aller*, and needs a little more work. This may be due to the fact that *venir de* also involves an aspectual feature of punctuality as observed by Ruwet (1983). However, like *aller* in (60) and *devoir*, "must," in (61), *venir de* cannot be combined with perfective aspect:

(66)   Elle vient/venait/*est venu d'arriver à Bruxelles.
        She comes/came/has come from to-arrive in Brussels.
        "She just arrives/arrived in Brussels."

We would like to suggest that the incompatibility of *venir de* with perfective aspect is due to the same restriction that applies to *aller* in (60) and *devoir*, "must," in (61), namely the general incompatibility of perfective aspect with objective epistemic necessity.

The following chart illustrates the combinations of tense and modality in French raising verbs expressing Tense:[25]

(67) | | *Necessity* | *Possibility* |
|---|---|---|
| *Future* | aller | risquer |
| *Past* | venir de | avoir failli |

These epistemic modal (64) and generic/habitual (55) properties of raising verbs expressing Tense is rather unexpected: why isn't it the case that at least some raising verbs simply express a nonmodal tense similar to those expressed by inflectional bound morphemes in French? For instance, why don't we have a raising verb with a nonmodal meaning similar to the past or future tense? Under the approach outlined above, there is a partial answer to this question: in order to be licensed, raising verbs must incorporate (or select) an AgrSP with a head that has quantificational properties. Modal operators of necessity and possibility seem to play that quantificational role in the case of raising verbs expressing tense. On its own, the tense expressed by a raising verb would be insufficient to license the syntactic configuration that is necessary for complementation involving raising. The syntactic configuration of raising seems to require a quantificational element as an essential ingredient for licensing the infinitival complementation of raising verbs.

7. CONCLUSION

Lamiroy (1993) argues against a view of passive as a purely mechanical counterpart of an active sentence. She notes that Meillet (1938) had already observed that were passive just a counterpart of active, passive would be superfluous in the grammar. Lamiroy (1993) shows that Meillet (1938) echoes Von der Gabelentz (1861), who had described passive as *Ein Luxus der Sprache*. Lamiroy (1993) notes that the idea that active and passive are completely equivalent seems to be contrary to any principle of economy in the structuralist sense. Lamiroy (1993) then goes on to suggest that the originality of passive lies in the suppression of the external argument. The passive, then, is a "recessive diathesis" (Tesnière 1969).

I do not share this conclusion. First of all, it does not capture why the object moves to subject position. If the essence of passive were suppression of the external argument, it would be sufficient for the grammar to have an impersonal passive construction. Second, the suppression of the external argument is not just a property of passive, but it is shared by nominalizations which can realize the external argument as a *by*-phrase in the same way as passive participles (*The destruction of Tenochtitlan by Cortéz*).

The analysis presented here shows why passive is not at all a "luxury of language." It is the only way in which an internal argument NP can be syntactically construed in such a way as to express an essential, constitutive property of that NP. Passive diathesis essentially involves a quantificational part-whole dimension relating the NP in subject position to the participial predicate. The active-passive diathesis in fact reflects a diathesis between a voice in which no inherent or constitutive property is necessarily predicated of the subject (*John destroys his bike*) and a voice in which an inherent, defining property of the subject is predicated (*The bike is destroyed by John*). A quantificational analysis of passive has been developed in which no reference is made to thematic roles to explain what has traditionally been viewed as "exceptions" to passive. The analysis presented here now allows us to relate partitive passive to Binding. A puzzling property of both Romance and Scandinavian languages is that the element that can be used as a reflexive or a reciprocal (Swedish reciprocal *-s* in *vi ses*, "we will see each other," French reflexive *se* in *Ils se lavent*, "They wash themselves") can also be used as a (medio-)passive morpheme (Swedish *lax serverades klockan fem*, "the salmon was served at five o'clock" French *Le saumon fumé se mange froid*, "Smoked salmon is eaten cold"). The question we would like to address here is why an anaphor should start to function as a passive morpheme in the first place. It seems our analysis of passive as partitive diathesis can offer a tentative answer to this question. Pica (1988) has shown that anaphors in various languages derive from nouns denoting inalienable nouns such as body parts and kinship terms, and that these nouns in turn often syntactically function as anaphors (cf. also Postma 1993). If inalienability can be defined in terms of partitivity, anaphoricity clearly involves partitivity. If this characterization of anaphors is correct, and if our analysis of passive as a partitive structure holds, it should not be surprising that intrinsically partitive anaphoric elements such as Romance *se* and Scandinavian *-s* can start to function as passive morphemes. It is then an interesting question of technical implementation to find out how these functions of *-s/se* (reflexive/reciprocal/passive) can be formally related. We will leave this question for further research.

NOTES

I would like to thank Sjef Barbiers, Rose-Marie Déchaine, Marcel den Dikken, Yves D'Hulst, Teun Hoekstra, Pierre Pica, and Gertjan Postma for useful comments and discussions. Thanks to audiences at Tilburg University and the Université de Paris VIII, where I had a chance to present previous versions of this work, in particular to Henk Van Riemsdijk, Anne Zribi-Hertz, Jean-Yves Pollock, Carmen Dobrovie-Sorin, and Co Vet for incisive comments. Special thanks go to Béatrice Lamiroy, whose critical review of the analysis of passive in Generative Grammar partly inspired this essay. The usual disclaimers apply. Some of the ideas concerning partitivity were partially developed in collaboration with Pierre Pica during my stay at UQAM in June 1993. Our syntactic implementation of the notion partitivity has, however, developed separately and in quite different ways. It is therefore important to warn the careful reader that Pierre Pica's view of partitivity as developed in his own work on Romance SE and my own views as they are developed in this essay should not be regarded as identical or freely substitutable notions.

1. In German or Dutch the imperfective passive auxiliary is a variant of English *become*:

   i.   Het boek werd/is gevonden
      "The book became/was found"

Importantly, the alternation noted for *be* also applies to *worden*, "become":

   ii. Het geheel wordt zijn/*de/een aantal delen (door opsplitsing)
      "The whole becomes its/the/a number of parts (through splitting)"
   iii. De delen worden *hun/*het/een geheel (door samenvoeging)
      "The parts become *their/*the/a whole (by combination)"

2. I use the term predicational very loosely here, without making a necessary distinction between predicational and specificational, where predicational refers to a reading of (i), in which some property of John is unusual, such as his profession, and specificational refers to the reading in which John himself is unusual.

   i. What John is is unusual

See Higgins 1979, Williams 1983, Heggie 1988, Verheugd-Daatzelaar 1990, Heycock 1991, and Zaring 1993.

3. Alternatively, it might simply be the case that *be* is itself a partitive operator in all cases, including the predicational reading. A sentence such as *Jan is sick*, then, is to be interpreted as "sickness is part of Jan." This calls for a view on predication that goes against a well-established tradition in formal semantics to view this relation in exactly the reverse way, that is, "John is part of the number of sick entities." I will not go into this question here.

4. The structure in (5a) seems to be restricted to nouns indicating a nonpartitive maximal entity: note the ungrammaticality of *The group is its/a number of members* versus *A chain is a number of links*. This restriction is probably related to relation between the NP subject and partitive Q_p: the noun *group* itself is partitive in nature (*a group of fifteen members*), while the noun *whole* is not: (*a whole of fifteen parts*). It might be that a partitive Q_p^0 incorporated into *be* is incompatible with an NP that is lexically specified as partitive. The structure exemplified in (5a) is, however, less limited than it seems at first sight. Marcel den Dikken reminds me that a similar, although unproductive, construction exists in Dutch:

   i. Het is des duivels om te dansen op zondag
      "It is of the devil (devilish) to dance on Sundays"

Rose-Marie Déchaine likewise points out to me that English has an (idiomatic) construction similar to (13):

   ii. Sally [was [$_{QP}$ of a mind [$_{CP}$ to leave without warning]]]

Note that *of a mind* must be indefinite, which might be interpreted as an indication of partitive case (Belletti 1988). Moreover, the noun *mind* also refers to an inalienable body part, reproducing a part-whole relation between the subject and the partitive NP.

5. Although these inanimate NPs admittedly refer to human qualities: *sapientia*, "wisdom," *stultitia*, "stupidity." Note that this "possessive" genitive also refers to alienable possession: *omnia hostium erant*, "everything (the whole city) was in the hands of the enemy," *Plebs Hannibali erat*, "The rabble was on the side of Hannibal." The translations of these sentences suggest that the sentence is meant to indicate very "close" possession.

6. Interestingly, certain "container" verbs allow for the expression of the "container" argument in passive sentences as a Location argument.

    i.   Several services are included in/*by that price
    ii. Several interesting articles are contained in/*by that book

It might be objected that this shows that "container" verbs do have passives and that the *by*-phrase in this case is simply expressed as a Location PP. However, not all container verbs allow for the possibility attested in (i–ii):

    iii. *Several interesting articles are comprised in/by that book

I would like to argue that the use of the verbs *contain* and *include* exemplified in (i–ii) does not involve a passive configuration, but a predicational "stative" construction of the type *Ronnie is armed and dangerous*, which can be opposed to the "eventive" passive *Ronnie was armed by the druglords*. One important argument for this position is that the Location PP allows for Locative Inversion, which is otherwise attested for the Location use of *be*, which is certainly predicational, not passive:

    iv. In that price are included several services that will interest you
    v. *By the Spanish have been destroyed many empires of the New World
    vi. In the boat were several slaves who had come from Africa"

We will leave this problem and the problem of "stative" versus "eventive" passives for further research.

7. Note that partitive Case can be checked overtly, as in Latin (13).

8. Belletti's (1988) appeal to inherent Case in impersonal constructions served as an escape hatch from the Case Filter for internal argument DPs: the DP does not have to raise to subject position since it is already Case-marked; definite DPs in impersonal constructions cannot receive inherent Case and are ruled out by the Case Filter, since they fail to raise.

9. The judgment in (49b) is Lasnik's (1994). It seems however that there is a lot of variation with respect to this construction among English speakers. The analysis proposed here also allows for a representation of the impersonal construction in (i), where it can be assumed that the indefinite NP has raised overtly to the SpecQ$_p$P position:

    i. There were $[_{Q_pP}$ [various empires]$_i$ $Q_p^{\ 0}$ [$\ldots$ [$_{VP}$ destroyed t$_i$]]]

10. See den Dikken (1993) for a full discussion of the problems associated with Chomsky and Lasnik's *there*-adjunction analysis.

11. Although in general the beginning and endpoints of findings and discoveries coincide, as in *Jones found/discovered a gold coin*, it is not always the case, as in *Jones slowly found his way through the jungle*, or *Jones slowly discovered the similarity of Greek and Sanskrit/that the Ark wasn't all that important*. The important point here, however, is that both points are present in some aspectual representation of *find* and *discover*.

12. The asterisk refers here to the nonserialized reading of the sentence. Of course, *for an hour* is perfectly possible with a serial reading of *find/discover* in which several coin findings/discoveries are made within the hour.

13. See Verkuyl (1972) for the compositional nature of boundedness. It might be objected that the correlation between *for an hour* and the impossibility of the impersonal construction does not extend beyond Achievements. Accomplishments do allow for modification by *for an hour* and have an impersonal construction. This is precisely the point: Accomplishment verbs are lexically defined with both a beginning and an endpoint. Moreover, they are aspectually complex in that they involve a durative subevent and an endpoint. Durative adverbs such as *for an hour* refer to the durative subevent within the Accomplishment, not to the entire event. The interesting thing about the Achievements *meet* and *leave* is that *for an hour* modifies the result of the meeting or the departure.

14. It is fruitless to suggest that the Case assigned to PRO by an infinitive would be somehow different from the one assigned to a full NP. This would amount to a stipulation artificially distinguishing empty NPs from full NPs. Rather, the appearance of PRO in controlled infinitives and the concomitant impossibility of full NPs should be ascribed to properties of Control, presumably the anaphoric character of PRO (Manzini 1983) or the infinitival AgrSP. Note there are non-control and non-ECM infinitives with overt subjects: *En Jan maar lopen*, "And John run." This suggests that the infinitive can assign Case to overt subjects in at least some cases, and that the nonovert character of the infinitival subject in controlled infinitives must be due to independent factors.

15. Note that this position probably forces us to say that Q_pP is itself followed by a projection accounting for agreement on the participle.

16. Another syntactic correlate of the addition of *bien* is the possibility of coreference of the matrix and embedded subjects with *bien vouloir*, which is impossible with *vouloir*, "want":

    i. Je veux *(bien) que je sois le seul à travailler dans ce département
       "I want (admit) that I am the only one to work in this department"

In the terminology of the seventies, *bien* suspends the application of Equi-NP-deletion. This property of *bien vouloir* was first observed by Ruwet (1984).

17. The only difference between the incorporation of *bien* into non-raising verbs and *bien* in the context of raising verbs is that in the context of raising verbs, it could be claimed that the Q^0 *bien* heads the infinitival complement selected by the raising verb. As was pointed out to me by Sjef Barbiers, Latin *posse*, "can," can be analyzed as the combination of *esse*, "be," with the morpheme *pot-*, as is obvious in the third person singular *potest*, "s/he can." The bound morpheme *pot-* seems very close to the Latin invariable comparative quantifiers *tot . . . quot*, "(there are) as many . . . as . . . ."

18. The question might arise as to how *seem* and *appear* can be described as raising verbs with quantificational properties. Intuitively, *appear* translates the fact that one has direct evidence for the truth of the event: *it appears to be raining* involves certainty that the event at hand is a raining event. *Seem* only relates the idea of indirect evidence for the truth of the event: *it seems to be raining* does not require certainty about a raining event, it involves a more subjective impression. At first sight, then, it is not clear how any of this translates as quantificational properties. However, Smessaert's (1993) analysis of comparative quantifiers (*more, less,* and so on) as Generalized Quantifiers suggests that *seem* and *appear* might be viewed on a par with comparative quantifiers such as *exactly*. In the same way *continue* and *keep* correspond to the universal quantifier in ter Meulen's (1990) analysis, the raising verb *appear* corresponds to the quantifier *exactly*: *it appears to be raining*, then, should be glossed as *This event is exactly like a raining event*, while

seem corresponds to *not exactly*: *it seems to be raining* corresponds to *This event is not exactly/quite like a raining event*. If this correspondence is a real one, there is evidence that *seem* and *appear* can indeed be described as raising verbs with quantificational properties. Note that *seem* is morphologically very close to comparatives in various languages: French *sembler*, "seem," versus *ressembler*, "resemble, be alike"; Dutch *lijken*, "seem" versus *(ge)lijk*, "like."

19. Interestingly, ter Meulen (1989) has a corner of the square that is not lexicalized in English: *not-start*. Still, it might be argued that the aspectual raising verb *be about* fits in this position:

    i. It is about to rain.
       "It has not yet started raining (but it's going to)."

Similarly, the French aspectual raising verb *tarder*, "await," fits into this position:

    ii. Il tarde à pleuvoir.
       it awaits to rain
       "It still does not start raining."

20. We include these verbs in the set of raising verbs because they meet the test of thematic transparency: the subject position of the verbs quoted is selectionally empty and can be filled by any subject of the embedded verb, including meteorological expletives.

Within the set of raising verbs, it might be argued that *seem* and *appear* belong to the class of aspectual verbs: while aspectual verbs modify the internal temporal development of a situation, "phenomenal" verbs such as *seem* and *appear* modify the atemporal manifestation of a situation. "Phenomenal" verbs compare an entire situation to a similar situation (cf. note 16), whereas aspectual verbs relate a situation to one of its subparts. This makes "phenomenal" verbs into a special subset of aspectual verbs, which are radically different from either Tense and Mood in that Tense and Mood, but not Aspect, relate a situation to, respectively, the time and the (possible) worlds of the speaker.

21. It might be noted that something similar is the case for English *will* ("possible" future: *she will have two girls and two boys*) as opposed to *be going to* ("necessary" future: *She is going to have two girls and two boys*).

Cross-linguistically, the necessity meaning is nevertheless not always linked up with the counterparts of *go/aller*. In Swedish, the auxiliary *ska*, "will," expresses necessary future in the context cited, whereas the auxiliary *kommer att*, "go," expresses the "neutral" possible future.

22. Note that perfective aspect for the counterpart of *aller*, "go," and of epistemic *moeten*, "must," seems to be perfectly possible in Dutch:

    i. Het is gaan regenen.
    ii. Het had moeten regenen om de oogst te redden.

However, in these cases the usual perfective participle marked by *ge-* has been replaced by the infinitival form, a possibility that also exists in other complementation — even raising — structures where well-known word order differences are correlated with it:

    iii. Jan is begonnen/beginnen een boek te lezen.
        "Jan is begun a book to read."
    iv. Jan is een boek beginnen/*begonnen te lezen.
        "Jan is a book begin to read."   (Southern Dutch)

Importantly, in (i) and (ii) the perfective participle is impossible:

    v. *Het is gegaan regenen.
    vi. *Het had gemoeten regenen om de oogst te redden.

It seems then that the structures in (i) are saved by the switch of participial morphology to infinitival morphology. I have no further explanation for this intriguing fact.

23. Lyons (1977) makes the distinction between objective epistemic necessity and subjective epistemic necessity: the latter is necessity related to the world of the speaker, as in (i):

> i. Il doit/a dû faire chaud dans le Kalahari aujourd'hui.
> "It must be/have been warm in the Kalahari today."

Subjective epistemic necessity involves probability. Importantly, this subjective epistemic meaning of *devoir*, "must," can be combined with perfective aspect.

24. In this respect, it is significant that Italian can use *venire*, "come," and *andare*, "go," only as passive auxiliaries and not as raising verbs, while French uses *venir*, "come," and *aller*, "go," only as temporal raising verbs and never as passive auxiliaries. I have no explanation for this fact, but it seems that this distribution could be explained in a framework such as the one sketched here, in which passive and raising are both viewed as cases of complementation involving quantificational operators.

25. We leave out the raising constructions of *promettre*, "promise," *menacer*, "threaten," *avoir toutes les chances*, "have a chance." From a temporal and modal perspective, the raising construction of *promettre*, "promise," seems to be closely related to *aller* (*Il promet/*a promis de pleuvoir*, "It promises/has promised to rain"), while *menacer*, "threaten," *avoir toutes les chances*, "have a chance," seem to be basically variants of *risquer*, "risk," (*Il menace/a menacé de pleuvoir*, "It threatens/has threatened to rain").

REFERENCES

Baker, Mark, Kyle Johnson, and Ian Roberts. 1989. "Passive arguments raised." *Linguistic Inquiry* 20:219–251.

Barbiers, Sjef. 1993. "Modal verbs in Dutch: An LF analysis of the epistemic-root distinction." Ms. University of Leiden.

Belletti, Adriana. 1988. "The case of unaccusatives." *Linguistic Inquiry* 19:1–34.

Burzio, Luigi. 1986. *Italian syntax*. Dordrecht: Kluwer.

Chomsky, Noam. 1981. *Lectures on government and binding*. Dordrecht: Foris.

———. 1992. "A minimalist program for linguistic theory." *MIT Occasional papers in linguistics* 1. Department of Linguistics and Philosophy. MIT, Cambridge, Mass.

Chomsky, Noam, and Howard Lasnik. 1993. "Principles and parameters theory." In *Syntax: An international handbook of contemporary research*, ed. J. Jacobs, Arnim von Stechow, and Werner Sternefeld, 506–569. Berlin: Walter de Gruyter.

Cureton, R. 1979. "The exceptions to passive in English: A pragmatic hypothesis." *Studies in the Linguistic Sciences*. 9:39–53.

Déchaine, Rose-Marie. 1994. "One *be*." Paper presented at the TIN dag (Linguistics in the Netherlands), ms. HIL.

Dikken, Marcel den. 1993. "Binding, expletives, and levels." Ms. Free University of Amsterdam, HIL.

D'Hulst, Yves. 1992. *La sintassi del passivo italiano nel quadro della Grammatica Universale*. Doctoral diss., Katholieke Universiteit Leuven Campus Kortrijk.

Jackendoff, Ray. 1972. *Semantic interpretation in generative grammar*. Cambridge, Mass.: MIT Press.

Heggie, Lori. 1988. "The syntax of copular structures." Doctoral diss., Los Angeles, University of Southern California.

Heycock, Caroline. 1991. "Specificational pseudo-clefts and predication." Paper presented at the Annual meeting of the LSA, January.

Higgins, Roger. 1979. *The pseudo-cleft construction in English*. New York: Garland.

Hoekstra, Teun. 1984. *Transitivity*. Dordrecht: Foris.

———. 1993. "BE as HAVE plus or minus." Ms. University of Leiden.

Jaeggli, Oswaldo. 1986. "Passive." *Linguistic Inquiry* 17:587–622.

Kayne, Richard. 1981. "On certain differences between French and English." *Linguistic Inquiry* 12:349–371.

———. 1993. "Toward a modular theory of auxiliary selection." *Studia Linguistica* 47:3–31.

Krifka, Manfred, ed. 1988. *Genericity in natural language: Proceedings of the 1988 Tübingen Conference*. Tübingen: SNS-Bericht.

Kühner, Raphael, and Carl Stegmann. 1955. *Ausführliche Grammatik der lateinischen Sprache*. Leverkusen: Gottschalkse Verlagsbuchhandlung.

Lamiroy, Béatrice. 1987. "The complementation of aspectual verbs in French." *Language*. 63:278–298.

———. 1993. "Pourquoi il y a deux passifs." *Langages 109 'Sur le passif,'* ed. Gaston Gross, 53–72.

Lasnik, Howard. 1992. "Case and expletives: Notes toward a parametric account." *Linguistic Inquiry* 23:381–405.

———. 1994. "Lectures on minimalist syntax." Ms. University of Connecticut. Storrs: Connecticut.

Lyons, John. 1977. *Semantics*. Cambridge: Cambridge University Press.

Manzini, M. Rita. 1983. "On Control and Control theory." *Linguistic Inquiry*. 14:421–467.

Martin, Robert. 1979. "La tournure impersonnelle: Essai d'une interprétation sémantico-logique." In *Festschrift Kurt Baldinger zum 60-Geburtstag*. Tübingen: Niemeyer.

Meillet, Antoine. 1938. *Linguistique historique et linguistique générale*. Paris: Klincksieck.

Meulen, Alice ter. 1990. "Aspectual verbs as generalized quantifiers." *The proceedings of the ninth West Coast Conference on Formal Linguistics*, ed. Aaron Halpern, 374–360. Stanford: CSLI.

Moro, Andrea. 1990. "The raising of predicates: Copula, expletives, and existence." Ms. Università di Venezia, Venice, Italy.

Pica, Pierre. 1988. "Sur le caractère inalienable de l'être." *Transparence et opacité: littérature et sciences cognitives (Hommages à M. Ronat)*, ed. Pierre Pica and Tibor Papp, 207–221. Paris: Cerf.

Postma, Gertjan. 1993. "The syntax of the morphological defectivity of BE." *HIL manuscripts* 3:31–67.

———. 1994. "The argumental licensing of the perfect tense." *Proceedings of CGSW 9*, ed. Höskuldur Thráinsson and Samuel Epstein. Dordrecht: Kluwer.

Rooryck, Johan 1992. "Negative and factive islands revisited." *Journal of Linguistics* 28:343–374.

Ruwet, Nicolas. 1983. "Montée et contrôle: Une question à revoir?" *Revue Romane* (numéro spécial) 24:17–37.

———. 1984. "Je veux partir– *Je veux que je parte: À propos de la distribution des complétives à temps fini et des compléments à l'infinitif en français." *Cahiers de Grammaire* 7:76–138.

Smessaert, Hans. 1993. "The logical geometry of comparison and quantification: A cross-categorial analysis of Dutch determiners and aspectual adverbs." Doctoral diss., Katholieke Universiteit Leuven.

Tesnière, Lucien. 1969. *Éléments de syntaxe structurale*. Paris: Klincksieck.

Vanden Wyngaerd, Guido. 1993. *PRO-legomena: An investigation into the distribution and the referential properties of the empty category PRO*. Berlin: Mouton de Gruyter.

Verkuyl, Henk. 1972. *On the compositional nature of the aspects*. Dordrecht: Reidel.

Vet, Co. 1980. "Les constructions impersonnelles en français: une approche dans le cadre de la grammaire fonctionnelle de S.C. Dik." *Travaux de linguistique* 8:49–64.

Verheugd-Daatzelaar, Els. 1990. *Subject arguments and predicate nominals*. Amsterdam: Rodopi.

Von der Gabelentz, H.C. 1861. "Über das Passivum." *Eine sprachvergleichende Abhandlung. Abhandlungen der königlichen sächsischen Geselschafft des Wissenschaft zu Leipzig Klasse* 3:449–546.

Williams, Edwin. 1983. "Semantic versus syntactic categories." *Linguistics and Philosophy* 6:423–446.

Zaring, Laurie. 1993. "Two 'be' or not two 'be': Identity, predication, and the Welsh copula." Ms. Carleton College, Minnesota.

NINE

On the Syntax and Semantics
of Local Anaphors in French
and English

PIERRE PICA
& WILLIAM SNYDER

1. INTRODUCTION

Local anaphors in French and in English have a variety of lexical and morphological properties that are unexpected on conventional approaches to Binding theory. We propose an account in which these characteristics follow from the fact that reflexives are essentially *pronominals*. On our approach, Principle B is the core of Binding theory, and the surprising properties of local anaphors derive from the need for local anaphors to escape Principle B. We argue that all local anaphors are bimorphemic (sometimes in contrast to surface appearances), and that this structure is related to a semantics of "partition," by which local anaphors escape Principle B. In support of these views, we present a variety of facts that follow in a natural way from our syntactic and semantic proposals, but that to our knowledge have not previously been explained within the framework of generative grammar. Our theory is shown to have a modular character, with distinct roles attributed to Principle B, the morphological structure of local anaphors, and the broader architecture of human cognition.

2. ON THE LACK OF SAUSSUREAN ARBITRARINESS IN LOCAL ANAPHORS

Standard Binding theory assumes a lexical distinction between pronominals and anaphors. On this traditional view, pronominals are subject to a disjointness constraint (Principle B), while anaphors are exempt from Principle B but subject to their own locality requirement (Principle A). Such an approach crucially assumes a lexically encoded categorial distinction between pronominals and anaphors.

It is remarkable, however, that if languages provide elements marked as anaphors in the lexicon, and if these elements are exempt from Principle B, that anaphors should be subject to the variety of severe restrictions observed in natural languages. For example, there are few if any languages with an anaphor completely unrelated, in its phonology and morphology, to either the pronominal paradigm or the agreement paradigm. This pattern is a source of puzzlement on standard approaches, because the inventory of anaphors in the lexicon should be subject to Saussurean arbitrariness.

Restricting ourselves to strictly local anaphors, the lack of arbitrariness is illustrated by French, in which the following elements all involve, in one way or another, a pronominal or agreement element: (a) the so-called complex anaphor, *lui-même*; (b) the so-called pronominal clitics such as *nous* and *vous*; and (c) the reflexive clitic *se*. The complex anaphor is formed from the pronominal *lui*. The "pronominal" reflexive clitics are identical in form to the corresponding pronominals. The reflexive clitic *se* is also related to the pronominal and agreement systems, as suggested, for example, by its etymological relation to the so-called impersonal *si* of Italian, which is often taken as involving a pronominal use of *si* akin to English *one*. A more direct relation of *se* to the pronominal paradigm is the phonological (and etymological) relationship of *se* to the third person singular possessive pronouns *son*, *sa*, and *ses* (see Benveniste 1969).

Furthermore, across languages, the antecedent of an anaphor is often subject to constraints that have been stated in terms of animacy, agenthood, awareness, or point of view. (On the role of awareness in long-distance anaphors, see among others Kuno 1987; on point of view, see Cantrall 1974.) These constraints, which have generally been formulated in pragmatic terms, are likewise a source of puzzlement on the standard view, because they do not derive in an obvious way from known principles of the grammar. For example, (1) illustrates the well-known animacy constraint on the French clitic *se* in its reflexive use:

(1) a. Jean se lave.
         John self washes
         "John washes himself."
     b. *La table se lave.
         the table self washes
         "The table washes itself."

The examples in (2) illustrate what we take to be a less readily observed property, namely that the reflexive clitic must have an agentive antecedent:[1]

(2) a. Jean se frappe.   (agentive)
         John self hits
         "John hits himself."
     b. ??Jean s'apprécie.   (non-agentive)
         John self likes
         "John likes himself."
     c. Jean se détache de la chaise.   (agentive)
         John self unties from the chair
         "John is untying himself from the chair."
     d. ??Jean se connaît.   (non-agentive)
         John self knows
         "John knows himself."

The agentiveness constraint observed in (2b, d) is reminiscent of the awareness constraint discussed by Kuno and others for long-distance anaphora (and local anaphora involving anaphors in oblique positions), but, to our knowledge, has not previously been noted for local anaphoric relations (between a subject and a direct object).

3. THE ROLE OF PARTITION IN LOCAL ANAPHORA

All of the above observations run counter to the predictions of the standard Binding theory, and cast doubt on its accuracy. As an alternative, we propose, first, that there is no Principle A as such, and that Principle B, which is the core of binding theory, applies to both pronominals and anaphors. On this view, an anaphor can be understood as a type of pronominal whose internal structure allows it both to *approximate* coreference with a local antecedent, and at the same time to escape Principle B.

We will argue that local anaphors satisfy these conflicting requirements through a semantics of "partition," in which the anaphor is interpreted as related to, but distinct from, its antecedent. For example, in the case of the English anaphor *himself*, the morpheme *him* is interpreted as the same individual as the antecedent. Yet, the semantics of the morpheme *-self* causes the anaphor as a whole to be interpreted as an individual related to, but distinct from, the individual denoted by *him*. In our view, the necessity of creating a partition accounts for the lack of Saussurean arbitrariness in the form of local anaphors, including both the tendency for local anaphors to be morphologically complex, and the tendency for anaphors to bear a visible similarity to elements from the pronominal and agreement paradigms.

We have identified two principal types of partition that are compatible with local anaphora. One type of partition appears to divide an individual into an agentive aspect (the individual understood as the psychological agent of a reflexive action) and a physical aspect (the individual understood as the physical patient of the reflexive action). A second type of partition appears to distinguish the individual, understood as a conscious observer or possessor of knowledge, from the same individual understood as the object of knowledge. (We will present evidence that in the second type of partition, the object of knowledge is generally understood psychologically rather than physically.) These two types of partition are summarized in (3).[2]

(3) a. Agent (Psychological) versus Patient (Physical)
    b. Knower (Psychological) versus Object of Knowledge (Psychological)

Thus, in (4), the NP *John* is understood psychologically, as the agent of hitting, while the NP *himself* is understood physically, as the patient.

(4) John hit himself.

In (5), the predicate *likes* is non-agentive, and so the anaphor *himself* (5b) cannot be dependent on the type of partition in (3a). Instead, we argue, Principle B is satisfied in (5b) by the partition of John into "knower" and "object of knowledge"

(3b). We take the English verb *likes* to be ambiguous between a reading in which the subject's positive attitude toward the object is based on knowledge about the object, and a reading in which the reason for the subject's positive attitude toward the object is left vague. When the object is non-reflexive, both readings are possible, as in (5a).

(5) a. John likes Mary, but he doesn't realize it.
     b. John likes himself (?*but he doesn't realize it).

When the object is a reflexive, however, the conscious-knowledge reading is obligatory, as illustrated by the anomalous nature of the parenthetical clause in (5b). This follows because the reflexive, with a non-agentive antecedent, depends on a partition of the type in (3b).

In French, the conscious-knowledge reading of English *like* can be unambiguously expressed by the predicate *apprécier beaucoup*, as illustrated in (6a).

(6) a.?*Jean apprécie beaucoup Marie, mais il ne le sait pas.
         John likes much Mary, but he not it knows not
         "John likes Mary, but he doesn't know it."
     b. Jean s'apprécie beaucoup.
         John self likes much
         "John likes (what he knows about) himself."
         (Conscious knowledge implied)

As expected, the reflexive (6b) is fully grammatical with this predicate.

French provides several other predicates corresponding roughly to English *like*. The *verb aimer bien* is ambiguous between the conscious-knowledge reading of *like* and the reading in which conscious knowledge is not implied, while the verb *aimer* alone preferentially corresponds to the latter reading only. As expected, (7a) is fully acceptable, while (7b) is anomalous.

(7) a. Jean s'aime bien.
         John self loves/likes well
         "John likes (what he knows about) himself."
         (Conscious knowledge implied on the relevant reading)
     b. ??Jean s'aime.
         John self loves/likes
         "John likes himself."
         (Conscious knowledge not implied)

It should be noted that the judgements in (6) and (7) are somewhat delicate, and are sensitive both to individual variation in lexical semantics and to possible effects of focus. Nonetheless, the same patterns can be observed with a variety of non-agentive verbs, and are completely unexpected on the standard Binding theory, in which similar effects have generally been taken as falling outside of the grammar. For example, the sentences in (8), involving two senses of the verb *know*, are exactly parallel to the observations in (6) and (7).

(8) a. John knows Mary, but he's momentarily forgotten the fact.
     b. John knows himself (?*but he's momentarily forgotten the fact).
     c. Jean se connaît ?? (bien).

John self knows well
"John knows himself."

In (8c), *connaître bien* is again ambiguous as to whether conscious knowledge is implied, but *connaître* alone does not clearly imply conscious knowledge on the part of the subject.

Interestingly, the precise set of semantic partitions with which local anaphora are compatible is considerably more restricted than the full set of partitions that one could, in principle, impose on an individual. An example is given in (9).

(9) a. John hit his body.
　　 b. John hit himself.　　(physical)
　　 c. John likes his body.
　　 d. John likes himself.　　(psychological/??physical)

Examples (9a) and (9b) are at least approximately equivalent, as we expect if the partition in (9b) (= 4) is between John understood as a psychological agent, and *John* understood as a physical patient.

We might reasonably expect a partition into psychological and physical aspects to enable (9d) to have approximately the same interpretation as (9c), but this expectation is at most partially borne out. The English-speaking informants whom we have consulted find (9d) relatively odd on an interpretation in which *himself* is understood physically. Thus, we specify in (3b) that the relevant partition is between an individual as "knower" and an individual as "object of knowledge," in *both* cases understood psychologically. We propose that the restricted set of partitions found with local anaphora may reflect significant properties of human cognitive architecture, potentially of relevance to much more than Binding theory, and for the present we content ourselves with a description rather than an explanation. For present purposes, we simply take the anomalous character of the "physical" reading in (9d) as another indication that local anaphora are restricted in ways that are unexpected on the standard Binding theory, but that are compatible with a partition analysis.

Further support for the role of partition in local anaphora comes from the incompatibility of certain experiencer-object verbs with the reflexive. For example, the contrast in acceptability of (10a, b) versus (11a, b) corresponds to the degree to which the surface subject of these predicates is understood as an object of (the experiencer's) knowledge. This interpretation of the evidence is supported by the contrast in acceptability of (10c) versus (11c), on the reading in which it is the information that *Mary* knows about *John* that bothers, annoys, frightens, or worries her.

(10) a.?*John bothers himself.
　　 b.??John annoys himself.
　　 c. The more Mary learns about John, the more he ?*bothers/??annoys her.

(11) a. ?John frightens himself.
　　 b. ?John worries himself.
　　 c. ?The more Mary learns about John, the more he frightens/worries her.

While the precise degree of ungrammaticality of the examples in (10) and (11) is difficult to assess, and undoubtedly varies across speakers, we expect that the relative grammaticality of examples such as (10a, b) and (11a, b) will be correlated with the grammaticality of corresponding examples of the form in (10c) and (11c).

Again, the facts in English are highly similar to those of French. In (12a, b), we find a contrast between the approximate equivalents of *annoy* and *worry*, in which the former more strongly resists the reflexive. (Here, we are specifically evaluating [12a, b] on the readings in which they are *not* inherent reflexives; we are thus excluding the alternate reading, "John is becoming annoyed/worried.") This contrast is paralleled by the contrast in acceptability of the two predicates in (12c).

(12)   a. ?*Jean s'ennuie.
        John self annoys
        "John annoys himself."
    b. ??Jean s'inquiète.
        John self worries
        "John worries himself."
    c. Le plus de choses Marie apprend sur Jean, le plus cela ??l'inquiète/?*l'ennuie.
        The more of things Mary learns about John, the more that her worries/her
        annoys
        "The more Marie learns about Jean, the more this worries/annoys her."

The evidence from experiencer-object predicates as in (10), (11), and (12) is especially interesting because in (11a, b) the anaphor *himself* expresses the "knower" rather than the object of knowledge (in contrast to 5b). This suggests that the semantics of *-self* is relatively general, making reference to a contextually available partition, but allowing the interpretive component to fill in the details. In the following sections we will propose a modular view of local anaphora, comprising independent roles for a disjointness condition (Principle B), the lexical semantics of *-self* (or its approximate equivalents in other languages), and the varieties of partition allowed by the cognitive architecture.

4. THE FORMAL SEMANTICS OF PARTITION

We find it interesting to note that in the preceding discussion, philosophical notions such as the *de se/de re* distinction have played a tacit role (cf. Lewis 1970; Castañeda 1967, 1975; and Quine 1955, among others). We suggest not only that such philosophical notions may be relevant to the proper understanding of linguistic phenomena, but also that many of the philosophical questions, including questions about the concepts of mind, body, person, and identity (again cf. Quine 1955; Lewis 1970; and Castañeda 1967, 1975), may have an unrecognized source in the phenomena of natural language (including the semantics and syntax of partition).

In particular, there exists an interesting and extensive philosophical literature on the concept of "self," which is suggestive in light of our approach to local anaphora. A widespread observation in this literature is that the term "self," which originates as a nominalization of the *-self* from local anaphors, is invoked precisely when there is a real or apparent *contradiction* between two roles that are performed by a single individual. This is surprising on a view in which the concept of "self" expresses something more like integral/defining/persistent properties of an individual, for example. Yet, the observation is precisely what we should expect if the noun *self* derives its meaning from the semantics of the reflexive morpheme *-self*, and if *-self* has the semantic function of specifying some aspect of an individual that is related to, but distinct from, a second aspect of the same individual.

In this connection it is also interesting to note that a remarkable number of languages use, in the formation of local anaphors, a morpheme that ordinarily denotes a body-part: Hebrew "bone," Hausa "head," Basque "head," and so forth. This strikes us as natural on an account in which many uses of local anaphora depend on a partition between psychological and physical aspects of an individual, because a body-part relates both to the physical body and, as an inalienable possession, to a psychological possessor.

We can represent the semantic contribution of the English morpheme *-self* as in (13), where we assume an extensional semantics for ease of exposition.

(13) $\| \text{-}self \| = f: D_e \to D_e$
For any x an element of the domain of individuals, where x denotes a contextually salient "aspect" of a person or object, $f(x)$ denotes a salient, *distinct* aspect of the same person or object.

The important points about the characterization in (13) are, first, that *-self* requires an individual-type argument corresponding to the morpheme *him* in *himself*, and, second, that the result of combining *-self* with its argument is an element drawn from the domain of individuals, which denotes an "aspect" of a person or object.[3] A further point is that the denotation of *-self* does not directly determine the type of partition that allows the anaphor to satisfy Principle B. Instead, the denotation in (13) makes reference to the partition, if any, that is made contextually salient by the semantics of the other lexical items in the sentence.

We propose a slightly different analysis of the French local anaphor *se*. In the case of *se*, we are again led to a bipartite structure analogous to that of English *himself*. We take the surface form *se* to correspond to an underlying structure of the form [se ∅], in which *se* corresponds to *him* and ∅ corresponds to *-self*. In contrast to English, however, the null counterpart of *-self*, on our account, has a semantics closer to that given by Heim, Lasnik, and May (1991) for the English morpheme *other*.[4] We represent the proposed meaning as in (14).

(14) $\| ∅ \| = f: D_e \to D_{<et,t>}$
For any x, an element of the domain of individuals, and any predicate g, mapping individuals to truth values, $f(x)(g)$ is true if and only if for every y in the domain of individuals such that y is distinct from x and in a discourse-supplied context set containing x, $g(y)$ is true.

For present purposes, an important characteristic of (14) is that the semantics of the element ∅ does not make reference to "aspects" of a single individual, but is instead stated in the more general terms of a partition on a set. In the case of the reflexive, the difference from *himself* is not apparent, but the more general semantics has the effect of allowing reciprocal, neuter, and middle uses of *se* that cannot be formed with *himself*. In the reflexive, the relevant set contains the two salient aspects of an individual. Another important characteristic of (14), as distinguished from (13), is that (14) incorporates the semantics of a universal quantifier. This quantifier has no effect in the reflexive, but is motivated by the semantics we assume for reciprocal and neuter uses of *se*.

We will set aside the middle and neuter uses of *se*, and limit ourselves to a few brief remarks on the reciprocal. Given the semantics for the null reflexive morpheme in (14), we can readily derive the reciprocal meaning of (15):

(15)   Les enfants se regardent.
      the children self look-at
      "The children are looking at each other."

Following Heim, Lasnik, and May (1991), we assume that the DP *les enfants* in (15) is associated with a null distributive operator D, semantically analogous to the overt element *each*.[5] We take the relevant partition in (15) to be between any given member of the set of children, and the rest of the set. The universal quantifier in (14) ("for every *y*") ensures true reciprocity:

(16)   For each child *x*, for every child *y* distinct from *x*, *x* is looking at *y*.

Example (15) also has reflexive readings, which we derive (in the case of the distributed reflexive) by taking the relevant partition to be internal to each child, or (in the case of the collective reflexive) by taking the relevant partition to be a partition into "group as knower" and "group as object of knowledge."

A striking piece of evidence in favor of the semantics in (14), and in favor of our "partition" approach more generally, is that in the reciprocal (15), the partition between a distinguished element (*x*) of the set and the remainder of the set eliminates any need for a partition of the type that is found with reflexives (cf. [3]). Thus, a sentence of the type *Les enfants se connaissent* "The children know each other" is perfectly grammatical on a reciprocal interpretation. The same sentence is disallowed on either a collective or a distributed reflexive reading, because the lexical semantics of *connaître* does not implicate a partition of the type expressed in (3a, b).

5. THE SYNTAX OF LOCAL ANAPHORA

Let us tentatively assume, rephrasing the analysis of Pica (1987) in terms of the checking of phi-features, that the reflexive *himself* in an English sentence such as (17) has the complex internal structure in (18).

(17)   John hit himself.

(18)
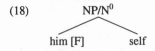

Here the complex element *himself* is formed by merging two X^0s in the lexicon, forming an element whose projection can be interpreted as both an X^0 and an XP. (See Chomsky 1994 on the double status of certain elements as X^0s and XPs.) We propose that the two X^0s constituting *himself* together form a word-level category, but still play distinct roles in feature-checking and semantic interpretation, for reasons related to the semantics of partition.

At Logical Form (LF) the whole complex (*himself*) moves to Spec/AgrOP (where the Case features of the XMax [*him self*] are checked).[6] *Himself* must, however, move further, as a kind of complex clitic (X^0) to the head of AgrSP, as partly illustrated in (19). Within AgrSP, the unchecked features of *him* (if any) are checked through a Spec-head relationship with *John*:

(19)

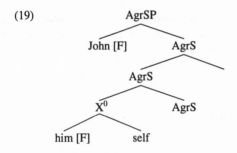

The fact that *himself* escapes Principle B, which amounts to saying that two distinct NPs or pronominals cannot "corefer" within a local domain, does not need to be stipulated in the grammar. This follows instead from the semantics of partition, as discussed above. The "reference" of *himself* is crucially distinct from that of *John*, and *himself* can consequently escape principle B.[7]

The parallelism observed above between *himself* and *se* strongly suggests that the anaphor *se* is not mono-morphemic, as usually assumed. (On the relationship between the morphological structure of the reflexive and its behavior, see in particular Pica 1984a, b.) Instead, we take *se* to have a bipartite morphological structure, as illustrated in (20).

(20)
```
        N⁰/NP
       /      \
    se [F]      ∅
```

The covert noun ∅ is interpreted as meaning a "part," and allows a partition of the kind discussed above.

In a sentence such as (21), for example, the complex clitic [se ∅] escapes principle B, because *Jean* and the complex clitic denote distinct aspects of the individual Jean.

(21)   Jean se lave.
       John self washes
       "John washes himself"

The complex [se ∅] moves first as an XP to Spec AgrOP, and then moves as an X^0 to AgrS, a position in which the features of *se* are checked through a Spec-head relationship with *Jean*, as partly illustrated in (22):

(22)

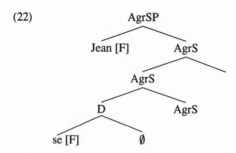

We believe that the equivalent of $\emptyset$ can sometimes be expressed overtly, as in Zribi-Hertz's (1978) example (23a), which, as she notices, can be paraphrased by (23b), and in (24a), which can be paraphrased as (24b):

(23) a. Jean se pose.
          John self seats
          "Jean is setting himself (down)."
          (that is, "Jean is sitting down")
      b. Jean pose son derrière.
          John seats his backside
          "Jean is setting his backside (down)."
          (that is, "Jean is sitting down.")

(24) a. Jean se convertit.
          John self converts
          "Jean converts himself."
          (that is, "Jean is undergoing a conversion.")
      b. Jean convertit ses idées.
          John converts his ideas
          "Jean is converting (that is, changing) his ideas."

Our analysis predicts the ungrammaticality of (25), where no type of partition that we have so far identified can apply. The sentence is therefore uninterpretable for semantic reasons.

(25) *La table se lave.
       the table self washes
       "The table washes itself."

The analysis explains, moreover, in very different terms than previous analyses (see in particular Kayne 1992) the well-known puzzle of why (non-reflexive) clitic pronouns such as *nous* can also be used as reflexive pronouns. In terms of the present analysis, pronominals can escape Principle B when they are subparts of a more complex structure (26), because then, for purposes of Principle B, they are in a domain distinct from that of their antecedent.

(26) N^0/NP

The element $\emptyset$ induces a partition (as in 3a, b), and the entire complex in (26) can escape the effect of Principle B, as illustrated in (27a, b).[8]

(27) a. Nous nous lavons.
  we us wash
  "We are washing ourselves."
 b. Nous nous croyons intelligents.
  we us believe intelligent-PL
  "We believe ourselves (to be) intelligent."

As predicted under the current framework, *se* and *nous* are subject to the same constraints when they cannot induce a local partition. This is illustrated by the parallelism between (28a) and (28b), in which *nous* cannot be interpreted as a reflexive:

(28) a. *Il s'apprécie.
  He self likes
  "He likes himself."
 b. *Nous nous apprécions.
  we us like
  "We like ourselves."

(Non-reflexive) clitic pronouns, as expected under the current analysis, are subject to Principle B, because they have a simple structure (29) in which there is no element $\emptyset$ to induce a partition.[9]

(29) DP/D^0
  |
  nous [F]

The pronominal *nous* moves as an XP to Spec AgrOP, where all its features are checked by Spec-head agreement with the head of AgrOP. There arises the question of why *le* cannot enter into a structure akin to (26) and be employed as a reflexive. This impossibility is illustrated by the ungrammaticality of (30):

(30) *Jean le frappe.
  John him hits
  "Jean hits himself."

We believe that this is due to independent factors, namely that *le* would give a referential status to $\emptyset$, and/or that the semantics of partition (somewhat similar to the semantics of possession) forces the use of a dative or genitive pronoun.[10]

Note that *lui-même* cannot express an agent-patient partition in French unless it doubles a clitic *se*, as illustrated by the following contrast:

(31) a. *Jean frappe sur lui-même.
  John hits upon him-self
  "John is hitting himself."
 b. Jean se frappe sur lui-même.
  John self hits upon him-self
  "John is hitting himself."

This observation can be reduced to the fact that *lui-même* is never used in direct object position in French, and consequently is not assigned the role of patient (occurring in positions more typically associated with location or goal). Hence, *lui-même* cannot, by itself, be interpreted in terms of an agent/patient partition.[11] As predicted by the present framework, (32), in which a knower/object of knowledge partition is possible, is permitted by the grammar:

(32)   Jean est fier de lui-même.
        John is proud of him-self
        "Jean is proud of himself."

Note furthermore that this type of partition (cf. [3b]) correctly predicts the following contrasts in French.

(33)   a.   *Jean se considère.
              John self considers
              "Jean is considering himself."
        b.   Jean se considère intelligent.
              John self considers intelligent
              "Jean considers himself intelligent."

(34)   a.   *Jean se croit.
              John self believes
              "Jean believes himself."
        b.   Jean se croit intelligent.
              John self believes intelligent
              "Jean believes himself (to be) intelligent."

In (33b) and (34b), *Jean* is taken as consciously attributing to himself a specific property; thus, there is a salient partition between *Jean* as knower (or at least "believer") and *Jean* as object of knowledge. In (33a) and (34a), there is no such partition, and Principle B applies.

Note that this last type of contrast casts very strong doubt on the accuracy of an analysis in terms of the argument-based notion "reflexivity" (Reinhart and Reuland 1993), in which any reflexive that is an argument of the verb can "reflexivize" the predicate of which it is an argument.[12]

6. CONCLUSION

In this paper we have presented evidence from French and English to show that local anaphors are possible only if they can be distinguished from their antecedent through a semantics of "partition." We have accounted for these facts by treating Principle B as applying to anaphors as well as pronominals. The result of the partition is that the anaphor is understood as related to, but distinct from, its antecedent: Coreference is thus *approximated* without violation of Principle B. On our view, local anaphors (including French *se*) are structurally complex. The semantics of partition arises in part from the compositional semantics of the two components of the anaphor, and in part from the context provided by the remainder of the sentence. We take the necessity of this bipartite structure to explain the surprising lack of Saussurean arbitrariness in local anaphors.

NOTES

Portions of this research have been presented in talks at CUNY Graduate Center, New York, the Universities of McGill, Geneva, Stuttgart, and York. Special thanks to A. Belletti, J. Bonneau, H.-N. Castañeda, N. Chomsky, C. Collins, A.-M. Di Sciullo, R. Fiengo, J. Greenberg, J. Gruber, A. Hestvik, R. Kayne, H. Koopman, H. Haider, K. Hale, I. Heim, H. Lasnik, L. Rizzi, J. Rooryck, K. Safir, C. Tancredi, and S. Vikner. All errors remain our responsibility. This work was partly supported by the Social Sciences and Humanities Research Council of Canada Grant n⁰ 411-92-0012, to A.-M. Di Sciullo. W. Snyder was supported by an NSF Fellowship in Linguistics, an NSF Research and Training Grant ("Language: Acquisition and Computation") to MIT, and the McDonnell-Pew Center for Cognitive Neuroscience at MIT.

1. This constraint can be superseded, however, under certain conditions, notably when focus is applied to either the surface subject (*Jean*) or the predicate (*s'apprécie*) in (2b). (Addition of the modifier *beaucoup* also renders [2b] acceptable, as will be discussed.) One explanation for the effect of focus would be that focus introduces a partition of the same type discussed in section 3. This would account for the effect of focus in (i), in which underlining indicates "coreference" and capitalization indicates a pitch accent. Yet, focus has more dramatic effects on possible binding relations than would be expected under a straightforward partition account, as illustrated by the example in (ii).

    i. John thinks Mary likes HER/*her.
    ii. John thinks Mary likes HIMSELF/*himself.

2. We do not, however, intend (3) as an exhaustive list. The task of characterizing the class of semantic partitions compatible with local anaphora is an ongoing research project. A possible third type, in addition to (3a, b), is the partition between an individual understood as a source and that individual understood as a goal. Such a partition may be responsible for the acceptability of examples such as (ia, b).

    i. a. John talks to himself.
       b. John sent a letter to himself.

An interesting possibility is that the relevant types of partition can be expressed entirely in a more restricted vocabulary of "thematic roles," such as those assumed in Hale and Keyser (1993) or Gruber (in preparation), but this remains a direction for future research.

3. Here we allow the antecedent of a local anaphor to be an inanimate object, although in many cases this will be ruled out by the nature of the available types of partition. For example, both of the partitions in (3) would seem to be incompatible with an inanimate object. Yet, there may exist other available types of partition that would not impose this constraint. Alternatively, it may turn out that apparent anaphors such as English *itself* have a status distinct from "true" reflexives, as might be inferred from the fact that *itself* was first attested in English more recently than the other reflexive forms, and also by the animacy constraint on reflexives in French.

4. The interpretation we propose is also reminiscent of the French word *partie*, which in its various uses can denote a person, a (sub)set of individuals, or a body-part, as suggested by the following expressions: *la partie adverse*, "the opponent," *les parties en présence*, "the parties present," *d'autre part*, "on the other hand," *à part* (exclusion) "separately."

5. Alternatively, the semantics of distribution may be encoded in the determiner *les*. On such an approach, *les* would be lexically ambiguous, with distributive and non-distributive lexical entries.

6. For purposes of exposition, we will assume a non-ergative treatment of French reflexive constructions. Few if any of our suggestions, however, are incompatible with the slightly more complex ergative analysis advocated by authors including Marantz (1983), Bouchard (1984), and Kayne (1992), as well as in Snyder (1992a).

7. We could tentatively assume, as in Pica (1994), a version of Principle B, reminiscent of the Rule of Disjoint Reference of Chomsky (1973), according to which two distinct Agreement nodes cannot be related to the same cognitive value v (in the sense of Heim 1993, in which a *cognitive value* for x differs from an *index* for x in that it takes into account not only the "reference" of x, but also the way x is interpreted in a given structure or discourse.

> i. Principle B (reformulated): For a given Predicate P, no more than one
> Agreement node can be associated with any single cognitive value v.

The semantics of partition that we assume amounts to saying that in (ii), for example, the relationship between *John* and *himself* is not subject to our reformulation of Principle B, because *himself* and *John*, both of which have their features checked in Spec AgrP positions, refer to distinct aspects of John. We term this reformulation of Principle B the Disjoint Agreement Principle (DAP).

> ii. John hit himself.

As suggested to us by A.-M. DiSciullo (personal communication), it might be possible to reduce (i) to an Economy Principle, according to which the presence of two Agreement nodes (at least Agreement nodes that check Case) is legitimated only by the presence of two arguments associated with two distinct cognitive values. We hope to explore this interesting possibility in subsequent work. We further note that both the DAP and the concept of partition tend to reduce the syntactic role of co-indexing, since *himself* is not strictly identical to its antecedent; this result is consistent with the intuition that interpretative indexing should not play any direct role in the syntax.

8. As pointed out to us by N. Chomsky (personal communication), an alternative approach would be to say that anaphors move to AgrS at LF, and escape Principle B because they cannot reconstruct to Spec AgrOP; (non-reflexive) pronominal clitics, in contrast, adjoin to V^0, an A'-position from which they obligatorily reconstruct. Pronominal clitics, unlike anaphoric clitics, would be visible to Principle B, on the hypothesis that Principle B applies only to (non-trace) XPs.

9. We believe that a strong pronoun such as French *eux* in (i), in which the pronoun can refer only to an animate antecedent, might have a more complex structure than what is generally assumed, as illustrated in (ii):

> i. Il pense à eux.
>   he thinks about them
>   "He thinks about them."
> ii. [eux ∅]

In (ii), the pronoun can refer only to animate antecedents, and ∅ can be overtly realized as *autres* in *eux-autres*. We take ∅ to stand in a predication relation to *eux*, and to take an understood "contrast" argument (an idea reminiscent of Benveniste 1965); the resulting interpretation is something like "those other than (the contrast argument)." The structure in (ii) is thus intended to be quite different from that proposed for the reflexive clitic.

10. Note in this connection that English *him* in *himself* is historically a dative, rather than accusative, pronoun; the same is clearly true for *lui* of *lui-même*.

11. As with the restrictions on *se*, this constraint can be superseded by factors such as focus, which we hope to study in some forthcoming work.

12. We have chosen not to address, in the text, the obviously important question of why there exist Principle A effects. One possibility would be that they originate in constraints on the movement operation by which local anaphors have their phi-features checked. One type of constraint could be the Economy notion of Greed. So, for example, in a sentence such as (i), the anaphor cannot move further if it has satisfied all its morphological requirements in AgrSP of the embedded clause.

i. John said that Mary likes herself.

A puzzle for this approach, however, is the ambiguity in (ii), in which *himself* can take as its antecedent either *John* or *Bill*.

ii. John told Bill about himself.

A possible first step would be to relate the interpretation of *himself* in (ii) to the interpretation of *himself* in "picture" NPs. The idea would be to treat the predicate "tell X about Y" as having an underlying structure closer to that of "tell X information about Y" (cf. Snyder 1992b). We leave this topic to future research.

REFERENCES

Benveniste, Émile. 1965. "Le pronom et l'antonyme en français moderne." *Bulletin de la Société Linguistique de Paris* 60:71–87.

———. 1969. *Le vocabulaire des institutions indo-européennes.* Paris: Minuit.

Bouchard, Denis. 1984. *On the content of empty categories.* Dordrecht: Foris.

Cantrall, William R. 1974. *Viewpoint, reflexives, and the nature of noun phrases.* The Hague: Mouton.

Castañeda, Hector-Neri. 1967. "On the logic of self-knowledge." *Noûs* 1:9–21.

———. 1975. "Identity and sameness." *Philosophia* 5:121–150.

Chomsky, Noam. 1973. "Conditions on tranformations." In *A Festschrift for Morris Halle*, ed. Stephen Anderson and Paul Kiparsky, 232–286. New York: Holt.

———. 1994. "Bare phrase structure." *MIT Occasional Papers in Linguistics* 5. Department of Linguistics and Philosophy, MIT, Cambridge, Mass.

Couquaux, Daniel. 1977. "*Même* marque-t-il qu'un pronom est réfléchi?" *Le Français Moderne* 2:126–143.

Heim, Irene. 1993. "Anaphora and semantic interpretation: A reinterpretation of Reinhart's approach." *SRS Report* 07. Tübingen.

Heim, Irene, Howard Lasnik, and Robert May. 1991. "Reciprocity and plurality." *Linguistics Inquiry* 22:63–101.

Kayne, Richard. 1992. "Anaphors as pronouns." Ms. MIT, Cambridge, Mass.

Kuno, Susumo. 1987. *Functional syntax.* Chicago: Chicago University Press.

Marantz, Alec. 1983. *On the nature of grammatical relations.* Cambridge, Mass.: MIT Press.

Lewis, David. 1979. "Attitudes de dicto and de se." *Philosophical Review* 88:513–543.

Pica, Pierre. 1984a. "Subject, tense, and truth: Towards a modular approach to binding." In *Grammatical representation*, ed. Jacqueline Guéron, Hans-Georg Obenauer, and Jean-Yves Pollock, 259–291. Dordrecht: Foris.

———. 1984b. "On the distinction between argumental and non-argumental anaphors." In *Sentential complementation*, ed. Wim de Geest and Yvan Putseys, 185–195. Dordrecht: Foris.

———. 1987. "On the reflexivization cycle." In *Proceedings of the North Eastern Linguistic Society* 17, ed. Joyce Mary McDonough and Bernadette Plunkett, 483–500. Amherst: Graduate Linguistic Student Association.

————. 1988. "Sur le caractère inaliénable de l'être." In *Transparence et Opacité, Littérature et Sciences Cognitives*, ed. Tibor Papp and Pierre Pica, 205–221. Paris: Cerf.

————. 1994. "On the disjoint agreement principle." Ms. Université du Québec à Montréal, Montreal.

Quine, W.V.O. 1955. "Quantifiers and propositional attitudes." *Journal of Philosophy* 53:183–194.

Reinhart, Tanya, and Eric Reuland. 1993. "Reflexivity." *Linguistic Inquiry* 24:657–720.

Snyder, William. 1992a. "Chain-formation and crossover." Ms. MIT, Cambridge, Mass.

————. 1992b. "*Wh*-extraction and the lexical representation of verbs." Ms. MIT, Cambridge, Mass.

Zribi-Hertz, Anne. 1978. "Économisons-nous: À propos d'une classe de formes réflexives métonymiques en français." *Langue Française* 39:104–128.

————. 1990. "*Lui-même* argument et le concept de 'pronom A.'" *Languages* 97:101–127.

Index